To Melanie Simile
The most wonderful leading lady I've ever known

Contents

Illustrations

For the Sake of Social Justice
Opening Remarks

I AM HONORED TO WELCOME such a distinguished group of scholars to Duquesne University's Rome campus. This is a first-of-its-kind international meeting on the important topic of women in educational leadership. I am delighted that Duquesne is able to host this historic event. I am grateful to everyone who had a hand in bringing this meeting about, but I must single out Dr. Helen Sobehart for a special thank-you. It is her leadership that has made this meeting possible, as well as the forthcoming publications of the scholarship produced for this meeting. Thank you, Helen.

Duquesne University of the Holy Spirit is one of America's leading Catholic universities. Located in Pittsburgh, Pennsylvania, Duquesne has 10,000 students in 174 academic programs, 400 full-time faculty, and 4,500 other employees. We were founded in 1878 by the Congregation of the Holy Spirit or Spiritans. These priests and brothers came to Pittsburgh from Germany and Ireland to assist immigrants from those same nations who worked in coal mines and in the production of steel, glass, and paint. The working conditions in those days were appalling and many of the immigrants lived in poverty. The Spiritans founded Duquesne University to provide educational opportunities that would change people's lives profoundly and for the better. Five generations later, this remains our mission today.

Duquesne University has one distinction that is especially appropriate for your gathering. In 1909, Duquesne became the first Catholic university in America to admit a woman. That woman was Mary Shepperson, a Sister of Mercy, and she was admitted by the university president as a "special case." She excelled, earning both a bachelor's and a master's degree in just four years. Over the next twenty years, 214 women were also admitted as "special cases" and all earned degrees from Duquesne. This record of success led one program after another at Duquesne to open its doors officially to women; first the School of Law in 1918 and finally the College of Arts and Science in 1927. We are proud of this history and of the Duquesne women who led the way.

I am especially pleased to welcome you to our campus in Rome because of the importance of the topic of your meeting, women in educational leadership. Earlier, I mentioned our sponsoring religious congregation, the Spiritans. They have an explicit emphasis in their historical documents and in their apostolic works over the last 300 years on social justice, and always from the point of view of the least well off. This meeting is squarely in that tradition of concern for social justice and from the point of view of women who are underrepresented in leadership roles in education around the world from preschool through universities.

Why is this so? Plainly part of the answer lies in history and tradition, and the way that contemporary culture carries and reinforces that history and tradition. With rare exception, our modern world evolved from a time in which women were excluded by law, by religion, and by widespread cultural assent not only from leadership positions but also from meaningful participation in most of public life. The family was the sphere for women, as wives and mothers, while men controlled all the public institutions of society.

Even in developed nations that experienced successful movements for women's emancipation in the nineteenth and twentieth centuries, the impact of the gender imbalance enforced in earlier centuries is still evident. Women in the United States, for example, gained the right to vote in 1920, but today the number of elected women leaders in our federal and state governments remains disproportionately small, and we have not yet had a woman president.

In much of the world of education, the relative lack of women in leadership positions, as principals, supervisors, directors, deans, is especially ironic. In K–8 education in the U.S., for example, the workforce of teachers and staff is dominated by women but they are still significantly underrepresented in leadership.

Among the important and challenging questions you will grapple with in this first global conversation about these issues is to what extent there are prejudices against women in this area—explicit or tacit—by men, of course, but perhaps also by women themselves. We have all inherited the worldview and biases of our histories and culture. Are the opportunities in education truly there for women? In some nations, the clear answer is no because barriers to educational leadership are explicit. Even where there are no obvious barriers, our role models for educational leadership may have been so shaped by male images that there is de facto prejudice against women seeking leadership roles.

And you will ask if women themselves are actually choosing against these opportunities, not seeking or accepting leadership roles in education. If this is so, why is it? It is plain that even in nations where women have entered virtually all parts of public life, the family remains a special responsibility for women. Many women choose what is best for their families over what may more readily advance their public career. This may mean stopping out of a career for years to raise young children, working part-time, or opting out of more time-intensive or stressful leadership jobs for the sake of family commitments. There is no doubt that such choices are honorable self-sacrifices. But there is also little doubt that the women who choose them can appear less serious about their public roles, thus less likely to be regarded as potential leaders by those in their public world. The deeper cultural question, of course, is why so many women are willing to make these sacrifices for their families but so few men are.

You will also consider whether there are gender differences that make opportunities for leadership in education less attractive for women. I know you will ask whether women overall are drawn to a different style of leadership than men. It is easy to slip into stereotypes when speaking of the dispositions of a gender, so let me say the obvious. Even if there are dispositions about leadership that are related to gender, we all know plenty of exceptions. But there are some studies that suggest that women are more participatory and consensus-oriented in their conception of leadership than men. In the bureaucracies of contemporary educational institutions that kind of style of leadership may be a handicap. Effective leaders in education seek advice and try to build support, of course, but decisions have to be made and made expeditiously. Consensus building takes time and can thwart decisions, especially difficult ones. Looked at another way, perhaps when women see the kind of leadership style required by contemporary educational institutions, they decide that they prefer the classroom and choose to exercise leadership in other contexts where a consensus-building style is more welcome and more

successful. Speaking for myself, I generally enjoy the administrative role I play, but there are days that I recall my years in the classroom not only with fondness but also with longing.

If there is credible evidence that a gender dimension to leadership style exists, we are left with the perennial nature-nurture question. If women generally prefer a different style of leadership to men, is it due to biology or culture, or to some subtle admixture of the two? And if there is a gender difference, what is the best path ahead to increase the numbers of women leaders in education? Shall we try to change our schools so that they place a greater stress on consensus and are friendlier to women's family commitments? Shall we mentor women so that they more easily adapt to the prevailing leadership styles in our educational institutions? Is it possible to succeed at both strategies at once?

I believe as a matter both of faith and experience that society is richer when all human contributions can be given their fullest expressions. If women as women have something special to contribute as leaders, then our schools and our societies will be better for whatever measures we can take to make the number of women leaders more proportionate to their total presence in education. On the other hand, we may conclude that there is no substantial gender difference in leadership styles. Or, we may find that there is a difference at present but that it is largely cultural. If so, perhaps the difference will diminish in significance as more women enter more fully into public life and role models for successful educational leadership become gender neutral.

Even if we were to find that gender dispositions regarding leadership play little or no role in accounting for the underrepresentation of women in educational leadership, we are still left with the fact that women are underrepresented. This fact, whatever its cause, is unjust on its face. For the sake of justice, we must make efforts to bring the number of women with leadership positions into closer proportion with the number of women in education. We owe this effort especially to our daughters, but to all future generations who will benefit from more inclusive educational institutions.

On behalf of those beneficiaries, I applaud your work here and wish you every success. I look forward to seeing your scholarship in published form. And I thank you for advancing the mission of Duquesne University of the Holy Spirit to change people's lives profoundly and for the better.

Charles Dougherty

Acknowledgments

WE WANT TO EXPRESS OUR most sincere appreciation to the following individuals and organizations whose support and talents contributed greatly to the success of the Rome conference, July 2007, the conference which inspired this book.

Duquesne University

Dr. Charles Dougherty, President

Dr. Ralph Pearson, Provost/Academic Vice President

Dr. James Henderson, Director, Interdisciplinary Doctoral Program for Educational Leaders Sponsorship

Dr. Roberta Aronson, Director, Office of International Affairs

Ms. Alison Conte, Assistant Director, Web Communication and Marketing

Ms. Taylor Tobias, Graphic Artist

University Council for Educational Administration

Dr. Michelle Young, Executive Director

American Association of School Administrators

Ms. Sharon Adams-Taylor, Associate Executive Director

Special thanks to Pearson Education for their collaborative support through AASA

Pittsburgh Council on Higher Education

Dr. JoAnne Burley, Executive Director

Duquesne University Italian Campus

Sister Miriam Joseph Mikol, Director, International Development

Michael A. Wright, Resident Director

PERSONAL THOUGHTS

I would like to thank Michelle Young, Margaret Grogan, Charol Shakeshaft, Sharon Adams-Taylor and leaders of the University Council for Educational Administration (UCEA) Women's Special Interest Group for their invaluable support in the development of this conference and their passionate commitment to the cause of women in educational leadership. I am also most grateful to President Dougherty and Provost Pearson for not only their financial support but their sincere moral support of this effort. Diane Wuycheck carried out the tedious job of technical editing, but with the same passion for the subject as those of us who participated. Dr. Pam Lenz supported technology and Dr. Katherine Houghton's photographs around the room gave face to our words.

Words are insufficient to express my appreciation to Melanie Simile for her devoted efforts to ensuring that every detail of the conference and this book were handled to the highest quality standard and for her ongoing care and modeling of what it means to "share the spirit." Her flame guides me every day as we work together.

Prologue

Fire, Ice and the Journey

Helen C. Sobehart with Liv Arnesen and Ann Bancroft

BACKGROUND

Ann Bancroft, half of the first all-woman team to traverse Antarctica, described her learning from an aborted earlier expedition. "I allowed myself to be influenced by the pilots who were in a hurry to leave, so I didn't thoroughly check each detail. After we were dropped off at the arctic site, we realized that the stoves and fuel which our supplier packed were not compatible. The only way we get water at the polar caps is to melt ice. No fuel, no fire. No fire, no melting ice into water. No water, no food or energy for survival. No energy, no ability to move forward" (Bancroft, 1998).

Though she could not have known at the time, her description is a powerful metaphor for not only the successful traverse that she subsequently shared with Liv Arnesen, but also for the difficult journey faced by those of us interested in gender, equity in educational leadership and social justice. It is about our ability to move forward, to transcend.

On July 24–27, 2007, 37 scholars gathered at the Rome, Italy, campus of Duquesne University, a 130-year-old institution located in Pittsburgh, Pennsylvania in the United States. It was a seminal event. Invited scholars from every continent, including Liv representing the Antarctic duo, gathered in Rome for two reasons: first, to develop and share research-based papers which highlight the situation of women in basic and higher education leadership in major regions of the world, and, second, to arrive at consensus around a common international research agenda and related work.

The level of scholarship was high and the representation was broad. We spoke for indigenous cultures from Melanesia and New Mexico; Hispanic and Brazilian people; Far East and Pacific views including China, Hong Kong, Australia and New Zealand; Middle Eastern perspectives in Pakistan, Bangladesh and Turkey; varied places in Africa such as Tanzania, Uganda and South Africa; and Western societies including the United Kingdom, Germany and the United States. Though most participants were female, since women are the majority who study this issue, three men participated, including keynote speaker Dr. Charles Dougherty, Duquesne University's president. Finally, Liv Arnesen of Norway delivered a keynote speech on behalf of herself and her colleague Ann Bancroft of the United States regarding their Antarctic journey.

The Women's Special Interest Group (SIG) of the University Council for Educational Administration (UCEA) gave birth to the idea for this conference at the national meeting in 2006. UCEA began over fifty years ago as a professional organization seeking to motivate universities which offer doctoral programs in educational leadership toward a continually higher standard. Members engage in ongoing research in the field, the use of best practice in teaching and learning, and dissemination through publication, presentation, mentoring and networking among noted scholars in the field.

In 2006, participant experts realized that no one source existed to provide a global overview of issues related to gender and educational leadership. As the new chair of the Women's SIG, I had the honor of facilitating this discussion. Our goals were to compile an initial source of information from major regions of the globe and to disseminate that information through various venues to scholars, practitioners and the public at large. Members of that public commonly believe that the "woman issue" has been "taken care of" by the regulations and movements so prominent in the 1960s and 1970s, especially in Western society. It has not.

Another prestigious professional organization, the American Association of School Administrators (AASA), had for many years demonstrated an interest in the issue of women in public education leadership. They had sponsored a national Women Administrators' Conference for a quarter of a century. They even disseminated a monograph of the conference so that the wisdom and experiences of women could be shared with men and women alike. I had the good fortune of being the inaugural editor of that monograph. So the confluence of the three organizations seemed meant to be. This book is the first fruit of that gathering, and though we have not yet met you, the reader, you are about to be affected by research and stories from around the globe, developing an understanding which you and we would never otherwise share, save for this one special book.

Join us now on this journey as I return to Ann Bancroft's words and the metaphor of the arctic expedition as we traverse the global path of women in leadership. Join us as we explore the "fuel, fire, ice and water" which challenge yet inspire us along the way. Finally, in the last chapter, join me in considering the ethereal energy we create by melting ice with the fire of our passion and the water of our work. Energy spreads like a spirit far into time and space, touching those in the future whom we will never know, but who will be touched by the light of our flame.

THE TRAVERSE

Ann's story of the cycle from fuel to fire to water and steam provides a metaphor for the arctic journey she took with Liv. It also conveys the journey which women in general, and those in educational leadership in particular, have shared over centuries.

Aside from its practical use in the arctic environment, *fuel* is a metaphor for *information*. As Ann's story underscored, information is critical as a backdrop for success. In the arctic, Liv and Ann needed to gather and study an enormous amount of information both before and during their trek. They needed to know facts related to production, geography, clothing, fuel, their own mental and physical abilities, and even about the interaction between them. They intentionally spent time together to see if they could be a team that would overcome almost unimaginable challenges.

Likewise, our group of scholars realized that the fuel in our journey was information from across the globe regarding women in educational leadership. By strategically inviting scholars who study this issue in major regions of the world, assuring that every inhabited continent was represented by at least one person, we believed that we would produce an amazing picture. We did. I will introduce you to just a few facts which my colleagues discuss in detail later in the book. The information will, indeed, fuel your interest.

Returning to Ann's tale, she and Liv used fire that came from the right fuel. The *fire* provides *heat* necessary to melt the ice. It burns with *passion*, a striking vision to accomplish complex goals. Ann and Liv explained that visions "express your basic values, may be spiritual and ideological compasses, provide long term perspectives, indicate who you want to be for

someone, and must be kept alive!" (Arnesen, 2007). They turned their vision into four goals, "1) to be the first women to ski across the Antarctic continent; 2) to make the biggest interactive educational program on the Internet; 3) to remain friends on the other side; and 4) to have fun!" (Arnesen, 2007). Those of us who participated in the conference also have dreams and goals. We already accomplished our first goal to collect and convey a global picture. We had fun, and committed to remaining friends and colleagues "on the other side" of our own journey. We want to fuel the fire of your passion, both for women in education and, inevitably, for children. To light that fire, I'll stoke some white-hot embers in this chapter to ignite your own passion to act and to read on.

This leads to ice and water. Ironically, in the Arctic *ice* is both an enormous *obstacle* and a *solution*. It is influenced by fire to turn into the water necessary for sustenance. Through hope, courage and perseverance, Liv and Ann used the challenge, the ice, to their benefit—not only to sustain the two of them physically, but to "use the expedition to inform, ignite, collaborate and to change thought and practices" (Arnesen, 2007). Their challenges included not only the obvious demands of the awe-inspiring glaciers of Antarctica, but also the sometimes more difficult daily frustrations that cause anger, jealousy and acrimony. They experienced it all, but triumphed.

Evidence of their success includes 2 billion news media impressions, 3 million global educators and schoolchildren affected, 25 million hits on their website, collaboration with the Girl Scouts of the United States to affect 3.6 million girls and 7 million through the World Association of Girl Guides, and receiving 25,000 messages during their Antarctica crossing. As important, they are still friends, colleagues and collaborators with many organizations to keep sustaining the emotional and intellectual life of women and girls using the water of action they created by melting their icy foe.

In the coming pages, we will introduce you to some of the cultural, social, organizational and intellectual glaciers that we as female leaders face across continents. You will see how we melt barriers into the water of action, even though at times it seems only a trickle. Each droplet, nevertheless, has a powerful rippling effect.

Finally, fanning flames turns *water* into *energy*. In the Arctic, boiling water provides sustenance. Residual energy disperses into the atmosphere, going to far places that Ann and Liv would never see, yet they conceive their work as spreading ever outward, fueled by the flame of passion and with a shared spirit among those who walk with them. The curriculum they provide to young women addresses everything from self-esteem to global warming, yet they may never see the rippling future effect from those whom they inspire. Nevertheless, they believe in what they may never see. One needs only to be near them to feel the power of their beliefs and the energy which touches others in ways that we cannot easily explain. Those of us at the conference, though successful in our own right, all know we are better people because we were with Liv.

We all share a belief that the *fire* of our passion, the *water* of our actions, and the *energy* of our common *spirit* will touch you and others whom we may never know. Come and take this journey with us as you glimpse elements below of the *fuel, fire, ice* and *water* that we later describe in the chapters of this book. I have saved the energy of the *spirit* till the epilogue.

THE ELEMENTS

Fuel
If *information* is the *fuel* necessary for fire, consider the following excerpts as droplets from the many gallons to come.

- In *New Zealand,* Jane Strachan notes how difficult it is to obtain statistical data on the representation of women in educational leadership in Melanesia. She does find that women more typically lead difficult rural schools or those of the lower ranks, and usually not by choice.
- From *East Asia,* both Haiyan Qiang from China and Esther Sui-chu Ho from Hong Kong note that the proportion of women in the highest levels of educational leadership continues to be small. For example, in Hong Kong basic education, women make up 99.4% of teaching staff, yet only 30% of secondary schools are administered by women.
- In *England,* Marianne Coleman finds that women are represented in only 13% of university vice-chancellor roles and 17% of the professoriate.
- Also in the *UK,* Jacky Lumby adds complexity by suggesting that gender may not be an appropriate unit of analysis. She and other colleagues consider "intersectionality" of many identities which interlock, mutually influence, negate, heighten and transform in an ongoing metamorphosis.
- In *Turkey,* Mustafa Celikten observes there is more research available about the number of votes in a geographic region of the country than on the number of schools.
- Representing *Pakistan,* Saeeda Shah cites an analysis of 180 countries over twenty-five years which argues that gender is one of the few modes of differentiation that has social, cultural, political and economic implications everywhere in the world.
- In *Tanzania,* Sister Hellen Bandiho shares that out of thirty-one principals in the government teaching colleges, only 19% are females. In 122 basic education offices, 74% of the leadership positions are occupied by males and only 26% by females. Out of 112 surveyed academic positions, five were female and 107 male.
- In *Uganda,* Alice Kagoda emphasizes that women are only now establishing property rights in a traditionally male-dominated society.
- Studying *Greece, Cyprus and the United States,* Linda Lyman, Anastasia Athanasoula-Reppa, and Angeliki Lazaridou agree with colleagues who note that gender inequality in leadership is pervasive while perception of inequality is not.
- In *Dominica, in the West Indies,* Katherine Houghton uses the power of the photographic lens to bring an understanding of "what is" and "what it means to know" as she shares photographs of women and children in their beautiful and sad day-to-day activities.
- Sharon Adams-Taylor of the *United States* and Claudia Fahrenwald of *Germany* suggest that the issues keeping women out of the top positions are universal, not particular to industries or to countries.
- In *South Africa,* Thidziambi Phendla corroborates other findings noting that men constitute 80.2% and 89.3% in executive manager and director positions, respectively, while women represent only 19.8% and 10.3% in the same categories.
- In *New Mexico,* Maria Luisa Gonzalez and Flora Ida Ortiz express their frustration when they ask, "What is it about educational leadership that individuals persist in claiming that the theory and explanations offered by others don't really apply to them?"
- In *Africa,* Pam Lenz and JoAnne Burley lament a pilot study of the National Professional Qualification for Head Teachers which found that all candidates with low self-esteem scores were women.

Fire
If *passion* is the spark that ignites the fuel into *fire,* the following revelations should provide more than enough kindling.

- In New Zealand, especially in *Melanesia*, women experience very high levels of violence. Strachan cites a male teacher who said: "Women are raped regularly, which is taken about as seriously as schoolchildren stealing pencils or food from a garden. . . . There are no women's human rights."
- In *England*, the Boards of Governors which select head teachers are not only discriminatory to women, but to men who do not conform to the masculinist attitude. A male teacher says, "I missed an interview for head of department due to the birth of my second daughter. The interview was rearranged but one of the panel made a comment that I wasn't needed at the birth."
- In *Turkey*, Celikten quotes a female principal, "Male administrators come together outside of work and make decisions. Yet as a woman I cannot partake in these occasions."
- Continuing about life in *Pakistan*, Shah notes that power lies with those who have control over religious interpretations, and Muslim women traditionally have been barred from religious discourse and interpretation.
- Bandiho cynically compares women's chances at leadership in *Tanzania* to gambling. The pool of qualified females has to be large enough and composed of highly capable candidates with appropriate certifications to have a fair chance of winning. If someone weighted one side of a coin in probability tosses, it would be considered cheating, but not so regarding the underrepresentation of women.
- In *Uganda*, "sugar daddies" promise payment and other luxuries to school students in exchange for sexual favors.
- In *Australia*, Jill Blackmore notes that the question "What about the boys and men?" coincides politically with a conservative social agenda while diverting the attention from the impact of poverty and rurality on educational achievement.
- In *Brazil*, Rosangela Malachias quotes a noted female leader: "I have been an educator for 42 years. Undeniably, I have to fight every day to be respected. How do I fight? When I was a little girl my mother taught me to say with her, 'We are. We can.' For years we repeated this mantra together, and I have survived."
- Marilyn Grady and Bettie Bertram highlight the religions of the world and their influence on customs and practices as significant forces in the access women have to leadership positions. Yet religion can bring inspiration. The Sisters of the Holy Family of

Nazareth, our hosts at the Rome campus, remember eleven of their order as martyrs of World War II.

Ice and Water
Some work is melting glaciers of ice into *waters of action* that can begin to sustain each other.

- The *New Zealand* Educational Institute's women's website connects members to international organizations working for women's human rights.
- Regarding the Gender Mainstreaming movement in *Germany*, one of the measures and principles is to establish a family-oriented university where there is work/life balance for women and men.
- In *China*, recent laws have encouraged and supported the position of women in educational leadership.
- A ray of light comes from *Hong Kong* where studies show that female principals engage in more home/school collaboration, thus trying to affect the community around them.
- In the *UK*, a gender audit of a major professional development program strongly suggested that gender issues should be put at the heart of every aspect of the course.
- In *Bangladesh*, the Bangladesh Rural Advancement Committee (BRAC) operates informal primary education that controls 34,000 schools in rural areas. Over 70% of the students enrolled in the BRAC schools are girls.
- In *Pakistan* some women principals have found success by appropriating the role of "mother"—one who is to be obeyed and honored as a passport to heaven—in order to empower themselves.
- Joyce Dana of the *United States* suggests that the cultural lens developed by Edgar Schein is a useful way to unpack the complexities of cultural barriers and opportunities.
- Lumby poses the framework of intersectionality to provide increased understanding of how different identities can work together toward success.
- In *Uganda*, an innovative policy requires a male and a female administrator in every school, both public and private.
- In *Germany*, the manner in which Gender Mainstreaming statistics are shared widely, but without needless "blame" rankings, provides a beacon of light.
- Grogan and Shakeshaft in the United States believe that documenting collective leadership practice will provide useful information about the relationship

among women's approaches, promote effective leadership and frame possible solutions.

- Dorothy Bassett cites research which notes that better decisions can be made by a group of people than by an expert in a given field, even when they do not have advanced knowledge of the topic.
- Grady and Bertram recommend that scholars need to nest their research in the works of their predecessors.

Energy

So how does the *energy* of steam work its magic by transforming the environment even as it ascends into the atmosphere and beyond? How do we, fueled by the facts we know, fired by the passion of injustice and trying to make strides in the face of almost insurmountable obstacles, create the energy to transform and transcend current and future conditions? I will return to this question at the end of the book, after we traverse the globe in these pages.

Enjoy the wisdom of my colleagues. The work is collected by geographic region. Each group of chapters begins with a reflective overview by conference participants. References appear at the end of each chapter.

As one last bit of fuel for your journey, let me restate a comment from our other keynote speaker, Dr. Charles Dougherty, president of Duquesne University. His entire speech is this book's foreword. We hope that his words give you hope, courage and perseverance. "The fact that women are underrepresented, whatever its cause, is unjust."

REFERENCES CITED

Arnesen, L. (2007). Dare to dream. Conference keynote at the international Women Leading Education conference, Rome, Italy.

Bancroft, A. (Writer/Narrator.) (1998). *The Vision of Teams* (Videotape). United States: Lead Dog Productions.

REVOLUTIONARY CHOICES

The Brits, the Yanks and Gender Identity Itself

CHAPTER 1

Overview for Part I

DOROTHY BASSETT

THE MORE THINGS CHANGE, the more they stay the same. Coleman's account (2007) of discrimination against women in educational leadership in England indicates that little headway has been made toward shifting the biases against women in the workplace. As Coleman notes, although there are many women working in the field of education, there is a disproportionately low representation of women in positions of leadership. The glass ceiling, it seems, is still firmly in place. Despite broadly recognized laws and policies that support equal opportunity in the workplace, deeply held stereotypes and beliefs continue to hinder the ready progress of women into positions of higher authority in the field of education.

In the cases cited by Coleman, men in decision-making positions tended not to be supportive of the idea of women in leadership roles, maintaining that the demands placed upon them as wives and mothers would make it difficult for them to shoulder leadership responsibility. Generally speaking, male leaders tended to be largely free of the pull of any household or child-rearing responsibilities.

Interestingly, some of the women themselves who were interviewed mentioned the difficulties that they had with balancing both roles. Coleman's research also noted that men who shouldered significant levels of caretaking responsibility at home experienced similar difficulties with balancing work and family, and similar biases against them from the more traditional male decision-makers. In fact, it is difficult for anyone, whether male or female, to balance professional and family roles and responsibilities. From this very practical perspective, Coleman notes that there is a need for a cultural and structural shift that would provide more support for women (and men) with family and home responsibilities, freeing up more of their time and energies to devote to their work as leaders. At the same time, changes would also be necessary in the work environment to create a culture that recognizes the validity and importance of employees' family responsibilities (Coleman, 2007).

However, even if cultural and structural changes occur outwardly, the true challenge lies in uprooting the strongly held beliefs about the appropriateness of women in leadership roles and about their ability to carry out leadership responsibilities with, at a minimum, the same level of competence as their male counterparts. It is, in fact, these beliefs that have sustained the cultural, societal and organizational structures that have functioned to "keep women in their place."

As we as women look at the issue of stereotypes, it is important to remember that not only men, but women as well, frequently hold negative stereotypes about women. Some of these stereotypes may surface in our consciousness when we consider appointing a woman to a top-level, high-stress position and ask ourselves if she can handle the pressure. Others may come to mind when we wonder if we should assign "Jane" to handle an account with a firm that is headed up by "good ol' boys." We question whether she would be as effective in the role as a man.

Clearly, there are shifts in perceptions and stereotypes that also must occur in order for women to be more readily accepted as leaders. While Coleman's chapter focuses primarily on the stereotypes held by men in the educational field, it is interesting to note some of the stereotypes and stereotypical behavior that seem to be held by some of the women that Coleman interviewed as well.

Several women who were interviewed mentioned that they were able to use the prevailing stereotypes about women to their advantage. Some of these, such as the woman who felt that her gender caused others to perceive her as a more compassionate, empathetic listener (Coleman 2007), would tend to have a neutral effect. The behavior of others could be seen as undermining the efforts of women overall to establish themselves as credible professionals in a male-defined work world. This is particularly the case with the respondents who indicated that they would play into stereotypes about women and "charm" male coworkers or superiors into doing what they (the women) wanted (Coleman 2007). While this type of strategy may help these individual women to achieve their very short-term goals, reinforcing stereotypes about women in this manner may ultimately make it even more difficult for these (and other) women to advance professionally (or even to be perceived as a serious professional).

Another case hints at the level to which societal attitudes about stereotypical female roles have affected women. One respondent, when speaking about maternity leave noted that she had "adequate time but [it] left me feeling unconfident. [It was a] real challenge to be 'career woman' then 'mum' then 'career woman'" (Coleman, 2007, p. 12). It is interesting that this respondent's sense of confidence came from her professional role and only her professional role. Based upon this brief comment, it appears that this respondent has internalized a prevailing societal viewpoint that devalues traditional female roles, and that she gains a sense of personal worth and confidence only from her activities in the male-defined work world. While the paper focused on women in the workplace, not women in the home, it is interesting, nonetheless, to note that this particular respondent feels that her home responsibilities detract from her sense of self-esteem.

While it may be a leap of logic to derive this interpretation from a respondent's brief sentence or two on the one hand, on the other it does raise the question of how much women themselves internalize (in the case of this last respondent) and/or promulgate (in the case of the previous respondents) existing stereotypes of women. In addition to the structural and cultural changes recommended by Coleman, it also may be wise for women as a group to engage in a difficult practice of critical self-reflection and assess the level to which we ourselves play a role in the perpetuation of stereotypes that later serve as barriers to our own advancement.

Some stereotypes assert that women are constitutionally incapable of being leaders. They are too kind, too gentle, unable to make tough decisions. Of course, this stereotype is directly connected to a not uncommonly held assumption that an autocratic, command-control, male-defined leadership style is the correct and only leadership style. This assumption most likely had its origins in the fact that until recent years, most people in leadership positions were men. Men tended to handle leadership in a particular way, and so by association, the way that men handled leadership was the only way and the best way.

As women began to move into positions of leadership, research began to emerge that examined women's approach to leadership. However, unlike many studies on women and leadership, Grogan and Shakeshaft (2007) ventured away from looking at women's leadership styles in the context of their similarities and/or differences from male leadership approaches. Instead, their research focused purely on how women lead. They found that a collective approach to leadership, that is, an approach in which power is shared and decisions are made jointly, is a hallmark of women's leadership. They also maintain that women's focus tends to center on creating positive change through a participatory process characterized by working with, rather than ruling over, others.

As Grogan and Shakeshaft (2007) point out, the concept of collective (or participatory) leadership, viewed as being a more "feminine" style of leadership, has gained much more widespread acceptance, even among predominantly male business circles. Even though other disciplines tend not to actively acknowledge this as being an innately female leadership style, the value of a collective approach is being recognized more and more. For example, James Surowiecki's book *The Wisdom of Crowds* (2005) points out that better decisions can be made by a group of people than by an expert in a given field, even when the people in the group do not have an advanced level of knowledge in the problem that they are focusing upon.

In reality, neither a directive, hierarchical approach nor a participatory approach provides all the answers. While a participatory or a collective process is likely to yield better results in terms of quality of decision than an autocratic approach, the collective approach can take more time. When a leader needs to make a quick decision, as would frequently be the case when dealing with an urgent situation, she or he may not have the luxury of time. Given this situation, an experienced leader would flex within a range of approaches, reserving a directive approach for those decisions and tasks that are of a time-driven nature. For example, Goleman (2000) maintains that the most effective leaders draw from among six leadership styles, ranging from coercive to coaching, matching the appropriate approach to the situation at hand.

Following this line of reasoning, in situations that are urgent and sharply time-bound, a directive style will certainly be the best route to take. In other situations, a collective approach will help to ensure employee buy-in, long-term support and higher quality decision-making. For this reason, rather than identifying one style as being male and one as being female, and one or the other as being right or wrong, it would be wise to understand the merits of both, and the situations in which each is most appropriate. Needless to say, no leader, male or female, will be expert in all the nuances of both approaches.

However, removing the connotative labels of "masculine" or "feminine" from each, and recognizing that each is composed of a set of tools, tools that can be *learned*, targeted training can enable all leaders to greatly enhance their ability to lead effectively. This provides them, as it were, a much broader skill set of leadership tools from which to draw. Moreover, increasing women's arsenal of leadership skills in this manner also will serve to enhance their sense of leadership efficacy. This is particularly important for its own sake. Also, as Hoyt (2005) notes, women with high measures of leadership efficacy are more resistant to being negatively affected when confronted with stereotypical comments or actions that question their capacity as leaders. Not only do these women maintain their sense of confidence as leaders, but also they identify themselves even *more* strongly as leaders when faced with negative stereotypes. This, in turn, can help them to be more effective and more credible leaders. This active demonstration of excellence in leadership can only serve to gradually chip away at the stereotypes about women that have made it difficult for women to be taken seriously in high-level positions.

Up to this point we have looked at stereotypes of women in isolation of any other variables that also affect the level to which women are well received in positions of leadership. While it is tempting to remain at a certain level of two-dimensionality, the real world, of course, does not function that way. Instead, there is any number of reasons why a given woman might be well received in a leadership role in one organization but not in another. Gender is only one of a number of factors that come into play.

Recognizing this, Lumby (2007) presents a complex, multidimensional approach to understanding the dynamics of discrimination and gender bias. Rather than looking at gender as being a unique and isolated characteristic that drives women's experience of discrimination, Lumby maintains that gender is one of many characteristics that interact dynamically to determine how individuals see themselves as well as how others perceive them and behave toward them. Other factors such as race, religion, ethnicity, and social and economic status, also play a role. Depending upon the context, one characteristic (e.g., race) may come more

to the forefront than other characteristics (e.g., gender), as that foregrounded characteristic may define a woman as more markedly different or more "other" than the individuals around her (Lumby, 2007).

This context also plays a role in determining how negatively that otherness is perceived. For example, the only woman in a workplace occupied by men may be identified primarily based upon her gender as a woman. However, if she is the only physically impaired person in the workplace, she will likely be identified by that characteristic first, and her coworkers' and superiors' response to her will be driven by that characteristic of otherness (Lumby, 2007).

As a side note, this may have something to do with why the men with family caretaking responsibilities in Coleman's 2007 study were also discriminated against. While these men were similar to the male decision makers on the basis of their gender, their caretaking role made them more "other." Of course, not only did this role make them different from the stereotypical men, but also it linked them more closely with traditional female roles. To the extent that these decision makers made this connection, the caretaking men were "guilty by association" or at least guilty by similarity to women. Consequently their own capabilities and dedication to their jobs were called into question.

While some aspects of an individual's perceived level of otherness are out of her control, Lumby (2007) notes that women have utilized several approaches to reduce their otherness in order to overcome any obstacles that they may encounter stemming from others' perceptions of them. She goes on to outline three coping strategies that women use to manage these perceptions: decategorization (identifying not as a member of the group of women, or of disabled people, or of other minority status, but identifying as an individual unto herself); recategorization (identifying not as a member of the minority group, but as one of a group of professionals); and intragroup solidarity (identifying with a minority group that cuts across the boundaries of a particular workplace or a profession, e.g., a member of a women's activist movement) (Lumby, 2007).

It would be particularly interesting to learn if there are patterns to the coping strategies and if certain coping strategies are more commonly used with certain sets of minority characteristics or variables of "otherness" than others. Moreover, are there strategies that are more effective than others in general? Are there particular contexts within which one type of strategy works better than another? This would be of value, not only from a purely academic standpoint but also from a practical one as well. Until the structural and cultural changes are made, and until stereotypes are no longer in existence, it will continue to be incumbent upon women to adjust their own behavior and develop coping strategies with which to move up into and succeed in positions of leadership. While this has been going on for some time, to a large degree it has been going on in isolation as individual women somehow determine which approaches work best for them in particular settings. Lumby's work could well form the foundation for a solid set of strategies which women could consistently employ in order to surmount the societal boundaries and attitudes that impede women's acceptance into and success within the leadership realm.

In sum, the review of these chapters has brought several questions to mind:

- To what extent do women themselves internalize and/or promulgate stereotypes against women? What needs to occur for women themselves to accept and support themselves and other women without being influenced by (or taking advantage of) these stereotypes?
- Recognizing the need for effective leaders to flex between a directive and a collective approach, what would need to occur for the workplace to embrace the concept of a gender-neutral leadership model, one which draws upon the best of both male and female approaches to leadership? What role can training—of both men and women—play in a shift toward a gender-neutral view of leadership?
- Given the multidimensional view of discrimination that Lumby presents, is it possible to develop a framework of effective coping strategies, strategies that incorporate both identity as well as external contextual variables, that women can put into practice in order to support their career progression and overall success?

REFERENCES CITED

Coleman, M. (2007, July 24). Women in educational leadership in England. Paper presented at UCEA Conference on Gender, Rome.

Goleman, D. (2000). Leadership that gets results. *Harvard Business Review, 78*(2), 78–90.

Grogan, M., and Shakeshaft, C. (2007, July 24). Conscious leadership in a political world. Paper presented at UCEA Conference on Gender, Rome.

Hoyt, C. (2005). The role of leadership efficacy and stereotype activation in women's identification with leadership. *Journal of Leadership & Organizational Studies,11*(4), 2–13.

Lumby, J. (2007, July 24). Disappearing gender: choices in identity. Paper presented at UCEA Conference on Gender, Rome.

Surowiecki, J. (2004). *The Wisdom of Crowds.* New York: Random House.

CHAPTER 2

Women in Educational Leadership in England

MARIANNE COLEMAN

INTRODUCTION

THIS CHAPTER REVIEWS SOME major aspects of the current situation for women in educational leadership in England, drawing on relevant literature. Particular use is made of data from two rounds of survey research, which focused on the impact of gender on educational leadership (Coleman, 2002, 2005). The first round took place in the mid-1990s and the second in 2004, so a comparison between the two indicates something of the nature and extent of change in this period.

The chapter begins with a brief overview of the English context as it relates to women in leadership. The choice is of England rather than the UK, as the four countries that make up the UK—England, Scotland, Northern Ireland, and Wales—have somewhat different education systems although the broad trends are likely to be the same across the four countries. The focus of the chapter then turns to an overview of major issues for women in educational leadership in England indicating the nature of change; first in accessing and then carrying out leadership roles; and second exploring the impact of family responsibilities for women and men leaders and the questions that arise relating to work/life balance.

CONTEXT

Within the English educational system, as elsewhere, men are generally preferred for leadership roles and this is particularly true for institutions catering to older pupils and students. Government statistics show that women make up 31 percent of secondary head teachers (equivalent to high school principals), a rise from 26 percent in 1997, and 39 percent of deputies, out of a teaching force that is 55 percent women (DfES, 2006). In the nursery and primary (grade school) sector the proportion of women teachers is 84 percent and the proportion of women head teachers (principals) is around 62 percent (DfES, 2006) so that although women predominate numerically as primary school leaders, men leaders are disproportionately represented.

There also appears to be something of an urban/rural divide, with women more likely to be in senior roles in urban metropolitan areas and less likely to be leaders in rural and suburban areas. In London, women make up more than half of the secondary school head teachers, whereas in the areas outside the ambit of the capital or other major conurbations, the proportion is around one quarter (Coleman, 2005).

In tertiary education, women are particularly poorly represented in senior roles; they are 13 percent of university vice chancellors (the most senior role in the sector) (EOC, 2007) and 17 percent of the professoriate, a rise from 8.5 percent in 1997 (Tysome, 2007). This rise is larger than in many sectors, indeed an Equal Opportunities Organisation survey carried out in England earned the comment: "Progress on women's representation across a wide range of professions and sectors is painfully slow, and in some cases has gone into reverse" (EOC, 2007, p. 3).

The rate of progress may be slow, but general perceptions seem to be that gender problems have been addressed and dealt with (Oakley, 2002) and the small increase in the proportion of women in positions of authority is used as evidence to support this. In addition, the position of women is seen to be strengthened through the law. The original gender legislation of the 1970s has been updated in the UK through the Equality Act (2006), which imposes a specific gender duty on public authorities to eliminate unlawful discrimination and harassment; and to promote equality of opportunity. This is to be welcomed as a necessary provision for equity, but it applies only to the public sector (specifically local government, education, health, the criminal justice system, and transport), and of course legislation is only one strand of the complex structures and cultures that provide the context for gender attitudes.

Despite these positive changes, women when questioned are aware of discrimination, but tend to believe it happens to other women and deny that it has happened to them (Howard and Tibballs, 2003). This pattern of "denial" and "distancing" has been identified elsewhere, for example in the United States (Rusch and Marshall, 2006, p. 245). There is evidence of this also in the 2004 survey (Coleman, 2005) that will be drawn on in this chapter.

TWO SURVEYS OF THE IMPACT OF GENDER ISSUES ON WOMEN AND MEN HEAD TEACHERS

The more recent of the two surveys of women and men head teachers was funded by the National College for School Leadership (NCSL) in 2004 (Coleman, 2005), but an earlier version using the same survey instrument was sent to women head teachers in 1996 and men in 1998 (Coleman, 2002) so it is possible to compare the views of the two cross-sections of head teachers taken at these periods of time. An overview of the samples and response rates of the two rounds of surveys is given in table 2.1.

Issues for Women in Educational Leadership

Although the proportion of women in educational leadership is slowly rising, there are still both direct and subtle messages including the use of stereotypes that impede women from accessing leadership and also affect the ways in which they inhabit leadership roles. Overt discrimination may be much less common than previously, due to legislation and a gradually changing culture, but a comparison of the perceptions of head teachers in the first and second round of surveys mentioned above gives a clear indication of continuing issues.

Discrimination and Career Progress

The 2004 survey (Coleman, 2005) found perceptions of subtle and widespread discriminatory attitudes toward women, which require analysis and interrogation if equity is to be achieved. Despite the fact that sex discrimination had been illegal for around 30 years, half of the women head teachers who responded to the 2004 survey stated that they had experienced some form of sexism or discrimination related to their career progress and appointment. This proportion is likely to be higher than 50 percent, as some of the ambiguity about discrimination found elsewhere (Howard and Tibballs, 2003; Rusch and Marshall, 2006) is echoed in these data. Some of the head teachers who responded negatively when asked if they had experienced sexist attitudes then went on to give examples of discrimination.

The proportion saying that they had experienced discrimination had been two-thirds in the earlier survey of women head teachers in 1996, with some of these head teachers drawing upon experiences that predated the equal opportunities legislation of the 1970s. Women in this earlier survey had experienced direct discrimination, for example, being told that there was no point in applying for a particular job as a decision already had been made to hire a man. The attitude that the job was too much for a woman with children was more common in the earlier survey but still present in 2004, although generally implied rather than stated overtly.

The main focus of discriminatory comments reported by the women head teachers in both surveys was the perceived importance of their family responsibilities, particularly in relation to motherhood (see further discussion below in relation to work/life balance). Such responsibilities were inevitably seen as diverting the prospective head teacher from her work role. There was an assumption of potential conflict for women who have families generated by the needs of husbands and children clashing with the demands of running the school. For example, one young head teacher said in the 2004 survey that she experienced: "Constant comments regarding my role and how it sits with being a mother of four young children — implication is I'm not doing a good job either as mother or head teacher."

Comments also related to how their husbands might feel, with the implicit assumptions that the male career comes first and that the primary responsibility of the wife is to offer support to her partner. Women who are not married, particularly those who are child free, were not immune from discriminatory stereotypes and might, for example, be accused of not knowing enough about how to handle children, as they had not had the experience of motherhood.

The group of stakeholders who were most likely to be identified as discriminatory in their attitudes was

Table 2.1. Sample and Response Rates of Surveys of Secondary Head Teacher/Principals in England

	1996			2004	
	Women	Men		Women	Men
Number	670	670		490	490
Sample of whole population	100%	25%		50%	20%
Response rate	70%	60%		56%	40%

school governors. This group is largely made up of individuals who represent the community and who take responsibility for the governance of the school. One of their more important responsibilities is the appointment of a head teacher and they are seen to bring with them valuable expertise in recruitment and selection from outside the education sector. However, the reported views that emerge from this group tend to be somewhat macho. For example, in the 2004 survey a woman head teacher commented: "I overheard governors talking at an interview saying that I could not get the job as they needed a man on the staff! I didn't get the job." The attitudes of governors are not only discriminatory to women, but also to men who do not conform to the hegemonic masculinist attitude. One man reported that: "I missed an interview for head of department due to the birth of my second daughter; the interview was rearranged but one of the panel made a comment that I wasn't needed at the birth."

Data from the head teachers in the 2004 survey indicated that the interview panels were weighted 2:1 men to women for both the primary and the secondary sectors. In the earlier surveys the proportion of men reported on the panels was even higher. The tendency for panels to appoint in their own image has long been a feature of research on careers and appointments (Hall, Mackay and Morgan, 1986) and the reported attitudes of some governors are not likely to provide an even-handed approach to the appointment of any candidate who diverges from the mean.

On the positive side there has been a development within schools in relation to stereotyping women into pastoral roles. In the earlier survey of 1996, women tended to be pigeonholed with responsibility for pastoral affairs. One woman summed this up as: "Expectations that I would be pastoral care—look after the girls/flowers/coffee/Tampax machines" (Coleman, 2002, p. 24). A corollary of this identification was that pastoral care was generally seen as not preparing women for the full demands of headship. At this time, men tended to dominate the management and leadership of the curriculum in secondary schools. In 2004 this situation had changed considerably as can be seen

in table 2.2, where the important curriculum area was being accessed almost equally by men and women.

Discrimination related to gender is particularly apparent in relation to interview and appointment but does not stop there. Women are regarded as outsiders in leadership and therefore continue to face gender-related challenges once in post and need to "win over" their community before they are accepted.

EXPERIENCING THE LEADERSHIP ROLE

For women, the experience of leadership is likely to vary somewhat according to the age of the students for whom they have responsibility. Although men are sought after as leaders and teachers in the primary sector of education, these schools are predominantly staffed by women. Therefore, once women head teachers in the primary sector are in post they are unlikely to experience difficulties related to their gender.

The situation is somewhat different in the secondary sector. Women head teachers there are operating in a context where they are seen as "outsiders," unlike men in the primary sector, where they may be rarities from the point of view of their sex but are widely welcomed as head teachers. As the proportion of male teachers in primary schools is steadily decreasing, the men who are in the sector are much in demand. For example, in the 2004 survey a male head teacher recalled: "As a man teacher in a primary school I was 'chased' professionally by female heads."

In connection with appointment, about half of the women in the secondary sector said that they had experienced sexism/discrimination while in their posts and gave examples of how their gender had negatively affected their role. The negative experiences tend to relate to other people's perceptions of women's suitability as leaders. One female secondary head summed up the relatively hostile atmosphere in which she worked (referring to sexist and discriminatory attitudes): "Too many to enumerate—mostly in the way parents/other professionals speak to women in my position—I've got hundreds of anecdotes!"

Once in post, governors' attitudes toward a female head also can be a problem. For examples a young female head teacher reported: "Governors said I should not be paid while on maternity leave—I was irresponsible and had no right." Another said that: "Governors are not sympathetic to the need for meetings being at a time when I can arrange child care—there are lots of evening meetings!"

Issues for women are not only with governors. They reported difficulties with male support staff and with

Table 2.2. Curriculum and Pastoral Responsibilities as a Deputy Head for Women and Men %

| | 1996 | | 2004 | |
	Women	Men	Women	Men
Curriculum	54	77	76	82
Pastoral	38	14	56	51

teachers: "e.g., caretaker [janitor] who questions my every decision"; teachers, both men and women: "I faced a challenging staff room—a significant number of people did not want me to succeed"; and with parents, particularly fathers. Women also reported experiencing particular difficulties with gatherings of other head teachers. Such gatherings in rural and suburban areas tend to be very male dominated. A woman secondary head commented that she is the "only female head in the LEA [local government area]—heads' meetings started with a full English breakfast and talk about rugby and cricket." A woman in the same age group stated that: "My current LEA has several senior officers who treat me differently, as I am the only female secondary head in the LEA. This is a very serious issue, which affects my working life."

The women also noted more positive experiences as women leaders, but these are generally due to the relative rarity of women as leaders in the secondary sector and their relationships with mainly male gatekeepers. Half of women secondary head teachers in 2004 reported advantages in being a woman in the leadership role, although the advantages mentioned were often linked with stereotypes about women: being able to placate angry males, being more empathetic, and being able to use feminine charms, as in the following examples:

- Aggressive fathers soon mellow.
- Parents see you as a mother as well as a head, that is, feel that you understand in difficult times.
- I can usually gain "extra" and more discount when negotiating with male reps. You can charm when necessary, for example, when trying to raise £50,000 [$100,000] for specialist school sponsorship.

Although men are clearly advantaged in becoming and being a head teacher, men in the secondary sector tended not to recognize this. In the primary sector, half the men did feel that their gender was an advantage. It seems that having minority status and/or being the "outsider," that is, men in primary schools and women in secondary schools, does have some advantages.

The tertiary sector of education has traditionally been seen as "masculine" whether in relation to the market-oriented vocational training provided through further education or the more academic offerings of the universities, particularly those with long histories, that offer "chilly climates" to women. Whitehead (2001, p. 79) comments on the situation in further-education colleges: "Firstly, the continued numerical dominance of men in management and, secondly, the masculinist work cultures now entrenched across both public and private sectors."

CURRENT DISCOURSES OF LEADERSHIP

In the period between the two surveys of head teachers, there has been a move in England to a more managerialist culture throughout education, in schools and in further and higher education and also in the public sector generally. There has been an increase in accountability in schools and colleges related to quality assurance, inspection, "naming and shaming" and target setting. There is also a more entrepreneurial climate, with schools expected to bid competitively for money or to raise money from industry that will then attract matched funding from the government, for example, for specialist college status. In higher and further education there is more stress on efficiency, value for money and entrepreneurialism than in previous years.

Perhaps as a result of this change in ethos, women leaders appear to feel more constrained. In 1996 in the first survey of women head teachers, a number of the women commented positively on their freedom from confining expectations in comparison with their male colleagues who were expected to act out the stereotype of the authoritarian traditional head. In 2004 there was no reference to this freedom of action. Despite their ability to enumerate the advantages of being a woman head teacher, 70 percent (10 percent more than in 1996) felt that they had to "prove their worth" as a woman leader. This may well be related to changes in educational policy which have left head teachers, particularly women, feeling vulnerable and exposed. One woman head teacher commented in 2004 on dealing with difficult situations or people: "I am more aware people put expectations on you, more than on men. Sometimes people want you not to succeed."

In schools the emphasis on inspection and on schools "failing" has the effect of exposing the leadership team, particularly the head teacher, to public scrutiny and blame. Since women in any case are often seen as "outsiders" in leadership they may, therefore, experience this effect to a greater degree than their male colleagues (Coleman 2005; Moreau, Osgood and Halsall, 2004). The ethos generated by recent educational policy is one that may make women in leadership feel more vulnerable, but they may also find the macho tone inimical. Lambert (2007) has analyzed the discourse of educational speeches made by Labour politicians, and argues that the variety of transformational leadership that is endorsed is essentially masculinist. Lambert quotes key phrases from education ministers' speeches such as "forging ahead," being "imaginative and at the cutting edge" and being able to "thrive in any walk of life," phrases that equate with traditional masculinist strategies of control. She goes on to say that while women are as capable as men in taking on these attitudes in leadership, it involves fewer risks for men who already "embody masculinity as the norm" (Blackmore, 1999, p. 173).

Commenting on the current managerialist culture that has been created not only in schools but also in teacher education, Thompson (2007) points out that although women are increasingly moving into management and leadership positions, in this case in teacher education, the work is unrewarding and increasingly unprofessional. Managers felt less in charge of their own work and increasingly that they were responding to external demands. As a result it is no longer seen as an attractive career for men: "It seems that former male managers in teacher training have moved out of what might now be seen as a stressful and demanding job with little power, reduced status and a heavy workload. By opting out, men may have, by default, created a space for women to move back into" (p. 346). However, this space may not be attractive to either women or men. A similar analysis of discourse in a public sector environment showed that the dominant leadership styles of men and women could be termed "macho-management . . . valued over the more feminine qualities" (Ford, 2006, p. 96).

SUPPORT

Leadership in education in England is less popular than it was as a career option. Vacancies for head of a school often stay unfilled, and re-advertisement is relatively common, particularly in the more challenging urban settings. There are more women head teachers in areas such as inner London than anywhere else in the country perhaps because there is less competition for these vacancies. Under these circumstances it may be particularly important that support and development opportunities are available for all head teachers, but particularly for women who may also face discriminatory attitudes not experienced by their male colleagues.

About three-quarters of all the respondents to the surveys of head teachers commented on the importance of the support of a previous head teacher. Only about half had been actively mentored, although this

proportion rose for the youngest cohort of head teachers in the 2004 survey. Respondents to the surveys recognized family, colleagues and primarily their own head teachers as encouraging and supporting them.

Support also can come from formal and informal networking and it is often felt that men benefit more from this. As a result networking for women may be recommended as a way of promoting women in leadership. Women's support groups were mentioned in 1996, but not in 2004. It could be that their demise is a symptom of the feeling that gender is no longer a problem referred to above or that the support offered by women to other women tends to be entirely informal and therefore taken for granted.

WORK/LIFE BALANCE ISSUES

Women have long been identified with the domestic private world and men with the wider public world of work. Despite times when there has been a need for women to be drafted into work, during World War II, for example, the gendered nature of work and home has continued to be conceptualized along traditional lines:

> Discourses of masculinity and femininity continue to be embedded in the work-family discourse, modified only to allow for greater movement between domains, that is, women are "allowed" to work, while maintaining stinging indictments of those who fail to do so seamlessly. (Runte and Mills, 2006, p. 714)

Given these difficulties in reconciling work and home, it is not surprising that women leaders in education and elsewhere are much less likely to have children than their male counterparts. There is a falling birth rate among professional women. At the age of 35, more than 40 percent of university-educated women in England born in 1970 were childless, compared with only 32 percent of those born in 1958 (Leapman, 2007). The younger women head teachers in the 2004 survey are similar to the 1958 cohort quoted above, as almost a third did not have a child or children at the time of the survey. However, 90 percent of their male colleagues had a child or children. It is interesting to compare the situation for women in 1996 when the contrast between men and women was even greater, with just over half the women having a child or children compared to 94 percent of the men (see table 2.3).

Combining a senior position at work with motherhood is a difficult prospect that may lead women to make choices about which to prioritize. Trying to

Table 2.3. Partnerships and Children %

	1990s		2004	
	Women	Men	Women	Men
With partner	67	95	78	96
Separated	3	1	2	1
Single (including widowed)	19	1	11	1
Divorced	11	2	9	2
Having child or children	52	94	63	90

successfully manage both can lead to role conflict and guilt. For both women and men there are issues of how best to try and balance the demands of a home life and a stressful job. In the two surveys men and women both identify the ability to work hard as the most likely reason for their success. Some claim to work up to 70 hours a week on a regular basis. The climate of accountability is likely to place more pressures rather than less on those in senior roles. In these circumstances there are inevitable tensions for men or women who are conscious of home responsibilities. One woman in the 2004 survey commented on "the long hours culture at Deputy Head level. I was the only female on the senior team. The men all stayed late/came in holidays. There were expectations that I would do the same."

In the 2004 survey there was a larger minority of men who also experienced some tension as a result of the demands made on them to put work before family. For example, one commented, "Pressure was brought to bear on me to lead a college meeting on the evening when my wife left hospital with my daughter."

Although men also express the wish to spend more time with their families, women generally carry most of the domestic responsibility and are more likely to experience the tensions involved in dealing with home and work. Men are less likely to carry most of the strain although in both surveys there were two or three men who had been widowed or whose partner was incapacitated by illness and who therefore had major responsibility for children. These men identified the same difficulties as were identified by the women with children. A more common response from men was that their wife/partner had put their children first and put her own career "on hold." Table 2.3 shows the proportions of principals who were married/partnered and had children in the first and second round of surveys.

We have already seen how women head teachers reported criticism of their attempts to combine the roles of motherhood and school leader. Although it is increasingly seen that men as well as women do

wish to combine work and family responsibilities, it is particularly difficult to shake the established norms that equate women with the home and the supportive role and men with careers. A study of women who were head teachers and mothers (Bradbury and Gunter, 2006) showed that despite feeling intense guilt at times in relation to perceived shortcomings due to role strain, the mothers did find ways of reconciling their conflicts and operating with their two identities:

> Not combined or integrated but coexist[ing] in a flexible state, with one sometimes growing and encroaching on the territory of the other, at other times vice versa, and at yet other times overlapping, underpinning or supporting each other, always balanced on their profile as woman. They are secure as women in their roles, positioning themselves within the dialogic identities; they live within complexity and work their way through it (p. 501).

This study goes some way to reconceptualize the role of women who both work in senior positions and have families, and moves beyond the stereotypes to show how despite tensions they can be "secure as women in their roles."

It is clear that there are varied patterns in the ways that individuals in marriage or partnership order their lives. For the women leaders in my surveys, there was some evidence that they shared responsibilities with their partners, often in running a dual-profession household, sometimes taking it in turns for one to move ahead in their career while the other "took a backseat." However, the male head teachers in the surveys, in contrast to their female peers, still tended to operate a fairly traditional division of labor within the family with the career of the male being dominant for both of the pair (see Evetts, 1994) and the female partner putting much less emphasis on her own career and carrying most of the domestic responsibility. For the male head teachers there had been virtually no change in the sharing of domestic responsibilities between the two surveys (see table 2.4).

Table 2.4. Sharing Domestic Responsibilities with Partner (Secondary Principals) %

	1990s		2004	
	Women	Men	Women	Men
More responsibility taken by respondent	43	4	33	2
Responsibility shared 50/50	38	24	35	26
More responsibility taken by partner	19	73	32	72

The career pattern for both men and women is generally expected to be a straight ascension to the top, although there are always some exceptions to the rule. However, taking time out for bearing and raising children does raise particular questions for women about the amount of time they take, the legal protection for their career status and the impact of managing a family while pursuing a demanding career.

CAREER BREAKS

Although some career breaks are taken for professional development the most common form of break is that taken by women who interrupt their career for motherhood. The reasons for having career breaks have changed somewhat between the two surveys (see table 2.5). In 1996 most women took a career break and of these about a third took a longer break for child care. In some cases breaks were up to ten years and the women were still able to return to a successful career. This pattern of longer breaks had become very much less common by 2004, when women were less likely to take a career break of any sort and were more likely to take a shorter maternity leave than an extended break.

Most of the women in the 1996 survey who had taken a longer break were in the older 50–60 age group, and this group was more likely to have children (62 percent). The younger 40- to 49-year-old women in the 1996 survey were the least likely of any cohort to have children (only 44 percent) and were more likely to have taken briefer maternity leave. By 2004, the expectation was of a much more male model of career for women, where having a child takes a central part of a woman's life for a short time only. The advent of statutory maternity leave in England has been beneficial in many ways, but ironically it may have limited the option of longer career breaks for women who wish to combine career and family.

Women in the UK are now entitled to up to a year of maternity leave, which guarantees that their employee status is protected (Clayton, 2007). This entitlement has only recently been increased so the women in both

Table 2.5. Changes in the Nature of Career Breaks for Women High School Principals %

	1996	2004
No break	29	60
Maternity leave	34	26
Longer term child care	27	11
Qualifications/experience	13	7

Note: Some have had more than one break.

surveys would have been entitled to a maximum of six months. In both cases income is not fully protected and Statutory Maternity Pay would represent a considerable drop in income to professional women. As a result many women would have taken less than the maximum time because of financial reasons or other pressures. Some women answering the survey referred to timing their babies so that they arrived during the summer vacation so that they did not have to take time off at all. Women in the 2004 survey identified the tensions related to maternity leave: role strain, financial hardship, being penalized on the return to work, and the pressure to take off as little time as humanly possible:

> "Adequate time but left me feeling unconfident. Real challenge to be career woman then mum, then career woman."
> "I took 13 weeks; it wasn't enough."
> "In part it was finance-led that I returned so soon, but I wanted to pursue a career and have children—have best of both worlds."
> "I returned and was asked to lose one of my management points. That was silly really as I still did the job."
> "My seniors thought the work I was leading would fall apart when I became pregnant. I took four weeks maternity leave and it did not."

CONCLUSION

This chapter has included a review of some of the findings of the two rounds of surveys I undertook in the 1990s and in 2004 considering the difficulties women have in accessing and holding leadership roles in education in England, particularly in the current managerialist culture.

In the chapter we have considered some of the issues relating to work/life balance and how our gendered perceptions affect the ways in which women and men see their responsibilities. There is no doubt that there is some progress toward a more equitable society for women. Legislation has been strengthened and culture has changed, with more men expecting a greater involvement in their family. However, gender is an important factor that continues to differentially determine and affect the ways in which individuals operate and work and perceive each other. Work/family tensions affect both women and men, but women tend to be more deeply affected. Successful educational leaders need to be informed and to reflect on the ways that gender affects them as individuals but also those they lead and the students they teach.

REFERENCES CITED

Blackmore, J. (1999). *Troubling women: Feminism, leadership, and educational change.* Buckingham, Open University Press.

Bradbury, L., and Gunter, H. (2006). Dialogic identities: The experiences of women who are head teachers and mothers in English primary schools. *School Leadership and Management, 26*(5), pp. 489–504.

Clayton, G. (2007). Relevant legislation. In Myers, K., Taylor, H., Adler, S. and Leonard, D. *Genderwatch still watching,* Stoke on Trent, Trentham Books.

Coleman, M. (2002). *Women as head teachers: Striking the balance,* Stoke on Trent, Trentham Books.

———. (2005). *Gender and headship in the twenty-first century,* Nottingham, NCSL. http://www.ncsl.org.uk/mediastore/image2/twlf-gender-full.pdf.

DfES (Department for Children, Schools and Families). (2004, 2005). Statistics of Education: School workforce in England, www.dfes.gov.uk/rsgateway/DB/VO:?v000380/index.shtml.

EOC (Equal Opportunities Commission. (2007). *Sex and power: Who runs Britain?* Manchester, EOC.

Evetts, J. (1994). *Becoming a secondary headteacher,* London, Cassell.

Ford, J. (2006). Discourses of leadership: Gender, identity and contradiction in a UK public sector organization. *Leadership, 2*(1), pp. 77–99.

Hall, V., Mackay, H. and Morgan, C. (1986). *Head teachers at work,* Buckingham, Open University Press.

Howard, M., and Tibballs, S. (2003). *Talking inequality.* London, Future Foundation.

Lambert, C. (2007). New Labour, new leaders? Gendering transformational leadership. *British Journal of Sociology of Education,* 2(2), pp. 149–163.

Leapman, B. (2007). Third of graduate women will be childless, *Sunday Telegraph,* 24 April.

Moreau, M.-P., Osgood, J. and Halsall, A. (2005). *The career progression of women teachers in England: A study of barriers to promotion and career development,* London, IPSE.

Oakley, A. (2002). *Gender on planet Earth,* Cambridge, Polity Press

Runte, M. and Mills, A. J. (2006). Cold war, chilly climate: Exploring the roots of gendered discourse in organization and management theory. *Human Relations, 59*(5), pp. 695–720.

Rusch, E. (2004). Gender and race in leadership preparation: A constrained discourse. *Educational Administration Quarterly, 40*(1), pp. 16–48.

Rusch, E., and Marshall, C. (2006). Gender filters and leadership: Plotting a course to equity, *International Journal of Leadership in Education, 9*(3), pp. 229–250.

Thompson, B. (2007). Working beyond the glass ceiling: Women managers in initial teacher training in England. *Gender and Education, 19*(3), pp. 339–352.

Tysome, T. (2007). Sex parity 50 years off. *The Times Higher Education Supplement,* 19 January.

Whitehead, S. (2001). The invisible gendered subject: Men in education management. *Journal of Gender Studies,* 10(1), pp. 67–82.

Young, M., and Mountford, M. (2006). Infusing gender and diversity issues into educational leadership programs. *Journal of Educational Administration, 44*(3), pp. 264–277.

CHAPTER 3

Conscious Leadership in a Political World

MARGARET GROGAN AND CHAROL SHAKESHAFT

IN THIS CHAPTER, WE EXPLORE the literature on women's approach to educational leadership in the United States, examining strategies and approaches that women choose to negotiate the political, and male, world of school organizations. Building on research describing the intersection of political and nontraditional approaches to educational leadership, this chapter explores the possibilities for women's engagement with political frames, ways to define and negotiate agenda setting, to map the political terrain, networking and coalition building, and bargaining and negotiating. Moving beyond the current knowledge of the challenges and opportunities for women educational leaders in the United States (Shakeshaft et al., 2007), this chapter explores the idea of collective leadership that we see as conscious leadership in a political world. We consider what we can learn from women's approaches to leadership in a political and gendered world that nurtures a collective experience. In this chapter, we consider how the notion of leadership can be expanded by building on women's experiences of leadership.

STATUS OF WOMEN SCHOOL ADMINISTRATORS IN THE UNITED STATES

Numbers and Role

Although the representation of women in administrative positions in K-12 and higher education institutions is increasing, they are still not present in proportion to their number in teaching. For instance, although women are 75% of all teachers, they are only 44% of all principals and 18% of all superintendents. In the United States, women are twice as likely as men to hold a doctorate in education, but men are more than five times more likely to lead school districts (Shakeshaft et al., 2007).

The proportion of women by ethnicity in the superintendency is nearly impossible to determine in the United States because of the ways in which sex and race/ethnicity are reported. There are reports by sex or by ethnicity, but not by both sex and ethnicity. In the United States, female representation in the principal-ship is more robust than in the superintendency, but still not proportional to the number of women teachers; 34.5% of all public school principals and 53.6% of all private school principals are women, but only 3.2% of school principals are women of color (NCES, 2004).

BARRIERS TO WOMEN BECOMING ADMINISTRATORS

Although women have been underrepresented in leadership in the United States (and perhaps because they are underrepresented), there is a robust literature on women in educational leadership spanning the last three decades. Of most interest has been the attempt to understand why there are so few. At the same time, there has been considerable interest in knowing how women lead. Most of the research has looked at women principals and superintendents. There is also a growing interest in women leaders in higher education at the level of dean and president.

We have learned much from this scholarship. We now have a sense of what women leaders face in getting the positions and how they lead once they are there. Most of the literature has focused on white women mainly because there are still so few women of color in educational leadership positions, as noted above. However, some of the more recent work gives us a profile of these understudied women (see Alston, 2005; Benham, Sanders-Lawson, and Smith-Campbell, 2006; Brunner and Grogan, 2007; Mendez-Morse, 2004). Two chapters in *Handbook for Achieving Gender Equity through Education* (Cooper et al., 2007; Shakeshaft et al., 2007) are particularly helpful in summarizing what we know about women educational leaders. We draw upon these comprehensive literature reviews to provide a background for moving forward the conversation about women in leadership.

The review by Shakeshaft et al. (2007) notes changes in barriers from documentation in the mid-1980s. Women no longer lack confidence in their abilities and they aspire to most administrative positions. While family and home responsibilities still play a part in career decisions of women educators, there has been increased support and encouragement for women to become administrators. While women are no longer underrepresented in preparation for doctoral programs, these programs do not yet meet the needs of women students. Institutional racism and sexism still discourage and impede women's move into administration as well as their ability to progress through the system to the top positions.

HISTORY AND BACKGROUND OF U.S. RESEARCH ON WOMEN ADMINISTRATORS

The relationship of gender and leadership has almost always been studied within the political context of organizational and societal inequities. Although not always acknowledged by the researcher, many of the early studies of leadership style compared females to males in an attempt to provide documentation that either there were no differences between the two groups or that women were better school and organization administrators than men. This research was conducted in the larger context of few women being hired as administrators. This was partly because women were believed to be "unfit" for administrative jobs due to their supposed inability to discipline, to work with men, to "command" respect, and to possess rational and logical approaches to leadership. Thus, the research was not so much about identifying and isolating the gender aspects of leadership but to provide evidence that would support equitable treatment of women.

Moreover, in these early years, studies that did not compare women to men were deemed "inadequate." At this time, it was difficult to publish studies that focused only on women. Critics argued that research on women was valid only if it was linked to research on men. Male behavior was the measuring stick against which all studies of women were compared.

A number of researchers have noted that leadership theory is based primarily upon studies of males (Brown and Irby, 1995; Grogan, 1999; Shakeshaft and Nowell, 1984). These scholars point out that current leadership theory is not representative of the ways in which many women lead. These theories are not focused on collaborative, collective leadership, often perpetuate practices that are barriers for women, and are not inclusive of advocacy perspectives. Grogan (1999) suggests that new conceptions of leadership theories are needed not only so that we might better understand practice, but also because current leadership theories have contributed to inequities. She states, "It is reasonable to imagine that because women's lived experiences as leaders are different from men's, new theoretical understanding of a leadership that is premised on social justice might emerge" (p. 533).

Young and McLeod (2001) warn that "traditional leadership literature [including leadership theories] essentially legitimizes traditionally male behavior and perspectives and delegitimizes the behavior and perspectives of women" (p. 491). Additionally, Young and McLeod found that "exposure to nontraditional leadership styles is a key element in facilitating women's paths into administration" (p. 491). If women observe variations in leadership styles and expectations, they are more likely to believe that leadership is not only something they can do, but also something they might want to do. Traditional command and control structures discourage many women and men from pursuing leadership opportunities.

However, as more women moved into school administration and as scholars argued that women's styles should be researched in their own right, studies that observed, interviewed and surveyed only women administrators emerged. These studies sought to identify the ways in which women lead as well as to describe best practice, regardless of whether or not there were differences in the ways that men administer schools. These studies often concluded that female approaches were effective and could serve as models of best practice. Comparison studies by gender have continued to be published but the bulk of the studies from 1985 to 2007 are single-sex inquiries. This scholarship has attempted to describe aspects that relate to what is believed to be the female experience.

GENDER AND LEADERSHIP

Gender Differences in Leadership

The studies that compare female and male approaches to leadership are mixed. Further, method of inquiry interacts with conclusions: 100% of the qualitative studies and 14% of the quantitative studies document differences.

Where differences are reported, women are more likely than men to be rated by both those who work with them and by women administrators themselves as instructional, task oriented leaders (Nogay, 1995; Spencer, 2000). Women are identified as more relational and interpersonal, logging in more one-on-one contacts with staff (Counts, 1987; Nogay, 1995; Perry, 1992). However, men send more memos and write longer memos to staff than do women (Rodgers, 1986). Genge (2000) found that women are more likely to use humor as part of their leadership style and to defuse conflict. For women, a loyal staff member is one who is competent. For men, the most loyal staff members are the ones who agree with them publicly.

According to Gardiner, Enomoto and Grogan (2000), Gardiner and Tiggerman (1999), and Eagley and Johnson (1990), the gender context of the workplace makes a difference in leadership styles. Women are likely to be more interpersonal than males in female-dominated workplaces, but equally interpersonal in male-dominated workplaces. Women are equally task oriented in female-dominated organizations, but more task oriented than men in male-dominated organizations. Among the twelve female secondary principals that Applewhite (2001) studied, leadership approaches were strategically chosen based upon the context, with women sometimes using more female-identified strategies and sometimes using more male-identified strategies. Barbie (2004) and Rottler (1996) both describe a mix of traditionally male and female styles. Anatole (1997) found no specific Myers-Briggs pattern among the high school principals studied, although Harris (1991) determined that the female high school principals she studied used primarily holistic or whole-brain cognitive patterns.

Female Leadership Styles
Examining what the "work" of women's leadership looks like—whether or not it is qualitatively different from the "work" of leaders who are men—may provide insights into alternative models of leadership. The body of research that examines leadership behaviors suggests several components of women's leadership, although the gender-comparative studies fail to support that only women employ these approaches. The existence of a feminine leadership style, separate from the leadership strategies of "tokens," as defined by Kanter (1993), is not yet agreed upon. While women may employ particular styles that lead to success, the reason why they use these styles is unclear, as is the connection to gender. Nevertheless, researchers have identified at least five themes that are likely to be part of women's leadership.

SOCIAL JUSTICE Commitment to social justice is a thread that runs across a number of descriptions of what motivates women to enter administration and what keeps them focused (Sanders-Lawson, 2001; Shapiro, 2004; Smith-Campbell, 2002; Strachan, 1999, 2002). These studies describe behaviors that are compatible with moral leadership (Sergiovanni, 1999), servant leadership (Schlosberg, 2003; Sergiovanni, 1992), and value-added leadership (Covey, 1990; Sergiovanni,

1994), and synergistic leadership theory (Brown and Irby, 2006).

Women discuss their desire to "make things better," right social wrongs, and increase support for underserved groups. Several studies cast women's approach as "servant leadership" (Alston, 1999; Brunner, 1999) in which women seek to serve others by being the facilitator of the organization, bringing groups together, motivating students and staff and connecting with outside groups. In these studies, women "minister" to others in the spirit of the Latin roots of "administer." For instance, the ten women superintendents of African descent in Collins' (2002) study described their jobs as "a mission." Although not specifically identified as striving for or achieving a social justice mission, the work of Hines (1999) categorizes women administrators as transformative leaders on the Leadership Practices Inventory. Burdick (2004) found that teachers were more likely to rate women principals, as opposed to men, as reform leaders.

SPIRITUAL Several studies document an additional dimension that some women add to their social justice, moral or servant leadership approach. For instance, studies of African American women extend the ministerial aspect of their leadership and include a spiritual dimension (Benham et al., 2006; Bloom, 2001; Collins, 2002; Jones, 2003; Logan, 1989; Sanders-Lawson, 2001). Donaldson (2000), Stiernberg (2003), and Millar (2000) noted the spiritual dimensions of white women administrators.

These women administrators discuss the relationship between spirituality and the ways they model behavior and inspire others. Further, these women acknowledge the importance of their spirituality to their success and ability to push forward, often in conflictual and difficult situations.

RELATIONAL A number of researchers document the importance of relationships for women leaders that connect with communication, work in teams, collaboration, and community connections. Several studies document women's propensity to listen to others (Bynum, 2000), whether in teamwork or one-on-one. Researchers explore the themes of nurturing, emotional connections and interpersonal relationships among women administrators.

Among others, Formisano (1987), Carnivale (1994) and Smith (1996) note women's discomfort with being described as powerful or as having power. Women often describe power as something that increases as it is shared. In order for women to be comfortable with the notion of holding power, power needs to be conceptualized as something that is shared with others and that is not power over, but rather power with. The connection of power issues and the importance of relationships to women are crucial. Power used to help others strengthens relationships, while power used to control damages relationships.

INSTRUCTIONAL FOCUS Similar to learning-focused leadership recommended by Beck and Murphy (1996), a number of studies note that instruction is central to women. Women administrators are likely to introduce and support strong programs in staff development, encourage innovation and experiment with instructional approaches. Women are likely to stress the importance of instructional competence in teachers and to be attentive to task completion in terms of instructional programs. The importance of instruction overlaps with the social justice agenda of many women administrators.

STRIVING FOR BALANCE Women's leadership styles are developed within a framework of balancing personal and professional needs and responsibilities (Smulyan, 2000). Women administrators often report that it is difficult for them to determine the line between the personal and professional and describe decision-making strategies and management time allocation resolutions that balance both.

CONSCIOUS AND COLLECTIVE LEADERSHIP

Within the traditional leadership literature, the "great man" scholarship offers analysis of profiles of charismatic, heroic leaders. In contrast, women's leadership often has been described as creating a context that promotes shared meaning-making within a community of practice grappling with issues of equity and diversity. This seems to be consistent with the trend in the leadership literature focusing on cognitive leadership, sense-making, and the way a collective works. Women leaders are likely to provide rich examples of experiments in collective leadership. Gauthier (2006) notes that in many non-Western cultures, "leadership is considered a collective rather than an individual capacity; leadership is defined then as a relationship or process, not a person" (p. 3). This characterization often holds true for women in the Western world as well.

Traditional leadership literature often focuses on the "executive" aspects of leadership, drawn from the world of commerce, that rely upon formal organizational authority and power. School and other social justice and social action organizations are more likely to need to operate from a legislative perspective or one which relies upon shared interests or the ability to persuade.

However, more recently, it has been suggested that leadership requires brokers or "midwives" who help partners work together to collaboratively decide on and deliver the goals of the organization. There is increasing interest in understanding this work of leadership, as "the contextualized outcome of interactive, rather than unidirectional causal, processes" (Gronn, 2002, p. 444). Depending upon the disciplinary background and organizational base of the writer, this approach is variously called socially constructed, collected, distributed, shared, or co-leadership. Scholars argue that collective leadership is largely unexplored (Foldy, Goldman and Ospina, 2007; Pearce and Conger, 2003). We argue that examining the processes that women educational leaders engage is fertile ground for understanding this "work" of leadership.

For example, in the postsecondary arena, according to Cooper et al. (2007), particularly in the early years, women were known for their activism, through which they increased the numbers of women faculty and women students in their institutions. They were described as willing to change course, to forge alliances with supportive others, and to gain the necessary funds to achieve their goals. Throughout the latter half of the twentieth century, as the numbers increased, women were known for engaging in generative leadership practices to encourage participation, creativity and open communications. These descriptions highlight the contrast between the heroic male leadership stance, which was lauded for its individuality, decisiveness and vision. Women were described as forming webs in their institutions rather than pyramids, especially when institutional governance structures provided the necessary space. Under these circumstances, they were seen to involve others in decision-making and to enhance others' self-worth. Research literature notes that women presidents of community colleges, in particular, are thought to be able to use the power of the position to carry out an action agenda—particularly to reshape gender- and race-related institutional policies.

Scholars researching women in higher education as well as K-12 leadership pose the same question we do. If we can expand what it means to lead complex organizations in the twenty-first century, we may be able to move away from the male norms that continue to cast women as the "other" in leadership terms. Thus, in the spirit of such an endeavor, we explore some theoretical constructs that may shed light on how leadership can be reconceived.

We argue that the idea of collective leadership gaining ground in some of the literature has been built on the foundations of the kinds of leadership approaches that research attributes to women—although many men are gravitating toward the same approaches as we all inquire into their utility. Considering the notion of collective leadership, we suggest that advances in our knowledge of leadership, emerging from women's lives and experiences as leaders, offer ways to grasp promising nuances and opportunities embedded in these theories.

Collective Leadership

The above summary of current research suggests that women often use a leadership approach that engages others in leadership events and that is conscious of the use of power in a political context. Much of women's leadership experience coincides with change projects—particularly with challenges to the status quo on behalf of marginalized populations that have not been well served. Collective leadership theory suggests that:

> Leadership is relational: the group as a whole is a leader just as members within the group can be leaders within the group. Leadership emerges out of specific situations: the process of defining vision and setting direction, as well as exercising influence over other people and organizations, becomes a shared function of the group. (Benham et al., 2005, p. 4)

This is an important departure from the individualized account of leadership still prevalent in much of the business and educational literature today. Although some scholars have moved away from heroic accounts of leadership to acknowledge its distributed nature (see Gronn, 2000, 2002; Spillane, 2006), many are still interested in the notion of leadership as actor directed or coordinated. While distributed leadership considers the importance of collaboration and interdependence among organizational members, collective leadership offers us an opportunity to focus on the relationships, events and activities—particularly the unstructured intra- and interorganizational ones that contribute to organizational direction setting and goal achievement. This approach also allows us to pay attention to the fact that all organizations operate in relationship with their external environments. Instead of viewing schools and districts as closed systems, if leadership is about collective or shared frames of reference, then an open system offers more possibilities for evolving ideas that lead to productive change.

Benham et al. (2005) argue that what emerges from this kind of leadership is the notion of collective power. The idea is that relationships and alliances help create effective and sustainable organizational change. But we have not learned to think of leadership in consciously political terms. Many superintendents, for instance, while involved in various communities have not always thought of them as providing opportunities for deliberate support building activities. Escobar (2005) makes the point that knowledge of the various networks in a community can increase the capacities for mobilization and change for those involved. Drawing on de Landa (2005), he asserts that there are advantages and disadvantages to the kinds of low density or dispersed networks that are found in most communities in contrast to a network that has been actively focused on achieving a particular goal:

> Low density networks, with more numerous weak links, are . . . capable of providing their component members with novel information about fleeting opportunities. On the other hand, dispersed networks are less capable of supplying other resources, like trust in a crisis, the resources that define the strength of strong links. They are also less capable of providing constraints, such as enforcement of local norms. The resulting low degree of solidarity, if not compensated for in other ways, implies that as a whole, dispersed communities are harder to mobilize politically and less likely to act as causal agents in their interaction with other communities. (2005, p. 7)

Thus, the hard work of collective leadership would necessarily operate within and through the spaces created by various networks that are available to individuals or groups who participate in the formal and informal business of a school district. Literature on women's leadership suggests that women leaders have been possibly unconsciously engaged in some of these kinds of activities.

REFERENCES CITED

Alston, J. A. (1999). Climbing hills and mountains: Black females making it to the superintendency. In C. C. Brunner (Ed.), *Sacred dreams: Women and the superintendency* (pp. 79–90). Albany: State University of New York Press.

———. (2005). Tempered radicals and servant leaders: Black females persevering in the superintendency. *Educational Administration Quarterly, 41*(4), 409–422.

Anatolem, M. J. (1997). *The characteristics of female secondary principals*. Doctoral dissertation. University of Southern California.

Applewhite, A. S. (2001). *Factors influencing Colorado female secondary principals' leadership practices*. Doctoral dissertation. Colorado State University.

Avolio, B. J., Gardner, W. L., Walumbwa, F. O., Luthans, F., and May, D.R. (2004). Unlocking the mask: A look at the process by which authentic leaders impact follower attitudes and behaviors. *The Leadership Quarterly, 15*(6), 801–812.

Balkundi, P., and Kilduff, M. (2005). The ties that lead: A social network approach to leadership. *The Leadership Quarterly, 16*, 941–961.

Barbie, J. A. (2004). *Narratives of women's life experiences and how it informs their practice as school district superintendents.* Doctoral dissertation. University of Denver.

Beck, L., and Murphy, J. (1996). *The four imperatives of a successful school.* Thousand Oaks, CA: Corwin Press.

Benham, M., Militello, M. and Price, R. (2005). *Lessons in collective leadership.* [Online]. Retrieved May 7, 2007, from http://creatingspace.pbwiki.com/f/KLCC_Lessons_Collective_Leadership.pdf.

Benham, M., Sanders-Lawson, R., and Smith-Campbell, S. (2006). Wholistic visioning of leadership from the perspectives of Black women. In C. Marshall and M. Oliva (Eds.), *Leadership for social justice: Making revolutions in education.* Columbus, OH: Allyn and Bacon.

Bloom, C. M. (2001). *Critical race theory and the African-American woman principal: Alternative portrayals of effective leadership practice in urban schools.* Doctoral dissertation. Texas A&M University.

Brown, G., and Irby, B. J. (Eds.) (1995). *Women as school executives: Voices and visions.* Huntsville, TX: Texas Council of Women School Executives, Sam Houston Press. (ERIC Document Reproduction Service No. ED401252).

———. (1996). Effectiveness of the career advancement portfolio for women. *Catalyst for Change, 26*(1), 21–24.

———. (2006). Expanding the knowledge base: Socially just theory in educational leadership programs. In Fred Demobowski (Ed.), *Unbridled spirit* (pp. 7–13). Lancaster, PA: Proactive Publications.

Brunner, C. C. (1999). "Back talk" from a woman superintendent: Just how useful is research? In Brunner, C. C. (Ed.), *Sacred dreams: Women and the superintendency* (pp. 179–198). Albany: State University of New York Press.

Brunner, C. C., and Grogan, M. (2007). *Women leading school systems: Uncommon roads to fulfillment.* Lanham, MD: Rowman & Littlefield.

Burdick, D. C. (2004). "Women hold up half the sky": Is principal selection based on gender and leadership style? Doctoral dissertation. Arizona State University.

Bynum, V. (2000). An investigation of female leadership characteristics. Doctoral dissertation. Capella University.

Carnevale, P. (1994). An examination of the ways women in school administration conceptualize power. Doctoral dissertation. Hofstra University.

Carroll, W., and Ratner, R. (1996). Master framing and cross-movement networking in contemporary social movements. *The Sociological Quarterly, 37*(4), 601–625.

Cohen, J. (1999). Trust, voluntary association and workable democracy: The contemporary American discourse of civil society. In M. Warren (Ed.), *Democracy and trust* (pp. 208–245). Cambridge: Cambridge University Press.

Coleman, J. (1990). *Foundations of social theory.* Cambridge, MA: Harvard University Press.

Collins, P. L. (2002). *Females of color who have served as superintendent: Their journeys to the superintendency and perceptions of the office.* Doctoral dissertation. Seton Hall University.

Cooper, J., Eddy, P., Hart, J., Lester, J., Lukas, S., Eudey, B., Glazer-Raymo, J., and Madden, M. (2007). Improving gender equity in postsecondary education. In S. Klein, B. Richardson, D. A. Grayson, L. H. Fox, C. Kramarae, D. Pollard, and C. A. Dwyer (Eds.), *Handbook for achieving gender equity through education* (3rd ed., pp. 631–653). Florence, KY: Lawrence Erlbaum Associates.

Counts, C. D. (1987). *Toward a relational managerial model for schools: A study of women and men as superintendents and principals.* Doctoral dissertation. Harvard University.

Covey, S. (1990). *The 7 habits of highly effective people.* New York: Simon & Schuster.

Donaldson, C. A. M. (2000). *Together and alone: Women seeking the principalship.* Doctoral dissertation. University of Calgary.

Eagley, A. H., and Johnson, B. T. (1990). Gender and leadership style: A meta-analysis. *Psychological Bulletin, 106*(2), 233–256.

Escobar, A. (2007). The "ontological turn" in social theory: A commentary on "Human Geography Without Scale," by Sallie Marston, John Paul Jones II, and Keith Woodward. *Transactions of the Institute of British Geographers, 32*(1), 106–111.

Flora, J., Sharp, J., Flora, C., and Newlon, B. (1997). Entrepreneurial social infrastructure and locally initiated economic development in the nonmetropolitan United States. *The Sociological Quarterly, 38*(4), 623–645.

Foldy, E. G., et al. (2008). Sensegiving and the role of cognitive shifts in the work of leadership. *The Leadership Quarterly,* doi:10.1016/j.leaqua.2008.07.004.

Formisano, J. (1987). *The approaches of female public school principals toward conflict management: A qualitative study.* Doctoral dissertation, Hofstra University.

Gardiner, M., and Tiggemann, M. (1999). Gender differences in leadership style, job stress and mental health in male- and female-dominated industries. *Journal of Occupational & Organizational Psychology, 72* (3), 301.

Gardiner, M. E., Enomoto, E., and Grogan, M. (2000). *Coloring outside the lines: Mentoring women into school leadership.* Albany: State University of New York Press.

International Labor Organization (2002). *International women's day 2004.* Retrieved March 9, 2005, from http://www.ilo.org/public/english/bureau/inf/magizine/5.

Gardiner, W. L., and Avolio, B. J. (1998). The charismatic relationship: A dramaturgical perspective. *Academy of Management Review, 23*(1), 32–58.

Gauthier, Alan. (2006). *Developing collective leadership: Partnering in multi-stakeholder contexts.* Leadership is global: Bridging sectors and communities. [Online]. Retrieved May 7, 2007, from http://www.leadershiplearning.org/creating_space/2007/GauthierArticle.pdf.

Genge, M. C. (2000). *The development of transformational leaders: The journeys of female and male secondary school principals, alike or different?* Doctoral dissertation. University of Toronto.

Gioia, D. A., and Chittipeddi, K. (1991). Sensemaking and sensegiving in strategic change initiation. *Strategic Management Journal, 12,* 433–448.

Granovetter, M. (1973). The strength of weak ties. *American Journal of Sociology, 81,* 1287–1303.

Grogan, M. (1999). Equity/equality issues of gender, race and class. *Educational Administration Quarterly, 36*(1), 117–142.

Gronn, P. (2000). Distributed properties: A new architecture for leadership. *Educational Management and Administration, 28*(3), 317–338.

———. (2002). Distributed leadership as a unit of analysis. *The Leadership Quarterly, 13,* 423–451.

Harris, P. B. (1991). Profiles in excellence: Leadership styles of female principals in high schools of excellence. Doctoral dissertation. University of North Carolina, Greensboro.

Hines, J. A. (1999). A case study of women superintendents in the state of Ohio in their roles as transformational leaders in creating school district climate. Doctoral dissertation. University of Akron.

Johnston, C. (1996). *Unlocking the will to learn.* Thousand Oaks, CA: Corwin Press.

Jones, S. N. (2003). The praxis of black female educational leadership from a systems thinking perspective. Doctoral dissertation. Bowling Green State University.

Kadushin, C. (2004). Some basic network concepts and propositions.[Online]. Retrieved July 5, 2007, from http://home.earthlink.net/~ckadushin/Texts/Basic%20Network%20Concepts.pdf.

Kanter, R. M. (1977). *Men and women of the corporation.* New York: Basic Books.

Logan, C. B. M. (1989). Black and white leader perception of school culture. Doctoral dissertation. Hofstra University.

Masson, D. (2006). Constructing scale/contesting scale: Women's movement and rescaling politics in Quebec. *Social Politics, 13,* 462–486.

Mayo, M., Meindle, J. R., and Pastor, J. C. (2003). Shared leadership in work teams: A social network approach. In C. L. Pearce and J. A. Conger (Eds.), *Shared leadership: Reframing the hows and whys of leadership* (pp. 193–214). Thousand Oaks, CA: Sage Publications.

Melucci, A. (1992). Collective action between actors and systems. In M. Diani and R. Eyerman (Eds.), *Studying collective action* (pp. 238–257). Newbury Park, CA: Sage Publications.

Mendez-Morse, S. E. (2004). Constructing mentors: Latina educational leaders: Role models and mentors. *Educational Administration Quarterly, 40*(4), 561–590.

Millar, V. J. (2000). The organizational entry and socialization of women in educational leadership positions: A case study. Doctoral dissertation. Eastern Michigan University.

NCES (National Center for Education Statistics). (2004). *The digest of education statistics, 2004. Chapter 2: Elementary and secondary education.* Retrieved on March 6, 2005, from NCES Web site: http://nces.ed.gov/programs/digest/d03/ch_2.asp.

Nogay, K. H. (1995). The relationship of the superordinate and subordinate gender to the perceptions of leadership behaviors of female secondary principals. Doctoral dissertation. Youngstown State University.

Osterman, K., and Kottkamp, R. (2004). *Reflective practice: Professional development to improve student learning* (2nd ed.). Thousand Oaks, CA: Corwin Press.

Pearce, C. L., and Conger, J. A. (2003). *Shared leadership: Reframing the hows and whys of leadership.* Thousand Oaks, CA: Sage Publications.

Perry, A. B. (1992). A comparison of the ways that women and men principals supervise teachers. Doctoral dissertation. Hofstra University.

Rogers, E. J. (1986). An examination of the written communications of male and female elementary school principals. Doctoral dissertation. Hofstra University.

Rottler, J. M. (1996). The women superintendents of Iowa: A 1990's analysis. Doctoral dissertation. University of Northern Iowa.

Sanders-Lawson, E. R. (2001). Black women school superintendents leading for social justice. Doctoral dissertation. Michigan State University.

Schlosberg, T. V. (2003). Synergistic leadership: An international case study: The transportability of the synergistic leadership theory to selected educational leaders in Mexico. (Doctoral dissertation, Sam Houston State University, 2003.) *Dissertation Abstracts International, 64,07A.*

Senge, P. (1990). *The fifth discipline.* New York: Doubleday/Currency.

Sergiovanni, T. J. (1994). *Building community in schools.* San Francisco: Jossey-Bass.

———. (1999). *Rethinking leadership: A collection of articles.* Arlington Heights, IL: SkyLight Training and Publishing.

Shakeshaft, C. (1990). The struggle to create a more gender inclusive profession. *Handbook of Research on Educational Administration.* San Francisco: Jossey-Bass.

Shakeshaft, C., Brown, G., Irby, G., Grogan, M., and Ballenger, J. (2007). Increasing gender equity in educational leadership. In S. Klein, B. Richardson, D. A. Grayson, L. H. Fox,

C. Kramarae, D. Pollard, and C. A. Dwyer (Eds.), *Handbook for achieving gender equity through education* (2nd ed., pp. 103–130). Florence, KY: Lawrence Erlbaum Associates.

Shakeshaft, C., and Nowell, I. (1984). Research on theories, concepts, and models of organizational behavior: The influence of gender. *Issues in Education, 2(3)*, 186–200.

Shamir, B., House, R. J., and Arthur, M. B. (1993). The motivational effects of charismatic leadership: A self-concept based theory. *Organizational Science, 4*(4), 577–594.

Shapiro, L. (2004). Disrupting what is going on: Women educational leaders make art together to transform themselves and their schools. Doctoral dissertation. Union Institute and University.

Smircich, L., and Morgan, G. (1982). Leadership: The management of meaning. *Journal of Applied Behavioral Science, 18*(3), 257–273.

Smith, S. J. (1996). Women administrators: Concepts of leadership, power and ethics. Doctoral dissertation. University of Wyoming.

Smith-Campbell, S. I. (2002). Exploring the world of Black women middle school principals. Doctoral dissertation. Michigan State University.

Spencer, W. A., and Kochan, F. K. (2000, January 24). Gender-related differences in career patterns of principals in Alabama: A statewide study. *Education Policy Analysis Archives, 8*(9).

Spillane, J. P. (2006). *Distributed leadership.* San Francisco: Jossey-Bass.

Stiernberg, P. W. (2003). The relationship between spirituality and leadership practices of female administrators in K-12 schools. Doctoral dissertation. Baylor University.

Strachan, J. (1999). Feminist educational leadership: Locating the concepts in practice. *Gender & Education, 11*(3), 309–323.

Terranova, T. (2004). *Network culture.* Ann Arbor, MI: Pluto Press.

Wheatley, M. (2006). *Leadership and the new science: Discovering order in a chaotic world* (3rd ed.). San Francisco: Berret-Koehler.

Young, M. D., and McLeod, S. (2001). Flukes, opportunities, and planned interventions: Factors affecting women's decisions to become school administrators. *Educational Administration Quarterly, 37*(4), 462–502.

CHAPTER 4

Disappearing Gender

Choices in Identity

Jacky Lumby

LOCATING GENDER

THIS CHAPTER LOCATES GENDER as one of the multiple identities that comprise the fluid kaleidoscope of an individual existence. It suggests that its effects may mutate as it intersects with other characteristics and as the individual in question chooses to foreground, conceal or transform how gender is self-perceived and projected to others.

The chapter challenges a focus on gender as a single characteristic. The concerns it reflects are longstanding. At the start of the twentieth century W. E. B. Du Bois insisted that race be linked to gender and class in analyses of disadvantage (Du Bois, 1903/1968; Hancock, 2005; hooks, 2000). In the same tradition, black writers have deplored "'race free' feminism" (Rooney, 2006, p. 359) and a critique has been sustained of "white middle-class feminists who have held the gatekeeping positions in terms of feminism and feminist journals" (Valentine, 2007, p. 12). Queer theory equally challenges essentialist notions (Sloop, 2005). Consequently, an insistence that gender be considered alongside race, class and sexuality has been evident for some time. More recently still, there has been an insistence that other characteristics such as status (Stets and Harrod, 2004), religion (Rooney, 2006; Shah, 2006), and culture (Sen, 2006) be considered simultaneously and holistically when discussing issues such as diversity, inclusion and equality.

As a logical development, the concept of intersectionality has emerged within the social sciences. This theoretical framework assumes that identities, including gender, are multiple, fluid, in part self-constructed and in part socially and organizationally constructed; that a perspective on a single characteristic such as gender risks active harm in encouraging the "appalling effects of the miniaturization of people" (Sen, 2006, p. xvi) and is in research terms unhelpful in privileging one characteristic over another. Intersectionality is a developing framework intended to support increased understanding of how different identities work together to create or avoid a response from others that advantages or disadvantages an individual or group.

One premise of this chapter is therefore that rather than focusing on gender, there may be great utility in locating gender within the complexity of individual identities and considering the relationship of the latter to inclusion or exclusion in leadership. The chapter adopts a concept of gender as "a practice of improvisation within a scene of constraint" (Butler, 2004, p. 1). Rather like improvisation in a theater, the performance of gender is constructed in response to others but within the implicit or explicit parameters exerted by the individual, organizational and social context. In summary, the chapter aims to place gender within "geometries of oppression" (Valentine, 2007, p. 11) by considering the nature of identity and the theoretical framework of intersectionality.

A second premise is that gender not only intersects with many other characteristics but also apparently appears and disappears within the identity performance. In contexts where being a woman leader provokes anxiety in others, suppression or disguise of gender or misdirection strategies may be utilized by the individual to circumvent possible negative responses (Goffman, 1986; Gurin and Nagda, 2006; Stone and Colella, 1996). Gender for women may be one identity that retreats behind or emerges from smoke screens, each time metamorphosed by its intersection with other identities.

IDENTITY

The concept of identity is hotly contested within a very large body of literature (Bauman, 2004). Identity formation is understood as "an interlocking personal and social project under particular discursive conditions of possibility" (Walker, 2005, p. 42); that is, identity is the creation of a self-concept, in part self- and in part socially constructed, always in response to the limitations of what is acceptable. The limitations may be accepted or resisted, but either way, they shape identity. The relevance of the concept of identity to gender is that it places the latter within a system of negotiated, fluid choices that are in part controlled by the individual and in part imposed. Identity is a performance in which what is constructed is part of the battery to create, maintain, defend and enhance self-worth and status in the eyes of others (Bauman, 2004; Goffman, 1959). It is intimately related to notions of power. Identities are adjusted to ensure that the response from others validates our self-concept. Such processes may not be, or be only in part, conscious (Stets and Harrod, 2004).

That identities change over time is not in dispute. Burke (2006) suggests that they can change in a number of ways. First, the nature of the single identity can change. How a woman characterizes her identity as "leader" or "spouse" might mutate. Second, the identity of leader or spouse that is foregrounded in the performance or given priority might change over time. Third, the characteristics of two distinct identities might align themselves more closely, so that discrepancies or tensions between being a leader and a spouse may be lessened. The catalyst of change may be small everyday decisions, or more noticeable changes in life circumstances. Equally Burke (op. cit.) suggests that large external changes may affect identity. For example, the changing expectations and conditions of education may challenge notions of identity as a leader.

Identities may not be congruent in the eyes of the individual or those with whom the individual comes into contact. The incongruity drives change. Identity theory challenges us to consider the experience of each individual who uniquely comprises multiple identities related to her history, personal and professional selves. It also demands that we link the mutations in identity to power. Bauman (2004) asserts that the degree of control over identity is related to the resources held by individuals, including their status, and also the financial resource to create a different identity through the symbolic adoption of a particular lifestyle or workplace setting (Bauman, 2004). Those who have less power are less able to resist their identity being defined by others and the negative or limiting consequences of imposition. Equally, the security of belonging to a high-status group, or longing for such security, may be powerful shapers of identity.

The mechanisms of changing identity in educational leaders are poorly researched and understood. Linking such mechanisms to an ability to lead effectively in a way which one values and is valued by others, is as yet a distant dream. Intersectionality is a framework that offers some promise of progress.

INTERSECTIONALITY

What problems or limitations in previous approaches to researching and theorizing gender does intersectionality address? The literature suggests a number of issues:

Identity, and specifically gender, is fixed; that is, to be a woman is taken as an essentialist common feature of the biologically female who can therefore be researched as part of a homogeneous group. Intersectionality assumes that gender is a fluid performance and but one of multiple identities, created in part by self and in part by other individuals, groups and structures. Its meaning is elusive and plural (Butler, 2004).

Oppression is primarily related to a few selected identities; that is, it is appropriate to consider gender, ethnicity/race, class, disability and sexuality. Intersectionality demands the incorporation of the full range of identities that may affect the individual's experience. In education this might include subject background, first language and hierarchical position in the school or college (Lumby with Coleman, 2007).

Oppression can be understood by an additative method. Understanding individuals' experience can be achieved by adding together what we have learned from researching the response to single characteristics. For example, if we add what we know of sexism and racism, we will get a complete picture of the experience of black women. Intersectionality rather insists that identities interlock, mutually influence, negate, heighten and transform in an ongoing metamorphosis. Oppression is experienced in relation to the complex unfolding tale of multiple identities, the sum of which is qualitatively different to the addition of the parts (Butler, 1990).

Identity is created by social structures. For example, patriarchal and capitalist systems position gender. Intersectionality adds to this understanding by focusing on identity as created by the minutiae of context-specific interactions between individuals and groups (Valentine, 2007).

Status is insufficiently included in analyses; the differential power which accrues to an individual because of any characteristic may be heightened or negated by status. The powerful impact of status is underestimated (Stets and Harrod, 2004).

Intersectionality is therefore a theoretical and empirical attempt to push on our capacity to understand the lived experience of women and men in a way that engages more fully with the complex, contradictory and constantly transforming experience of their lives. It does not negate previous learning about how gender may disadvantage. Rather it potentially challenges us to view work to date as part of the process in the evolution of our understanding and action, and to press on.

DISAPPEARING GENDER

As well as interacting with other characteristics, the impact of gender on leadership relates to its mutability in individuals' perception of themselves and others. Identities are colored as positive or negative attributes by reference to the standards of what is "normal" in a particular context. Being female may therefore be viewed as highly positive in the family context, but as problematic within leadership groups where it may be seen as deviant from a male norm. "Woman" and "mother/wife" construe as consistent. "Woman" and "educational leader" may not (Coleman, 2002). Consequently in educational leadership, being female may be seen by colleagues, children or parents as a stigma—"an attribute that is deeply discrediting" (Goffman, 1986, p. 3). The degree of stigma relates to the specific context. A woman elementary/primary school principal among a staff of women may be less stigmatized than a female high/secondary school principal in a majority male staff. Equally, the stigma that attaches to her gender may be insignificant compared to that which attaches to one or more of her other characteristics.

Whatever its degree, the effects of a stigma are multiple and complex. For example, explanation of the achievement of the stigmatized may differ from that related to the majority group. Appointment to a leadership post of a stigmatized person may be interpreted as the result of outstanding courage, persistence or ability. Relationships also are affected. Whatever others profess, they may not accept the stigmatized person fully or unproblematically. The reaction of both men and women to the stigmatized female leader has layers of complexity that would not be the case with the "default identities" (Walker, 2005, p. 49) or "normals" as Goffman (1986) names those who conform to the standards of the group. The normals' response to the stigmatized may be to consider whether they need to be especially sensitive or considerate, or if such sensitivity is in fact likely to be considered insulting. The interaction is uncomfortable for both:

> Each potential source of discomfort for [the stigmatized] when we are with him [sic] can become something we sense he is aware of, aware that we are aware of, and even aware of our state of awareness about his awareness; the stage is then set for the infinite regress of mutual consideration. (p. 18)

In response the individual may adopt "defensive cowering" or "hostile bravado" or oscillate between the two (op. cit., p. 17). And once the stigmatized reaches the highest layer of hierarchy, she may then become a representative of those who have overcome the stigma; in the case of gender, a "successful" woman. Whether she wishes it or not, her gender is now a badge of honor as much as a stigma. She is viewed as a representative of the group of which she is atypical.

In summary, the negativity that attaches to a single identity such as gender may vary by context, for example, depending on how rare or otherwise a female leader is in a schooling age phase or in a particular country/cultural group. The stigma may be deepened by the presence of other attributes perceived as deviant, such as minority ethnicity, atypical educational background, or minority sexuality. Alternatively it may be negated, virtually obliterated as a negative identity by the overpowering stigmatizing force within a particular context of an alternative characteristic such as ethnicity. It may be transformed into the opposite of stigma, a badge of honor, by the powerful cleansing force of status.

MANAGING IDENTITY

The performance of gender is therefore likely to be intended to manage responses. In order to do so, it is in part a choice of whether to place gender in the foreground or to make it disappear entirely. Stone and Colella (1996, p. 357) write of the wide variety of "impression management strategies" employed by those with disabilities to shape not only the cognitive but also the affective response of others. Women may use similar strategies to manipulate how others see their gender, or even to misdirect them to focus elsewhere.

Two prevalent strategies which suppress identities perceived as "other" by the majority are described by Gurin and Nagda (2006). *Decategorization* strives to encourage seeing people as individuals rather than as members of a group, thereby avoiding group stereotypes: "I am uniquely me, not a woman seen predominantly as indistinguishable from the group categorized as women, or any subgroup such as African American women." *Recategorization* draws out-groupers into the in-group through common tasks and symbols of identity, sidestepping difference to emphasize one single group rather than an in-group and out-groups: "My identity is a member of the senior leadership team, not a woman." A third strategy, *intragroup solidarity,* intends the opposite effect, placing the stigmatized characteristic into the foreground. This emphasizes differences through establishing groups that share a characteristic, such as black groups or gay/lesbian groups. This is evident in feminist writing and in groups that form a mutually supporting "circle of lament" (Goffman, 1986, p. 20).

In the remainder of the chapter, the conceptual frameworks of identity, intersectionality and Gurin and Nagda's (op. cit.) strategies are used to analyze the self-perception of a sample of women, exploring how they see their gender identity in relation to leadership, and the circumstances in which it has been foregrounded, disappeared or mutated.

WOMEN LEADERS' EXPERIENCE—METHODOLOGY

The analysis draws on interviews with women who were part of two studies constructing cases around the intersection of leadership and diverse identities undertaken in England and South Africa. The research was intended to explore with leaders at a variety of levels in differing roles the interrelationship of identities, group membership and leadership inclusion/exclusion (Lumby et al., 2007).

A rich data set resulted. This chapter does not present the analysis and implications of the full set. Rather it uses interviews with selected women leaders to explore how we might understand their construction of a leadership identity, where gender fits or does not in their own estimation, and in what ways their self-perceived gender had become more or less significant or had changed during their careers. As such it makes no claim to be representative of women or any subgroup of women. Rather the interviews selected are used "to exemplify critical points" (Walker, 2005, p. 45) and to search for questions rather than answers.

Interviews are viewed as a mutually constructed performance that reflects the respondent's performance of gender and other identities. Scheuerich (1995) argues that in interviews, language "is persistently slippery, unstable, and ambiguous from person to person, from situation to situation, from time to time" (p. 240) and that attempting to resolve and wrest unambiguous meaning from interviews "borders on a kind of violence" (p. 242). Accepting such ambiguities, this analysis nevertheless attempts to arrive at some understanding of how each respondent believes her identity has been shaped and relates to her leadership, or at least what she believes at that point in time. Rather than the interviews being conceptualized as in some sense giving access to "real" experience, the analysis rests on the assumption that the chapter reflects the construction by the researcher

of a construction by the respondents; my narrative of their narrative, which acknowledges the "radical indeterminacy at the heart of the interview interaction which cannot be overcome by any methodology" (Scheuerich, 1995, p. 250).

Maintaining confidentiality renders it problematic to provide detailed contextual information about the women and their organizations, so limited background is provided. Pseudonyms are used throughout.

WOMEN LEADERS' EXPERIENCE: THE DATA

Gender as Significant and Insignificant

SUMEY Sumey is an Asian-origin head of department in an elementary school in South Africa, of the group previously categorized as "colored" during the apartheid era. She is one of very few nonwhite members of staff and the only one who holds a leadership role. She believes she brings new ideas, flexibility and a willingness to listen:

> If I specify my role, I will be sitting there thinking how we can do something new; how we can approach in a different light . . . I like to think of as many options as possible. I never believe that there is one way, a right way of doing things . . . I really like to look at things differently and to try and understand other people's points of view.

In adopting this leadership identity, she battles with stereotypically limiting notions of both her youth and her ethnicity.

> Some people's reaction was "You will learn with time." Other people's reaction is "You will just have to do as we say," you know. They want to enforce their way type of thing. And then of course there is also I think, simmering beneath somewhere, that I would think differently because I am not white. . . . So you know [they think] I would not want to follow because I am not white.

She also faces a belief that she is a token:

> Although I know what I am worth to the school, I sometimes think I am just like a token in the school to be able to say that they have somebody who is colored and she has been on the committee and she has done this at the school and it's a good face to wear to the public.

and that she is betraying her own community:

> I know there are people in the community who think, ah, she thinks she is there but she is being used. I don't

think I am being used because just as much as they are using me I use them in return. I also want to get somewhere. I also want to promote myself.

Asked if her gender influenced people's reaction to her, she believed not:

I don't think so, especially not in primary schools as there are only about five or six men on roll and in primary schools you are going to find women in leadership roles.

Being a woman is congruent with leadership in this school. Minority ethnicity is not and youth is not. Sumey believes her primary battle is to overcome the negative legacy of racism and apartheid:

There is still an undercurrent of distrust, not distrust but of not really being able to accept that people of color could also have a good point to make, could also have something strong and something worthwhile to bring.

In this case, the intersection of two identities perceived as incongruent with leadership, youthfulness and minority ethnicity, and the relative lack of status compared to senior leaders are apparent. Gender appears a nonissue to Sumey because it is congruent with leadership and because it is submerged beneath identities that have much greater stigmatizing force. The intersection of identities, historical and current contexts is clearly visible. The experience of being a minority ethnic woman in a specific context may metamorphose the construction of gender by self and others in an infinite number of ways. In this case, not only ethnicity but first language and age were important chromosomes in the identity DNA. And just as in DNA, extremely small differences can have huge effects on the physical and psychological nature of the individual, so small shadings within identities will provoke disproportionately differentiated responses from others.

Being of Asian origin was assumed "other" in a particular way in South Africa, related to decades of institutionalized white belief in the lesser abilities of nonwhite races and the particular stereotypes related to Asian people. The ethnicity-related assumptions about lesser competence intersects with youth, also assumed to be less competent than the more aged and experienced. Ethnicity and youth appear to interact to heighten the stereotype of lesser competence in a way that makes leadership more problematic for this

woman than for white men and women or for older staff.

MARGARET Margaret, a faculty leader in a UK college, is black and disabled. She believes she is subject to stereotypical assumptions. Her appointment was seen to offer an advantage to the institution in that it was assumed that she could communicate better with the local black community. She questions why she is assumed to have better skills of communicating with a community of which she has no more knowledge than many other staff. "It's like, why? Why? Oh, because I'm black." She was aware of the negative response of some to her appointment. "It left me at the disadvantage of never feeling equal to the people at the same level as me. . . . I work twice as hard to be just about equal and that's not good for morale." Like Sumey, she also feels like a token person. "They did not have anybody . . . that was ethnic minority and now there are two of us, one girl, one boy, so good; ticked that box." Even more disturbingly, she believes the response to her disability combines ignorance and manipulation. "They have never kind of got it that I'm in pain most of the time." Requests for particular facilities have consequently not been granted. She believes that this is in part a strategy to ensure she does not aspire too high or value her status too much: "a deliberate ploy, immoral, nasty, malicious . . . so I don't get an idea above my station, to make sure that I'm in pain." The intersection of two identities and its devastating effect on her capacity to lead is evident. Gender is also a factor, though relatively minor in her view:

There is no doubt that my immediate line manager sees me as needy and neurotic. He never says that. It's just the way he kind of behaves to me, kind of pats me on the head. Are you a bit stressed today? No, I am not, you know. Does he behave with the men that way?

The three identities related to ethnicity, disability and gender intersect with her personal choices in projecting her identity. Where Sumey tried to "sweet talk" people into agreeing, Margaret is assertive:

Being black, I have been brought up in a culture where you're the black awkward chip on the shoulder blah, blah, blah, whatever. I have been brought up that the majority of people aren't going to like me so blah, blah that's what I am expecting. So the risk for me to say something is not a very great risk.

While being strong and assertive may correlate with leadership, this is undermined by the three identities that are not congruent. The latter are met with attempts at "managing" her identities, by pats on the head, by manipulating her environment to be painful, by limiting her contribution to that seen as stereotypically appropriate. The result is, in her estimation, that the way people perceive her impacts on her ability to lead "hugely and it is going to be an issue for me all my career, the way I am, the person I am." In this case gender has not disappeared, but sits alongside other identities. Margaret does not place her gender in the foreground. Nor does she make it disappear. Her interwoven identities are complex and, she believes, perceived so negatively by many that she has little influence over the perception of her identity by others.

It may be that multiple incongruence cumulatively disempowers the leader's ability to shape identity in the eyes of others, and each identity suggests strategies for undermining not only the single identity but one or more other identities as well. The response to her disability in her view is used to ensure she remains subjugated. Her disability has become a tool for the white majority to ensure it remains in control of her as a black woman. She is denied both recategorization and decategorization. That is, she is not recategorized as a manager or leader. Nor is she decategorized, becoming just "Margaret." She remains firmly located as a black, disabled woman. The remaining strategy, in Gurin and Nagda's terms, is to join "a circle of lament" (Goffman, 1986, p. 20). She has not chosen to do this, but instead to expect and accept a career-long imposition of identity by others with all the limitations it places on her leadership.

Stone and Colella (1996) offer a number of possible explanations for the effects of the intersection between two characteristics. For example, they suggest that the negative attributes associated with minority ethnic groups may coincide with those associated with disabilities. For instance, if African Americans are stereotypically assumed to be unintelligent and lazy, these attributes enter into synergy with the stereotypical attributes of the disabled having limited physical and mental stamina. As a consequence, the intersection of the two identities augments the negative response to each. The effect is not additive but exponential, and the response from others is also augmented, an amplified negative or positive attitude as people react antithetically or, being aware of this, overcompensate in the contrary direction. They also suggest that disability may be seen less negatively in women, because the stereotypical correlates of disability, "lack of physical strength or endurance" (p. 367), are incongruent with

the male stereotype and congruent with the female stereotype. The complex interrelationships of disability and other characteristics are evident. However, while Stone and Colella consider dyads of identities, gender and disability, social status and disability, they do not explore the effect of more than two identities intersecting. In Margaret's case she potentially projected three stigmatized identities within leadership: being a woman, disabled and black. In her own estimation two stigmatized identities, being disabled and black, heightened each other to result in instances where people experienced her as very disquieting. Her characterization of people's response to her melds reactions to her ethnicity, her disability, her gender and her personal approach to communicating.

HELEN Helen, a white UK college curriculum leader in a male-dominated area, described the evolution of her identity from a shy teenager to someone who was assertive and seen just like the men, as one of them:

> You can't walk in and say I am different because I am a woman. You're as good as them. . . . As long as you can do the job, that's it—the be all and end all. It doesn't matter what color you are or what gender, disabled or not, can you do it and that's it.

Gender has disappeared, through a process that was traumatic at times. "I've always felt I had to prove myself . . . I used to go home crying my eyes out. It was tough, really tough." The identity of competent professional has been placed in the foreground in order to take a place as an equal. The process of having to prove herself to colleagues appears to have ceased and gender has, in her eyes, disappeared. She has become a quasi male, or in Gurin and Nagda's terms, recategorized.

Youth was a factor as well as gender. Among her colleagues, Helen's youth appeared to her as a positive identity, met by others with the assumption that she would bring fresh ideas. Unlike Sumey's experience, the intersection of professionalism and age created a positive and confident leadership identity where gender had apparently disappeared.

Goffman (1986, p. 41) suggests that those who are different may attempt to escape the "careful disattention" given to the discrediting identity by cooperating in a pretense of sameness. "The cooperation of a stigmatized person with normals in acting as if his [sic] known differentness were irrelevant and not attended to is one main possibility in the life such a person" Goffman (1986, p. 42). How is one to interpret the disappearance of gender? Clearly being a woman with female characteristics was perceived by Helen as so deeply incongruent with the role of leader in this context that she chose to, and was able to, recategorize, to choose youth and professionalism as primary identities. As a consequence, she says, "I don't see myself as different. I am just the same as them" and, tellingly, "everyone is treated just normally." Her language is significant. Helen has joined the normals.

Paradoxically, though gender has disappeared, it is central in Helen's identity, the aspect of herself most important to control in self-perception and in the response of others. To adapt Walker's (2005) phrase, gender is nowhere and everywhere in Helen's life and leadership. The need to obliterate gender highlights its centrality in shaping her identity. Ironically, among the sample of women Helen, who assessed her gender as unproblematic, may have been the most profoundly affected by it in her identity.

ANN Ann, a white UK college leader with responsibility for managing resources, considers gender to be an important factor that had an impact on her ability to lead. Her role is one generally undertaken by men. She believes that her gender was the primary identity of significance to others, and that it results in prejudiced assessments of her ability and achievement. In response to others' persistent lack of confidence in her ability to do her job, she feels the need to work harder, be smarter than her male colleagues and never make mistakes, as she tried "not to let standards drop and not to give them the opportunity [to criticize] I suppose as well. . . . You do get to the stage where you think 'I should not have to keep doing this.'" The process of proving herself was unending. She did not appear to have the option to recategorize as Helen had done. Nor, being an older woman, did she have an alternative positive identity, that of youth.

The data suggest that one woman was permitted by others to recategorize and felt the process of proving herself had finished while another faced an unending demand for proof of competence. Does the willingness of one to adopt a particular affective stance, not showing emotion or weakness, explain the discrepancy? Much gender literature has asserted this for some time. Goffman (1986) recounts examples of the stigmatized who attempt to correct their failings in the perceptions of others. In this case, Helen had undergone a process of toughening up and becoming assertive, and had over time removed what would be perceived as stereotypically feminine characteristics.

However, the data suggest that issues of age and status were also key. Ann, a middle leader, was of higher status than Helen. Is recategorization more acceptable when intersected with status at the extremes of the hierarchical spectrum? At one end of a leadership hierarchy, a woman team leader is but one of a large group. The competition she presents to the others for resource or promotion is relatively small. The intersections of status and gender render the latter less problematic than at middle level, where a woman who is very unusual in a particular role is one of a smaller group and so presents a higher level of competition. Once a principal, competition is irrelevant. Gender acquires the luster of status and is lauded. In Helen's case, intersections of status and age (youth) shape how her gender is perceived. In Ann's case, the same characteristics of status and age (middle age) interact with gender in quite different ways.

EDITH Gender also can be set in the foreground as significant in a positive sense. A white female principal, Edith, celebrated her gender. Others in the organization also saw her gender as a significant identity and one that was powerful and positive:

> Everything here was run by white males, middle class. They were given power and now we have a new team to engender trust and respect. We have turned the corner . . . before there was a lot of male domination, but now that has changed because we have a female principal.

Edith described a previous era as paternalistic, when the male principal looked after staff, even at a cost to students. She has taken on that role but with a twist:

> I want to be seen as a good leader, as someone who is visionary, someone who takes the college forward, someone who is passionate and stands up for the college, someone who listens and puts the student first, which is part of the paternalistic thing and I suppose it is part of the maternalistic thing isn't it, that you want to put the children first.

She describes her role here as both father and mother. However, her religion was also an important aspect of her self-constructed identity, in its turn shaping how she saw the identity of "mother." This woman used multiple identities, as woman, as leader, as spouse, as mother, as father, as a member of her church, to construct her leadership. Her status was sufficiently powerful so that gender was not a stigma to the extent experienced by many other women. She was consequently able to place gender in the foreground and adopt an intragroup solidarity stance, supporting other women.

Two points emerge. First, Edith's multiple identities do not simply function additively. They interact so that her leadership is founded on a complex transformation of the constituent elements. A matriarchal approach is flavored by religion. It is also mutated by a patriarchal impetus that is related strongly, in her estimation, to the changing public sector accountability context. Second, and consequently, intersectionality appears to provide a more promising framework for understanding her leadership than gender theory alone, which would distort and impoverish. It rather demands a wider view on the intersection and changes within multiple identities.

BARBARA A final example illustrates the complex interrelationship of gender with other identities. Barbara, a white department head in a UK college, is highly critical of the dominance of men within the leadership at the middle level of the organization. In meetings:

> They have more authoritative voices and they speak more. They dominate time. . . . They dominate time because they are louder and have more presence irrespective of what the issue might be. They have more authority in every aspect. Their length of service here, their role here.

She links other identities to that of masculinity: role and length of service, which is a proxy for age. The dominance of particular individuals is related to an intersection of their gender, age and specific role.

The last is highly important in her own case. She believes that while gender is undoubtedly a highly significant feature in how she and others perceive her identity, her curriculum area—and specifically its status—was more decisive than gender in locating her identity for others. The decline of her curriculum area had led to a sharp drop in her status in the eyes of others and, in her own view, a consequent negation of her ability to lead: "Because I don't feel that I have that much input anymore and any valid input to make, I feel inferior. I feel professionally that I have really lost my status."

The reshaping of her department led to greater investment and development in courses that were run by staff with a vocational rather than university education and from a lower socioeconomic class than those leaders previously in the ascendant. Her perceived exclusion from leadership was not prevented by her higher level class or education. On the contrary, in her perception, these act to her disadvantage. For Barbara, leadership demands a position where influence is founded on status and power. Both are created through a perceived identity where gender, age, educational background, class, role and curriculum responsibility intersect. The fluid and shifting complexity of her identity and the relationship of identity to leadership was painfully apparent to her in her waning ability to exert influence.

AN AGENDA FOR FUTURE RESEARCH

The "interlocking systems of oppression" (Hill Collins, 1990, p. 222) have long been evident. Nearly two decades ago Hill Collins signaled a paradigmatic shift as a result of recognizing that each system of oppression needs the others to function, and that if race, class and gender intersect, then age, sexual orientation and religion must also be considered. So much then is not new. This chapter builds on this position in two respects. First, it suggests that the identities that interlock to include or exclude from leadership and to shape the enactment of leadership are more varied than those in the stock list that is increasingly embedded in equality legislation throughout the world. Some of the women interviewed accounted for their inclusion or exclusion from leadership primarily in terms of the identities historically related to oppression, gender, ethnicity, disability and age. However, not all of the accounts cited gender as a primary shaping identity. In Sumey and Barbara's case, other identities related to curriculum area, educational background and language were critical to understand their experience.

Second, this chapter queries why, if the interreactive nature of oppressions has been recognized for so long, have we made so little progress in researching the interactions? One possible answer is the political nature of research. Individuals and organizations compete for recognition and for funding, both of which are structurally related to oppression, as a result of lack of cooperation. There are more often funds to address gender or race or disability issues, rather than all three, let alone more messy conflations of multiple factors.

The interests of researchers also may reflect particular standpoints (Hill Collins, 1990). While there is an eagerness to expose the degree to which scholarship is controlled by white male ascendancy, there is less emphasis on the degree to which feminist scholarship may be dominated by white females, or to acknowledge the degree to which black feminist scholarship may distort by homogenizing the experience of all minority ethnic women by adopting the perspective of a particular subgroup. Instead of an inclusive fight for rights and opportunities for all, individuals and groups "focus on their own tender, sore and touchy spots" (Bauman, 2004, p. 37).

Engaging with the multiple identities of women also raises issues about voice. Being biologically female has appeared enough to write about "all women," the homogenized group. Once the group is disaggregated so that other characteristics surface—such as ethnicity, disability, sexuality, language, cultural positioning and subject area, among others—the researcher's capability and moral right to research and write about women with characteristics other than her own may be questioned. Can I, as a white, "abled" woman, legitimately write about black women or disabled women without violating or intruding on an area of experience that is unknown to me? It is an irony that no one would question my right to research all women, but the right to understand better by looking beneath the surface of this homogenized group might be seen as illegitimate. Such incursion into the territory of the oppressed is, of course, a politicized act, and the differential power of those writing and those written about is sensitive. However, if progress is to be made in understanding the rich, mutable, enabling and disabling intersection of identities and leadership, then researchers and writers need permission to explore that which is "other." It may be done hesitatingly, uncertainly, with errors and false routes. The alternative of remaining in the safe, de-racialized, de-sexualized, de-individualized world of gender conceptualized as all women risks more. The obligation is both personal, to increase individual understanding of the experience of others, and public, as Fraser suggests, "to *render visible* the ways in which societal inequality infects formally inclusive existing public spheres" (Fraser, 1994, p. 83, original emphasis).

There also may be practical reasons why research has not progressed on interlocking systems. Valentine (2006) suggests that it is very hard to cover multiple identities and oppressions in one article. This chapter is a point in question, as it has had space to do no more than suggest questions and frameworks that may be helpful. There also remain philosophical and methodological difficulties. How identities might be understood, how we might respond to the multiple constructions by individuals and by those with whom they interact, requires ontological resolution (Sanchez et al., 2007). Longitudinal studies are implied by the notion of the fluid and changing nature of identities (Abes et al., 2007). The political, ethical, methodological and practical barriers to pursuing an intersectionality approach to gender are formidable.

Nevertheless, this chapter suggests that such an approach offers a promising path to understand better how one identity, such as gender, may trump another in attracting or repelling influence, and thereby create or inhibit possibilities for leadership. It directs attention to explaining the impact of context and of the factors that impel one identity to the foreground or make it apparently invisible to self and/or others. Valentine (2006) sets out an agenda:

This approach means looking at, for example, accounts of the multiple shifting, and sometimes simultaneous ways that self and other are represented, the way that individuals identify and disidentify with other groups, how one category is used to differentiate another in specific contexts, and how particular identities become salient or foregrounded at particular moments. Such an analysis means asking questions about what identities are being "done" and when and by whom, evaluating how particular identities are weighted or given importance by individuals at particular moments and in specific contexts, and looking at when some categories such as gender might unsettle, undo or cancel out other categories such as sexuality. (p. 15)

Valentine's suggested approach implies that focusing on how identities are created may be of equal utility in unraveling the complexities of inequality, rather than remaining within the limitations of the default focus on groups deemed to be particularly oppressed, such as "women."

Some may argue that all research selects a focus, that we must make choices of where to look and that there is utility in focusing on an area such as gender. While this argument seems logical, the issue is that feminist literature has habitually made such a choice, not pointing out that the selection of gender is a limited focus. Rather it is taken as a given and so has miniaturized women by writing of them as if being a woman was a universal concept and shared experience.

The evidence presented briefly in this chapter has suggested that gender is a phenomenon continually created by self and others; that its perceived value in supporting inclusion in leadership and shaping leadership varies significantly in differing contexts; that its impact cannot be understood fully without taking account of the metamorphosis of gender as it collides with, permeates and transmutes in the presence of other identities. While research on the demographics of women's presence in educational leadership and on the difficulties they encounter as women will continue to be of value, this chapter suggests that to make progress in understanding the mechanisms of oppression, an intersectionality approach is likely to be more fruitful.

Questions emerging from this small data set include: why and how women choose to attempt or are denied de-categorization or re-categorization; why and how does the stigmatizing force of one identity overwhelm other identities so they disappear in some cases and in others work in parallel, mutually magnifying the effects of two, three or multiple identities; how far do the positive and negative stereotypes of stigmatizing identities align with or counter gender stereotypes; and how might women most effectively manipulate their identities in order to gain access to leadership and to lead in a way they and others value. There is undoubtedly a substantial agenda for research using the intersectionality frame to interrogate the experience of gender.

ACKNOWLEDGMENTS

Research was undertaken in the UK with Kalwant Bhopal, Martin Dyke, Felix Maringe and Marlene Morrison, and in South Africa with Jan Heystek. The UK project was funded by but does not necessarily reflect the views of the Centre for Excellence in Leadership.

REFERENCES CITED

Abes, S. A., Jones, S., and McEwen, M. K. (2007). Reconceptualizing the model of multiple dimensions of identity: The role of meaning-making capacity in the construction of multiple identities. *Journal of College Student Development, 48*(1), 1–22.

Bauman, Z. (2004). *Identity.* Cambridge: Polity Press.

Burke, P. J. (2006). Identity change. *Social Psychology Quarterly, 69*(1), 81–96.

Butler, J. (1990). *Gender trouble: Feminism and the subversion of identity.* New York: Routledge.

———. (2004). *Undoing gender.* New York: Routledge.

Coleman, M. (2002). *Women as head teachers: Striking the balance.* Stoke-on-Trent, U.K.: Trentham.

Du Bois, W. E. B. (1903/1968). *The souls of black folk.* New York: Johnson Reprint Company.

Fraser, N. (1994). Rethinking the public sphere: A contribution to the critique of actually existing democracy. In H. A. Giroux and P. McLaren (Eds.), *Between borders: Pedagogy and the politics of cultural studies.* New York: Routledge.

Goffman, E. (1959). *The presentation of self in everyday life.* London: Pelican.

———. (1986). *Stigma: Notes on the management of spoiled identity.* New York: Simon and Schuster.

Gurin, P., and Nagda, B. R. A. (2006). Getting to the what, how and why of diversity on campus. *Educational Researcher, 35*(1), 20–24.

Hancock, A. (2005). W.E.B. Du Bois: Intellectual forefather of intersectionality? *Souls: A Critical Journal of Black Politics, Culture and Society, 7*(3–4), 74–84.

Hill Collins, P. (1990). *Black feminist thought: Knowledge, consciousness and the politics of empowerment.* London: Routledge.

hooks, b. (2000). *Feminist theory: From margin to center* (3rd ed.). Cambridge, MA: South End Press.

Iles, P., and Kaur Hayers, P. (1997). Managing diversity in transnational project teams. A tentative model and case study. *Journal of Managerial Psychology, 1*(2), 95–117.

Lumby, J., with Coleman, M. (2007). *Leadership and diversity.* London: Sage.

Lumby, J., Bhopal, K., Dyke, M., Maringe, F., and Morrison, M. (2007). *Integrating diversity in leadership in further education.* London: Centre for Excellence in Leadership.

Milliken, Frances J., and Martins, L. L. (1996). Searching for common threads: Understanding the multiple effects of diversity in organizational groups. *Academy of Management Review, 21*(2), 1–32.

Rooney, E. (2006). Women's equality in Northern Ireland's transition: Intersectionality in theory and place. *Feminist Legal Studies, 14,* 353–375.

Sanchez, A. K., Zogmaister, C., and Arcuri, L. (2007). When "They" becomes "We": Multiple contrasting identities in mixed status groups. *Self and Identity, 6,* 154–172.

Scheuerich, J. J. (1995). A postmodernist critique of research interviewing. *International Journal of Qualitative Studies in Education, 8*(3), 239–252.

Shah, S. (2006). Educational leadership: An Islamic perspective. *British Educational Research Journal, 32*(3), 363–386.

Sen, A. (2006). *Identity and violence: The illusion of destiny.* London: Allan Lane.

Sloop, J. (2007). In queer time and place and race: Intersectionality come of age. *Quarterly Journal of Speech, 91*(3), 312–326.

Stets, J. E., and Harrod, M. M. (2004). Verification across multiple identities: The rowel of status. *Social Psychology Quarterly, 67*(2), 155–171.

Stone, D., and Colella, A. (1996). A model of factors affecting the treatment of disabled individuals in organizations. *Academy of Management Review, 12*(2), 352–401.

Valentine, G. (2007). Theorizing and researching intersectionality: A challenge for feminist geography. *The Professional Geographer, 59*(1), 10–21.

Walker, M. (2005). Race is nowhere and race is everywhere. *British Journal of the Sociology of Education, 26*(1), 41–55.

DESERT, RAINFOREST AND GROWING OASIS
Traversing Challenges and Opportunity in Africa

CHAPTER 5

Overview for Part II

JoAnne E. Burley and Pamela Lenz

INTRODUCTION

A CURRENT VIEW OF WOMEN serving in positions of leadership in Africa shows a continent in transition. Geographically, the nations within the African continent are still defined by the desert, rainforest, plains and savannahs. But the continent of Africa today is also a growing oasis that finds women at a pivotal point. Women offer their leadership in roles that have traditionally belonged to men and as a result, women are facing new and greater challenges.

The following three chapters examine the challenges and the many opportunities that lie ahead for women in leadership roles in today's Africa. The first (Bandiho, 2007) presents an examination and review of educational leadership in Tanzania and the emergence of female participation. In the second, Kagoda and Sperandio (2007) present the prospects and challenges for women seeking careers in school administration along with accompanying professional development, specifically in Uganda. Finally, Phendla (2007) views the rise of women in leadership roles and the resultant social, political, economic, and cultural impact in South Africa.

CONCEPTUAL FRAMEWORK

Exploratory in nature, each of the three chapters presents a focus on the participation of women in educational leadership from primary school through university. The conceptual framework for the collection of chapters includes the history of women at work in each country, major obstacles and challenges to advancement, women's rights and the government's commitment to gender equity, and the economics of educating the entire citizenry. Each chapter concludes by raising questions regarding women's presence in African educational leadership that provide rich opportunities for future study.

CONTENT

In general, the three chapters in this section present a very strong argument for educational reform and the inclusion of trained women who could assume a leadership role at all levels of education. Bandiho (2007), Kagoda and Sperandio (2007), and Phendla (2007) all demonstrate similar issues regarding women in leadership within three countries. According to Bandiho, a distinction in educating girls and boys is noticed in elementary school. There are primary school equity issues with girls' academic preparation and leadership training falling behind when analyzed statistically. Thus over the years, women's leadership roles in higher education were presented as being bleak. The evidence to support such statements is well documented in charts and test results.

The prospects and challenges for women seeking careers and professional development in education in the Ugandan educational system are similarly stated (Kagoda and Sperandio, 2007). Specific reference is given to Uganda being a male-dominated society even though women make up approximately 52 percent of the population. Another issue that has a negative impact on the progress of women assuming a leadership role in Ugandan education is health concerns including HIV, early pregnancy and inadequate general health screening.

Overachieving women also were conscious of social issues, such as finding marriage partners. This is only one example of many other societal considerations that were shown to be parallel to those faced by women in other nations, including the United States.

Each chapter presents similar issues that must be faced by women leaders in Tanzania, Uganda and South Africa. The list includes poor opportunities for advancement, navigating the politics within the educational setting, sexism and lack of support for other staff members.

The strength of the authors' arguments is evident from the research and documentation compiled and the emotional depth attached to each. The prerequisite facts and documentation speak volumes for each study, and the emotional investments clearly demonstrate the sincerity of the researchers' work.

NEXT STEPS

As exploratory studies, each chapter lays the groundwork for research related to increasing the opportunities for women in the educational leadership of Africa. To fully explore the questions raised in these preliminary studies, it will be necessary to investigate the data in light of gender-related issues presented in both the literature of women's studies and leadership in general. Particular areas of focus include national culture and multiple femininities, as well as opportunities for gender-specific mentoring and training.

Regarding culture, the emergence of Tanzania, Uganda and South Africa from patriarchal societies to those of gender equity necessitates more in-depth study. All three authors reference the continent's policy enactments calling for gender parity in education. Looking at this in light of Schein's (2004) cultural lens could yield insights that would further pave the way for aspiring women leaders. Of greatest relevance to the studies is his third, or deepest, level, that of tacit assumptions. Consisting of cultural elements that are not cognitively identified in everyday interactions, these unspoken rules exist without the conscious knowledge of society, causing its membership to become acclimated to their existence and thus reinforcing the invisibility of their practice. This is important in that the creation of gender equity policy, in itself, does not ensure that parity will actually occur.

In her inquiry, Phendla (2007) states, "Black women's lives can only be understood through the interlocking categories of various constructs including race, ethnicity, gender, class, language, culture, and traditional norms." Such an assertion calls for further examination of the interaction between gender and social contexts in what Connell (1995) posits as a theory of multiple femininities. His view calls for abandoning unitary typecasting in favor of a model that considers multiple social variables. Two metaphors for guiding further study are the blending of primary colors into more complex hues and peeling back an onion's layers to reveal the complexities that lie within a seemingly simplistic whole. Conversation around the latter stimulates considerable interest in studying the multiple facets of women as they relate to their role as educational leaders.

The training and mentoring opportunities available to women who aspire to roles of educational leadership in Africa are likewise a field ripe for future study. Statistics cited by Bandiho (2007), Kagoda and Sperandio (2007) and Phendla (2007), indicating deficits in schooling options and the number of women presently holding positions in educational leadership, call to mind the writings of Blackmore (1999) as well as Young and Mountford (2006). These studies speak of the underrepresentation of women in leadership and the need for coaching and mentoring within and across gender lines.

Self-perceptions of African women also are critical when examining their aspirations to positions of leadership. That women are less likely than men to view themselves as leaders was apparent in a pilot study of the National Professional Qualification for Head Teachers (NPQHT). In reviewing this work, Cubillo (1998) pointed out that all candidates with low self-evaluation scores were women. The interplay of self-perception, mentoring and training is a critical avenue of study for those wishing to assist future generations of women in realizing career goals in educational leadership.

These lines of inquiry, as well as others that the authors choose to incorporate, will anchor their research to the existing body of literature while also allowing them to explore that which is still uncharted in African women's studies. As the continent itself is in a stage of transition, so will future investigations based on these papers afford increasing opportunities for women to assume positions and make a difference in the educational leadership of Africa.

REFERENCES CITED

Bandiho, H. (2007, July). Status of educational leadership and female participation: The case of Tanzania. Paper presented at the International Conference on Women and Educational Leadership, Rome, Italy.

Blackmore, J. (1999). *Troubling women: Feminism, leadership and educational change.* Buckingham: Open University Press.

Connell, R. W. (1995). *Masculinities.* St. Leonards, NSW: Allen and Unwin.

Cubillo, L. (1998). Women and NPQH—An appropriate leadership model? Paper presented at the British Education Research Association Conference, Belfast, Northern Ireland.

Kagoda, A. M., and Sperandio, J. (2007, July). Prospects and challenges for women seeking careers and professional development in school administration and leadership in the Ugandan education system. Paper presented at the International Conference on Women and Educational Leadership, Rome, Italy.

Phendla, T. (2007, July). Women on the rise: Navigating across social, political, economical, and cultural arenas to claim their stake in educational leadership positions in South Africa. Paper presented at the International Conference on Women and Educational Leadership, Rome, Italy.

Schein, E. H. (2004). *Organizational culture and leadership* (3rd ed.). San Francisco: Jossey-Bass.

Young, M., and Mountford, M. (2006). Infusing gender and diversity issues into educational leadership programs. *Journal of Educational Administration, 44*(3), 264–277.

CHAPTER 6

Status of Educational Leadership and Female Participation

The Case of Tanzania

SISTER DR. HELLEN A. BANDIHO

A NEED FOR EDUCATIONAL LEADERSHIP IN TANZANIA

GIVEN THAT LEADERSHIP is a valuable addition to the repertoire of every organization (D'Souza, 2003), a need for good leaders is echoed throughout the corporate, educational, political, business, social and religious worlds. In most countries of the East African region, new private universities, high schools and grade schools are being founded, which is a positive sign. As a result, enrollment of students has increased tremendously. In Tanzania, for example, the government requires each ward to have a secondary school, a dramatic turnaround from a few years ago when the entire country had a handful of secondary schools. Ten years ago in this country, there were only three accredited universities. In 2007 there are more than 28 universities and affiliated colleges (Tanzania Commission for Universities, 2007). The number of secondary schools has increased from 781 with 6,291 classrooms in 1998 to 3,485 with 14,921 classrooms in 2007 (BEST, 2007). This is another call for educational leadership.

Most African countries are witnessing shifts in their overall educational philosophy in which institutions aim to serve the masses, rather than simply the elite. The trend in Africa also is to value partnerships over insularity as well as accelerating the participation of female students and staff to a stage of gender parity (Court, 2000). To make all these developments a reality, education and training are key items. Is the continent prepared to provide good educational leaders to administer and sustain these new expansions and challenges?

Relying on data from education centers, Tanzanian universities and a variety of educational institutions, this chapter explores the status of educational leadership in Tanzania—a country whose situation may mirror that of many other African countries whose independence came about in the 1960s. It also explores the status of women in educational leadership at various levels of education.

CHAPTER STRUCTURE

As mentioned earlier, the goal of this chapter is to show the participation of women in educational leadership at different levels of education in Tanzania, as well as the status of women with potential for educational leadership. Literature on leadership, the basic education of current female educators and educational information about young women in Tanzanian schools and universities are discussed. The author concludes that, without such women being educated, future women educational leaders cannot exist.

LEADERSHIP

Road to Academic Leadership

Success of different organizations, especially educational institutions, depends on effective and efficient leaders. How do educational leaders assume educational leadership positions? Is it because of their education, training, experience, political beliefs or a combination of the above? Gmelch and Wolverton (2002) conducted a study to examine American deans' ascensions to their positions. The main questions for this study were to find out where the road to leadership begins, whether it is in the home, at high school and colleges, or from the teaching ranks in the academy. They concluded that the metamorphosis that deans experience as they transition from academicians to administrators is murky at best, but it is clear from literature on business executives that the process begins long before an individual reaches the professional ranks of the academy. In another study, conducted by Madsen (2007), it was concluded that various career paths could lead to top leadership positions in academe. It is important, therefore, for African educators to determine what helps to nurture future leaders within the African context while remaining conscious of global realities.

Leadership today continues to be more challenging and involving, and it requires preparation. New environmental challenges continue to emerge, and educational leaders have to adapt to changing environments.

Leadership calls for new ways of being in the world, not in oppositional isolation or confrontation, but in convivial cooperation with our evolving universe which, if adopted well, may lead to fresh horizons of wholeness, new hope and possibilities for Africa and the world.

Role of Educational Leadership

Academic leaders have multidisciplinary, interwoven roles. Schools and universities of the twenty-first century are compelled to have instructional leaders who are community sensitive and visionary. These are principled leaders who also demonstrate energy, commitment and entrepreneurial spirit. Educational leaders need the ability to communicate effectively, generate human interaction and use information to transform their institutions into learning organizations. They have to inquire, evaluate information and allocate resources. Today's leaders require an understanding of the impact of technological advances, decision-making processes and methods of becoming agents of change for the new era (Swanson and Rezik, 2000). Education today is shaped and threatened by global competition, and leaders must be able to move to a different beat (Hoffman and Summers, 2000).

My friend Edwardina, who is a graduate of Scranton University, was recently appointed principal of a new boarding high school in Dar es Salaam, Tanzania. Her responsibilities as principal include negotiating contracts for building construction, hiring new teachers, fundraising, obtaining registration for the school and many others. During an hour visit with Edwardina, a student came to her office complaining of stomach pain, a parent called her regarding delay of tuition for her child, a board member wanted some statistics, a teacher wanted to see her and the chief cook was out of cooking gas. She alternated between roles of a nurse, a counselor, a principal, a public relations officer and a purchasing officer. Thus, we can see that some educational leaders' roles are directly educational but others are political, similar to what Edwardina went through before she could obtain registration for her new school. Clearly, educational leaders need adequate preparations.

Training: Fundamental to Leadership

More often, leadership instructors are faced with a question of whether leaders are made or born. Similar to accountants, artists, athletes and all other professionals, leaders also are born. Leadership is not a place, it's not a gene, and it's not a secret code that cannot be deciphered by ordinary people. All it takes are skills and abilities that are useful and that could be strengthened, honed and enhanced through education, training and coaching (Kouzes and Posner, 2002).

Over the years, management-related careers have been taken for granted, and experience alone was thought to be a leading factor for such professions. Today's needs are numerous, making training an important ingredient for leadership. It is through training that a cadre of leaders can be developed (Fenstermacher and Smith, 1999). A study of deanship conducted by Griffiths and McCarthy (1980) examined 181 deans, 10% of whom were females. The sample was drawn from colleges and universities across the United States. This study revealed that work-related stress was one of the major problems faced by many deans and lack of preparation was a major contributor to stress.

Such consequences may affect academic leaders more today than in the 1980s because of various developments that are shaping educational institutions. Experience alone is not enough. Today's educational leaders need to possess a broad variety of skills that enable them to function comfortably and effectively in changing environments and under highly politicized conditions where change is the only constant (Swanson and Rezik, 2000). Through well-prepared training programs, leadership candidates can begin to study what characteristics must be developed to assure that they are reflected later in school leadership behaviors (Glasman and Glasman, 1997). Thus, the importance of preparation for academic leadership cannot be overemphasized.

Role of Women in Leadership

Women are as important as men in leadership. Some researchers (Winter, Neal and Waner, 2001) assert that women tend to be more participative, relationship-oriented leaders while men are more task oriented. Others (Stelter, 2002) claim that women often use styles of leadership such as relationship building, inclusiveness, participation and caring, that are highly effective in today's turbulent, culturally diverse environment. Some researchers (DeSmet and Martell, 2001; Kolb, 1999; and Shimanoff and Jenkins, 1992) conclude that men leaders and women leaders are more alike than different in their leadership behaviors.

If studies reveal that men and women have different talents, we should also agree that inclusion of both genders in leadership roles would make a positive difference. Effective leadership is not the exclusive domain of either gender because each can learn from the other (Appelbaum, Audet and Miller, 2003). Besides, the challenges that organizations face today are remarkable and likely to increase in scope and complexity. Thus, the difference in men's versus women's leadership styles is particularly important in light of these new trends. Each person's talents are enduring and unique and each person's capacity for growth is that person's greatest strength. Needless to say, an organization has much to gain by employing both men and women in building a strength-based school or university.

Failing to maximize the potential of female employees, organizations are at a loss. They do not fully benefit from the unique talent and perspective that women can impart (Appelbaum, Audet and Miller, 2003). A gender-balanced leadership will provide a broader and deeper base of experience for creativity and problem solving, essential for building learning organizations. Such collaborative leadership is what Allen and Mease (2002) call energy optimization. Thus, enabling participation of both genders means honoring the diversity of gifts and releasing energy that is already present in the system.

EDUCATIONAL LEADERSHIP: TANZANIAN EXPERIENCE

Tanzania has had a Ministry of Education since its independence in 1961. Over the years, this ministry has dealt with educational institutions of different levels. The following section will discuss some of the institutions under the Ministry of Education, educational leaders and their roles.

Teachers' Training Colleges: Who Trains Them?
Teachers' colleges in Tanzania offer courses leading to certificates or diplomas in teacher education. Educators in these colleges are themselves educational leaders with a responsibility of training future educational leaders. In 2007 there were 31 government and 22 nongovernment teacher training colleges. Out of 31 principals in the government teaching colleges, only six (19%) were females; 25 (81%) were males (Ministry of Education and Vocational Training, 2007). In 2007, these colleges (government and nongovernment) had 29% female educators. Also, out of 392 academic staff with at least a B.A. degree, only 88 (22.4%) were female. This indicates not only that women are few but also that they are less educated than their male counterparts.

Regional and District Educational Officers
Tanzania is divided into regions and districts. Regional Educational Officers and District Educational Officers are heads of education in their regions and districts. As of this writing, Tanzania is divided into 21 regions. Each region has a Regional Education Officer (REO). Regional Education Officers are assisted by several District Educational Officers in the districts within their regions. In 2007, when a survey for this chapter was conducted, 20 positions out of 21 were filled. Out of 20 REOs in Tanzania, 16 (80%) were males and four (20%) were females (Ministry of Education and Vocational Training, 2007).

As of January 17, 2007, there were 122 District Educational Officers in the 122 educational districts. Out of 122 established educational offices, 90 (74%) were occupied by male educational officers and 32 (26%) by female educational officers (Ministry of Education and Vocational Training, 2007). It may be interesting in the future to determine whether female teachers are not interested in such educational leadership positions, whether they are denied those positions, or whether they are not qualified for such positions.

Tanzanian Secondary Schools
One cannot talk about academic leadership in isolation from potential future educational leaders. It is therefore important to discuss enrollment of students by gender at different levels. UNESCO reports that secondary education in Africa represents a major challenge, especially for girls. Although most countries of the region are still striving to achieve universal primary education (UPE), the stream of learners knocking on the doors of secondary schools keeps growing. At present, the gross secondary school enrollment rate exceeds 20% in half of sub-Saharan African countries, yet remains below 8% in 10 of these countries.

In Tanzania, there have been some achievements in the secondary education sector in terms of enrollment as well as the number of new schools. In 1961, for example, only 151 males and 25 females were enrolled in Form 6—the highest secondary school level in Tanzania. In 2007, there were 12,002 males and 8,333 females enrolled in Form 6. Thus, female enrollment at Form 6 level had increased from 25 in 1961, to 417 in 1981, and to 8,333 in 2007. In percentage form, this increase is from 14% of total enrollment, to 22% and to 41% in respective years (BEST, 2007).

As indicated in table 6.1, the overall increase of secondary education participation is gradual and encouraging; but as shown in table 6.2, there is a declining trend when compared to enrollment in the higher education. These statistics are a clear indication that the higher you go in the education ladder, the less you find female participation. We need excellent female students to have exemplary teachers and educational leaders, as well as a satisfactory pool of educational leader candidates to choose from.

Women Teaching in Tanzanian Schools

Careers in education have traditionally been a woman's expected choice. A survey of secondary school teachers in Tanzania, however, reveals that men still dominate teaching positions in secondary education while more women are found in grade schools. These teachers either have degrees, diplomas (obtained after advanced level of secondary education plus teaching training) or Grade A teaching certificates (obtained after ordinary secondary education plus teacher training). For the purposes of this chapter, I mainly concentrated on teachers with at least an undergraduate degree—those with more potential for leadership positions in the near future.

Data obtained from basic education statistics in Tanzania (BEST, 2007) reveal that in Tanzanian secondary schools, there were 29,858 teachers. These teachers include those with degrees and diplomas, as well as Grade A teachers. Out of 29,858 total secondary school teachers, 20,963 (70.2%) were male and 8,895 (29.8%) were female. Out of all teachers, only 4,891 (16.4%) had degree qualifications and out of 4,891 teachers with at least the first degree, only 1,305 (32%) were females.

These statistics show that only 16.4% of the secondary school teachers hold degrees. It also should

be noted that only 1,305 (4.4% of all teachers) female teachers hold at least undergraduate degrees and might therefore qualify for educational leadership in the near future.

A mathematical theory of probability can be used to guide a reader in distinguishing and justifying educational equity between genders—a justification that may enable both males and females to have equal chances of winning. Probability experts inform planners that when flipping a coin in a large number of trials, it tends to yield about 50% heads and 50% tails (Cryer and Miller, 1994). This predictable behavior could only be true for future educational leaders when the number of qualified males and females is relatively equal. Thus, equality in educational leadership is obviously justifiable when there are equal chances of winning.

More opportunities need to be made for females in higher education and leadership training. Population statistics of 2002 indicate the gender ratio is about 1.1 female to male (National Bureau of Statistics, 2006). It is therefore reasonable to apply equity by raising female teachers' educational qualifications. In order to apply probability theory, the pool of qualified females has to be large enough and composed of highly capable candidates with appropriate certifications. This will enable them to qualify and compete for higher levels of educational leadership.

Slightly different circumstances are found in primary schools. In 2007, there were 156,664 teachers. Of these, 79,881 were males and 76,783 (49%) were females. However, only 367 (0.23%) primary school teachers hold bachelor's degrees. The rest have diplomas, Grade A's or other lower qualifications. Of the 367 with degree qualifications, 217 (52.3%) are males and 150 (47.9%) are females. In this category of teachers, we see fewer teachers (both males and females) with degrees, but the ratio of male to female degree holders is almost 1 to 1.

SCHOOL LEADERSHIP IN SECONDARY EDUCATION

Participation of Female Leaders in Primary and Secondary Schools

In 2006, there were 14,700 primary schools with a total enrollment of 7,959,884 students. The ratio of students per head teacher was about 1 to 542 students. Data for their sex were not available. There also were 2,286 secondary schools in 2006, with 2,286 principals responsible for 675,672 students. Of these principals, 290 (12.7%) were female and 1,996 (87.3%) were

Table 6.1. Secondary School Enrollment by Gender, 2003–2007

Year	Female	Male	Total
2003	157,863 (46%)	187,578	345,441
2004	199,963 (46%)	232,636	432,599
2005	244,571 (47%)	279,754	524,325
2006	317,544 (50%)	358,128	675,672
2007	477,314 (47%)	543,196	1,020,510

Table 6.2. Total Student Enrollment in Higher Learning Institutions, 2002/2003–2006/2007

Academic Year	Female	Male	Total
2002/2003	10,486 (34%)	20,575	31,061
2003/2004	11,782 (29%)	28,402	40,184
2004/2005	15,782 (33%)	32,454	48,236
2005/2006	17,885 (32%)	37,411	55,296
2006/2007	26,890 (36%)	48,456	75,346

males (Ministry of Education and Vocational Training, 2007). As Tanzania and other countries continue to create new schools, the importance of having more qualified and motivated educational leaders is more than we can imagine. At the same time, girls need more role models in education to help them become motivated and interested in education in general and educational leadership in particular.

Participation of Women in Higher Education
There seems to be a serious recognition by some African governments and universities of the need to increase the number of women students, faculty and administrators. As Court (2000) puts it, "This signifies not just a concession to a notion of equity but an understanding that this will influence for the better changes in the quality, practice and structure of universities."

The Tanzanian Universities Act 7, Section 22(2)(ii) stipulates that universities need to have a "clear statement on gender and opportunities for persons from disadvantaged groups." Also, Section 44(2)(c) says that "the composition of the council or governing Board shall as far as possible consist of members of both sexes on an equal basis, and so that, in any event, at least one-third of the membership shall be women." The same gender ratio is applied to the composition of a senate or an academic committee (Universities Act, Section 46(3)(b)). The same act stipulates that grants committees have an obligation to find means of "funding of higher education especially for women, the disabled and other persons in other disadvantaged groups" (University Act, Section 11(1)(g)). These are some of the policies in place. However, there is still much more to be desired.

As shown in table 6.2, total enrollment in higher learning institutions in Tanzania has increased more than 100% in five years. Although this increase is very significant in both genders, enrollment of women still lags behind. In the 2005–2006 academic year, for example, enrollment of female students in higher learning institutions was 32% and in 2006–2007 enrolled female students represented 36% (Basic Statistics on Higher Education, 2007).

In addition, statistics from the Ministry of Higher Education, Science and Technology published in July 2007 indicate that out of 951 Ph.D. holders teaching in all Tanzanian higher learning institutions, only 102 (11%) were women. The same statistics show that of 1,321 academic staff with master's degrees, only 261 (20%) were female. As indicated earlier, there are few educators from basic education who hold higher degrees. Therefore it is from higher education teaching cadres where one could find future educational leaders. These alarming statistics indicate a need to educate more women if we need them to occupy educational leadership positions.

Consequences resulting from unequal representation of gender in higher education may contribute to a disparity in gender distribution across university leadership positions in Tanzania. University leadership encompasses many levels, but a survey conducted in January 2007 concentrated on the top four levels of university leadership.

More than 98% of accredited universities in Tanzania were surveyed and, in general, females are underrepresented in educational leadership in higher learning institutions. As of January 2007, there was only one female university chancellor in Tanzania, at the Muslim University in Morogoro. The rest of the chancellors were male. There is only one female deputy of academics and only three female deputies of administration. Thus, out of the 112 surveyed academic positions, five (4.5%) were held by females and 107 (95.5%) by males. Clearly, women are underrepresented at top leadership levels in higher learning institutions in Tanzania. There is a claim that more females are deans or department chairs, but concrete data were not available. Further research may reveal the authenticity of this conclusion.

SUMMARY AND CONCLUSION

This chapter explored educational leadership in Tanzania and female participation in academic leadership. It showed their participation at different levels of education and leadership. In secondary schools, girls make up almost 50%, but their numbers dwindle as they move toward higher levels of education. Likewise, more women teachers and leaders are found in primary schools than in colleges.

The journey of educational leadership is continuous and life-long. Leadership is not something that we can "do to" people like fixing their hair or teeth. It involves unlocking people's minds by giving them the potential to become better. Leadership is about opening new horizons at all times through integration of gender, education, cultures and collaborative ventures. Educational stakeholders need to play their part in bringing the importance of educational leadership to the global map and equal participation of all.

Efforts in working together should be inclusive of gender, nationalities, universities, policy makers and all stakeholders. As noted above, equal participation of gender signifies not just a concession to a notion of equity but an understanding that this will influence for the better changes in the quality, practice and structure of universities (Court, 2000). We ought to discover unifying links that transcend all the divisions and distinctions developed by the human mind. We can begin to address the issue of human participation in educational leadership only when women are educated, trained and exposed to leadership roles. Meanwhile, equity will and should prevail.

REFERENCES CITED

Allen, K. E., and Mease, W. P. (2002). Energy optimization and the role of leadership. In C. Cherrey and L. R. Mutusak (Eds.), *Building leadership bridges* (pp. 137–148). North Carolina: The International Leadership Association and Center for Creative Leadership.

Appelbaum, S. H., Audet, L., and Miller, J. C. (2003). Gender and leadership? Leadership and gender? A journey through the landscape of theories. *Leadership and Organizational Development Journal, 24*(1), 43–51.

Basic Statistics on Higher Education: 2002/2003–2006/2007 (July 2007). Ministry of Higher Education, Science and Technology. Dar es Salaam, Tanzania.

BEST: Basic Education Statistics in Tanzania (June 2007). Ministry of Education and Vocational Training.

BEST: Basic Education Statistics in Tanzania (June 2006). Ministry of Education and Vocational Training.

Court, D. (2000, March/April). Challenge and response in African higher education. *Tanzania World Education News and Reviews, 13*(2).

Cryer, J. D., and Miller, R. B. (1994). *Statistics for business: Data analysis and modeling* (2nd ed.). Belmont, CA: Duxbury Press.

DeSmet, A. L., and Martell, R. F. (2001, December). A diagnostic ration approach to measuring beliefs about the leadership abilities of male and female managers. *Journal of Applied Psychology*, 1223–1232.

D'Souza, A. (2003). *Leadership: Trilogy on leadership and effective management.* Nairobi: Paulines Publications Africa.

Fenstermacher, G. D., and Smith, W. F. S. (Eds.) (1999). *Leadership for educational renewal: Developing a cadre of leaders.* San Francisco: Jossey-Bass.

Glasman, L. D., and Glasman, N. S. (1997). Connecting the preparation of school leaders to the practice of school leadership. *Peabody Journal of Education, 72.*

Gmelch, W. H., and Wolverton, M. (2002). *College deans: Leading from within.* Westport, CT: Oryx Press Series in Higher Education.

Griffiths, D. E., and McCarthy, D. J. (Eds.) (1980). *The Dilemma of leadership.* Danville, IL: Interstate Printers and Publishers.

Hoffman, A. M., and Summers, R. W. (Eds.) (2000). *Managing colleges and universities: Issues for leadership.* Westport, CT: Bergin and Garvey.

Kolb, J. (1999). The effect of gender role, attitude towards leadership, and self-confidence on leader emergence: implications for leadership development. *Human Resource Development Quarterly, 10*(4), 305–320.

Kouzes, J. M., and Posner, B. Z. (2002). *The Leadership challenge* (3rd ed.). San Francisco: Jossey-Bass.

Madsen, S. R. Women university presidents: Career paths and educational backgrounds. Academic Leadership: The Online Journal. Retrieved June 23, 2007, from http://www.academicleadership.org/empirical research/Women University Presidents Career Paths and Educational Backgrounds.shtml: Volume 5, Issue 1.

Ministry of Education and Vocational Training (2007). Dar es Salaam, Tanzania.

National Bureau of Statistics (Tanzania). Retrieved on December 27, 2006, from www.nbs.go.tz.

Shimanoff, S. B., and Jenkins, M. M. (1992). Leadership and gender: Challenging assumptions and recognizing resources. In R. S. Cathcart and L. Samovar (Eds.), *Small Group Communication* (6th ed., pp. 504–522). Dubuque, IA: Wm. C. Brown.

Stelter, N. Z. (2002). Gender differences in leadership: Current social issues and future organizational implications. *The Journal of Leadership Studies, 8*(4), 88–99.

Swanson, D., and Rezik, T. (2000). *Fundamental concepts of educational leadership.* Upper Saddle River, NJ: Prentice Hall.

The Tanzania Commission for Universities (January 2007). Raw Data. Dar es Salaam, Tanzania.

The Universities Act 7. (2005). The Government Printer. Dar es Salaam, Tanzania.

Winter, J., Neal, J., and Warner, K. (2001). How male, female and mixed-gender groups regard interaction and leadership differences in the business communication course. *Business Communication Quarterly, 64*(3), 43–59.

CHAPTER 7

Ugandan Women

Moving Beyond Historical and Cultural Understandings of Educational Leadership

Alice Merab Kagoda and Jill Sperandio

INTRODUCTION

UGANDAN WOMEN HAVE moved slowly into school leadership. Expatriate women missionaries led the first girls' schools founded in the 1880s during the colonial period in Uganda. But not until the 1960s and the country's independence from Britain did Ugandan women take on the roles of school administrators and educational leaders in any numbers. Leadership, however defined and practiced, has been a strictly male preserve in traditional Ugandan society, and jealously guarded.

This situation is changing. The development of a strong women's rights movement in Uganda, help from international human rights agencies, and a national government committed to international gender equity goals have increased opportunities for women to move into decision-making and leadership at all levels in the education system. An innovative policy now in place requires a male and female administrator in every secondary school, both public and private. This policy not only addresses the underrepresentation of women in school leadership, but is a very visible endorsement of the government's commitment to gender equity.

However, while the policy sends a clear message of support to women, its implementation has been less straightforward. In this chapter we construct the historical record of women's education leadership in Uganda and use statistics obtained from the Ministry of Education and Sport (MoES) to illustrate the current representation of women in educational leadership in Uganda. We draw on data collected for a qualitative study of 12 Ugandan female heads and deputy heads of schools and 60 female teachers collected in 2006 to examine past and current barriers facing women seeking leadership positions in education.

For those women who do become school leaders there is the challenge of personalizing the theories and practice of leadership given the very different models to which they have been exposed. These models include traditional Ugandan male leadership, which is closely associated with the wielding of personal power and influence. At the other extreme is the service or servant leader model provided by expatriate male and female missionaries whose leadership was intimately linked to strong religious belief and the exemplar and experience of private boarding schooling in western Europe.

Personal understandings of school leadership influence the approach that women educational leaders adopt to specific country and culture problems. These problems include a largely rural, low-income population of children who must walk long distances to school and undertake house- and farm work on their return. In addition, school heads must cope with an enormous population of AIDS orphans who are often emotionally scarred by watching parents and relatives die from the disease. They must provide a safe school environment for adolescent girls. Uganda's recent commitment to universal secondary education, which will bring more girls into the education system at higher levels, will create a further demand for women sensitive to the needs of adolescent girls to be present at all levels of decision-making in the education system.

We conclude this chapter by considering the type of formal preparation for educational leadership most appropriate for women motivated to take on these problems as Uganda seeks to expand and improve education. We ask whether Ugandan women school administrators bring special skills, understanding and experience to school leadership. If they do, how can they be helped to use these to best effect in the schools they lead to the benefit of all their students, particularly those disadvantaged by gender or socioeconomic status? How can these women best be prepared to cope with community interactions and gender discrimination in the very varied communities that exist in Uganda to which women, as school heads, may be called to serve? Placing these questions in a wider context, we consider whether school leadership preparation that incorporates best practices from around the world is enough, or whether such preparation should be tailored or developed from grassroots experience for a specific context.

THE PHYSICAL AND SOCIAL CONTEXT OF UGANDAN EDUCATION

Uganda is a landlocked country in East Africa, bordered to the south by Lake Victoria and the west by the East African Rift Valley. Despite these natural borders, the country is a construct of British colonial mapmaking and encompasses over 50 tribal identities. For this multilingual nation, the use of English as a national language is now a unifying factor. With a population of 27 million growing at 3.6 percent a year, Uganda has one of the highest growth rates in the world (Uganda Bureau of Statistics, 2006). It is a predominantly rural country, with only 12 percent of the population living in the urban areas of the capital city, Kampala, and a handful of large market towns. The rural population is mostly engaged in subsistence farming, producing the country's food staple, *matoke* bananas, supplemented with a variety of cash crops including rice, tea and coffee, and cattle raising. The 2 percent of the population regarded as wealthy are mostly bureaucrats, private businessmen and expatriate employees of multinational companies (Banugire, 1989).

Education is of major concern to the government of Uganda given the increasing youth of the population. The median age is 15.3 years, and the proportion of children in the population has increased from 51 percent in 1969 to 56 percent in 2002. There is a high incidence of adolescent motherhood in Uganda, with 18 percent of the 2.4 million females aged between 12 and 19 years having already given birth to a child. Fertility rates have remained high over the past three decades, with an average birthrate of seven children.

Education for girls has become an important part of the political agenda in recent years for a number of reasons. The threat faced by women of contracting AIDS and giving birth to HIV-positive babies has demonstrated the importance of providing health and life skills education for adolescent girls in addition to academic and vocational skills.

In the formal educational system, a four-tier model is followed. It involves seven years of primary education, four years of ordinary level secondary education, two years of advanced secondary education and finally tertiary education in the form of vocational courses or three- to four-year university degree courses. Students take a national examination at the end of each level. Uganda introduced Universal Primary Education (UPE) in 1997 and Universal Secondary Education (USE) in 2007, providing free schooling to every child (MoES, 1997, 1998, 1999). Faced with limited financial resources that have restricted the expansion of government schools, and the growing school population as a result of UPE and USE, the government has encouraged the growth of the private education sector at all levels, requiring licensing and inspection of private institutions by MoES officials.

The government of Uganda has a long history, stretching back to the colonial period before independence in 1962, of articulating a strong commitment to promoting social equity and modifying societal attitudes and beliefs that discriminate against women (Sperandio, 2003). A national gender policy has been developed (Ministry of Gender, 2000). There is a well-organized and vocal women's movement. Nongovernmental organizations (NGOs) and aid donor agencies all have given support. Academics are developing a body of research focusing on specific Ugandan gender issues (Burns, 2001; Kyomuhendo, 1997; Muanga, 1997). Women are only now establishing civil and property rights in what has traditionally been a male-dominated society. Their movement into educational management and leadership has been equally slow (Brown and Ralph, 1996).

THE HISTORY OF WOMEN'S EDUCATIONAL LEADERSHIP IN UGANDA

Colonial Education (1877–1962)

Before the arrival of the first missionary group in 1877, boys were sent to the homes of tribal chiefs and influential persons to learn tribal law and acceptable behavior. Girls were taught by their mothers, relatives and friends to be homemakers, good wives and mothers and efficient workers on the family farm, the *shamba*. Missionaries arriving from the British Christian Missionary Society (CMS) and French missionaries from the Roman Catholic order of the White Fathers imposed a formal system of schooling onto this traditionally informal education (Castel, 1968; Furley and Watson, 1978). After converting a number of tribal chiefs to their respective religions, the missionaries persuaded them to send their children to the Euro-Christian environment of the mission schools. Thus the first schools, of which King's College, Budo, is an example, were boys' schools set up to train future tribal chiefs. These schools modeled British educational practices and propagated a clear moral and religious code, promoted high academic standards and encouraged participation in sports and music.

The first girls' schools did not appear until the early 1900s. Catholic nuns at Nsambaya established a primary school offering boarding facilities in 1903 and CMS did so at Gayaza in Mengo district in 1905. Gayaza opened with an enrollment of five daughters of tribal chiefs. The goal of these schools was to prepare girls to be future wives of kings and chiefs and other influential people in government, to join their husbands in their role as leaders of the new religious faith. Other schools followed, some offering six years of schooling and some only four; most of these schools survive to the present day. The first generation of women leaders in Uganda was the product of these missionary-founded boarding schools.

The head teachers of these schools were appointed by the education office within the archdeaconry/diocesan office of a particular region. In the early missionary period (lasting until 1945) the head teachers were male missionaries, wives of missionaries, nuns or unmarried female missionaries. Their duties included implementing Christian moral practices and the academic curriculum, management of school funds and school materials, organizing national examinations, attending meetings at local and district level and ensuring that teachers and workers in the school were morally upright, including the dismissal of female teachers who became pregnant.

There were few incidences of educated Ugandan female head teachers being appointed, largely because few women received an education past the primary level. Even if they did gain such an education, they were still expected to undertake domestic work in the home for their husbands and children. The very small pool of educated women who became teachers and aspired to become heads of schools could only look to European female school heads for role models, not easy given the racial and social taboos operating in this period.

Pre-Independence (1940–1962)

This period was marked by an increasing number of students enrolling in primary schools as urban and semi-urban areas grew in response to economic development. Junior and secondary schools also developed, but were still few in number and catered predominantly to boys because parents were unwilling to pay even small school fees to educate girls. In Busoga region, for example, there were only two girls' schools but eight boys' schools and one coeducational school. All schools had been single sex until this time.

By the end of the 1950s, a limited number of secondary schools developed as recommended by the Binns (1951) and De Busen (1953) commissions. Both commissions emphasized the Africanization of education. The children of rich Ugandans were sent to boarding schools, while poorer parents used the day schools. Parents favored girls' day primary schools as they offered a means of reducing the incidence of early interactions with boys. Like boys, girls started school when they were relatively old, usually about seven years or older. Ugandan male teachers were recruited to head the schools, although most girls' schools continued to be headed by white missionary teachers.

In this period the roles of the head teachers increased as a result of increased enrollment and the demands of preparation for independence, which resulted in rising expectations and political agitation among male secondary school students.

Attitudes toward girls' education remained relatively unchanged since Gayaza Girls' School's first headmistress, Miss Allen, maintained that the purpose of educating girls was "to develop their character and make them good, sensible women who are not afraid to work" (Bantebya, 2004). Marriage, motherhood and the domestic sphere continued to be linked to notions of respectability and gentility, and women were not prepared to take leadership roles by their upbringing, nor did their education motivate them to acquire technical and administrative skills and competencies (UNESCO, 1993). There were few cases of Ugandan female head teachers leading primary schools by the time Uganda obtained independence. Those women who did accept such positions remained single because of social taboos regarding the relative education levels of marriage partners.

During this period only two institutions, Kyambogo Teacher Training College and Makerere University, trained diplomates or graduates for secondary school teaching. The few women who completed a secondary education were in competition with many qualified male students for teacher training places. Very few were selected, as it was assumed they would get married, become pregnant and leave their jobs, thus wasting their training. This further limited the pool of female teachers from whom future female head teachers could be drawn.

The path to top management was built on gaining experience as the head of a department, boarding school matron or other positions of responsibility in the school. Female teachers often failed to gain this experience, in part because of the interruption of their careers due to marriage, childbearing or the lack of their spouse's support of their progress. In some instances, their male peers and superiors in the schools would engineer their exclusion from the official promotion procedures. This lack of experience would result in aspiring female teachers failing to meet the basic qualifications needed for the official promotion procedures.

Independence and Civil War (1962–1985)

After Uganda gained independence in 1962, and influenced by the Castle Report (1962) and the World Bank Survey Mission (1963), government attention focused on the provision of secondary education to ensure the human capital necessary to spearhead economic and social development. The government took over a number of missionary schools, which allowed it the right to post teachers and appoint head teachers of their choice. However, many of the parent religious bodies retained some school governance rights, including that of accepting or rejecting a head teacher appointed to their school.

Wanyuange Girls' School appointed its first Ugandan female head in 1966. Tororo Girls' School, a vocational secondary school set up in collaboration with the University of Massachusetts, Amherst, gained a Ugandan headmistress in 1970.

Uganda experienced a devastating civil war between 1972 and 1980 that halted the development of the education system. The war forced both foreign residents and many educated Ugandans to flee the country, including teachers who were often employed in neighboring Kenya, and displaced large numbers of the rural population. As stability returned in the 1980s, education was influenced by a government program of recovery aimed at the rehabilitation of destroyed schools and educational facilities and services. Also included in the program was a rapid expansion of secondary schooling, resulting in the number of secondary schools increasing from 178 in 1981 to 512 in 1988. All coeducational schools continued to be headed by men.

However, the number of female students in secondary school did not increase at the same rate as that of their male counterparts. While parents were increasingly accepting of the idea of educating girls, conditions in the schools often discouraged them from doing so. Countering these conditions became an additional role of head teachers. Parents wanted the school to ensure girls were not exposed to bad company and early sex, which would ruin their daughters' chances of a favorable marriage with a high bride price or well-paid employment, the payback for parents' investment in a daughter's education.

The duties and responsibilities of school heads increased with the demand for the implementation of children's rights, increasing student strikes and protests about poor facilities, and increasing student drug use in urban areas. Absenteeism among teachers was also a problem as the government found it increasingly difficult to meet salary commitments, forcing teachers to take on several jobs. Heads were increasingly at the mercy of parent associations and school boards who had stepped in to provide the financial support that the government could not supply. Many of these women lacked the experience in financial management that was now necessary for survival in schools acting as independent entities.

From 1985 to the Present

By 1988, only 63 percent of girls were attending primary school, 7 percent were enrolled in secondary school, and 38 percent of women were still illiterate. While the government addressed the problem of unequal access in a White Paper (1991), there was no systematic policy of nonsexist education to overcome cultural and social barriers to participation of girls in education (Kagoda, 2000; Sperandio, 1998, 2003).

Current female heads and deputy heads of secondary schools recall the many difficulties they experienced in gaining promotion during this period (Sperandio and Kagoda, 2007). Although in theory the merit principle was used to guide the selection of head teachers by the Civil Service Commission's Appointment Board, most positions were filled on the basis of trust and rapport, patronage or cloning. Women's challenge was in part due to their exclusion from the professional networks that Perry (1993) and Coleman (1994) note help with the interpretation of government policies and learning from the experience of others. Women were accustomed to a female community-based culture that frowned upon upward social mobility and self-promotion and made it next to impossible to socialize with males in a semiformal or informal context. They were not comfortable with male communication patterns or humor. Female teachers also needed the official support of their head teachers and community members together with encouragement and support from family and spouses to apply for promotion. Rarely were all of these forthcoming.

Women could not contemplate taking on a headship position, which would almost certainly involve leading male teachers. Okello (2004) investigated this problem, concluding that in Ugandan society it was doubtful whether male teachers would "accept to perform any task delegated to them by their female heads since these men are brought up to believe women cannot lead them." One of our female head interviewees noted the common lack of self-esteem among the women with whom she grew up in the period before 1985, when traditional male attitudes to women prevailed. She explained "women are mothers and by nature are nurturing and very accommodating and this is often interpreted as a weakness by society." She continued "society criticizes decisions made by a woman leader because she is female."

All of the head and deputy head teachers we interviewed recognized that they would be expected to perform their domestic roles even if they gained promotion. They acknowledged the widespread acceptance in Uganda prior to 1985 of the belief that a successful woman was one who got married, raised a family and submitted to her husband. Most of the women had no expectation of their husbands being prepared to help with the domestic duties should they be appointed to leadership positions.

The women we interviewed also noted that a further deterrent to applying for school leadership was the fear of being posted to a rural area. Women understood that the chances that husband and family would be prepared to move to a rural area lacking access to modern health and recreational facilities, educated peers, and low employment opportunities, so most opted to stay in the classroom rather than seek promotion.

AFFIRMATIVE ACTION

Pressure from the international community for Uganda to commit to globally recognized standards of gender equity in the 1990s resulted in the government's adoption of a number of affirmative action measures. These were designed to limit discrimination and encourage women to aspire for leadership positions in various sectors of the civil service. Uganda adopted a new constitution, which included the statement that "women shall have a right to equal treatment with men and that right shall include equal opportunities in political, economic and social activities" (RoU, 1995). Following this, a national gender policy (RoU, 1997) was developed with the collaboration of a number of NGOs including Action for Development, Women Lawyers, and the National Association of Women's Organizations in Uganda. The Ministry of Gender and Social Development was created, as well as "gender desks" in all government departments. All government departments are now

required to ensure that they meet a 30 percent female employment quota.

In education, the opening up of opportunities for girls to receive free secondary education was supplemented by an affirmative action policy to bring more women into university and college education. The establishment of the Department of Distance Learning at Makerere University, and the opening of additional universities both publicly and privately funded, provided women with the opportunity to obtain the required minimum education criteria needed to head a school.

The MoES now requires that each coeducational school have both a male and female administrator. This requirement applies to both government-supported schools and private schools licensed by the government. In theory, this should have opened many new opportunities for women to move into educational leadership.

WHERE ARE UGANDAN WOMEN IN EDUCATIONAL LEADERSHIP IN 2007?

Women are still in the minority as both school head and deputy head teachers (see table 7.1). This is of particular concern given the increasing numbers of girls now entering secondary schooling at a time in their lives when they are most vulnerable to harassment from male students and teachers, and from "sugar daddies" who promise payment of school fees and other luxuries in exchange for sexual favors, all too common characteristics of life for adolescent girls in Uganda (Sperandio, 1998).

The number of women at the policy-making levels of the MoES is equally worrying (see table 7.2). Typically, policy makers at ministry level are recruited from the ranks of school administrators. Given the small pool of women who hold this rank, it is not surprising that they are poorly represented in the educational policy-making hierarchy. This places the burden of insuring gender equity and sensitivity in new developments with watchdog women's organizations, such as the Ugandan chapter of the University Women's Association.

UNDERSTANDING CHOICES ABOUT LEADERSHIP: A RESEARCH AGENDA

Women's Career Choices

Research on what influences women teachers' decisions to apply for leadership roles and success in accessing them is clearly needed. There is no indication that the number of women in school leadership has

Table 7.1. Distribution of Male and Female Head and Deputy Head Teachers in Government-Aided and -Licensed Private Secondary Schools in Uganda, February 2006

School Type	Position	Females	Males	Total
Government-aided schools				
Boys only	Head	0	29	29
	Deputy	3	46	49
Total		3	75	78
Coed	Head	78	555	633
	Deputy	119	571	690
Total		197	1,126	1,323
Girls only	Head	46	6	52
	Deputy	31	52	83
Total		77	58	135
Grand Total		277	1,259	1,536
Private schools				
Boys only	Head	0	15	15
	Deputy	2	17	19
Total		2	32	34
Coed	Head	85	752	837
	Deputy	116	731	847
Total		201	1,483	1,684
Girls only	Head	22	10	32
	Deputy	13	14	27
Total		35	24	59
Not stated	Head	0	2	2
	Deputy	0	1	1
Total		0	3	3
Grand Total		238	1,542	1,780

Source: MoES, 2006b, cited in Sperandio and Kagoda, 2007.

Table 7.2. Positions Held by Women in the Ministry of Education and Sports, April 2006

Position	Female	Male
Ministers	1	3
Permanent Secretaries and Undersecretaries	0	3
Commissioner and Assistant Commissioner	8	16
Principal Officers	6	24
Senior Officers	9	28

Source: MoES, 2005, cited in Sperandio and Kagoda, 2007.

significantly increased. Are women choosing not to seek leadership positions, or are they being prevented from accessing them?

A senior member of the Department of Educational Foundations at Makerere University when asked to comment on this situation suggested that career choices are different for men and women in Uganda. She observed, "The majority of male teachers who choose to study for the Master's of Education degree do so within a year or two of getting their undergraduate degree while the majority of female teachers do so five or ten years after obtaining their undergraduate degree." She observed that women teachers also fail to take advantage of opportunities to upgrade their qualifications. She noted that of the 60 students enrolled for the educational management course in 2006, only 10 were female, and only three of the 30 students enrolled for a master of arts course in the Department of Higher Education were female. These courses provide the management component for educational leadership, thus very few women appear to be gaining this qualification, needed for promotion to school headships.

Barriers to Promotion

A second line of research should explore the barriers encountered by the female teachers who do aspire to leadership. Facing the District Service Commissions and the Education Service Commission can be a daunting prospect for many women. Harassment of female teachers and even newly appointed female leaders is still common. One woman head described how, at her first appearance at the district level meeting, a male school head teased her, asking, "Are you now a man?" Women teachers may be reluctant to take up positions in private schools that would give them much needed leadership experience because of the loss of seniority and pension rights in the government system, and can be fired at will by the school owner.

A third line of research could explore the factors that would make educational leadership an appealing career choice. Interviews with teachers who stated they were *not* interested in seeking promotion mentioned the number of school strikes occurring. They had become increasingly dangerous, and in some cases fatal, when students burned classrooms, offices and dormitories. With more women forced to seek work outside the home, the traditional respect shown by children to adults is breaking down.

Head teachers also must cope with teachers who lack motivation and are not prepared to do anything to improve the schools without a promise of financial recompense. Teachers' salaries are very low. Primary teachers' salaries are the equivalent of US$120 a month, while secondary school teachers' salaries are below US$300 a month. Head teachers also are under pressure from the MoES, parents and the local school community to improve the school and must often go to considerable lengths to find funding to do this.

The Effects of HIV/AIDS

Head teachers are on the front line in Uganda's continuing fight against HIV/AIDS. The country has registered significant achievements in combating the disease over the past 20 years (Ugandan AIDS Commission, 2005); however, the prevalence rate is once again on the rise, from 6 percent in 2005 to more than 7 percent in 2006 (Ministry of Finance, Planning and Economic Development, 2006). Adolescents and young adults between the ages of 13 and 30 are at highest risk of acquiring the disease through unsafe sexual practices (MoES, 2005; Piacy, 2005). With large numbers of infected students, head teachers must not only ensure adequate health education, but also cope with the consequences of the disease. Many schools have teachers living with the disease. The national response policy requires that they cannot be replaced even when they are no longer able to perform their duties, creating large gaps in the schools' human resource capacity.

Schools frequently have large populations of orphans, some of whom may also carry the disease. While this is a challenge that confronts both men and women in educational leadership, female school leaders find themselves especially involved. This is due in part to the community perception of women as nurturing family-builders, and partly due to the particular need to educate girls about sexual issues and provide them with support and strong role models. Research that provides a clearer picture of the expectations being placed on female educational leadership with respect to measures to combat the effects of AIDS is urgently needed.

Leadership Preparation

Ways must be sought to encourage more women to view educational leadership as a career path, and to smooth that path for those interested in pursuing it. Research needs to be undertaken to establish whether the provision of gender-differentiated educational leadership preparation would meet the first of these goals, giving confidence to those women who have the formal qualifications but are afraid to seek promotion. Current undergraduate foundation courses have a very small component focusing on administrative management skills.

Research is also needed to establish the priorities for ongoing training and help for those women already in leadership positions, or who have firm aspirations to obtain them. The popularity of the master of education degree with women who are currently heads, deputy heads or directors of studies in primary schools suggests that women are actively seeking additional training. Over 70 percent of the students admitted to this course at Makerere University since 2000 have been women. They come from all over Uganda. If new forms of training and leadership preparation are to be developed they must be specific to the context of Uganda and consider what is needed to prepare women for the particular challenges female leaders in Uganda must face. The experiences and opinions of the few women who have faced the challenges and are now successful school leaders are important in this respect and must be sought out and analyzed.

CONCLUSION

Ugandan women have made important advances into educational leadership in the past 10 years, with women leading increasing numbers of primary schools together with a small number of the most prestigious secondary schools. Government policies have created opportunities for women to get the practical experience of leadership as deputy heads and are helping to overcome the legacy of both history and cultural norms and understandings of leadership defined by men.

The challenge now is to establish through research the adjustments to the present process of leadership preparation, recruitment and selection that are most helpful in motivating women to seek leadership positions. By nature and socialization, Ugandan women are strong, hardworking, nurturing, cooperative and adaptable, all characteristics of successful leadership in the Uganda of today where schools face a multitude of social problems including those resulting from the AIDS epidemic.

Gender differentiated leadership programs could provide an opportunity for women to develop their specific skills and approaches to leadership that are often very different from those of their male peers. Such preparation also could be a crucial factor in encouraging more women into educational policy making and implementation to the benefit of all Ugandan children, but especially girls.

REFERENCES CITED

Beijing Declaration and Platform for Action (BPA). Fourth World Conference on Women. 15 September 1995. Retrieved 8 August 2006 from http://www.un.org/women-watch/daw/beijing/platform/plat1.htm.

Bantebya-Kyomehendo, G. (2004). The role of national mechanisms in promoting gender equality and the empowerment of women: Uganda experience. Paper prepared for the Experts' Group Meeting. 29 November 2004. Rome.

Banugire, F. R. (1989). Employment, incomes, basic needs and structural adjustment policy in Uganda, 1980–1987. In Onimode Bade (Ed.), *The IMF, the World Bank, the African debt and the social and political impact*, pp. 95–110. London: Zed Books.

Bitamazire, N. G. (2005). Status of education for rural people in Uganda. Unpublished paper presented at the Ministerial Seminar on Education for Rural People in Africa, 7 September 2005, Addis Ababa, Ethiopia. Retrieved 8 August 2006 from http://fao.org/sd/erp/ERPevents37_en.htm.

Brown, M., and Ralph, S. (1996). Barriers to women managers' advancement in education in Uganda. *International Journal of Educational Management, 10*(6), 18–23.

Castle, E. B. (1996). *Growing up in East Africa.* London: Oxford University Press.

Coleman, M. (2001). Achievement against the odds. *School Leadership and Management, 21*(1), 75–100.

Furley, O., and Watson, T. (1978). *A history of education in East Africa.* New York: NOR Publishers.

Kagoda, A. M. (2000). Determinants of career professional development of female teachers in Uganda. Unpublished paper delivered to the Human Services Today Conference, Makerere University, Kampala, Uganda.

Kwesiga, J. (1998). *Women in Uganda. Uganda 1997/98.* Yearly Review. Kampala, Uganda, 144–150.

Kyomuhendo, G. (1997). *Household economics: Implications for the attainment of enrolment of girls in schools in Uganda.* Nairobi: Academy Science Publishers.

Ministry of Education and Sports (MoES) Republic of Uganda. (1997). *National strategy for girls' education in Uganda.* Kampala, Uganda.

———. (1998). *Guidelines on policy, roles and stakeholders in the implementation of primary education.* Kampala, Uganda.

———. (1999). *Education for all (EFA) 2000 assessment.* Kampala, Uganda.

———. (2004a). *Annual school census.* Kampala, Uganda.

———. (2004b). *The development of education in Uganda at the beginning of the 21st century.* Report to the 47th Session of the International Conference on Education, Geneva, Switzerland. 8–11 September, 2004. Kampala, Uganda.

———. (2004c). *Annual education performance report.* Kampala, Uganda.

———. (2005). Staff list. Retrieved from www.education.go.ug/email addresses.htm 23 January 2006.

———. (2006a). *The education sector annual performance report, 1st July 2005–30th June 2006.* Retrieved from www.education.go.ug/Final/20ESAPR/202006.htm.

———. (2006b). Unpublished statistics generated for the author by the Statistics Office of the MoES. 20 February 2006.

Ministry of Gender and Community Development and the Statistics Department, Ministry of Planning and Economic Development. (1998). *Women and men in Uganda: Facts and figures, 1998.* Kampala, Uganda.

Ministry of Gender, Labour and Social Development. (1999). *The national action plan on women.* Kampala, Uganda.

Ministry of Gender, Republic of Uganda. (1997a). *National gender policy.* Kampala, Uganda.

———. (1997b). *Household survey.* Kampala, Uganda.

Mutibwa, O. M. (1988). *Ugandan women in high-level decision making positions.* Unpublished paper, February 1986. Kampala, Uganda.

Nsubuga, Y. K. *The case for the Universal Secondary Education in Uganda.* Retrieved 8 August 2006 from http://www.education.go.ug/USE.htm.

Nuwagaba, A. (2001). Situation analysis of women in the Ugandan political economy. *Africa Social Science Research Review, 17*(1), 15–30.

Okello, J. F. (2004). Effects of female head teachers' administrative styles on the performance of male teachers of primary schools in Lira District (1999–2003). Unpublished dissertation. Department of Foundations, Makerere University, Kampala, Republic of Uganda.

———. (1990). Educational Policy Review Commission. *Education for National Integration and Development.* Kampala, Uganda.

———. (1992). *Government White Paper on the Education Policy Review Commission Report.* Kampala, Uganda.

———. (1996). *The Constitution.* Article 32, and also Local Governments Act Amendments, 2000. Kampala, Uganda.

———. (2002). *Education Service Act.* Article 31. Kampala, Uganda.

Sperandio, J. (1998). Girls' secondary education in Uganda: Unintended outcomes of well-intentioned policy. Doctoral dissertation. University of Chicago.

———. (2003). Leadership for adolescent girls: The role of secondary schools in Uganda. *Gender and Development, 14*(4), 391–410.

Sperandio, J., and Kagoda, A. M. (2007). Advancing Ugandan women into educational leadership (in press).

Uganda Bureau of Statistics (UBS). (2006). Statistical Abstracts. Kampala, Uganda.

Wakoko, F., and Labao, L. (1996). Reconceptualizing gender and reconstructing social life: Ugandan women and the path to national development. *Africa Today, 43*(3) 307–322.

Xiaoyan, L. (2002). Uganda post-primary education sector report. Africa Region Human Development Working Paper Series, World Bank. Retrieved 8 August 2006 from www.worldbank.org/afr/seia.

CHAPTER 8

Women on the Rise

Women Navigating across Social, Political, Economic and Cultural Arenas to Claim Their Stake in Educational Leadership Positions in South Africa

Thidziambi Phendla

INTRODUCTION

RECENT MERGERS IN HIGHER education in South Africa have served to reduce rather than increase the number of women leaders in higher education institutions. At the beginning of 2007, Professor Gumbi was the only woman vice chancellor (VC) at a traditional university in South Africa. It was not until recently that three more women VCs were appointed, but at former technical institutions (now referred to as universities of technology), which do not enjoy the same status as traditional universities. Although the increase from one to four may be seen as substantial, this number is appalling given that there are 23 institutions of higher education in the country. Undoubtedly, this number (that is, four women in VC positions) does not represent the current situation, in which there are 58.5% male and 41.5% female professionals with permanent appointment in higher educational institutions in South Africa (Hemis Database, 2006). The four women represent a mere 17.4% in leadership positions.

It is clear from the 2006 database that women are marginalized by race, gender, age, rank and personal category. Women are underrepresented in the academic and administrative hierarchies of the university. The questions that come to mind are "How many women are in senior leadership positions in higher education institutions in South Africa? How are they represented in terms of the racial demographics of the country? What is the distribution in terms of personnel category? Where do we find more women—in the professional or nonprofessional categories?

Very little statistical data are available and even less is published about the status of women in the higher education sector in South Africa. As a Black South African woman and a professor at a university, I am confronted by the desire to establish what the representation of South African women leaders in higher education institutions is. Largely due to traditional mainstream educational scholarship, which has not addressed the influence of race, gender and other social constructs on educational policy and practice, there is a knowledge gap about the role these constructs play in influencing the upward mobility of women in senior positions in the country.

Framed by this complex background, the main compelling question that I propose for this study is: How are women represented in professional and non-professional positions in higher education institutions in South Africa? Finally, and perhaps most important, I hope this study raises as many, if not more, questions than it answers.

THE NATURE OF EDUCATION IN SOUTH AFRICA PRIOR TO 1994

Apartheid is defined as "a legalized repression and exploitation of the Black majority to regulate the destiny and fate of legalized discrimination" (Njobe, 1990, p. 44). Similarly, Smith (1992) says that "apartheid" is an Afrikaans word that means "apartness." It is a word that has come to connote racial segregation, and hence the system of government in South Africa based upon total supremacy of the White minority population. The salient feature of education in South Africa was the differential pattern of education development for different race groups.[1]

On the one hand, Whites received a very high level of education, comparable with the best in the industrialized world. On the other hand, Black education was characterized largely by an inequitable allocation of resources, overcrowded classrooms, high dropout rates, and insufficient numbers of teachers, most of them poorly qualified. Various scholars argued that even before the Bantu education was introduced in 1953 for Africans, vast differences existed in the provision of education for Blacks and Whites.

Christie (1986) indicated that education also was divided according to mother-tongue instructions for all population registration groups. For instance, the Venda speakers were separated from the Sotho speakers and the Afrikaans speakers were separated from the English speakers. Schools also were divided in terms of city and rural with vast differences between rural and farm schools, rich schools, private schools and religious schools (Christie, 1986, pp. 125–126, cited in Phendla, 2000).

Molteno (1986) argues that Bantu education was created to reinforce the system of Bantustans. The education was designed to control the direction of thought, to delimit the boundaries of knowledge, to restrict lines of communication, and to curtail contact across language barriers. In addition, apartheid education aimed to dwarf the minds of Black children by conditioning them to servitude positions in order to serve the White minority government and provide cheap labor (p. 94). Certainly, apartheid education was a plan designed to remove Black people psycho-ideologically and resettle them in their place of subordination (p. 93). In Verwoerd's notorious words:

> There is no place for him in the European community above the level of certain forms of labor. Within his own community, however, all doors are open. For that reason it is to no avail for him to receive a training which has as its aim absorption in the European community, where he cannot be absorbed. Until now he has been subject to a school system which drew him away from his own community and misled him by showing him the pastures of European society in which he was not allowed to graze (Christie, 1986, p. 12; Molteno, 1986, p. 92).

In terms of disparities in race and gender in South Africa, White people still hold the majority of senior positions in general and higher educational institutions in particular. The 2004 Census of South African Women in Corporate Leadership, conducted by the Business Women Association of South Africa (BWASA) in association with Catalyst USA, surveyed the women on boards of directors and in executive management in public companies listed on the JSE (Johannesburg Stock Exchange) as of September 30, 2004 (BWASA, 2005) (cited in Booysen and Nkomo,

Table 8.1. Percentage of Females in Permanent Appointments in Higher Education Institutions in South Africa

Position	Number of Positions	Females	%
Professor	2,000	370	18.5
Associate Professor	1,421	424	29.8
Directors	89	14	15.7
Associate Director	234	65	27.7
Senior Lecturer	4,048	1,597	39.4
Lecturer	6,157	3,139	50.9
Junior Lecturer	662	373	56.3
Below Junior Lecturer	66	37	56.0
Undesignated/Other	638	342	53.6
Total	15,315	6,361	41.5

Source: Hemis, 2006.

2006, p. 27). The survey shows that men constitute 80.2% and 89.3% in executive manager and directorate positions respectively. Women make up 19.8% and 10.7% in these positions respectively.

In my opinion, these differences are a direct result of Verwoerd's notorious apartheid philosophy of divide and rule. From the statistics obtained among 23 institutions of higher education in this study (tables 8.1 and 8.2), it is clear that an overwhelming majority (more than 61%) of senior leadership positions are still occupied by White academics. In the same way it is safe to claim that the legacy of apartheid provided fertile ground to breed inequalities in higher educational institutions since Blacks and women, in particular Black women, are still occupying lower ranks in academia.

WHERE ARE WOMEN ON THE EDUCATIONAL LEADERSHIP LADDER IN SOUTH AFRICA?

Data for this study were obtained from the Hemis Database (2006). The data were collected from 23 South African institutions of higher education. The data represent a percentage of females in permanent appointments in higher education institutions in the following positions: professor, associate professor, director, associate director, senior lecturer, lecturer, junior lecturer, below junior lecturer and undesignated or other.

Table 8.2. Percentage of Females in Permanent Appointment According to Gender and Race in Higher Education Institutions in South Africa

Position	Race					Total	% Female
	White	Colored	Indian	African	Other		
Professional	12,439	1,155	1,548	4,880	59	20,081	42.9
Nonprofessional	6,720	3,373	1,484	11,635	43	23,255	56.6
Total	19,159	4,528	3,032	16,515	102	43,336	50.3

Source: Hemis, 2006.

The distribution of professionals in South African universities does not reflect the demographic profile of the larger society. The system is highly polarized by race and gender, with more prestigious positions like full professor occupied predominately by White males. Blacks and women tend to be consigned to lower rungs of the employment ladder, with a disproportionate number in nonprofessional positions that provide basic services in the unskilled labor environment.

Table 8.1 shows that of a total of 2,000 professors, 1,630 were male and 370 were female. This represents a mere 18.5% of women holding professorial positions. There were 289 men and 373 women in junior lecturer level, and 29 men and 37 women below junior lecturer level. This represents an average of 43.8% men and 56.2% women in the two lower levels. The disparities are much higher given that the margin between men and women represented in the whole workforce in higher educational institutions is slight: 49.5% and 41.5% for men and women, respectively. According to table 8.1, of a total of 6,157 lecturers, there were 3,139 female and 3,018 male lecturers. This represents 50.9% of all women in this level. It is clear from this database that women are more visible in junior positions.

Even though there have been major changes in terms of educational provision since the new democratic government led by the African National Congress (ANC), Africans are still disaggregated by race and acutely underrepresented, as reflected in table 8.2. Of a total of 20,081 professional staff, 12,439 were White, 1,155 Colored, 1548 Indian, 4,880 African and 59 "all other." This means that 61.4% professional staff are White, 5.8% Colored, 7.7% Indian and 24.3% representing the African group. Contrary to the above picture, Africans are in the majority in South Africa. Of the 45 million people in South Africa in 2002, Africans were 30.5 million, Whites 4.5 million, Coloreds 4.1 million, and Asian/Indian 1.2 million. These numbers constitute 79%, 9.6%, 8.9% and 2.5% for these groups respectively (Census, 2002).

The data depicted in table 8.2 have major implications for South African higher educational institutions, let alone the still huge disparities in terms of race and gender.

The proportion of women by ethnicity in leadership in higher educational institutions is nearly impossible to determine in South Africa because of the ways in which gender and race/ethnicity are reported. There are reports by gender or by race, but not by race, gender and ethnicity. In South Africa, female representation in the senior instruction/research professions has increased in recent years to at least 42.9%, but is still not proportional to the number of women teachers in the country.

Without a doubt, the ANC government has made huge strides toward gender balancing and equalization. There were only six women in Parliament during the apartheid regime. This number escalated to 27% during President Mandela's reign. President Mbeki's first term saw a rise of 3% more, taking the number to 30%. As of 2008, women occupy 42% of Parliament seats in the South African government. It is the present government's mission to see a 50/50 representation in all spheres of government and institutions. Given the current situation in higher educational sectors it is unlikely that a 50/50 representation will occur in the near future unless dramatic changes occur. A mere 18.5% of women holding professorial positions is a far cry from what the ANC government advocates.

The major issue that may influence the movement of women within the ranks of educational leadership in South Africa is the issue of political leadership. While the South African government has demonstrated its commitment to gender equity, parity and balance in all the government structures, it is only when the commitment translates to changes in other sectors like higher educational institutions that we begin to experience and witness gender equity and parity in the real sense.

ARE YOU BLACK FIRST OR ARE YOU A WOMAN FIRST? WHAT ROLE DO RACE AND GENDER PLAY IN ENSURING LEADERSHIP IN SOUTH AFRICA?

Race continues to be a major construct that plays a significant role in the creation of differences in academic professors in South African higher education. Gender claims a second position, but the intersection of race and gender seems to be a dynamic combination that requires much attention. White males continue to dominate and occupy leadership positions in the country. Although White women were also dominated and oppressed by the apartheid policies of the former government, they stand to gain more when compared with their Black counterparts.

The Affirmative Action (AA) and the Employment Equity (EE) Acts of 1997 in South Africa were legislated to address the imbalances of the past and include "previously disadvantaged individuals" (PDIs)—that is, Blacks, women and youth—in the socioeconomic fabric of the country. Much has been achieved in this area; however, individuals who are currently benefiting are Black men and White women. Therefore, Black women remain in the background and stand to lose from the interventions.

There are several schools of thought around the issue of AA policy in South Africa. Some advocate a total exclusion of White women from benefits of AA interventions; some suggest a stance in which White women train and mentor Black women. The bottom line is that AA and EE policies are seen as strategies to reverse apartheid while posing fears to Whites in general and White males in particular, a group which is now referred to as "currently disadvantaged individuals" (CDIs).[2] Although there is a broad band of ideas and astute suggestions on how these policies should work, the reality is that these are met with weak plans of action. Policy is confronted with the perennial problem of practice.

A recent study conducted by Booysen and Nkomo (2006) reveals that there is a slow progress in the implementation of the Employment Equity Act. They argue that, while it appears that momentum is building up in the increase of employment of Blacks (5.7%) in general and females in top and senior management positions, there seems to be a drop in the representation of Blacks and women at the professional and middle management levels (p. 26). In addition, the increase fails to benefit Black women as they continue to be poorly represented in top management (13.8% in 2002 from 12.4% in 2000) and in senior management (21.6% in 2002 from 21.0% in 2000) (Commission for EE (CEE), 2003, as cited in Booysen and Nkomo, p. 26).

With the foregoing in mind, the pattern that emerges from the data in this study suggests that women are being appointed at the lecturer level but either get stuck at this level or drop out of academic work, unable to combine family responsibilities with academic commitments. Furthermore, more women than men are found in nonacademic categories and undesignated levels. In general, there are fewer women in senior positions, consistent with apartheid patterns that favored men over women. In particular there are fewer Black women on the leadership ladder because Black women were and to an extent are still oppressed by both race and gender.

Table 8.3 shows disproportionate distribution regarding gender: females account for 26% and males for 74% of all senior management positions. According to unconfirmed statistics regarding race and gender in senior leadership positions in the business sector in South Africa, in 2000, White, Indian, Colored and African males constituted 53%, 5%, 4% and 11%,

Table 8.3. Percentage Distribution of Legislators by Race and Gender in South Africa

Race	2000		2003	
	Male	Female	Male	Female
White	53	20	51	17
Indian	5	2	5	2
Colored	4	3	5	3
African	11	2	13	4
Total	73	27	74	26

Source: Commission for EE, 2 003.

respectively. In 2003, there was a slight increase of 2% especially for African males and females. The distribution accounted for 51%, 5%, 5% and 13% White, Indian, Colored and African males, accordingly.

Also, table 8.3 illustrates huge disproportions in terms of race and gender where White females still occupy second position on the leadership ladder. The statistics show that in 2000, White, Indian, Colored and African females accounted for 20%, 2%, 3% and 2%, respectively. There was a slight change in that the number of White females dropped to 17%, still positioning them in second place in the echelons of leadership. The statistics show that in 2003, White, Indian, Colored and African females constituted 17%, 2%, 3% and 4% accordingly. The racial imbalances in senior management are evident in that the White group constitutes 68%, in particular White males making up 51% and continuing to dominate all the groups (Booysen and Nkomo, 2006).

The BWASA Census of 2004 also provides more insight into the workings of race and gender in that it reveals the deep division among the South African citizens. It centers the race/gender debate on another level that questions the commitment of the policy makers. The survey brings clarity and coherence into the already distorted picture, where, after more than a decade in a democratic government, the power and decision making are still in the hands of men, and in particular, White men.

WHY ARE THERE FEW WOMEN ON THE EDUCATIONAL LEADERSHIP LADDER IN SOUTH AFRICA?

Booysen (2007), in her work on effective management of diversity, draws a desolate picture of South Africa wherein it is caught between two worlds, the Eurocentric and Afrocentric. Booysen contends that the influence of both globalization and internalization present a unique profile, given the continuing internal struggles presented by cultural diversity, including language, religion, race and gender issues (Booysen,

2007, p. 52). There are still vast differences between African ethnic groups in South Africa, where Xhosa-speaking people continue to dominate other ethnic groups, especially in government structures.

Table 8.4 shows the percentage breakdown of official languages and ethnic representation in the Cabinet of South Africa as of January 2006. In terms of official spoken languages the statistics reveal the following: IsiZulu 23.8%, IsiXhosa 17.6%, Afrikaans 13.3%, Sepedi 9.4%, English 8.2%, Setswana 8.2%, Sesotho 7.9%, Xitsonga 4.4%, IsiSwati 2.7%, Tshivenda 2.3%, IsiNdebele 1.6%, and other 0.6%. Although spoken language does not necessarily constitute ethnicity of an individual, it is close enough to provide a basis for speculation. For instance, on the one hand, Colored people speak either English or Afrikaans, with a large number using Afrikaans as their first language. On the other hand, the majority of Indian people consider English as their first language, given that Indian languages are not considered official languages.

Table 8.4 reveals that IsiXhosa is the second most spoken language in the country. It is unsettling to note that the Xhosa group takes up the first position in parliamentary Cabinet seats, with 32.8% representation, while the Zulu group occupies the second position with a mere 15.5%. An analysis of the statistics in terms of ethnic classification reveals that the Xhosa group by far exceeds its share of representation in the country, let alone in the Cabinet. There is a general feeling among ordinary South Africans that people of Xhosa origin seem to dominate, especially in leadership positions.

In my 2000 study of women in leadership, I argue that ethnicity is still a purely divisive and negative phenomenon that needs to be balanced by recognition of the positive dimension in the intellectual, political and academic levels. Contrary to these sentiments, politicians, academics and intellectuals in South Africa are reluctant to address the persistent surfacing of ethnic rivalries. This demonstrates the complexity of the South African cultures beyond race and gender discrimination.

This chapter clearly underscores what Booysen (2007) calls "cultural diversity management challenges facing South African organizations." She identified four challenges, but for this chapter, I will pursue only two:

Challenge 1: The Disparity in Numbers Between Male and Female and Between White and Black Managers

According to Booysen (2007), and also demonstrated in this chapter, White males are still overrepresented in management, with White females in second place and Black females at the bottom of the ladder. Several surveys have shown a slowly closing racial gap, but with persistent gender gaps at senior management level.

Challenge 2: The Relative Ineffectiveness of Affirmative Action in Closing Disparity in Numbers

While there have been several regulatory reform efforts since the democratic elections in 1994, policies such as affirmative action and employment equity are weakened by the gap between theory and practice. Booysen (2001) argues that the way in which affirmative action is being implemented is still subject to the dominant White male value system because of the disparity in numbers between male and female and Black and White managers. This raises some issues in

Table 8.4. Percentage of Females According to Official Language and Ethnicity in the Cabinet in South Africa

Ethnicity	% Official Language	Total Positions	Females	%
Zulu	23.8	9	7	77.7
Xhosa	17.6	19	10	52.6
Afrikaans	13.3			
White		8	2	25
Pedi	9.4	3	0	0
Tswana	8.2	3	3	100
English	8.2			
Sotho	7.9	3	1	33.3
Shangaan	4.4	2	1	50
Swati	2.7	0	0	0
Venda	2.3	2	1	50
Ndebele	1.6			
Colored		4	2	50
Indian		5	1	20
Other	0.6			
Total	**100**	**58**	**27**	

Source: South African government, 2006.

terms of the approach to and effectiveness of affirmative action, namely:

- the perceived addressing of racial rather than gender imbalances;
- the need for White males, who still hold most positions in senior management, to be serious about advancing women in management;
- the dual disadvantage of Black women in management (Booysen, 2007, pp. 72–73).

There are few surveys conducted to address the scarcity of women in higher educational institutions. Nevertheless, one may safely deduce from the current debates that women are grossly underrepresented at South Africa's higher education institutions.

THEORIZING BLACK FEMINISM

Various scholars suggest that the form of our understanding depends upon the genre in which our experiences are created (Collin, 1998; hooks, 1984; White, 1984). For Black women the question is, "How are you oppressed most—as a Black person or as a woman?" Collins' matrix of domination rejects the Eurocentric dichotomy of "either/or" and embraces the view of "both/and."

Instead of starting with gender and then adding other variables such as age, sexual orientation, race, social class and religion, Black feminist thought sees these as distinctive systems of oppression being part of one overarching structure of domination. Collins (1998) argues that what is significant is how these systems interconnect within the systems of economic, political and ideology that support them. Viewing the world through a "both/and" conceptual lens of simultaneity of race, class and gender oppression and of the need for a humanist vision of community creates new possibilities for an empowering feminist knowledge (Collins, 1998 Phendla, 2000, 2004a, 2004b and 2007). For example, although White women are penalized by their gender, they are privileged by their race, and both these constructs penalize Black women.

Because White people write about Black people without adequate concrete knowledge of and contact with them, the "politics of difference" should incorporate the voices of displaced, marginalized, exploited and oppressed Black people, especially Black women. This practice of silence by "those who are written and talked about, and by those who speak it," hooks (1990) says, is a measure to minimize Black people as outsiders looking into the discourse.

Collins (1991) provides a platform for the creation of the new paradigm based on the fact that Black women intellectuals create Black feminist thought using their own concrete experiences as "situated knowers" in order to express a Black woman's standpoint (p. 17). Furthermore, to embrace this epistemological framework, Collins suggests that we should reject the pronouns "they" and "their" when describing Black women and our ideas and replace them with the terms "we," "us" and "our" (p. 17). As a result, Black feminist thought cannot challenge race, gender and class oppression without empowering African American women.

Democratic elections in 1994 in South Africa indicated the death of apartheid government and White minority rule and the birth of a nonracial government of national unity. However, some of the most significant issues central to the oppression of women in general, and Black African women in particular, remained unchallenged—insignificant and unremarked in the eyes of the policy makers.

Although the statistics from the Hemis Database (2006) are silent on the issue of ethnic classification in the national head count of personnel with permanent appointment in higher education, it appears ethnicity has a role to play. Also, in consideration of the fact that there are few previously disadvantaged institutions (at least five, although some were merged), they are still bearing a particular ethnic group profile, according to previous demographic classification. For instance, universities like Venda, Zululand and Limpopo were situated in the former homeland demarcated for the Venda, Zulu and Pedi people respectively. Unconfirmed statistics show a prevalence of these ethnic groups at these institutions.

One may conclude that historical White institutions by virtue of the apartheid era, which placed them on a higher footing than their Black counterparts, would have a majority of either Afrikaans- or English-speaking personnel. Therefore ethnicity still has a role to play in securing leadership positions in higher education institutions since there are more previously White higher education institutions in South Africa.

Mabokela (2000) argues that there must be an intense endeavor to create a supportive environment for Black faculty since they are persistently marginalized in higher educational institutions in South Africa. She further maintains that to address the challenge of lack of Black academics, a systematic program of recruitment should be implemented to go above and beyond the traditional sources such as newspapers and the old boys' network (Mabokela, 2000, p. 155). In addition, junior lecturers should be supported through mentorship programs where a nonthreatening culture of scholarship is created and encouraged. These and other similar measures may work to support Blacks, women and Black women in particular, who happen to be on the lowest rung of the leadership ladder.

CONCLUDING THOUGHTS

In the mid-1990s, Whites owned and controlled 98% of the JSE, and now they own a little more than 50% (*Financial Week Report*, April 2005). While there is already visible progress regarding economic redress, it is by no means an indication that Blacks are approaching economic parity with Whites. The road toward economic equality is still a long and steep one. On a relative basis White males still hold greater power than other groups. They are still disproportionate in their share of the working and general population and in most decision-making positions. The latest training figures indicate that White men are still the biggest beneficiaries of training and skills development in both the private and the public sectors.

The picture in South Africa reveals that Blacks have the power in the supra-system, not yet in management or organization, due to the ineffectiveness of the AA and EE plans. Policies and formal procedures for good employee relations are in place; however, there seems to be a disconnect between the policy and practice. In response to the major question raised in this study, "How many women are in senior leadership positions in higher education institutions in South Africa?" the resounding answer is that there are fewer than expected, and those who are there do not represent the racial demographics of the country since there are only a handful of Black men in leadership positions and an even smaller representation of Black women in professional categories.

What happens to leadership when a South African woman is at its center? The poor representation of women in management and academic positions may reflect the unwillingness of top management to appoint women to these positions or may be the outcome of unwillingness on the part of women to apply for such appointments. What appears to be the case is that women in general and Black women in particular are expected to perform, compete and lead in unfamiliar and hostile environments with little support. At times women feel overwhelmed and refuse to expose themselves to these harsh conditions.

There is still a lack of cultural sensitivity, a lack of cultural awareness programs in White-male-dominant organizational culture. Black people are still viewed as tokens and are not being fully integrated into leadership positions. They are not given real responsibility or decision-making authority. Last but not least, there is a lack of training of Blacks, and especially Black women, hence, the proportion of women decreases significantly along the academic ladder. Women deans, directors and professors are a minority group and women vice chancellors and chancellors are still a rarity.

NOTES

1. *Black* in this context refers to all those South Africans classified as Africans, Coloreds and Indians, although in the day-to-day usage of the language, the term *Black* generally referred to people of African origin, while the other two groups preferred to be called Indians and Colored. It is interesting to note that after the 1994 democratic government, both the Indian and Colored groups prefer the term "African" to either "Indian" or "Colored."
2. There is a surge of fear from different racial groups in South Africa. Indians and Coloreds argue that they were not White enough during the apartheid era to benefit as Whites, now they are not Black enough to be regarded as AA and EE candidates. Whites, on the one hand, are reluctant to train Blacks because they fear that Blacks will take their jobs. White males, on the other hand, regard the AA and EE policies as tools to undermine them, not as fast-tracking mechanisms to address imbalances in the workplace.

REFERENCES CITED

Benham, M. K. P., and Cooper, J. E. (1998). *Let my spirit soar!* Thousand Oaks, CA: Corwin Press.

Bennet, J. (2001). Companies bleeding skilled Blacks at a rapid rate. *Sunday Times*, March 25.

Booysen, L. (2001). The duality in South African leadership: Afrocentric or Eurocentric. *South African Journal of Labor Relations*, 25(3/4), 36.

———. (2007). Managing cultural diversity: A South African perspective. In K. April and M. Shockley (Eds.), *Diversity in Africa: the coming of age of a continent*. Basingstoke, U.K.: Palgrave Macmillan, pp. 51–92.

Booysen, L., and Nkomo, S. (2006). Think manager—think (fe)male. *The International Journal of Interdisciplinary Social Sciences*, 1(2), 23–34.

BWASA (Business Women's Association South Africa, Catalyst USA) (2006). *South African women in corporate leadership: Census 2005*. Sandton: Nedbank Press.

Christie, P. (1986). *The right to learn: The struggle for education in South Africa*. Johannesburg: Ravan Press.

Collins, P. (1991). *Black feminist thought: Knowledge, consciousness, and the politics of empowerment.* New York: Routledge.

———. (1998). *Towards a new vision: Race, class and gender as categories of analysis and connections.* A publication for the Research Clearinghouse and Curriculum Integration Project, Center for Research on Women. Memphis State University.

———. (1998). *Fighting words: Black women and the search for justice.* Minneapolis: University of Minnesota Press.

Denzin, N. K., and Lincoln, Y. S. (1994). *Handbook of qualitative research.* Thousand Oaks, CA: Sage Publications.

Hemis Database (2006). National headcount of senior instruction/research with permanent appointment for the year 2005.

hooks, b. (1984). *Feminist theory: From margin to center.* Boston: South End Press.

———. (1989). Marching for justice: Feminist interventions. *Journal.* 32–41.

———. (1990). *Postmodern Blackness.*[Online]. Available: http://www.allaboutbell.com/postmodern.htm. Accessed 31 July 2003.

Mabokela, R. O. (2000). Voices of conflict: Desegregating South African universities. New York: RoutledgeFalmer.

Molteno, F. (1986). The historical foundations of the schooling of Black South Africa. In P. Kallaway (Ed.), *Apartheid and education: The education of Black South Africans.* Johannesburg: Ravan Press.

Njobe, M. W. (1990). *Education for liberation.* Johannesburg: Skotaville Publishers.

Phendla, T. S. (2000). *Musadzi u fara lufhanga nga hu fhiraho: Black women elementary school leaders creating socially just and equitable environments in South Africa.* Dissertation, Michigan State University.

———. (2004a) Musadzi u fara lufhanga nga hu fhiraho: Life stories of Black women leaders in South Africa and their struggles to forge social justice in schools. *Perspectives in Education, 22*(1), 51–63.

———. (2004b). Metaphors of leadership, metaphors of hope: Life stories of Black women leaders in South Africa. *Africa Education Review, 33*(2).

———. (2007). The paradox of Luselo-Lufhanga metaphor: African women defining leadership for social justice. *International Studies in Educational Administration, 36*(1).

Rautenbach, F. (2005, April 8). Indirect BEE through JSE: Is South Africa making progress? *Financial Week Report,* pp. 1–37.

South Africa. (1996). Constitution of the Republic of South Africa. Government Printers: Pretoria.

———. (1997). Employment Equity Bill Draft 91. Government Printers: Pretoria.

———. (1998). Employment Equity Act. No. 55 of 1998. Government Printers: Pretoria.

Statistics South Africa. (2003). *Census 2001.* SSA: Pretoria.

White, E. F. (1984). Listening to the voices of Black feminism. *Radical America, 18*(2/3), 7–25.

Young, M. D. (2000). Considering (irreconcilable?) contradictions in cross-group feminist research. *International Journal of Qualitative Studies in Education, 13*(6), 629–660.

A MODERN/ANCIENT PARADOX

Issues in China, New Zealand, Melanesia and Australia

CHAPTER 9

Overview for Part III

JOYCE A. DANA

FACING A PARADOX MAY not be a frequent life experience; however, a primary paradoxical context of particular interest to the research in this publication exists in communities worldwide where strong cultural norms require women to be the culture's domestic workers. When women have strong desires to be educated and to become leaders in their professions they are likely to face a considerable burden. The picture is clear: women must meet their domestic duties whether or not they commit themselves to years of study and entry into educational leadership positions. The workload—both professional and domestic—is heavy. Cultural norms are strong.

Although "culture" can be a somewhat ambiguous term, culture and the expectations embodied in a culture are present wherever a group of people share or hold common beliefs, common practices, and common expectations. It is the culture that most frequently creates the paradox for women who aspire to being professionally educated and to leading in an educational profession. "Culture is both a dynamic phenomenon . . . being constantly enacted and created by our interactions with others and shaped by leadership behavior, and a set of structures, routines, rules, and norms that guide and constrain behavior" (Schein, 2004, p. 1). As an abstraction, culture can be described and understood by the concrete evidence and interactive behavior that exists in a particular society.

Schein (2004) identifies 11 categories that guide the identification and description of a culture: (1) observed behavioral regularities when people interact (language, customs, etc.); (2) espoused values; (3) formal philosophy (policies and ideological principles); (4) rules of the game (unwritten rules for getting along with others); (5) climate (the feeling conveyed by physical factors in the environment); (6) embedded skills (skill in making things that is passed on through the generations); (7) habits of thinking, (8) mental models, linguistic paradigms (shared cognitive frames that guide perceptions, thought, language used by group members); (9) shared meanings; (10) root metaphors or integrating symbols (the ways in which groups characterize themselves); (11) formal rituals and celebrations (pp. 12–13).

The research presented by Qiang, Han and Niu (2007), Ho (2007), Strachan (2007) and Blackmore (2007) is compelling. Individually, and as a collection organized under the theme of challenges to women, the combined research rings with familiarity, yet adds insight to the challenges within those cultures for women who want to be educators and, furthermore, want to acquire positions of influential leadership. The search for gender equity in leadership continues.

Qiang, Han and Niu (2007) report that supporting conditions for an increasing number of women seeking education and leadership equity exist in China. Relatively new legislation and new policy have been developed and implemented to meet the objective of achieving equity between men and women, not only in acquiring university degrees but also in accessing influence and leadership in businesses, organizations and communities. Thus women have the opportunity now to develop and demonstrate competence in their areas of interest, including educational leadership. Also, China's Fundamental State Policy of Equality of Men and Women, coupled with the Plan for Chinese Women's Development for 1995–2000 and 2001–2010, was intended to increase the number of women participating in policy-making and management in national and social affairs.

So, how did that fare with the culture? Many embraced the concept and worked diligently to achieve degrees of equity. The data illustrated the remarkable increase in numbers of women in university and college study and their proportion compared to men. However, acquisition of positions at the university/ college level was most revealing. The higher the status and greater the voice or power in the position, the smaller the number of women who reached that status, voice or power.

To provide a clear picture of influences of the equity legislation, Qiang, Han and Niu (2007) present data illustrating inequities that exist for women serving in educational leadership positions. Where preschool education was delivered predominantly by women, the leaders were predominantly women. The situation was similar at the elementary level. The norm for women, as childbearers, is to care for children and serve as nurturers. The younger the children, the stronger the norm appears to be. Leadership in secondary education still reflects a notable inequity. Clearly, the role expectations of the culture, the norms for women and men, are witnessed in the reality of the existing inequity. The number of women in leadership positions in secondary levels was not proportionate to the number of women who were teachers. A sharp drop in the presence of women leaders occurred at the secondary levels. An even greater difference existed in higher education where the highest rank (professor and/or administrator) was achieved by a small number of women. The data have a similar profile to the data in the United States and other developed and/or developing countries.

What is of particular interest is that the first goal of the Plan for Chinese Women's Development, developed in 1995, was to increase the number of women participating in policy-making and management in national and social affairs by appointing more women in professional positions typical of those where women work—industries, departments and enterprises. The specific intent of the goal is to create a proportional representation of female leaders to the number of female employees in the professions. The question that arises is whether or not that policy language broadly addresses social justice, specifically (a) equity of access and (b) outcome when the focus is on "female domain professions."

While it is wise to start somewhere and while organizations catering to or fulfilling the organizational and leadership needs of women provide good beginnings, social justice is not necessarily the outcome. Female domain professions are likely smaller in number than male domain professions. Additionally, and most worrisome, is the fact that domains in a society become bifurcated, reinforcing the mental model of a culture regarding "women's places" and "men's places." In many cultures, the professions with the most desirable conditions (salary, satisfying work and many benefits) are those still led by males, the decision makers.

It is no surprise that the writers' research reflects the need for cultural support of women aspiring to become educational leaders in the more senior positions. Although there certainly is evidence of some

steps and commitment toward achieving gender equity, the mental models ("female domain") need to be adjusted and the norms need further challenge. Women who seek development and full participation in the leadership and decision making of their cultures, whether local, regional, national, or international, will find great difficulty in achieving that end without the support of sponsors, advocates, colleagues who open doors and so forth.

The paradox remains—the culture identifies role expectations (women take care of domestic responsibilities and childrearing), reinforces norms in large part ("women's" professions, industries, departments and enterprises), and establishes policy that reduces the paradox a bit but does not necessarily assure that the requirements for equity in leadership are met, certainly not in educational leadership, except at the lower levels where the power of voice is lessened.

Ho (2007) presents research data from a home-school-community collaboration study in Hong Kong that is similar in profile to the data from Guangzhou City and Nantong City reported by Qiang, Han and Niu (2007). Ho cites the GLOBE study of gender egalitarianism and societal practices as recognizing Hong Kong as egalitarian. The recognition occurred even though the international mean of 3.37 (4.0 was the reference point) indicated that social practices are still slightly discriminating against women.

Additionally, the Hong Kong data for women at decision-making levels of leadership at the universities had a similar profile. Using the United Nations Economic and Social Council's motion to have 50% of the decision-making positions filled by women by 2000, Ho notes that women's involvement was highest at 56% representation in the community/social and personal services sector, in particular, and 65% representation in the education/medical/community/social services sector.

Particularly of interest is that Ho extracted data from a larger study to explore the leadership nature of women and men, who were working with parent volunteers in schools in a large decentralization effort in Hong Kong. Ho investigated the difference in leadership between women and men leaders in heading decentralizing efforts in their schools which included parents in decision making and involved the development of site-based management.

Findings were surprising. As might be expected, given the role of women as childrearing and nurturing, parent volunteers who were women composed approximately 84% of the volunteer population. The average number of volunteers who were mobilized by female principals was significantly higher than those mobilized by male principals. Where the surprising shift in the data existed was in male principals' acceptance of parents as decision makers, actively participating in the governance of the school. The difference was significant between men who accepted parental roles in the governance function and women who were less willing to accept parental roles in governance.

The finding related to governance begs for further study. Considerable data have informed descriptions of how women lead and how men lead. Strong evidence exists that where women are more collaborative in their leadership decisions and governance, men are more inclined to have a central council of administrators making policy and governance decisions.

Where countries and geographical areas are quite diverse, the challenges for women in leadership can be more complex. Culture itself raises barriers for women's aspirations simply because of the attitudes, learned behaviors and routine practices that are practiced and reinforced. Strachan's portrait of New Zealand and Melanesia (2007) demonstrates the point.

While New Zealand experiences female leadership in major governmental and corporate CEO positions, women remain underrepresented in key areas of educational leadership. This is particularly poignant in the case of ethnic minorities—an all-too-familiar and undesirable situation. The native Polynesian population in New Zealand remains underrepresented in educational leadership with neither role models of educated women nor advocates for their leadership. Mirroring the circumstances in the United States for female superintendents, female principals in New Zealand tend to be located in economically poor schools, rural schools or schools that require hard work, increasing the ever-present challenge for women leaders of balancing home and work. The poorer the school, the more likely that the woman principal is Maori or Pacific in ethnicity.

Melanesia presents even more disturbing circumstances, particularly without efforts by the government to identify the descriptors of culture for women. Consequently, anecdotal evidence provides the picture of women's circumstances related to education and educational leadership. Although teaching may be a desirable profession in the Pacific countries, it is closed for the most part to women and, when women are interested, their struggle in accessing education is an experience in discrimination. The culture in

Melanesia painfully illustrates its stance in denying educational access to women. However, there seems to be acceptance of women in informal leadership positions—positions that complement and support the leadership of men. If there is hope, it comes in the form of Christianity, which practices servant leadership and reinforces women's roles within their culture. Servant leadership asserts that, as leaders, we are all servants of others, no matter what our formal role. So, for example, priests and nuns both serve the needs of the faithful. That there is value in women's leadership is intermittently recognized, as it was from 1998 to 2003 during the time when the Women for Peace movement negotiated between the warring factions in the country. Their efforts found only men at the negotiation table. Strachan (2007) notes that women played a central role in the struggle, but their presence was not invited when it came to sharing power after independence was gained. The cultural norm for women was so strong that there appeared to be no discussion about whether it was appropriate to omit women from the negotiation table regardless of the fact that women had contributed extensively to the negotiation process that put the leaders of the factions at the table.

That the cultures of the Pacific countries, specifically Papua New Guinea, the Solomon Islands and Vanuatu, openly value males as superior and females as subordinates is most disturbing. This mental model restricts the culture's potential by assuring that an estimated one-half of the population must subordinate itself to men. Unforgivable is the violent treatment of women in New Zealand and Melanesia when they try to take on a different role, assert their rights, or take on a behavior that differs from the culture's expected role that they must fill. This clearly presents a human rights issue for New Zealand, as well as Melanesia. Although there are efforts to change the value system and, ultimately, the norms, governmental legislation and policies that are developed must have a will to penalize the violence on women and to actively take on the sponsorship of women who desire to be educated and to become educational leaders.

Additionally, the government must establish and enforce data collection and public reporting regarding the status of girls in schools receiving an education, of women in universities receiving an education and serving in leadership positions, and of women serving in educational leadership positions in primary (kindergarten through grade 12 or 13) schools. To do differently, to do nothing at all or to fail to enforce the legislation calling for equity in education and in leadership, is to deny a significant portion of the population their human rights. This simply is not acceptable.

Globalization, movements back to efficiency, consolidations, mergers and poststructuralism—all have had an effect on women in leadership. As organizations have merged, it is notable that women CEOs lose their influential positions while men retain the CEO positions. Blackmore describes this effect as the "simultaneous radical restructuring of education along corporate lines to link it more instrumentally to the economic needs of the state, industry and the individual." Consequently, a regression of women in leadership positions has taken place since the 1970s, not only in Australia, but also in the United States. Furthermore, Blackmore's data regarding women in higher education positions mirror what was cited by Ho and Strachan: the higher the level of decision making, voice and power, the lower the number of women occupying those positions.

Blackmore (2007) provides an in-depth analysis and understanding through the lenses of cultural categories and, as such, demonstrates understanding of the abstract and powerful nature of culture, as well as understanding the concrete realities of the effects the categorical cultural behaviors have on aspirations for equity in women's educational leadership.

Obviously, there is a need for women worldwide to become activists on behalf of their own gender. The authors of the following four chapters have identified areas for further research. Sponsorship, activist voices, mentoring and encouragement are all called for from other women. To choose to remain a woman who assumes the domestic work is admirable. To choose to be educated is necessity. To choose the opportunity to be a decision maker regarding policy and governance in one's culture will have the same outcomes identified in the preceding research—unless we do something to move the gender equity and awareness of human rights violations to the front of national and international discussions.

WHAT CAN WE DO?

We can begin by studying the culture in which girls and women are educated—or not educated—and collect facts and examples of cultural practices and behaviors that will help us understand where there might be an opportunity within that culture to begin to effect change. We can join international organizations that will combine the strengths of activists into a strong global voice for improved policy, practice and governance that more equitably serves the needs of women and ends human rights violations. To remain silent is to allow gender bias to continue and to become even more deeply embedded in the status quo of culture.

To illustrate how cultural descriptors might be used to develop a knowledge and understanding of a culture, Schein's categories of culture appear in table 9.1 with brief descriptors from each of the cultures in the research discussed in these chapters. Until the culture is understood in which women hope to be educated, aspire to complete higher education, work to become educational leaders and eventually experience access to the top positions of power and decision making to achieve equity, activist efforts on behalf of the women in that culture are likely to be counterproductive. Table 9.1 illustrates the connection between a sample of the descriptors of cultures from which the data were collected. Although incomplete, the descriptors should help the reader develop an idea of how an extensive collection of examples of each descriptor might assist activists with knowing and understanding the culture in order to develop intervention plans that might have some opportunity to succeed on behalf of women.

REFERENCE CITED

Schein, E. H. (2004). *Organizational culture and leadership* (3rd ed.). San Francisco: Jossey-Bass.

Table 9.1. Examples of Cultural Categories Represented in Four Research Papers

Categories	Qiang, Han, Niu	Ho	Strachan	Blackmore
Observed Behavioral Regularities	Number of women in higher education and education leadership	Collaborative women; delegative men	New Zealand: Women have leadership opportunities; Melanesia: Low socioeconomic status; low literacy rate	Number of women in educational leadership positions is regressing; disengagement of women; no opportunity
Espoused Values	Equity (legislation/ policy)	Equity; Egalitarianism	Melanesia: Women are lower class w/o essential human rights	Efficiency; Globalization (though it results in fewer women leaders)
Formal Philosophy	Develop women leaders	Leadership needs to be more democratic and collaborative	New Zealand: Girls can do anything	Acceptable for women to be middle management rather than CEO; reliance on Equal Opportunity Initiatives
Rules of Game	Women's access to higher educa-tion (law)		Melanesia: Violence against women	Mergers result in lost CEO jobs for women
Climate	Women's equity opportunity is is hopeful	Women have a stronger focus on people and interaction	New Zealand: Some major leadership positions are held by women Melanesia: Data not collected about conditions for women; violence practiced against women	Labor markets
Embedded Skills		Collaborative women; delegative men; exception is in decentralized school governance		Past equity practices now embedded into logic of managerial practices in schools
Group Norms	Double burden of domestic work and education for women; women not in power leadership positions	Women are primary caretakers of children and domestic work; not in power in leadership; sex discrimination	Maori/Pacific: Few opportuni-ties for women; absence of role models Melanesia: Where Christianity exists, some women lead	

Categories	Qiang, Han, Niu	Ho	Strachan	Blackmore
Habits of Thinking, Mental Models, Linguistic Paradigms	Primary descriptor is woman as domestic worker; use women's organizations to increase policy and governance leadership of women	Female leaders will be more collaborative; male leaders will be more delegative; men more knowledgeable about politics	Girls are as successful as boys on educational exams, but less likely to win admission to higher education programs	Culture of overwork for women
Shared Meanings Root Metaphors or Integrating Symbols	A fence needs the support of three stakes and an able fellow needs the help of three other people (Chinese proverb)		"Big man" leadership	
Formal Rituals and Celebrations		New Zealand women in major policy and government leadership		

CHAPTER 10

Re/positioning Women in Educational Leadership

The Changing Social Relations and Politics of Gender in Australia

JILL BLACKMORE

WOMEN AND THEIR underrepresentation in leadership are recurrent "problems" in education. But this is part of a wider political and increasingly economic problem in "globalized" democratic societies. This chapter first provides the historical context for gender equity reform in Australia. The relationship between feminism as an epistemological and political movement vis-à-vis the state and the individual shapes equity discourses and organizational practices as well as research on gender and leadership. History also indicates that there is no simple linear progress toward gender equity. Context and policy shape the possibilities and practices of educational leadership, both formal and informal.

I then outline the most recent "re/positioning" of women with regard to educational leadership in schools and universities over the past decade. I identify issues around the discursive construction in policy and practice of gender and educational leadership in high-risk and low-trust times, arguing that increasing the representation of women in leadership is no longer an adequate measure of success. Finally, I map out a feminist research agenda that seeks to advance thinking and research about gender and leadership in the context of emerging challenges to contemporary education.

AUSTRALIAN GENDER EQUITY REFORM: RESEARCH, POLICY AND PRACTICE

During the 1970s, with the rise of the new social movements in most Western democracies, feminists were able to exert external pressure on a newly elected Australian Labour federal government to address patterns of discrimination against women and girls identified by research. The positioning of "femocrats" (feminist bureaucrats) within the federal and state governments (similar to the state feminism of Scandinavian countries) led to gender equity legislation and policies nationally, including women's budgets and audits, a practice replicated at the state government level in the 1980s. As in the United States and UK, within a liberal feminist theoretical frame Equal Employment

Opportunity (EEO) policies initially focused on removing legal and structural barriers and gaining equal pay with the intent that individual women could access organizations and therefore positional leadership (e.g., principalship and deanship). Such policies were quickly adopted in education, then seen to be a major site of social change, employment of and equity for women. Investment in public education by the welfare state was viewed to have individual and public benefits.

Identity politics around difference during the 1980s aligned with feminist theories focusing on women's ways of being and doing. Previously, leadership research had been by men on men in leadership, producing dominant notions of particular forms of masculinity as the leadership norm—being rational, unemotional and objective.

This "cultural feminist" approach re/positioned women as offering a positive contribution to organizational life, rather than the earlier deficit and psychological view that women as a group lacked the necessary skills, vision and aspirations. Drawing from the wider theoretical debates over educational change and organizational cultures, feminists focused on changing "masculinist culture(s)" as sites of male resistance to gender equity with the aim to make them more "inclusive" of alternative models of leadership. Feminist scholarship also drew on theorizations of the social relations of gender and how different masculinities (homosexual, working class, etc.) and femininities (emphasized feminism, lesbianism, etc.) were created in relation to each and relative to the norm of dominant "hegemonic masculinities"(Connell, 1995, Kenway et al., 1998).

Internationally, Australian feminists and femocrats were key players in organizations of the global women's movement such as Unifem, developing strategies for, and measures of, gender equity, as well as providing exemplars of how equity policy can be developed through the state, such as women's budgets (Sawer, 1999).

At the same time, the discourse of women's style of leadership was readily co-opted and incorporated into

EEO policies to either complement or soften "hard" masculinist cultures (see, for instance, Blackmore, 1992). While EEO strategies successfully improved the skills and raised the aspirations of individual middle-class women during the 1980s, the gendered images of leadership and the "masculinist" cultures of educational bureaucracies remained intact (Lingard and Limerick, 1995). While empowering for women collectively, this cultural feminist discourse treated women (and men) as a unified group, with little regard for racial, ethnic, class and indeed value differences among women (and men) (see also Reay and Ball, 2003).

Under the pressure of globalization, neoliberal reforms of the1990s saw significant shifts by Australian federal and state Labour governments toward "economic rationalism" and "corporate managerialism." Femocrats, gender equity practitioners and educators in general were increasingly marginalized by the twin mantras of efficiency and effectiveness. Educational restructuring, in the form of devolution of risk and responsibility for outcomes to locally competing units, such as self-managing schools, did not deliver the promise of increased autonomy. Instead, devolution was accompanied by stronger policy frames and external accountability to government with the reassertion of executive management and to volatile student markets.

This cycle of policy-delivery-accountability produced cultures of performativity, leading individuals and institutions to increasingly focus on outward performance as measured against multiple performance indicators, such as standardized tests rather than internal improvement. Simultaneously, schools and universities were experiencing intensified consumer demand to meet the needs of cultural and educational diversity arising from increased retention in schools, the massification of higher education after the unification of colleges with universities in 1989, and the emergence of international students as a new source of income for universities and schools (Blackmore and Sachs, 2007). Leadership was seen to be invested in executive positions, and the success of the leader was equated to the success of the school or university (Thomson, 1999).

The trend toward privatization and marketization of public education (universities and schools) accelerated with the election of the socially conservative but economically neoliberal Howard federal government in 1996. Howard sought to re-regulate the social by reconnecting Australian national identity to a narrow and nostalgic version of the nuclear family and border protection against refugees, and deregulate the economy with attacks on unionized collective bargaining. The federal equity infrastructure was steadily dismantled and the funding of the Status of Women's Office was radically reduced, although the office was retained for its "symbolic value" but with weak monitoring powers (Hancock, 1999). Women who went out to work or relied on welfare were denigrated for not being good mothers. Yet due to the re-privatization of the costs of health and education, women were forced to enter a more casualized and deregulated labor market just to maintain familial class status at the same time child care was privatized.

Gender equity policy also significantly changed focus away from its move toward considering the social relations of gender and different modes of masculinity and femininity and toward boys' academic underachievement. This was fueled by the federal policy emphasis on outcomes and standards as mechanisms of control over teachers and state governments (Lingard and Douglas, 1999; Mills, Martino and Lingard, 2004).

The backlash against feminism merged with the "crisis in masculinity" discourse, mobilized by the media, the federal government, numerous parliamentary inquiries and a small lobby of male activists who saw boys as victims of feminism (Blackmore, 1997; Lingard, 2003). Together with the privatization of education arising from federal funding policies favoring "user pays" and private schools relative to public universities and schools, the effect has been a polarization of wealth and poverty, increased concentration of poverty, poor health, inadequate educational and community infrastructure, unemployment and educational underachievement. In 2007, one in five Australian children lived in poverty.

These moves regressed previous feminist equity work theoretically and politically. Politically, the "what about the boys and men" school of thought coincided with Howard's conservative social agenda and diverted attention from the impact of poverty, rurality and indigeneity on educational achievement. The femocrats fled, or were expelled, from the chilly climate of educational bureaucracies now driven by accountability of the public service up to their political masters to whom they were "contracted" rather than to "the public" (Taylor, 1997).

Feminist academic-teacher connections were lost as all felt the brunt of restructuring and intensification of labor. Equity units in many state governments that worked for such groups as indigenous populations, girls and women, persons of low socioeconomic status, students with disabilities and so on were dissolved and mainstreamed (Sawer, 1999). The policy discourse shifted from equal opportunity and social justice to a more individualized discourse of diversity (Bacchi, 2000). In the area of theory, the 1990s were also a period in which feminists were enticed by poststructuralism and its focus on identity because of its linguistic sophistication and explanatory power with regard to the experiences of individual women and women leaders. But the poststructuralist focus on identity, language, and text and the contradictions, ambivalences and contestations between the multiplicity of leadership identities and discourses distracted from the wider and highly gendered economic and material restructuring of education and the professions that was gendered (Dillabough and Acker, 2003; Pyke and Ward, 2003).

Paradoxically, in the first decade of the twenty-first century, the discourse is about lifelong learning, innovation and teacher leadership. Yet teachers and academics, schools and universities endure increased regulation through the disciplinary technologies of market and managerial accountability as well as the intensification of work and precarious tenure. The institutional flexibility necessary for survival in local, national and international education markets is now contingent on labor flexibility, exemplified in the casualization of educational labor in Victoria schools increasing from 8% to 16% and in universities from 8% to 30% since 1996 (AVCC, 2005). This is not about family-friendly workplaces, but rather encourages increased expectations for unpaid overtime, which invades private lives. In 2006, the latest Gender Equity Index report indicates that with regard to democracy and women's position in Australian society, women are, as in the United States, in a regressive position relative to a decade ago. Australia has been listed by the ILO (International Labour Organization) in 2007 in the top 20 countries where workers are at risk. What does this mean for the possibilities for individual women in leadership, the gender politics of education as a field and the gender micropolitics of educational organizations?

THE POSITION OF WOMEN LEADERS IN AUSTRALIA

Restructuring during the 1990s meant government school systems and the higher education sector (38 universities) tapped into the growing pool of female aspirants fired up by equal opportunity programs and feminist discourses about women leading organizational change. So how have we progressed? Broadly across government, nongovernmental organizations

(NGOs) and business, there is ongoing underrepresentation. Women in Australia in 2005 are still not well represented in executive positions in industry (only 3%) and parliaments (28% federal government, 27% New South Wales, 30% Victoria, and 43% in the Australian Capital Territory), with women being 28% of federal ministers in the Howard government, which has generated the backlash against feminism and undermined women's working and familial conditions.

In local government, previously an avenue for women's political careers, women average 25% of local councilors. Women are still on average only 37% of the judiciary (EOAW, 2005). In education, with regard to organizational position and power, women in higher education (HE) are still largely concentrated in the lower nontenured ranks as lecturers and senior lecturers and in marginalized contract or casual positions as assistant lecturers and research assistants, as they were in 1992 (Castleman, Allen, Battalich and Wright, 1995). Table 10.1 indicates that restructuring HE with a focus on quality and research has meant that more males *and* females are in professorial positions, in part as universities seek to attract research leadership.

What these full-time employment (FTE) figures in HE do not show is the actual high rate of part-time work undertaken by female academics (Probert et al., 1998, p. 62). Research performance of senior tenured staff is invisibly supported by numerous contracted research assistants, whose job positions are largely undefined but who often work as tenured staff's domestic as well as academic laborers (Reay, 2000; Bell and Bentley, 2005). At the same time, there has been a numerical feminization of teachers in HE, with the proportion of women employed full time rising from 33% in 1996 to 40% in 2005.

Paradoxically, the most significant rise has been at the executive level in HE. In 2005, of the 38 universities, three had female chancellors and 11 had female vice chancellors (up from two vice chancellors

Table 10.1. Percentage Distribution of Academic Staff, Australian Universities, by Gender

Full-time estimated	1996		2005	
Level	Female	Male	Female	Male
A Tutor	29	14	26	15
B Lecturer	45	21	41	29
C Senior lecturer	18	28	21	26
D Associate Professor	5	14	7	14
E Professor	2	11	5	15
	100	100	100	100

Source: Australian Vice Chancellors Committee, 2006.

in 1995 and six in 1999)(AVCC, 2005). In 2002, 24% of the 153 deputy and pro vice chancellors and 37% of the senior administrative staff were women (AVCC, 2002). This was the effect of the escalated expansion of the middle management infrastructure of teaching and research in universities encouraging academics to market and meet external accountability and quality requirements. Of the 66 Technical and Further Education (TAFE) institutes, 19 had female directors compared to four in 1995. Yet the numbers of senior academic women remain low, with full female professors, like vice chancellors, being predominantly white, middle class, in their 50s, living with a partner and with children, a profile not representative of the ethnic diversity of Australia (Ward, 2000). More women remain at associate professor level, dispirited, worn out or stuck in the multiplying number of administrative positions that are proliferating as part of the multi-tasking required of academic leadership; for instance, international students, teaching and learning, and the like are proliferating in more managerialized universities (White, 2003).

One explanation for the low numbers of female professors is that it is faster for women to take the managerial rather than research track to get a promotion. Achieving a research chair requires negotiating careful career moves such as establishing a career before children, completing a doctorate before becoming an academic, doing a post-doctorate fellowship rather than being an early career researcher and teaching at the same time (Currie, Thiele and Harris, 2002; White, 2003). Those who seek promotion or get promoted into executive levels of university management tend to be those who meet the male norm or who fit a particular model and have survived previous positions within the HE culture with little opportunity or little desire to challenge the dominant models of corporate leadership (Blackmore and Sachs, 2007; Currie, Thiele and Harris, 2002).

Against the HE situation, women seem to have progressed relatively better in schools. In state schools in 2005, women were 62% of principals (principal and assistant principal, primary and secondary) in the Australian Capital Territory, 42% in New South Wales, 53% in Northern Territory, 43% in Queensland, 49% in South Australia, 48% in Tasmania, 46% in Victoria and 38% in Western Australia (AEU, 2005). Women now constitute over 74% of the teaching force, compared to 70% in 1996, fueling concerns about the lack of men, particularly in primary schools (Mills et al., 2004). But as with the academy, teachers are still a homogenous middle class and white workforce.

The South Australian Department of Education cites 5.8% of employees born overseas compared to 20.3% of the general population and 1.23% of Australian and Torres Strait Islanders (ATSI) employees (many of them Aboriginal education workers) compared to 2% benchmark (Department ECS, 2005, p. 58). The Department of Education in New South Wales (the largest and most populous state) in 2005 cited that 1.4% of its employees were from ATSI background, 12% from racial, ethnic and ethno-religious minority groups, and 11% from a non-English-speaking background (NESB).

Yet as with universities, women teachers are in more precarious work situations. In New South Wales, women in 2005 constituted 70% of all full-time and part-time staff (up from 68% in 2001; 65% of the permanent full-time positions; 91% of permanent part-time; 74% of temporary full-time; and 85% of temporary part-time. At the upper end, in 2002 women were 33% of the senior executive service level and seven of the 46 district superintendents, critical positions with regard to the selection of principals (NSW Department of Education, 2003). There continues to be an ongoing gender differential between primary and secondary, as indicated by Victoria in 2005 where women constituted 50% of primary principals and 83% of primary teachers; 42% of secondary principals and 60% of secondary teachers (DE&T Annual Report, 2004–2005). The Catholic sector (20% of all Australian students) has the highest ratio of women principals, this sector being more amenable to women leaders with its history of nuns as principals, although always under the paternalistic gaze of the local parish priest and bound by Catholicism's patriarchal view of leadership.

As women get to the same levels as their male managers, resistance can become the ploy (Burton, 1998). Dispersal of responsibility downward also shifts responsibility for action away from the executive level. Yet evidence suggests that it is the lack of political will on the part of executives in universities and schools to commit to equality for women that is a major obstacle (Sinclair, 1998).

Then there is the localized belief of many men in particular, that women have done well and were indeed advantaged due to gender equity policies despite systemic patterns indicating the contrary: women's experience that they are not doing well (Castleman, Allen, Battalich and Wright, 1995; Currie, Thiele and Harris, 2002). Evidence from interviews with middle managers suggests ongoing discrimination because women have discontinuity in careers, familial responsibilities, and the like (Blackmore and Sachs, 2007). A dominant feature of universities during the 1990s, Currie et al. argue, was the normalization of the male culture of competitive individualism, a "blokiness" that makes men feel comfortable and women excluded, a culture in which men's sexuality is ruled in and women's sexuality ruled out (e.g., child care, breastfeeding) (Chesterman, Ross-Smith and Peters, 2004; Eveline, 1998). While largely invisible, this culture is normalized and indeed exacerbated in the field of education, which has become highly politicized and managed because education is now seen to be critical to knowledge-based economies.

Finally, there are new phases of restructuring in schools and universities emerging with pressures resulting from international "quality assurance" and professional standards movements. The approaching Australian Research Quality Framework has the potential to create new hierarchies. Women in all education sectors often enter the field late, experiencing career discontinuity, and so will be further disadvantaged by such quality regimes (Morley, 2001).

In aggregation, these factors mean that women are moving into leadership to manage downsizing, outsourcing and casualization of an increasingly feminized education labor force working under more precarious and underresourced conditions at a time of intensification of labor and increased surveillance. Women principals in schools and as vice chancellors in universities tend to be concentrated in the more difficult to staff and less resourced institutions seeking to meet the needs of more diverse student populations, compared to more selective elite schools and universities. Thus through choice and selection, the burden of equity continues to lie with individual women rather than men, systems or the state.

It is risky for both men and women who resist the managerial discourse, as the bottom line is ultimately about institutional survival in national and international markets that rank and reward in increasingly simplistic and reductionist ways—on student evaluations or test scores, market reputation, abstracted notions of quality of research, or just money won. At the middle management level, where many women are now located, many women simultaneously resist and comply with the regimes of performativity. All are in some ways complicit through better managing themselves and others to reach organizational objectives while also seeking to mobilize the discourses in more equity-oriented ways, accommodating, rejecting

and revising what they can at the local level (Blackmore and Sachs, 2007). Many women thrive in this entrepreneurial and managerial context, some with little regard for their female or male colleagues, being more committed to their own self-advancement than equity for others. In the lower ranks, there is significant dissatisfaction and alienation among women as public universities and schools rely on the unfunded overtime and commitment and goodwill of their staff to maintain quality, at risk to teachers' and academics' health, well-being and family life (Probert, 2001b).

At the same time, some things have changed. During the 1990s, EEO policies successfully led to increased numbers of women in middle management: principal and assistant principal class, deans and heads of school. While there is weak central monitoring of EEO outcomes, equity is often the outcome of self-regulating universities, for example, which seek to be perceived as EEO employers at a time when it is difficult to attract quality academics. Similarly, schools are undergoing redesign in order to be able to better prepare students for the twenty-first century. Teachers are now seen to be the critical factor in improving student outcomes. Teacher leadership is an emerging discourse within school reform that recognizes, as feminists have long argued, that many people do leadership, and that leadership is a collective and relational practice, whereas positional leadership is often reduced to management. But as most equity researchers argue, it is the capacity of EEO to be so readily incorporated into the process and procedurally driven management frame that is its major weakness and strength.

EQUITY ISSUES

The overarching question is whether women's representation in leadership is an adequate measure of progress within the current re-formation of gender within globalized economies. Furthermore, what is the role of the "post-welfare" state with regard to gender equity? What types of strategies are required within institutions and within education in more deregulated times?

Policy Frames

Policies in the 1980s recognized that there was systemic structural and cultural disadvantage that required remediation. EEO policies provided a language and legitimization of reform for women and by women. Much professional development and equal opportunity policy continues to focus on changing the status of women by adopting similar practices that have worked for men. Currie et al. point out (2002, p. 82) that unless the "peak male culture" in executive positions in universities or in education bureaucracies recognizes that discrimination is often intangible, and that male advantage is likewise invisible and unnamed, then a major cultural shift will not occur.

Diversity as a Conceptual Strategy

What gender equity practitioners know is that naming the problem is critical (Bacchi, 2000). The 1990s have seen the language of equal opportunity, social justice and equity supplanted by that of diversity, but with what effect? Diversity is more descriptive than normative. Diversity therefore fits well within the neoliberal framework of the individual's right of choice as the primary mechanism of distribution of educational resources (Blackmore, 2005). With the corporatization of education, the discourse of diversity has been readily appropriated for its symbolic value: diversity is productive in that it mobilizes all talent within an organization as long as it does not challenge the dominant economistic mode of operations, the entrepreneurial cultures or strategic leadership.

The lack of diversity in educational leadership is problematic, not merely because it is counterproductive within a culturally diverse society, but also because excluding the voices of "the other" questions the legitimacy of democratic institutions (Sinclair, 2000b).

Disengagement and Alienation from Leadership

Numerous reports on teacher and principal as well as academic demand and supply indicate that governments face ongoing shortages in part due to demographics with the retirement of the large baby boomer cohort (Blackmore, Thomson and Sachs, 2006). But research in Australia as elsewhere indicates that there is a "disengagement" with leadership seen in diminished numbers of applicants for formal leadership positions in schools and in universities, and that women in particular are tending toward refusal (Blackmore and Sachs, 2007; Gronn and Rawlings Sanaei, 2003).

Two issues emerge. One is the extent and nature of the workload involved with the principalship and middle management in universities and the physical, emotional as well as ethical cost that it often brings. Resistance to leadership arises out of awareness of teachers and academics of the intense pressure and scrutiny executives and managers experience.

Collectively, performance management, mission statements, strategic plans, outcomes-based education, performance indicators and performance appraisal have produced a subtle but intrusive web of power that captures and exploits the desires of teachers and principals, academics and deans to do well. It also directs their emotional, intellectual and physical energy toward specific and often narrow organizational ends that may not include equity. Add to this political pressures for professional standards and performance-based pay; the media bashing of teachers (lowering standards) and academics (low quality of research); multiple government reports on teaching and teacher education; quality assurance regimes; and teachers' and academics' declining rate of pay relative to other professions. When women do get into positional leadership, they undertake the emotional management work of systems in ongoing crisis. In particular, for women with dependent family, the culture of overwork, long hours and the like means exclusion or self-exclusion (Chesterman, Ross-Smith and Peters, 2004, p. 10). Most see formal leadership as being about management, not educational leadership.

The second "turn off" identified in Australian research (as in the UK and United States) is rejection of the implicit and explicit value systems promoted in management and the politicization of education. Positional leadership for many women is perceived as being more about "being good" in alignment with system priorities or market demand rather than "doing good" in alignment with educational principles and what is best for the students and colleagues (Blackmore and Sachs, 2007). Many are passionate about education as a means of social change and personal empowerment and making a difference, with a professional commitment to "the public." When leadership is limited to individual or organizational success and focused on performativity (i.e., being seen to be doing more for less) they are disinterested (Blackmore and Sachs, 2007; Probert, 2001a; Sinclair, 2006).

Australian research has identified an emerging values dissonance as part of a wider cultural shift in education in which the field has been restructured toward more instrumental and vocational ends. Broadly, education has become an industry and a field subjugated to politics and journalism. Institutionally, there has been a concentration of power in line management and consequent marginalization of the academic and teacher voice. Australian universities became less of a democratic/collegial community of scholars transmitting and expanding knowledge and more a corporate business delivering education *products* (Currie, Thiele and Harris, 2002). This is indicative of how education is being framed by the new contractualism of educational governance, which positions education as an individual position rather than a public good. This contractualism has implications for the role and responsibilities of educational professionals with regard to "the public" and for how leadership is understood and enacted locally as a democratic or managerial, individual or collective, practice, least of all about social justice in and through education (Blackmore, 1999).

FUTURE RESEARCH AGENDA: BEYOND WOMEN AND LEADERSHIP

Feminist researchers in Australia have argued that gender equity for women has stalled, if not regressed (Probert, 2001b). Most agree that gender equity policies have benefited middle-class white women, but even they are now questioning their capacity to effect change.

Politics of Leadership and Gender Research

What is also evident is that mainstream research in educational administration has not been informed by feminist research. The numerical increases of women in leadership (particularly executive leadership) are now seen to mean that all women are equal and the issue of the underrepresentation of women and leadership is resolved. Even the token chapter in many educational administration texts, typical of the 1990s, has disappeared. (There is no such chapter in the 2005 International Handbook on Educational Administration and Leadership.) This is indicative of the overall failure of the field to be informed by critical organizational theory outside the field and feminist, black and postcolonial theory within the field that sees organizations as cultural sites structured by the social relations of gender, class and race (e.g., Alvesson and Due Billing, 2002; Aschraft and Mumby, 2004; Hearn, 2002).

Gender Division of Labor

Probert (2001a) argues cogently for the need to review certain mythologies about the nature of "the problem." She argues that Australian equity reforms have been effective in providing a range of policies and practices (family leave, maternity leave, mentoring, etc.) that seek to reduce structural and cultural discrimination against women.

She cites two dominant explanatory frames for women's ongoing underrepresentation, one being that unequal outcomes are due to unequal treatment and the second being that women lack human capital in the form of experience and qualifications due to different career choices. Researchers agree that level,

age, full-time work and time out of the labor markets were the most important determinants of the gender salary gap with years worked the strong predictor of level (Blackmore and Sachs, 2007; Probert, 2005, p. 53; Ward, 2001).

Probert suggests that promotion systems in themselves in universities and schools are premised upon merit and provide a range of supports and recognition of women's position, and that when women do apply they have a higher ratio of success than men who apply more often (Burton, 1998). Women are more likely to get promoted as teaching is recognized and valued in most institutions, but less likely to apply as men are more aggressive about career and self-advancement. Second, while women and men are both affected by casualization, the issue is now the underrepresentation of women in continuing employment because of the difficulty in moving from sessional to continuing (Probert, 2005, p. 53). Women start lower in academic careers (Level A) but generally with lower qualifications (no Ph.D.). They also are less likely to earn a Ph.D. (in University of New South Wales women 52.9% compared to 61.9% of men) or progress beyond Level C (Probert, 2005, p. 53).

Third, the issue is not that women teach more and therefore are unable to do research, as is often claimed, but that both men and women are experiencing higher workloads. Similarly in schools, women are more likely to undertake more professional development than men. The gender difference lies not in formal workloads, but more in the extent of informal work, that is, the emotional management work and welfare/mentoring that women undertake with students and colleagues, which is often not done by male colleagues (Blackmore and Sachs, 2007; Probert, 2005). Thus, the longer in the system, the wider the female/male wage gap, with the greatest gap occurring between ages 40–49 for women, a period which feeds into upper levels of management.

The real problem is that while men and women both experienced the detrimental effects of "greedy organizations," women also felt intensified domestic demands at home that were not experienced by men (Franzway, 2005; Pocock, 2006). Mobility, extracurricular activities and undertaking the additional responsibilities necessary for promotion are therefore difficult. Those women who become principals tend to have supportive, often retired, partners, are single, and nearly all are without dependent children (Blackmore and Sachs, 2007). The logistics of child care have become too hard for many women to take up leadership positions given the unrealistic demands (Probert, 2005, p. 68). Multiple factors arising from differential responsibilities to men due to the uneven and unequal distribution of domestic and emotional labor at work and at home therefore affect women's "choices" about formal leadership.

Gender and Difference: Which Women and Which Men?

Much of the research continues to focus on mapping women's location within educational organizations and systems, identifying patterns and obstacles to progress, and on the successes/failures of EEO policies. While this resesrch is important to inform policy, theoretically there have not been significant advances beyond poststructuralist accounts of women leaders experiencing ambiguity, contradiction and ambivalence. Many, regardless of their politics and personal dispositions, readily call upon discourses about women's leadership style in ways that are self-affirming but rarely challenged. There is less research that considers the relationship between leaders and their colleagues. As women increasingly move into positional leadership, there is greater scope and less political damage associated with investigating women leaders who do not "fit" the caring and sharing style and who promote values that are not about equity, and indeed could be seen to be about bullying and intimidation. The field needs to move its focus away from gender difference to consider differences among women such as indigenous, "ethnic," religious and linguistic difference (Moreton-Robinson, 2000; Ngurruwutthun and Stewart, 1996; Oplatka and Hert-Lazarowitz, 2006) and not to privilege gender as the analytical frame.

This would lead to different questions for feminist educational researchers. First, the structures that enable or disable particular career "choices" need to be understood more widely. Discrimination is no longer constrained to workplaces but is part of wider structural and cultural relations between family, work and community that are being reconstituted in ways that simultaneously detraditionalize and retraditionalize gender relations.

This has policy implications that can be mobilized. First, there is a need to redesign the job of leadership to be more inclusive of a range of practices. Until there is a recognition of different structures of leadership (e.g., shared leadership, co-principalships, etc.), there must be a focus on educational leadership, making formal positions less demanding physically, emotionally, intellectually and ethically, or there will continue to be

a leadership supply crisis. This supply crisis could be enduring, as more mobile, well qualified and aspiring women feel less committed to education as a vocation, and since educational work is now less attractive for both academic and teaching women relative to other more family friendly and lucrative jobs. Teaching and research may be episodes in a portfolio career (Blackmore, Thomson and Sachs, 2006).

Second, we need to move beyond current conceptualizations of leadership that equate leadership with formal position. This would mean considering the range of leadership practices in different communities of practice, for instance teacher leadership in schools, academic leadership, but also alternative leader positionalities that derive from black, indigenous and ethnic literature (e.g., AhNee-Benham, 2003; Battiste, 2005; Mabokela, 2007).

Third, research is needed to explore further the significance of the relations between context and leadership practices in order to comprehend how context (policies, politics, location, etc.) shapes the practices of leadership. This involves considering the impact of wider educational reform, the impact of globalized discourses and policies (Lingard, 2006) and how they are conceptualized and implemented, as well as investigating what is happening to education as a profession. As a field, education is increasingly being made subordinate to politics, the media and the economy (Blackmore and Sachs, 2007; Dillabough and Acker, 2002). What does this mean for how women work with/against the nation state and the regionalized state and global policy communities, such as the Office of Education and Child Development (OECD) (Lakes and Carter, 2004)?

Fourth, feminist poststructuralism has theoretically provided a more sophisticated tool to understand the complexities of the positioning of women leaders with regard to multiple subjectivities based on gender, race, class, ethnicity and religion. But in continuing to place gender and identity at the foreground, it has been at some loss to investigate the wider material conditions and specificity of contexts within which leadership is practiced. There is now the need for new theoretical trajectories, such as feminist social geography, to integrate this with feminist materialist theories around the impact of local/global articulations.

Fifth, as we have learned from feminist poststructuralism, essentializing gender will take the analysis no further. The focus on women and not gender has taken this field to its theoretical limit (Alvesson and Due Billing, 2002; Blackmore, 1999; Reay and Ball,

2000). It is critical that feminist and profeminist researchers shift the conceptual focus from women to the social relations of gender, and how different masculinities and femininities are constructed in relation to each other in specific contexts. Issues of race, class, ethnicity and indigeneity then take on significance in understanding leadership in particular situations. The question should be, "Which men and which women are advantaged/disadvantaged within this specific context?" "Which men and which women get to be leaders and why?"

Finally, we need to consider the implications historically, as well as futuristically, of the relations between gender, globalized education and social change. This requires comparative studies that recognize the complexity of gender relations in educational leadership and that identify key issues and strategies, including the local and global, tactical and strategic. Brooks (2006) highlights how globalization has transformed not only the economies of Singapore and Hong Kong but also the social relations of gender in context-specific ways. How are women being located within transnational flows of educational ideas, goods, policies and people and how do these translate into local and transnational practices of educational leadership and gender equity reform as a possible trajectory (Lingard, 2006)? How are notions of leadership shaped by national and diasporic cultures and how will this further transform the social relations of gender (Narayan, 1997)? Add to this the foregrounding of and association between nationalism, citizenship and religion as a mix that has significant potential to inform the micropolitics of gender in schooling and universities.

Feminist academics and researchers need to reconnect with the wider social movements of feminism across nations. Much of the work on women and educational leadership has tended to neglect the impact of feminism as a social, political, economic and transnational movement (Narayan, 1997). This is largely because research has worked within a liberal and arguably masculinist framework of the field of educational administration and leadership. Scholars now need to theorize from postcolonial as well as materialist and poststructuralist perspectives about how the politics of feminism meshes with, interacts with, and subverts research on "women and leadership" (e.g., Tuhiwa Smith, 1999).

As I have indicated, there is no linear progress of equity, and different imperatives for reform have a capacity for both regressive and progressive tendencies for gender equity. While gender equity is ultimately what most researchers and practitioners alike agree is

the intent, how we understand and frame our notions of social justice in globalized societies is yet to debated (Fraser, 2006).

REFERENCES CITED

AhNee-Benham, M. (2003). "In our mothers' voice": A Native women's knowing of leadership, in M. D. Young and L. Skrla (Eds.), *Reconsidering: Feminist research in educational leadership*, pp. 223–246. Albany: SUNY Press.

Alvesson, M., and Due Billing, Y. (2002). "Beyond body-counting": A discussion of the social construction of gender at work. In I. Aaltio and A. Mills (Eds.), *Gender, identity and culture in organizations*. London: Routledge, pp. 72–91.

Ashcraft, K., and Mumby, D. (2004). *Reworking gender: A feminist communicology of organization.* Thousand Oaks, CA: Sage.

Australian Vice Chancellors' Committee. (2006). *Selected Statistics.* Canberra: AVCC.

Bacchi, C. (1999). Managing diversity: A contested concept. *International Review of Women and Leadership, 5*(2), 1–8.

———. (2000). The see-saw effect: Down goes affirmative action, up comes workplace diversity. *Journal of Interdisciplinary Gender Studies, 5*(2), 65–83.

———. (2001). Managing equity: Mainstreaming and diversity in Australian universities. In A. McKinnon and A. Brooks (Eds.), *Gender and the restructured university: Changing management and cultures in higher education.* Buckingham: Open University Press, pp. 119–135.

Battiste, M. (2005). Leadership and Aboriginal education in contemporary education: Narratives of cognitive imperialism reconciling with decolonization. In J. Collard and C. Reynolds (Eds.), *Leadership, gender and culture in education, male and female perspectives.* Buckingham: Open University Press, pp. 150–156.

Bell, S., and Bentley, R. (2005). Women in research discussion paper. Prepared for AVCC National Colloquium of Senior Women Executives.

Benhabib, S. (2000). *The claims of culture: Equality and diversity in the global era.* Princeton, NJ: Princeton University Press.

Blackmore, J. (1996). Doing emotional labour in the educational market place: Stories from the field of women in management. *Discourse, 17*(3), 337–350.

———. (1997). Disciplining feminism? Australian perspectives on feminism and the backlash in tertiary education. In L. Eyre and L. Roman (Eds.), *Dangerous territories: Struggles for equality and difference in education.* New York: Routledge, pp. 75–98.

———. (1999). *Troubling women: Feminism, leadership and educational change.* Buckingham: Open University Press.

———. (2005). Deconstructing diversity: Discourses in the field of educational management and leadership. *Educational Management, Administration and Leadership, 34*(2), 181–199.

Blackmore, J., and Sachs, J. (2007). *Performing and reforming leaders: Gender, educational restructuring and organizational change.* Albany: SUNY Press.

Blackmore, J., Thomson, P., and Sachs, J. (2006). *The declining supply of principal applicants.* Geelong, South Australia: Deakin University, Faculty of Education.

Boler, M. (1999). *Feeling power: Emotions and education.* London and New York: Routledge.

Brooking, K. (2005). Principals and school boards in New Zealand. Unpublished doctoral dissertation. Deakin University.

Brooks, A. (2006). *Gendered work in Asian cities: The new economy and changing labour markets.* Hampshire, U.K.: Ashgate.

Brooks, A., and MacKinnon, A. (Eds.) (2001). *Gender and the restructured university: Changing management and culture in higher education.* Buckingham: Open University Press.

Burton, C. (1997). *Gender equity in Australian university staffing.* Canberra: Department of Employment, Education, Training and Youth Affairs.

Carrington, K., and Pratt, A. (2002). How far have we come? Gender disparities in the Australian higher education system. *Current Issues Brief, 31,* 2002–03.

Castleman, T, Allen, M., Battalich, W., and Wright, P. (1995). *Limited access: women's disadvantage in higher education employment.* South Melbourne: National Tertiary Education Union.

Chappell, L. (2002). *Gendering government: Feminist engagement with the state in Australia and Canada.* Vancouver: UBC Press.

Chesterman, C., Ross-Smith, A., and Peters, M. (2004). *Senior women executives and the cultures of management: A brief cross sectoral comparison of public, private and higher education organizations.* http://www.uts.edu.au/oth/wex-dev/pdfs/culturesofmanagement.

Connell, R. (1995). *Masculinities.* Cambridge: Polity Press.

Connell, R. W. (1998). Masculinity and globalization. *Men and Masculinity, 1*(1), 3–23.

———. (2000). *The men and the boys.* Sydney: Allen and Unwin.

Court, M. (2003). *Different approaches to sharing leadership.* Nottingham: National College of School Leadership.

———. (2004). Talking back to the new public administration's version of accountability in education: A co-principal's practice of mutual responsibility. *Educational Administration and Management, 32*(3), 33–49.

Currie, J., Thiele, B., and Harris, P. (2002). *Gendered universities in globalized economies: Powers, careers and sacrifices.* New York: Lexington Books.

Czarniawska, B., and Hopfl, H. (2002). *Casting the other: The production and maintenance of inequalities in work organizations.* London: Routledge.

DE&T (Department of Education and Training), Victoria. (2004–2005). *Annual Report.* Melbourne: Victorian Government Printer.

De Groot, J. (1997). After the ivory tower: Gender, commodification and the "academic." *Feminist Review, 55*(Spring), 130–142.

Deane, E. (1996). *Women, research and research productivity in post-1987universities: Opportunities and constraints.* Canberra: Higher Education Division, Department of Education, Training and Youth Affairs.

Deem, R., and Ozga, J. (1997). Woman managing for diversity in a postmodern world. In C. Marshall (Ed.), *Feminist critical policy analysis.* Vol. 2. London: Falmer Press, pp. 25–40.

———.(2000). Transforming post-compulsory education?: Feminists at work in the academy. *Women's International Studies Review, 23*(2), 153–166.

Department of Education and Children's Services, South Australia. (2005). *Annual Report.* Adelaide: Government Printer.

Dillabough, J., and Acker, S. (2002). Globalization, women's work and teacher education: A cross national analysis. *International Studies in Sociology of Education, 12*(3), 227–260.

Eveline, J. (1998). Heavy, dirty and limp stories. Male advantage at work. In M. Gatens and A. MacKinnon (Eds.), *Gender and institutions.* Cambridge: Cambridge University Press, pp. 90–106.

Franzway, S. (2001). *Sexual politics and greedy institutions.* Annandale, N.S.W.: Pluto Press.

Fraser, N. (2006, November). Reframing justice in a globalizing world. *New Left Review, 36,* pp. 1–17.

Gewirtz, S. (1998). Conceptualising social justice in education: Mapping the territory. *Journal of Education Policy, 13*(4), 469–484.

Gronn, P., and Rawlings Sanaei, F. (2003). Principal recruitment in a climate of leadership disengagement. *Australian Journal of Education, 47*(2), 172–184.

Hancock, L. (Ed.), (1999). *Women, public policy and the state.* South Yarra, Victoria: Macmillan.

Hearn, J. (2002). Alternative conceptualisations and theoretical perspectives on identities and organizational cultures: A personal review of research on men in organizations. In I. Aaltio and A. Mills (Eds.), *Gender, identity, and culture in organizations.* London: Routledge, pp. 39–56.

Hey, V., and Bradford, S. (2004). The return of the repressed?: The gender politics of emergent forms of professionalism in education. *Journal of Education Policy, 19*(6), 691–714.

Husu, L., and Morley, L. (2000). Academe and gender: What has not changed? *Higher Education in Europe, 259*(2), 137–138.

Johnson, S., and Birkeland, S. (2003). Pursuing a "sense of success": New teachers talk about their career decisions. *American Educational Research Journal, 40*(3), 581–617.

Kerfoot, D., Pritchard, C., and Whitehead, S. (2000). (En)gendering management: Work, organization and further education. *Journal of Further and Higher Education, 24*(2), 157–171.

Lakes, R., and Carter, P. (Eds.). (2004). *Globalizing education for work. Comparative perspectives on gender and the new economy.* Mahwah, NJ: Lawrence Erlbaum.

Leonard, P. (1998). Gendering change?: Management, masculinity and the dynamics of incorporation. *Gender and Education, 10*(1), 71–84.

Limerick, B., and Anderson, C. (1999). Female administrators and school-based management: New models in an era of change? *Educational Management & Administration, 27*(4), 401–414.

Lingard, B. (2003). Where to in gender policy in education after recuperative masculinity politics? *International Journal of Inclusive Education, 7*(1), 33–56.

———. (2006). Globalisation, the research imagination and deparochialising the study of education. *Globalisation, Societies and Education, 4*(2), 287–302.

Lingard, B., and Douglas, P. (1999). *Men engaging feminisms: Pro-feminism, backlashes and schooling.* Buckingham: Open University Press.

Lingard, B., Rawolle, S., and Taylor, S. (2005). Globalizing policy sociology in education: Working with Bourdieu. *Journal of Education Policy, 20*(6), 759–177.

Mabokela, R. (Ed.). (2007). *Soaring beyond boundaries: Women breaking educational barriers in traditional societies.* Netherlands: Sense Publishers.

Meadmore, D., and Meadmore, P. (2004). The boundlessness of performativity in elite Australian schools. *Discourse, 25*(3), 375–388.

Mendez-Morse, S. (2003). Chicana feminism and educational leadership. In M. D. Young and L. Skrla (Eds.), *Reconsidering: Feminist research in educational leadership,* pp. 161–178. Albany: SUNY Press.

Mills, M., Martino, W., and Lingard, B. (2004). Attracting, recruiting, and retaining male teachers: Policy issues in a male teacher debate. *British Journal of Sociology of Education, 25*(3), 355–371.

Moreton-Robinson, A. (2000). *Talkin' up to the white woman: Indigenous women and feminism.* St. Lucia: University of Queensland Press.

Morley, L. (2000). The micropolitics of gender in the learning society. *Higher Education in Europe, 25*(2), 229–235.

———. (2003). *Quality and power in higher education.* Buckingham: Open University Press.

Narayan, U. (1997). *Dislocating cultures: Identities, traditions and third world feminism.* London: Routledge.

Ngurruwutthun, N., and Stewart, M. P. A. (1996). "Learning to walk behind; learning to walk in front": A case study of the mentor program at Yirrkala Community Education Centre. *Unicorn, 22*(4), 3–23.

Oplatka, I., and Hertz-Lazarowitz, R. (Eds.) (2006). *Women principals in a multicultural society: New insights into feminist educational leadership.* Netherlands: Sense Publishers.

Ozga, J., and Walker, L. (1999). In the company of men. In S. Whitehead and R. Moodley (Eds.), *Transforming managers: Gendering change in the public sector.* London: UCL Press, pp. 107–120.

Probert, B. (1998). Working in Australian universities: Pay equity for men and women? *Australian Universities Review, 42*(2), 33–42.

———. (2001a). Researching Australia's gender culture: From shared expectations to profound ambivalence. *Dialogue, 20*(2), 21–27.

———. (2001b). "Grateful slaves" or "self-made women": A matter of choice or policy? Clare Burton Lectures. Melbourne: RMIT.

———. (2005). I just couldn't fit it in: Gender and unequal outcomes in academic careers. *Gender Work and Organization, 12*(1), 50–71.

Pyke, J., and Ward, K. (2003). Recasting our understanding of gender and work during global restructuring. *International Sociology, 18*(3), 461–489.

Reay, D. (2000). Dim dross?: Marginalized voices both inside and outside the academy. *Women's Studies International Forum, 23*(1), 13–21.

Reay, D., and Ball, S. (2000). Essentials of female management: Women's ways of working in the education market place? *Educational Management & Administration, 28*(2), 145–159.

Sawer, M. (1999). The watchers within: Women and the Australian state. In L. Hancock (Ed.), *Women, public policy and the state.* South Yarra, Victoria: Macmillan, pp. 36–53.

Sinclair, A. (2000a). Teaching managers about masculinities: Are you kidding? *Management Learning, 31*(1), 83–101.

———. (2000b). Women within diversity: Risks and possibilities. *Women in Management Review, 15*(5/6), 137–145.

Strachan, J. (1999). Feminist educational leadership in a New Zealand neo-liberal context. *Journal of Educational Administration, 37*(2), 121–138.

Tuhiwa Smith, L. (1993). Getting out from under: Maori women, education and the struggles of Mana Wahine. In M. Arnot and K. Weiler (Eds.), *Feminism and social justice in education. International perspectives,* pp. 145–165. London: Falmer Press.

Ward, M. (2001). The gender salary gap in British academia. *Applied Economics, 33*(13), 169–181.

White, K. (2003). Women and leadership in higher education in Australia. *Tertiary Education and Management, 9,* pp. 45–60.

CHAPTER 11

Women's Leadership in Educational Decentralization and Parental Involvement

The Case of Hong Kong

Esther Sui-chu Ho

INTRODUCTION: CURRENT STATUS OF WOMEN'S LEADERSHIP IN HONG KONG—THE BIG PICTURE

In 1990, the UN Economic and Social Council adopted a motion demanding all member states to raise the number of women representatives at decision-making levels in all public offices to 30% by 1995 and to 50% by 2000 (United Nations, 1990). Hong Kong's performance is far below the target set by the UN. Women comprised 45% of the workforce in 2002 and the proportion of females in management and administration was only 26% in Hong Kong (Women's Commission, 2003; CEDAW, 2004, Annex R and O). The percentage of women managers and administrators has seen a very slow increase in Hong Kong since 1993. Women represented only 16% of all managers and administrators. Yet female managers represent only 4.9% of all employed females, in contrast to 11% for males (Kershaw and DeGolyer, 2006).

Of all the major economic sectors in Hong Kong, women's involvement was highest (56%) in the community/social and personal services sector, in particular, education/medical/community/social services (65%). The field of education is numerically dominated by women laborers in the world. Yet school managers in education are predominantly male although there is some evidence of a growing number of women taking up leadership positions in education (Coleman, 1996, 2002; Cubillo and Brown, 2003).

WOMEN'S LEADERSHIP IN HONG KONG: HIGHER AND BASIC EDUCATION

In Hong Kong higher education, the total number of teaching staff was about 6,000 in 2001 (CEDAW, 2004, Annex L). Only 8% (27 out of 340) of those at professor grade, 10% (31 out of 321) of those at reader grade, and 15% (87 out of 591) of those at senior lecturer grade were women (CEDAW, 2004, Annex L).

For Hong Kong basic education, the total number of teaching staff was about 70,000 in 2001. Women made up 99.4% (9,061 out of 9,115), 77.4% (18,508 out of 23,916), and 68.5% (25,560 out of 37,331) of the teaching staff in kindergarten, primary and secondary school respectively. However, for the leader position, only about 20% of aided secondary schools were administered by woman principals in 1995 (Shum, 1995, p. 168). This percentage grew to 30% in 2007 (EMB, 2007). The percentage of primary school principals reached 50% in 2007, yet this percentage is still underrepresented since women comprise 77% of teaching staff in Hong Kong primary schools.

GENDER EGALITARIANISM IN HONG KONG FROM AN INTERNATIONAL PERSPECTIVE

The evidence suggests that the practice of Hong Kong in empowerment of women is far below the target set by the UN. Yet people in general, and even women, in Hong Kong often do not perceive gender discrimination, and when they do, they accept it as something to work around rather than as something that can be changed (Ford, 2007).

In a recent cross-cultural study (the GLOBE study) of gender egalitarianism conducted in 62 countries/regions in 2004 (Emrich, Denmark and Hartog, 2004, p. 365), Hong Kong was grouped into the "high" band of gender egalitarianism regions in terms of the measures of societal practice. A high-gender-egalitarian society is defined by the following criteria in the study (p. 359): (1) have more women in leadership positions; (2) afford women a higher status in society; (3) afford women a greater role in community decision making; (4) have a higher percentage of women participating in the labor force; (5) have less occupational sex discrimination; (6) have higher female literacy rates; (7) have a similar level of education of females relative to males.

Of the 62 countries participating in the study, Hong Kong (mean score of 3.47) and Singapore (3.70) were the only two Asian societies grouped into the societies with "high gender egalitarianism in societal practice." The majority of other Asian societies were grouped into the "medium" band of gender egalitarianism, among them Thailand (3.35), Indonesia (3.28), Japan (3.19), China (3.05), and India (2.90). South Korea

(2.50) was grouped into the "low" band of gender egalitarianism regions.

Gender egalitarianism in the GLOBE study was measured by the perceptions of sampled managers regarding the extent to which genders are treated equally in their societies. Managers were asked to report their perceptions of statements such as this sample item: "In this society, boys are encouraged more than girls to attain a higher education." Each item was measured on a seven-point scale, where "strongly agree" was coded as 1 and "strongly disagree" was coded as 7. Across all the 62 societies surveyed in the GLOBE study the mean index is 3.37 and standard deviation is 0.37 for the index of Gender Egalitarianism Societal Practices (GESP). The range of GESP is 2.50 to 4.08. The international mean of 3.37 indicated that social practices are still slightly discriminating against women when using the midpoint of 4 as reference. An alternative interpretation given by Emrich, Denmark and Hartog (2004, p. 362) is that "no society in the GLOBE study is perceived to be female dominated—that is to say, encouraging girls, more so than boys, to attain a higher education or having more women than men in position of high office." In my view, the mean score of 3.37 indicates a modest cross-cultural sex discrimination in the allocation of leadership roles between females and males.

Moreover, the international mean of GESP, 3.37, is actually lower than the index of Gender Egalitarianism Societal Value (GESV), 4.51. GESV measured the ideology or habits of people valuing gender equality with a 7-point Likert scale. A sample item is as follows: "I believe that opportunities for leadership positions should be: more available for men than for women (coded 1-2); equally available for men and women (coded 3-4-5) or more available for women than for men (6-7)." Consistent with the international pattern, Hong Kong managers do express a desire for their society to be more gender egalitarian (4.35) than they are in practice (3.47). This finding indicates that the expectation for moving toward gender equality was generally higher than what is seen in Hong Kong as well as many other societies.

MAJOR BARRIERS FOR THE MOVEMENT OF WOMEN INTO LEADERSHIP POSITIONS

The evidence from the GLOBE study suggests that Hong Kong has the *value* or *ideology* for gender egalitarianism, yet there is a gap in *practice* of gender equality. So, what are the main reasons that deter women from fully realizing their potential and why is there still low representation of women leaders in Hong Kong?

The Women's Commission in Hong Kong conducted a survey in 2002 to collect information on the current gender-related situation in Hong Kong. The survey identified the top three barriers for women's development in their careers: existence of sex discrimination (45%); need to take care of children (30.6%) and limitation in physical condition (23.2%). Moreover, about 17.2% of the people consider that "women are relatively less capable of making decisions than men." And about 18.4% disagreed that "Hong Kong needs to have more women to act as community or organization leaders." Moreover, about 34.0% of the people responded that "men are more knowledgeable about politics than women" (Women's Commission, 2002). While it was more evident that males engaged in gender stereotyping in the political arena, females on the other hand tended to agree that "mothers are responsible for taking care of children while fathers are not." This is possibly due to the traditional cultural norm dictating that women should take care of the family at home whereas men should earn the bread in the workplace.

Mahtani (2005) conducted a qualitative study on the leadership experience in various workplaces in Hong Kong. Twenty-two women leaders who achieved the top and senior management positions in Hong Kong were interviewed. Most of the women leaders believed that leadership is primarily about the "ability to inspire and lead others." However, when asked whether they were themselves leaders, most women hesitated, being uncomfortable with the term "leader." Most women leaders said differences between leadership styles are not gender specific. Nevertheless, the study found that "a key difference identified between women's and men's leadership styles was women's stronger focus on people and interaction" (Mahtani, 2005, p. 5). Several factors were identified by these women leaders as major barriers for women's moving into leadership positions. First, women leaders find it difficult to strive for a "balance of work and family obligations." Second, women leaders note a lack of patronage and sponsorship, a kind of social capital for development in their fields. Third, women leaders are usually relegated to the traditional role, especially in Chinese culture. That is, women are still expected to do the "taking care" more than the "taking charge." Yet "taking care" is still undervalued relative to the "taking charge."

Nevertheless, the women leaders in the study generally believe that Hong Kong is a good place for women to work because of good employment opportunities, the availability of interesting and challenging jobs, and the availability of reliable child care. However, a "glass ceiling" still exists because of the gender stereotype that women—even those in leadership—are the primary caregivers at home. Thus, women, especially those of childbearing age, have to work extra hard to prove their work commitment and ability.

WOMEN'S LEADERSHIP IN EDUCATIONAL DECENTRALIZATION AND PARENTAL INVOLVEMENT

Under the current global decentralization reform movement, parental participation in children's education and school governance has been taking hold in England, Wales, Australia, New Zealand, Israel, Singapore, Brazil, Germany, France, Italy, the United States and Canada (Beattie, 1985; Brown, 1994; Ho, 2003). Previous studies often associate decentralization policy with parental empowerment (Cochran and Dean, 1991; Comer, 1980, 1987; Comer and Haynes, 1991; Cooper and Christie, 2005). They contend that meaningful involvement of parents requires a restructuring of roles and a shift of power toward parents. Sarason (1995) argues that parental involvement in school governance is the basic right of the parents.

Other scholars support that when parents are involved in management decisions, they are more cognizant of school needs and are more likely to find ways to participate in school and at home (Comer and Haynes, 1991; Rowse, 1994). In Hong Kong, with impetus generated by the School Management Initiative (SMI) and Education Commission Report No. 7 (ECR7), the promotion of parental involvement in children's education has become a major concern for various stakeholders in the educational sector.

Previous studies suggested that principals are key players in determining the role of parents in children's education (Brown, 1994; Ho, 2003). Yet little has been done to clarify the principals' leadership habits and practices toward parental involvement in school activities and school governance, especially from a gender perspective.

Hall (1996) in the UK and Hope-Arlene (1999) in Canada found that female school principals are more likely to employ the "power through" leadership approach whereas their male counterparts are more likely to employ the "power over" approach. The "power through" approach tends to be associated with empowerment and participation of stakeholders and is framed as more consistent with feminine thesis. On the other hand, the "power over" approach is associated with control and dominance and is perceived as a more masculine leadership style. In brief, it appears that the "power through" approach is more consistent with the current educational decentralization movement, which emphasizes the empowerment and participation of parents, teachers and other stakeholders in the education system.

Other researchers suggest that there is little or no difference in traits and abilities of managerial and professional women and men (Davidson and Burke, 1994; Mahtani, 2005). For instance, evidence from studies by Butterfield and Powell (1981) and Mahtani (2005) suggested that leadership style is independent of gender. These studies argued that male and female leaders exhibit similar amounts of "task" oriented and "people" oriented leadership behaviors.

Eagly and Johnson (1990) conducted a meta-analysis on gender and leadership style. They compared the leadership styles of women and men based on 162 studies and found both a convergence and divergence of leadership style between women and men. They found that female and male leaders did not differ in the "person-oriented" versus "task-oriented" styles in organizational studies. However, women tended to adopt a more "democratic or participative" style and a less "autocratic or directive" style than did men. Eagly and Johnson argued that women are more likely to make decisions in a "collaborative" style for not only the soliciting of suggestions from one's peers and subordinates but also the preservation of good relationships with their peers and subordinates when evaluating and perhaps rejecting their ideas.

An alternative perspective, given by Appelbaum, Audet and Miller (2003), Coleman (2000) and Jirasinghe and Lyons (1996), is that male leaders are more "delegatory" than female leaders, whereas female leaders are more "collaborative" than male leaders. If that is the case, male principals may be more ready to delegate decision making to parents, but female principals may be more ready to collaborate with parents and involve parents as volunteers in different kinds of school activities. Thus, gender may be a key factor for principals' habits toward school governance and their practices in involving parents in school affairs.

KNOWLEDGE GAP AND RESEARCH QUESTIONS

Given the inconclusive nature of the research on gender and leadership, and the possible influence of decentralization and parental involvement policy in opening up the opportunities for women to be empowered, this chapter aims to explore gender difference in leadership habits and practice toward parental empowerment and involvement, that is, to discover if female principals are more collaborative with parents in school volunteering and male principals are more delegatory to parents for school administration. This chapter attempts to address the following two research questions:

1. Are female principals different from male principals in their views and practices toward collaboration with parent volunteers in school?
2. Are female principals different from male principals in their view and practices toward delegating decision-making authority to parents in school? If so, what are the possible factors related to these gender differences?

METHODOLOGY AND DATABASE SAMPLING

Data for this paper are mainly from the survey of principals extracted from a large-scale study of home/school/community collaboration in Hong Kong primary schools. Questionnaires were sent to principals at all 940 primary schools in Hong Kong in February 2004 at the first stage of the study. A total of 294 principals returned the questionnaires, a response rate of 32%. Descriptive analysis, t-test and logistic regression analysis were used to examine the convergences and divergences of female and male principals for their views and practices toward parental participation in school volunteering and parental empowerment in decision making.

GENERAL CHARACTERISTICS OF THE SCHOOLS AND PRINCIPALS

Of the responding principals in the general primary schools, about 47% are male and 53% are female. About 59% of the principals have a bachelor's degree; about 23% have a master's degree, and about 2% have a doctoral degree. About 43% of the schools have no religion; about 28% are Christian schools, and about 22% are Catholic schools. The majority of the schools (89%) are supported by external governmental funds. About 63% are whole-day schools and 35% are half-day schools (see table 11.1).

RESULTS AND DISCUSSION

Divergence of Female and Male Principals in Mobilizing Parents as "Volunteers"

Table 11.2 shows that the number (average number of parents) of volunteers mobilized by female principals in schools is significantly higher than the male principals. Moreover, the diversity (average number of works) of volunteering tasks initiated by female principals also is significantly higher than by the male principals. Table

Table 11.1. General Characteristics of the Sampled Primary Schools and Principals

	Frequency	Percentage
Principal's gender		
Female	144	53
Male	127	47
Principal's education		
Ph.D.	5	2
Master's	62	23
Bachelor's degree 161	59	
Associate degree	28	10
Higher Diploma/Certificate	2	1
Diploma/Certificate	13	5
School Religion		
None	116	43
Catholic	60	22
Other Christian	74	28
Buddhist	15	6
Taoist	3	1
Muslim	1	0
School Type		
Government	14	5
Aided	228	89
DSS	2	1
Private	9	4
English School Foundation	2	1
Length of School Day		
Whole day	170	63
Half day	93	35
Partially whole day	5	2

11.3 shows that the number of volunteers mobilized from Grade 1 to Grade 4 by female principals is significantly higher than by the male principals.

Divergence of Male and Female Principals in Accepting Parents as "Decision-makers"

The study asked a general question: "Do you (as principals) agree to introduce 'parent as decision maker' in the school management committee?" We found that more male principals accept parents as decision-makers in School Based Management (SBM) than female principals. Table 11.4 shows that about 58.8% of male principals agreed to have parents as decision-makers in the SBM reform, a significantly higher rate than that of 49.4% of female principals.

POSSIBLE REASONS FOR ACCEPTANCE OF PARENTAL INVOLVEMENT AS DECISION-MAKERS In the final analysis, a logistic regression analysis was used to examine the factors related to principals who accept parents as decision-makers. The acceptance of parents as decision-makers was analyzed as a function of four groups

Table 11.2. Number and Diversity of Parent Volunteers

	Sex	Mean	Std. Dev.	F	Sig.
Number of volunteers in school	Female	77.29	158.43	4.073	0.045
	Male	42.19	98.56		
Diversity of volunteers in school	Female	5.36	2.61	6.818	0.009
	Male	4.56	2.62		

Table 11.3. Number of Volunteers across Grade

	Female		Male		Total			
	Mean	Std. Dev.	Mean	Std. Dev.	Mean	Std. Dev.	F	Sig.
Grade 1	22.69	45.98	10.31	21.03	17.15	37.41	6.26	0.013
Grade 2	20.01	44.71	9.64	22.15	15.24	36.44	4.76	0.030
Grade 3	17.23	33.45	9.28	24.46	13.46	29.73	4.27	0.040
Grade 4	15.94	33.64	8.59	22.98	12.50	29.31	3.76	0.054
Grade 5	14.48	31.41	9.53	24.11	12.20	28.34	1.79	0.182
Grade 6	14.23	31.22	8.85	22.26	11.76	27.55	2.22	0.138

of factors: (1) gender; (2) socioeconomic context of school; (3) principals' ideology toward home/school collaboration; (4) principals' report of the function of their school parent-teacher association (PTA). A list of definitions and descriptive statistics of all the variables is given in appendix 11.1.

Table 11.5 indicates that there are significant gender differences in the likelihood of principals accepting parents as decision-makers. A female principal is less likely (0.339 times) to accept parents as decision-makers than is a male principal. Moreover, principals' attitudes toward accepting parents as decision-makers are not related to socioeconomic factors such as: percentage of immigrant students, percentage of students from single-parent families, and the average socioeconomic status (SES) of the schools. This finding challenges the view of the advantage of upper-class parents in their involvement in their children's education. In other words, whether or not principals accept parents as decision-makers is not significantly related to the social background of the parent community. Principals' views of parents as decision-makers also are not related to principals' teaching experience, principalship experience, whether principals take charge of

home/school/community (HSC), or if he/she delegates a senior teacher to take charge of HSC in school.

However, principals' acceptance of parent as decision-maker is significantly related to the history and functions of PTAs. Schools with more than one year of PTA were 1.256 times more likely to accept parents as decision-makers. Moreover, principals who perceived the functions of PTAs for consulting, decision-making and evaluating schools are more likely to accept parents as decision-makers. Principals who reported that the PTA's function is allowing parents to make decisions on essential school affairs were 13 times more likely to accept parents as decision-makers than those without this function of the PTA. In addition, principals with higher level of communitarian ideology are more likely to accept parents as decision-makers. In other words, when principals perceived parents as co-owners of schools, parents could be nurtured and teachers could collaborate with parents to create a better learning environment. Therefore, they were more likely to accept parents as decision-makers.

CONVERGENCE OF MALE AND FEMALE PRINCIPALS FOR THE LOW LEVEL OF ACCEPTANCE FOR CONCRETE PARENTAL EMPOWERMENT

The issue of parental empowerment is more complicated than just accepting parents as decision-makers. When we ask principals about authority to be delegated to parents with 15 concrete governance issues, principals are generally very conservative regardless of their gender. Results in previous analyses of tables 11.4 and 11.5 suggest that male principals

Table 11.4. Percentage of Principals Agree Parent as Decision Maker in School-Based Management

	Female Principal	Male Principal	t	Sig
Mean	45%	59%	2.343	0.020
SD	.50	.49		

Table 11.5. Logistic Regression of Acceptance for Parents as Decision Makers

	B	S.E.	Wald	Odds Ratio
Female Principal	−1.083	0.460	5.533	0.339
Socioeconomic Context				
Percentage of immigrants	0.010	0.011	0.821	1.010
Percentage of single parents	−0.028	0.025	1.197	0.973
Average of SES	−0.005	0.281	0.000	0.995
Principals' Background				
Teaching experience	0.017	0.027	0.412	1.017
Principalship experience	−0.009	0.032	0.081	0.991
Have HSC responsibilities	0.292	0.408	0.513	1.339
Have senior teacher take charge of HSC	0.557	0.540	1.063	1.746
PTA years	0.228	0.090	6.437	1.256
Principals' Ideology toward Decentralization				
Communitarian	0.439	0.211	4.341	1.551
Bureaucratic	−0.075	0.225	0.111	0.928
Utilitarian	0.216	0.212	1.041	1.241
Functions of PTA				
Parenting	0.555	0.971	0.326	1.741
Networking	0.161	0.536	0.090	1.174
Social gathering	−0.580	0.589	0.969	0.560
Volunteering	−0.667	0.612	1.187	0.513
Consulting	1.349	0.548	6.062	3.854
Decision making	2.609	0.634	16.924	13.587
Evaluating	−0.953	0.488	3.809	0.386
Constant	−2.196	1.733	1.606	0.111

are more ready to empower parents to be decision-makers in school governance than are female principals; however, when we asked about a set of more concrete school governance issues in which power would be shared with parents to make decisions, we did not find significant gender differences (see table 11.6).

Table 11.6 shows the t-test results of the gender difference of principals' degrees of acceptance of parental empowerment in decision-making on 15 school governance issues. The findings suggest that there is no gender difference in principals' attitudes toward involving parents to make decisions on any of the 15 items. Overall, both female and male principals have the greatest acceptance of delegating decision making to parents on "setting PTA policy" and "organizing parent activities." Student issues are the second category of decisions on which principals were more willing to consult parents. For issues concerning school budgeting, curriculum, instruction and staffing, principals appear to inform parents rather than having parents make the decision. Overall, all principals have a low acceptance of parents in decision making in Hong Kong except in issues related to parent activities and PTA, regardless of the principals' gender.

CONCLUSIONS AND IMPLICATIONS

The two questions formulated at the outset were: Are female principals different from male principals in their views and practices toward collaboration with parent volunteers and parental empowerment in school governance? If so, what are the possible factors related to these gender differences in parental volunteering and parental empowerment? Findings from the study show that there are gender differences in mobilizing parents as volunteers as well as in accepting parents as decision-makers. However, regarding concrete school governance issues, when asked when principals should be informed, consulted or participate in making decisions, both male and female principals are very conservative and there is not much gender difference. I will discuss these interesting findings in detail in this section and then explore some implications for policy, practice and further research.

Divergence in the Practices of Parent Volunteerism
Women are seen to be a new source of leadership talent because of their caring and sharing propensities, their communicative and organizational skills, and their capacity to listen to and empathize with the needs of parents and community members. These

Table 11.6. Zone of Acceptance of Parental Involvement in Decision Making

Decision Items	Female Principal	Male Principal	Mean Difference	t	Sig. (2-tailed)
Setting PTA policy	2.721	2.801	-0.081	-1.495	0.136
Organizing parent activities	2.516	2.526	-0.010	-0.133	0.894
Arranging student affairs	2.260	2.304	-0.044	-0.479	0.633
Evaluating school quality	2.013	1.955	0.058	0.745	0.457
Arranging extracurricular activities	1.813	1.754	0.059	0.591	0.555
Regulating quantity and quality of homework	1.623	1.640	-0.016	-0.189	0.850
Setting school educational goal	1.606	1.709	-0.103	-1.169	0.243
Making school development plan	1.600	1.701	-0.101	-1.134	0.258
Joining school management committee	1.510	1.615	-0.105	-0.874	0.383
Setting student disciplinary policies	1.503	1.537	-0.034	-0.344	0.731
Decision on the courses to be offered	1.252	1.154	0.097	1.051	0.294
Grouping students into classes	1.200	1.119	0.081	0.904	0.367
Drafting annual school budget and funds allocation	1.039	1.037	0.002	0.018	0.986
Selection of textbooks	0.882	0.956	-0.074	-0.831	0.407
Employment and assignment of teachers and administrator staff	0.561	0.467	0.095	1.146	0.253

Note: 0 = no involvement; 1 = inform parents; 2 = consult parents; 3 = parents make decision.

traits are deemed critical to the new decentralization and parental involvement movement in the field of education, which needs flexibility to change and respond to person-oriented demands.

Feminist research on women in leadership provides evidence that many female principals are more caring, collaborative, communicative, consultative, communitarian, consensus oriented and student and curriculum focused (e.g., Henry, 1996; Nakama, 2005). Yet such research has a tendency to produce a generalization that "all" women leaders are caring and sharing and collaborative in all aspects of organization, which is of course highly problematic. While this study finds that most female principals tend to be more collaborative with parents in general school volunteering, they are not more delegatory than male principals in terms of accepting parents in decision making.

Convergence in the Views of Parental Empowerment
Evidence from the principal survey suggested that both female and male principals are conservative in parental empowerment. One possible reason is that female principals, like the male principals, during their selection and socialization into the managerial role in schools, internalize a clear division of work between home and school. The decision making in school is always within the professional territory whereas parents' home-based involvement and school-based volunteering are welcomed only when that involvement supports school policy and practice.

Implications for Policy and Practice
Parents have been seen as an untapped resource for school reform since the 1980s and thus increasing parental involvement in every aspect of schooling appears to be a promising avenue for improving school quality and productivity in the current educational decentralization movement. Under this global movement, promotion of parental involvement provides the chance and challenge for women to be involved in the public sphere—the school. Evidence from Hong Kong suggests that, since the educational decentralization and parental involvement policy in the early 1990s, more parents have become involved in their children's education and the majority of these parents are women (Ho, 2000). Parental involvement appears to be quite successful in that women are getting more chances to step up, network and be advocates for themselves and their children in the field of education.

In fact, current evidence in Hong Kong indicates the number of parent volunteers increased substantially during the past decade and the majority of the volunteers are women (Ho and Kwong, 2007). Increasing numbers of female volunteers in schools might have transformed the way principals look at leadership from only "taking charge" of schools toward a hybrid approach of both "taking charge" of schools and "taking care" of children. This shifts the notion of leadership from an earlier version of a more masculine-bureaucratic approach to a more androgynous-communitarian mode. The androgynous-communitarian approach appears to be a more effective leadership style in the context of educational decentralization regardless of gender, and its advantages for teaching and learning have been widely recognized by many organizational theorists (e.g., Coleman, 2000; Henry, 1996; Hope-Arlene, 1999; Pounder and Coleman, 2002; Nakama, 2005; Shum and Cheng, 1997).

Implications for Future Studies

Moves to increase the inclusion of women into education leadership have resulted in partial success in Hong Kong. Female principals appear to be more equally represented in primary education (about 50% in 2007). Yet women are still underrepresented in secondary education (30%) and in higher education (less than 10%). In fact, women continue to be underrepresented globally in educational leadership, especially at higher levels of the field of education.

The global trend of educational decentralization and parental involvement opens up the opportunities for women principals to collaborate with parents and community members. In the study, the most interesting findings that emerged were the divergences and convergences between female and male principals in parental involvement and empowerment. The present study suggests that female principals have the advantage to mobilize parents by various communication channels and to provide diversified forms of volunteering opportunities. However, when comparing the views of delegating substantial authorities to parents in various governance issues, no gender differences could be found. An interesting research question emerges from the present study: Why doesn't the advantage of female principals in mobilizing parent volunteers enhance their attitude toward parental empowerment in decision making? Qualitative methods or mixed methods would be a promising approach to understand the reasons why principals, regardless of their gender, are conservative in concrete school governance issues.

Since this study was conducted in an Asian society, Hong Kong, it will be interesting to examine if gender differences and similarities revealed in this study are similar to those in other countries. Moreover, since this study focuses on principals' views on parental involvement and empowerment, it would be worthwhile to triangulate principals' views with that of teachers and parents in future studies since both teachers and parents are major stakeholders for children in education under the current educational decentralization reform.

REFERENCES CITED

Appelbaum, S. H., Audet, L., and Miller, J. C. (2003). Gender and leadership? Leadership and gender? A journey through the landscape of theories. *Leadership and Organization Development Journal, 24*(1), 43–51.

Beattie, N. (1985). *Professional parents: Parent participation in four Western European countries.* London: The Falmer Press.

Brown, D. J. (1994). Decentralization in educational governance and management. In T. Husen and Postlewaite (Eds.), *The International Encyclopedia of Education,* pp. 1470–1411. Oxford: Pergamon Press.

Butterfield, D. A., and Powell, G. N. (1981). Effect of group performance, leader sex and rater sex on ratings of leader behavior. *Organization Behavior and Human Performance, 28,* 129–141.

CEDAW. (2004). Convention on the Elimination of All Forms of Discrimination against Women, Second Report on Hong Kong Special Administrative Region (CEDAW). Hong Kong: Government Logistics Department. Compiled by the Health, Welfare and Food Bureau, Hong Kong Government.

Coleman, M. (1996). Barriers to career progress for women in education: The perceptions of female head teachers. *Educational Research, 38*(3), 317–332.

———. (2000). The female secondary head-teacher in England and Wales: Leadership and management styles. *Educational Research, 42*(1), 13–27.

———. (2002). *Women as head-teachers: Striking the balance.* Stoke on Trent: Trentham Books.

Cochran, M., and Dean, C. (1991). Home-school relationship and the empowerment process. *The Elementary School Journal, 91*(3), 261–269.

Comer, J. P. (1980). *School power: Implications of an intervention project.* New York: The Free Press.

———. (1987). New Haven's school-community connection. *Educational Leadership, 44*(6), 13–16.

Comer, J. P., and Haynes, N. M. (1991). Parent involvement in schools: An ecological approach. *The Elementary School Journal, 91*(3), 271–277.

Cooper, C. W., and Christie, C. A. (2005). Evaluating parent empowerment: A look at the potential of social justice evaluation in education. *Teachers College Record, 107*(10), 2248–2274.

Cubillo, L., and Brown, M. (2003). Women into educational leadership and management: International differences? *Journal of Educational Administration, 41*(3), 278–291.

Davidson, M. J., and Burke, R. J. (Eds.). (1994). *Women in management: Current research issues.* London: P. Chapman Publishing.

Early, A., and Johnson, B. T. (1990). Gender and leadership: A meta-analysis. *Psychological Bulletin, 108*(2), 233–256.

Emrich, C. G., Denmark, F. L., and Hartog, D. N. D. (2004). Cross-cultural differences in gender egalitarianism: Implications for societies, organizations and leaders. In R. J. Hourse, P. J. Hanges, M. Javidan, P. W. Dorfman and V. Gupta (Eds.), *Culture, leadership, and organizations: The*

GLOBE study of 62 societies. Thousand Oaks, CA: Sage Publications.

Ford, S. (2007). Women and leadership: The big picture. Paper presented at the Annual Workshop of Pushing the Boundaries: Women and Leadership. Hong Kong University, 9 June 2007.

Hall, V. (1996). *Dancing on the ceiling.* London: Paul Chapman Press.

Henry, M. E. (1996). *Parent-school collaboration: Feminist organizational structures and school leadership.* Albany: SUNY Press.

Ho, S. C. (2000). The relationships between family factors, institutional policies and parental involvement in children's education. *Educational Research Journal, 15*(2), 275–300.

————. (2003). Teachers' views on educational decentralization towards parental involvement in an Asian educational system: The Hong Kong case. *International Studies in Educational Administration, 31*(3), 58–75.

Ho, S. C., and Kwong, W. M. (2007). Parental involvement in children's education: What works and how it works. Final report of Earmarked Grant Research Projects: RGC Ref. CUHK 4335/01H.

Hong Kong Government: Women's Commission. (2002). Survey on the extent and level of positions taken up by women in the private and non-governmental sectors in Hong Kong.

Hope-Arlene, F. (1999). Power in the principal: Four women's experience. *Journal of Educational Administration, 37*(1), 23–50.

Jirasinghe, D., and Lyons, G. (1996). *The competent head: A job analysis of heads; tasks and personality factors.* London: The Falmer Press.

Kershaw, A. M., and DeGolyer, D. (Eds.). (2006). Women in power and decision-making. *The status of women and girls in Hong Kong 2006,* pp. 37–47. Hong Kong: The Woman's Foundation.

Mahtani, S. (2005). *Women leaders in Hong Kong: Insights into their workplace experiences.* Hong Kong: Community Business.

Nakama, D. A. (2005). Leadership, power, collaboration: Understanding women educational leaders' experiences through a feminist lens. Doctoral dissertation. Nayinal Chiayi University.

Pounder, J. S., and Coleman, M. (2002). Women—better leaders than men? In general and educational management it still "all depends." *Leadershisp and Organization Development Journal, 23*(3), 122–133.

Rowse, J. (1994). The home and school organization in the small elementary school. A major paper for the degree of Master of Education in the Department of Educational Studies (Educational Administration). The University of British Columbia.

Shum, L. C. (1995). Woman principals' leadership and teachers' work attitudes. Master's thesis. The Chinese University of Hong Kong.

Shum, L. C., and Cheung, Y. C. (1997). Perception of women principals' leadership and teachers' work attitudes. *Journal of Educational Administration, 35*(2), 165–184.

United Nations. (1990). Economic and Social Council Resolution E/RES/1990/15 (24 May 1990) of the United Nations.

Appendix 11.1. Definitions and Descriptive Statistics of All of the Variables in Chapter 11 Tables

	Mean	(SD)	Frequency	Percentage
Female Principal			144	53%
Socioeconomic Context				
Percentage of immigrants	15.0	(22.2)		
Percentage of single parents	11.5	(9.5)		
Average of SES	2.5	(0.9)		
Principals' Background				
Teaching experience (years)	26.2	(9.4)		
Principalship experience (years)	9.4	(8.7)		
Have HSC responsibilities (%)			141	48.0%
Have senior teacher take charge of HSC			220	75.0%
PTA years	6.4	(6.4)		
Principals' Ideology toward Decentralization (Factor Score)				
Communitarian	0	1		
Bureaucratic	0	1		
Utilitarian	0	1		
Functions of PTA (Factor Score)				
Parenting	0	1		
Networking	0	1		
Social gathering	0	1		
Volunteering	0	1		
Consulting	0	1		
Decision making	0	1		
Evaluating	0	1		

CHAPTER 12

Chinese Women's Participation in Educational Leadership

A Review and Analysis of the Current Situation

Haiyan Qiang, Juan Han and Xiaoyan Niu

THE CURRENT SITUATION OF WOMEN'S PARTICIPATION IN SCHOOL LEADERSHIP IN CHINA

Supporting Conditions Have Been Created for Women to Participate in School Leadership by the Chinese Government since the Early 1980s Reform and Open Policies

SINCE THE FOUNDING OF the People's Republic of China, great emphasis has been placed on improving women's political, economic and social status as well as creating conditions for the improvement. Especially since the earlier 1980s national reform and open policies, great efforts have been made and favorable conditions have been provided by the government in the domains of laws, policies and higher education opportunities for women to participate in educational leadership.

New Legislation Provides Legal Rights and Protection for Women's Participation in Educational Leadership

One of the prerequisites for women's participation in educational leadership is a university degree so that women may obtain the competence and qualification required for the career of education. At present a legal system that ensures women's participation in educational leadership has been established. Such a legal system is based on the Constitution of the People's Republic of China, principally the Law of the People's Republic of China on the Protection of Rights and Interests of Women, with the Education Law of the People's Republic of China included. Especially in 2005, the amendment of the Law of the People's Republic of China on the Protection of Rights and Interests of Women not only proclaimed the legal status of China's Fundamental State Policy of Equality of Men and Women but also proclaimed that the Party and the government should ensure that men and women enjoy equal rights in school admission, progressing from one grade level to the next, degree awarding and overseas studies. It also holds that women shouldn't be barred from employment and that employment standards for women shouldn't be raised simply because they are women.

China's Fundamental State Policy of Equality of Men and Women Provides Strong Policy Support for Women's Participation in Educational Leadership

Jiang Zeming, representing Chinese government, made a solemn proclamation to the Chinese people and the whole world that equality of men and women would be proclaimed as China's Fundamental State Policy to boost the social development at the Fourth World Women's Congress of the UN in 1995. Since then, two important plans for women's development have been framed and adopted by the Chinese government: the Plan for Chinese Women's Development (1995–2000) and the Plan for Chinese Women's Development (2001–2010).

The first goal formulated in the 1995 plan was to increase the degree of women's participation in policy making and management in national and social affairs. The detailed measure to realize that goal is to select and appoint more women in leading groups in the female domain: professions, industries, departments and enterprises (SCILSNC, 1997). In the 2001 plan, women's participation in policy making and management is ranked second among the six priorities that women should develop. The plan proclaims that the main goals for women's participation in leadership are to improve the level of women's participation in policy making and management in national and social affairs; to raise the proportion of women's participation in administrative leadership positions; to increase gradually the proportion of female cadres in the whole cadre group; and to reach an appropriate proportion between female leaders and female employees among the managerial levels in the female domain professions, departments and enterprises. In comparison, the orientations in the 2001 plan are more concrete and definite in women's participation in national and social affairs.

The Growth of Women's Enrollment in Higher Education Has Guaranteed Women's Competence to Participate in Educational Leadership

One of the most important guarantees of women's social participation competence is access to higher education. In fact, a university degree has an important effect on the range and extent of their participation. At present, receiving higher education is a prerequisite for Chinese women and men to pursue careers in education and further educational leadership participation. Much progress has been made in women's higher education opportunities since the early 1980s.

The proportion of the number of female college students has been increasing, from 33.6% in 1993 to 47.08% in 2005 (Jue Wei, 1995). Meanwhile, from 1993 to 2005 the number of female graduates has leaped more than elevenfold, from 6,486 to 71,157; the number of female holders of master's degrees by 10 times, from 6,176 to 63,322; the number of female doctorate students as much as 28 times, from 272 to 7,835 (DDPME, 2006). Furthermore, women will pursue even higher levels of education over the same period of time. The proportion of female graduates also has been growing rapidly. Overall, great progress has been made in the number as well as the proportion of women's higher education in the past decade, which creates prerequisites for women to work in education fields including taking leadership positions.

THE PRESENT SITUATION OF CHINESE WOMEN'S PARTICIPATION IN EDUCATIONAL LEADERSHIP

Differences exist in the power structures of higher education and basic education. The present situation of Chinese women's participation in educational leadership will be surveyed from two levels in this chapter—higher education and basic education.

THE CURRENT SITUATION OF CHINESE WOMEN'S PARTICIPATION IN THE LEADERSHIP OF HIGHER EDUCATION INSTITUTIONS

Two types of power exist in higher education institutions: academic and administrative. We will analyze the current situation of Chinese women's participation in terms of the two types of power or leadership in higher education institutions.

Women's Participation in Academic Leadership in Higher Education Institutions

With the rapid expansion of Chinese higher education since the 1990s, the number of college and university teachers has increased sharply. During the process, have similar great changes occurred as well in women's participation in academic leadership in higher education institutions? The following three groups of statistics will shed some light on this.

GROUP 1 *The number of full-time female college / university teachers:* In 1993, the number of full-time female college/university teachers was 119,000 and their proportion was 30.96%. In 1999, the number was 159,000 and their proportion was 37.35%. In 2004, the number grew to 364,500 and their proportion to 42.46% (Wei Yu, 1995). This group of statistics reveals that more and more women have been involved in teaching and research and have become an important force as full-time academic fellows in universities and colleges during the past 11 years.

GROUP 2 *The educational background of full-time female college/university teachers:* From 1993 to 2004, the number of female teachers with master's degrees has been growing most dramatically, from 17,127 to 94,045. The gap between males and females holding master's degrees is closing. However, despite a similar sharp increase in the number of female university teachers holding a doctoral degree, they represent only about one-fifth (22%) of all university teachers, and there still is a great gap compared with the number of male university teachers with the same degree (Jue Wei, 1995). The statistics reveal obvious improvement in the level of female university teachers' academic degrees.

GROUP 3 *The professional titles of full-time female college/university teachers:* The third group of statistics shows a larger number and proportion of female university teachers holding elementary and middle professional titles, and the number with middle professional titles approximates that of full-time male university teachers. Furthermore, the proportion of those holding a sub-high professional title (associate professor) is increasing rapidly, nearly 200%. A similar increase is also seen in the number of those holding a high professional title (professor), though their absolute proportion is rather small. It can be concluded that the proportion of full-time female university teachers with high professional titles is small, which puts them at a disadvantage in the structure of academic leadership. (See table 12.1.)

Now we are going to review the situation of female supervisors for master's and doctoral students in colleges/universities in China. Table 12.2 shows a rapid increase in the proportion of female supervisors under the age of 45, and the trend aligns with the growth of academic degrees of college/university female teachers. However, seen from the whole, the proportion of female supervisors is not large and increases very slowly. Women supervisors for graduate students are in a comparatively weak situation in the structure of academic leadership.

Table 12.1.   Professional Titles of Full-Time Female College/University Teachers

Year	Number of Female Professors and Proportion	Number of Female Associate Professors and Proportion	Number of Female Lecturers and Proportion	Number of Female Teaching Assistants and Proportion
1993	2,929 12.01%	20,921 21.93%	53,145 32.69%	34,667 41.36%
2004	16,045 19.28%	95,220 39.25%	127,825 45.5%	93,756 52.79%

Source: China Education Statistical Yearbook, 1993, 2004.

In all, women occupy a small proportion and lower posts in the administration of higher education. According to the statistics, there are only three female presidents, which is 4% among all the presidents in 71 universities and colleges affiliated with the Ministry of Education in China (Liu Liqun, 2002). A recent survey in Guangxi Province reveals that female university teachers represent about 40% in 10 universities and colleges. With regard to school administrators, there are only three women presidents, or 12.5%, among 24 university presidents or equivalent positions in these higher institutions; and there are only six women vice presidents, or 10.9%, among 55 vice presidents or equivalent positions (Liu Huagang, 2006). As for university administrative sections, such as in the Propaganda Department of a university party committee, Teachers Union, Students Union, or

Committee of Youth League, there are comparatively more women with middle-level administrative positions, and a majority of them have only vice or associate positions. Very few of them hold leadership positions in important university offices such as teaching affairs, academic affairs, and graduate programs management.

Chinese Women's Participation in School Leadership
Basic education in China has three levels: preschool education, elementary education and secondary education. Since school leadership in basic education is best represented by administrative positions, the review of women's participation in school leadership will focus on the number and proportion of school principals.

PRESCHOOL EDUCATION From the year 1999 to 2005, the proportion of female teachers, staff and principals in kindergartens in China remained high, over 92% respectively (DDPME, 2006). This shows that preschool education is, and is regarded as, a female profession. Meanwhile, the number of women involved in school leadership is proportional to that of female employees.

ELEMENTARY AND SECONDARY EDUCATION Elementary and secondary school education is a comparatively female-dominated profession. The proportion of female teachers and staff is around 50% (DDPME, 2006). What is women's participation in school leadership? At present, no publicized statistics from government are available. However, the situation can be estimated through reviewing the following statistics (Guangzhou Education Bureau, 2007; Yang Yuhong, 2004) on elementary and secondary school principals in Guangzhou, the third-largest city in China, and Nantong, a midsize city in the east of the country.

Tables 12.3, 12.4 and 12.5 show that women teachers/staff dominate numerically in elementary

Table 12.2.   Female Supervisors of Graduate Students in Colleges/Universities in China

Age	1993	1999	2004
Proportion of Female Supervisors	13.7%	16.8%	21.7%
Under 30	1.9	12.68	17.7
31–35	3.9	13.68	26.8
36–40	7.9	15.5	25.37
41–45	10.4	16.88	22.5
46–50	13.6	18.44	21.8
51–55	17.3	19.59	20.89
56–60	14.3	18.54	17.17
60 or over 60	10.0	13.56	12.2

Source: China Education Statistical Yearbook, 1993, 1999; Statistics of Female Supervisors in Colleges/Universities in China, 2004.

Table 12.3. Female Teachers in Guangzhou and Nantong

	Guangzhou		Nantong	
School Type	Female Teachers	Proportion	Female Teachers	Proportion
Primary School	30,111	73.4%	14,176	52.2%
Secondary School	18,545	57.6%	11,441	38.3%

and secondary schools in the two cities, especially in elementary schools. In contrast with the number of female teachers and staff, women participate in school leadership disproportionately. From elementary schools to secondary schools, the proportion of women involved in school leadership decreases gradually. Moreover, women hold more assistant or associate posts but fewer chief posts in school leadership.

In conclusion, the situation of women's participation in educational leadership is characterized by the following. First, from kindergarten until higher education, the proportion of women involved in school management is slumping, and the proportion of women involved in school leadership is small and disproportionate with the number of female teachers and staff in the profession. Second, from elementary school level to college/university level, women have

more chance to obtain lower or assistant/associate posts than chief leadership positions. Third, seen from the types of administration in which women participate, the proportion of women involved in academic leadership in higher institutions is greater than that in administrative positions.

BARRIERS THAT LIMIT WOMEN'S PARTICIPATION IN EDUCATIONAL LEADERSHIP IN CHINA

System Analysis

DUAL RETIREMENT POLICIES

The differences and the unfair policies in the retirement age between males and females in educational institutions hamper women from being promoted and shorten women's career life in their participation in educational leadership. Take the selection of administrative cadres. For instance, the fact that women retire five years earlier than men will be taken into consideration. Consequently, it is usually very difficult for women over 45 to be promoted to midlevel positions and impossible for those over 50 to be promoted to senior leadership positions. This means a great majority of women lose opportunities for promotion, are deprived of access to senior posts in educational leadership and brush past their second opportunity for leadership, despite the rich working and life experience they now have.

Table 12.4. Female School Principals and Vice Principals in Guangzhou and Nantong

School Type	Guangzhou			Nantong		
	Total Number	Number of Female Principals	Proportion of Female Principals	Total Number	Number of Female Principals	Proportion of Female Principals
Primary School	366	217	59.29%	1,652	248	15%
Secondary School	341	107	31.38%	1,032	47	4.6%

Table 12.5. Female School Principals in Guangzhou and Nantong

School Type	Guangzhou			Nantong		
	Total Number	Number of Female Principals	Proportion of Female Principals	Total Number	Number of Female Principals	Proportion of Female Principals
Primary School	201	106	52.74%	985	115	11.7%
Secondary School	119	27	22.69%	371	8	2.2%

LESS DEVELOPED WOMEN'S NONGOVERNMENTAL ORGANIZATIONS The success of women depends on diverse concrete help and ardent support from other high-level female mentors. If most mentors are female leaders or managers in their profession, a favorable environment for the success of women can be formed. Such models have been adopted in the success of women in American universities or colleges (Bao Lei, 2004). It will be beneficial for women's individual development and the improvement of their overall social status to found women's nongovernmental organizations and create more opportunities and conditions under which they can communicate with each other, learn from each other and encourage each other. Since the 1990s, women's nongovernmental organizations in China have developed, represented by the growth of Women's Federations. Women's professional organizations have been established, such as Capital Female Professors' Sodality and Chinese Female Judges' Association. However, due to the deficiency of social networks, lack of funds, people's lack of knowledge about nongovernmental organizations and other factors, these women's organizations are unable to meet the need for the growth of female groups.

Culture Analysis

WOMEN'S ROLE IN FAMILY AND MEN'S ROLE IN SOCIETY In contemporary Chinese society, the traditional ethic that men are superior to women no longer occupies the mainstream of thinking in social culture, and the notion that men and women are equal is gradually taking deep root among people. Women in the domain of education generally think highly of their own competence. Some surveys show that female intellectuals share similar opinions toward intelligence and talents, and that there is no inborn difference between sexes—each has its own merits. Some 91.1% of interviewees felt they would succeed in their career if they worked hard.

However, women are often caught between the pursuit of professional roles and prescribed traditional roles due to the gendered division of labor in traditional Chinese culture. Women administer the private domain of the home and family whereas men administer the public domains of work and the regulation of the wider society. This at times can seem irreconcilable. The traditional moral ethics for women is that woman should be a good wife and good mother, supporting her husband and nurturing her children. These are also social value identity and assessment criteria for women in China even today.

Xiudi Fan surveyed 110 male teachers and 127 female teachers in Tongji University on the perceptions of female faculty members regarding marriage, family and career in higher education. She found that 43.6% of female faculty members agreed that a successful husband makes a wife honorable and that working well is not better than marrying well; and 60.2% female faculty members would sacrifice their own career for their spouse if he had better prospects in his career development. Regarding personal energy, 17.9% female faculty members devote most of their energy to supporting their husband's work, while 26.0% spent most of their energy doing domestic chores and nurturing their children. These women are willing to sacrifice their own career, to transfer their entrepreneurial spirit and initiative to their husband, and to realize their own value through their husband's success. They even think that their husband's success is their own success (Wan Qionghua, 2002).

As can be seen from these responses, although female teachers don't have a lower assessment of their own competence, the standards of value orientation toward women in social culture make it very hard for female teachers to devote as much energy to their career as men do. The energy required by domestic and family life limits women's achievement motivation, initiative consciousness and orientation for their own professional development.

GENDERED PROFESSIONS FOR WOMEN It has been noted that the proportion of women's involvement in educational leadership declines as school levels proceed from preschool education to tertiary education. However, women involved in school and higher education leadership are not proportionate to those employed in preschool education. What can account for such unparalleled success in women's involvement in school and tertiary education leadership compared with that in preschool education?

The Chinese culture formed on the traditional division of gendered labor (that women administer the private domain of home/family whereas men administer the public domains of work and the regulation of the wider society) makes people live in the gender stereotype recognized by social culture. In China, it is universally agreed that women are suited to work in the domain of preschool education, which is seen as a woman's job. Women are thought to be born with a maternal instinct, demonstrated by the process of childbearing and nurturing; women show more affection to children by nature. Consequently, the public accepts that women are well engaged in preschool education, while men are considered to be impatient, crude, and not good at taking care of children. Social cultural character images make it extremely hard for men to want to take this job.

Furthermore, besides being one's means of earning a living, the occupation represents the social status of those engaged in this occupation. The traditional social notion is that everyone is able to take care of children, though in different ways. Therefore, preschool education is not professional and is regarded as having lower social prestige in comparison with other, more "professional" occupations. In addition, at present 55.3% of the kindergartens in China are privately run (DDPME, 2006). They thus have to raise funds on their own, so most kindergarten teachers are lower paid and have few benefits. Kindergarten teachers have lower social status, making it hard to attract men to work in kindergartens in China.

The traditional social images of women limit their participation in school leadership. It is thought in the traditional gender culture that women have innate traits characteristically described as emotional, careful and prudent, while men are thought to be assertive, rational and rugged. Women's character images don't quite coincide with the competence required for administrators, and so women are not thought to be as adaptable as men are to leading roles at school and university levels. For instance, a survey on elementary school and secondary school principals reveals that when asked, "Male or female, who do you think is more suited to be the principal?" a great majority of people think both can take the principal post and it has nothing to do with gender but with personal qualities. When further asked, "Who do you think are more suited to the leading role as secondary school principal or elementary school principal?" 78.30% people hold the view that women are more suited to be elementary school principals while men are more suited to be secondary school principals. In the interview, quite a few principals mentioned that working in elementary school is more concrete and trivial and female principals just naturally have such attributes as being careful, being prudent, etc. However, men are more suited to being secondary school principals because they are good at considering more "important" macro-level matters and issues (Bai Libo, 2005). Such findings coincide with those in our survey in Guangzhou: there are more female elementary school principals but more male secondary school principals. Given these female images and leading images at school level and the differentiation in the traditional division of gender

labor that men administer and women assist, it is quite obvious that women obtain more assistant managing posts in secondary and tertiary education.

DUAL ROLES OF WOMEN IN EDUCATIONAL LEADERSHIP Women are endowed with the physical abilities of childbearing and breast-feeding, which are extended culturally such that women's primary role is to shoulder all domestic work by the traditional division of gender labor. Although the notion of equality between men and women enables women to step out of the domestic domain and enter the public domain of work to pursue a career, the inertia of cultural moral ethics on the traditional division of gender labor still plays a role. Professional women in the public domain continue to shoulder the duty in their families, the personal domestic unpaid field. Social cultural norms call for their attention to both—to be fit for professional posts and to take good care of household work. According to the statistics in the survey on Chinese women's social status, on average women spend 2.73 times as much time as men on domestic chores and women spend 2.48 times as much time as men in urban settings in China (Zhang Aishu, 2006). When they are unable to combine their work and family roles, if they pay more attention to the former at the expense of the latter, not only won't they gain wide social identity but they also will feel ashamed in emotion and responsibility. Female teachers make more efforts to succeed in their career than men. Due to the differences in pressure, some female teachers have lower motivation for career success.

Moreover, it is well recognized in the modern social culture that successful female leaders should play dual roles, balancing their family duties and leadership responsibilities. In contrast with men, women are short of enough energy to devote to work, which is the main concern facing high-level leaders when selecting female candidates for leadership positions. Such realistic concern and the dual roles make women lose many opportunities to access and occupy educational leadership positions. Women leaders in education have much more pressure than male leaders, and they have to deal with a lot of conflicts in order to play the dual roles well. Compared with male leaders in education, women leaders must expend much more effort for career success because of the dual roles.

However, it should be noted that the increasing number of female research supervisors under 40 years old in tertiary education not only reflects our great progress in higher education in the last decade but also the improvement against those barriers for young women to participate in academic leadership at higher education levels.

REFERENCES CITED

Bai Libo. (2005). Investigation of decision-making images of primary and secondary school principals. *Journal of Education Development Research, 2B*, 80.

Bao Lei. Pushing more women to the level of social management exploration and free views. In Yang Yuhong. (2004). *Research on the growing of primary and secondary school female principals.* Nanjing: Nanjing Normal University, 26, 35.

DDPME (Department of Development and Planning of Ministry of Education). (2006). *China Education Statistical Yearbook 2005.* Beijing: People's Education Press, 6, 69, 145, 162, 181, 184–185.

Gan Kaipeng. (2006). Equality and segregation: An analysis of the present situation of women's higher education. *Journal of Learning and Education Research, 9.*

Guangzhou Education Bureau. Information collection and compilation in 2007 on the website of Education Bureau of Yuexiu District in Guangzhou and Education Bureau of Haizhu District in Guangzhou. (The statistics are incomplete.)

He Qiong. (2006). *The support to women's participation in politics since the reforming and opening.* Changsha: Hunan Normal University.

Jue Wei. (1995). *Women's education in China.* Hangzhou: Zhejiang Education Press, 387, 406.

Liu Huagang. (2006). The developing situation of women teachers in colleges in Guangxi in view of social gender. *Higher Education Forum, 4*(3), 6.

Liu Liqun. (2002). The perspective on the role of female administrators in the field of higher education. *Education Exploration, 6*(98), 100.

Liu Ping. (2006). *Problems and solutions of teachers' gender structure in kindergarten.* Changsha: Hunan Normal University.

Ma Wanhua. (2007). Development and participation: Some problems of female education of higher learning. *Journal of Hebei Normal University (Educational Science Edition), 3.*

SCILSNC (Selection and Compilation of Important Literature Since the 14th National Congress) (middle). Beijing: People's Publishing House, 1997, 1492.

Wan Qionghua. (2002). On initiative consciousness of women teachers in universities in respect of their participation. *Journal of Henan Vocational-Technical Teachers College (Vocational Education Edition),5*(25), 28.

———. (2004). Negative effects and solutions of traditional gender role on women teachers in higher education institutes. *Journal of Exploration and Free Views, 1.*

Wei Yu. (1995). *Women's education in China.* Hangzhou: Zhejiang Education Press, 405.

Xu Yanli. (2006). The analysis of the current situation of female administrators in the field of higher education. *Journal of Northwestern Polytechnical University (Social Sciences), 4.*

Yang Yuhong. (2004). *Research on the growing of primary and secondary school female principals.* Nanjing: Nanjing Normal University, 11, 26, 35.

Zhang Aishu. (2006). Moderate balance of female directors between self-recognition and social identity. *Journal of China University of Mining and Technology Social Sciences, 4*, 100–104.

Zhang Jianqi. (1997). The research on the status of female teachers in higher education. *Journal of Research on Education, Tsinghua University, 4.*

Zhang Mingyun. (2000). The status, barriers and trend of Chinese women's participation in higher education. *Journal of China Higher Education Research, 1.*

Zhao Xiezhu. (2007). The analysis of female teachers' group in higher education. *Journal of College (Study & Evaluation), 2.*

Zheng Haihang Cui Jiaying. (2006). Double factors of leadership ability and communication. *Journal of Economic Management, New Management, 5.*

CHAPTER 13

Women and Educational Leadership in New Zealand and Melanesia

Jane Strachan

INTRODUCTION

New Zealand is situated in the southern Pacific Ocean. It is a small island nation with a population of just 4.1 million (Statistics New Zealand, 2006). Maori are the indigenous people of New Zealand, the *tangata whenua*,[1] and make up 14.6% of the total population. New Zealand has the world's largest population of Pacific Islands people (6.9% of the total population), from Polynesia, Melanesia and Micronesia. The number of Pacific Islands nations represented is vast (Statistics New Zealand, 2006). New Zealand's strong connection to the people of these Pacific Island nations is not just to people resident in New Zealand. The New Zealand government's largest international aid program is to the Pacific (New Zealand Aid and Development Agency [NZAID]). Because of high levels of poverty, Melanesia[2] (Papua New Guinea, Vanuatu and the Solomon Islands) receives a high proportion of that aid, a great deal of which goes into the education sector (NZAID, 2007).

For the following reasons, I have chosen to focus on Melanesia as well as New Zealand. First, the Pacific is very diverse—there are as many cultural differences as there are commonalities. Although culturally diverse, the countries of Melanesia are relatively ethnically homogeneous. Second, as mentioned earlier, Melanesia is the region of the South Pacific that is poorest and therefore graphically illustrates some of the issues I elaborate on later. Finally, I have spent the last seven years working in Melanesia, in particular Vanuatu and the Solomon Islands, and I have some personal knowledge of life in those countries, particularly for women.[3] I speak the lingua franca (pidgin) and have people there I call family and who also call me family, including a Ni Vanuatu[4] granddaughter. I and her mother do not want her to have her opportunities limited because of her gender.

I focus mainly on the primary and secondary school sectors in New Zealand and Melanesia.[5] I also give examples from the early childhood and tertiary sectors. I first explore the position of women in educational leadership in New Zealand, including Maori and Pa-

cific women. Second, I explain some of the current issues faced by New Zealand women when in, and trying to access, educational leadership. Next, I present the situation for Melanesian women, including their representation in educational leadership and the factors that constrain their ability to be involved in formal leadership. Finally, because New Zealand is the largest and wealthiest South Pacific nation, I argue that New Zealand has an obligation to assist and support women in its wider Pacific neighborhood and that as privileged women we need to step out from our comfort zone and cross international borders in support of our Melanesian sisters.

This argument is not mine alone. It is predicated on years of working with Melanesian women and listening to what it is that they want for themselves and their daughters and how we might help them achieve that.

NEW ZEALAND WOMEN AND EDUCATIONAL LEADERSHIP

New Zealand has a reputation as a country where women are well represented in employment at all levels. On the surface that would appear to be so. In comparison to many other countries (for example Melanesia) women have gained ground. In 2005, our prime minister, chief justice, attorney general, governor general and the CEO of Telecom (New Zealand's largest company) were all women. However, if one digs deeper the picture is somewhat different. Women continue to be underrepresented in many key areas of employment; for example, 32.2% of politicians and 19.2% of newspaper editors are women (Human Rights Commission, 2006). The situation for ethnic-minority women is worse.

Since the 1970s in New Zealand, feminist scholars have been at the forefront of exposing the extent of women's underrepresentation in educational leadership positions and the reasons for that underrepresentation (for example, Court, 1993; Korndorffer, 1992; Malcolm, 1978; Neville, 1988; Strachan, 1993; Thomson, 1988; Watson, 1989; Whitcombe, 1979, 1980, 1995; Wilson, 1995). In 1980, the Department of Education in New Zealand produced the *Teacher Career and Promotion Study*, which for the first time presented sex-disaggregated data on the position of men and women in the teaching service. These reports provided data on, among other things, the representation of men and women in senior positions in schools and tertiary organizations, salary levels, rates of application for promotion, and the reasons why women do, or do not, apply for promotion. Annual sex-disaggregated data continue to be produced by the Ministry of Education (formerly the Department of Education). However, the data are now mainly statistical and lack some of the critical analysis of earlier reports.

Over the last two decades in New Zealand, teaching has become an increasingly feminized profession. For example, in 2004, 80.5% of primary teachers and 55.7% of secondary teachers were women (Ministry of Education, 2006). The only exception is early childhood education, which has always been the domain of women (92.4%). However, despite the increased feminization and the increased number of women in senior positions, women remain underrepresented in senior positions in state schools and universities and the extent of that underrepresentation is still large. In 2005 in primary education, 43.5% of principals were women, yet women made up more than 80% of the primary teaching workforce. In secondary education, 28.8% of principals were women, yet they were almost 56% of the secondary teaching workforce. The proportion of teachers by gender who are principals is 3% of women and 11% of men. That is, if you are a man you are almost four times more likely to be a principal than a woman is. However, at 80%, women's representation is much higher in management positions (Ministry of Education, 2006). So there is a pool of women gaining leadership experience that will help prepare them for more senior leadership.

The situation is no better in the university sector. In 2005, 13.8% of professors and 19.9% of associate professors were women, yet women were 35.8% of full-time academics. What is also cause for concern here is that over a two-year period (2003–2005) the percentage of women professors dropped by 1.9% (Human Rights Commission, 2006).

Maori and Pacific Women
Only recently has the New Zealand Ministry of Education collected data on the ethnicity of the teaching workforce and its representation in senior positions (Fitzgerald, 2003). However, Fitzgerald is correct when she asserts that "these data are not readily available in

publicly released documents" (2003, p. 437). To obtain the data for this chapter a special request had to be made to the New Zealand Ministry of Education. The raw data they supplied show that there has been an increase in the number of Maori who are principals, from 166 in 2002 to 290 in 2007, and women outnumber men. However, Maori are underrepresented in teaching (primary 11% and secondary 8%) when compared to their representation in the total population (14.2%) (Ministry of Education 2006; Statistics New Zealand, 2006). This is cause for concern, as Maori make up 21.4% of the student school population (Ministry of Education, 2004). Maori students lack male and female Maori role models in educational leadership. As Fitzgerald (2003) pointed out, many Maori will be principals of *kura kaupapa* and *wharekura* schools[6] where the ability to speak the Maori language and knowledge of Maori culture are considered essential. Few Maori are principals of mainstream schools. The lack of role models for Maori is a particular issue for students in mainstream schools.

Pacific people are grossly underrepresented in educational leadership. Pacific women are principals in approximately equal numbers to their male colleagues; however, in 2007 both men and women were just 0.5% of all principals (Ministry of Education, 2007, raw data). Pacific teachers in New Zealand are 3% of primary teachers and 2% of secondary teachers, yet Pacific people are 6.6% of the total population and 8.9% of the total student population (Ministry of Education, 2006; Statistics New Zealand, 2006). Pacific people are underrepresented in teaching and educational leadership and Pacific students have very few Pacific role models in educational leadership.

Underrepresentation in the teaching workforce results in underrepresentation in leadership, and this is a particular issue for minority cultures.[7] However, the issue goes farther, as fewer Maori and Pacific students than Pakeha (European New Zealander) or Asian students leave school with qualifications (Ministry of Education, 2006). This limits their access to tertiary education and their ability to enter the teaching profession.

These data alert us to a number of continuing issues. First, women continue to be underrepresented in leadership. Their numbers are increasing, but the rate of that increase is still slow. In 1988, I wrote that at the then-current rate of increase it would take women at least 50 years before they were represented in senior positions in proportion to their representation in the teaching workforce (Thomson, 1988). It is now 20 years since that prediction, and the increasing feminization of the teaching workforce has exacerbated women's underrepresentation and made it difficult for them to catch up in senior positions.

Second, the data available on women's representation in senior positions are not consistently reported, and the data on Maori women and Pacific women in senior positions are not regularly published. Finally, data on the type of schools women lead (for example, rural, urban, and decile ranking)[8] are also not routinely published, but are available on request. What the data reveal is that over a period of nine years (1998–2007), women are more likely to be principals of rural schools (52%) than urban schools (39%), and are more likely to be principals of low-decile (52%) rather than high-decile (45%) schools. In my doctoral study on feminist educational leadership, one of the participant principals ("Jill") commented that women were likely to be principals of low socioeconomic schools (those with low decile rankings) as they were more likely to have a social justice leadership agenda or be principals of schools that required hard work, such as rural schools with a teaching principal (Strachan, 1999). The data support her prediction.

THE ISSUES FOR NEW ZEALAND WOMEN
Even though some progress has been made with regard to women's participation in senior leadership in education, the issues today are similar to those of 20 years ago. There are issues related to school location, the socioeconomic status of the school (decile ranking), the ethnicity of the principal, women balancing family and work, women's resistance to managerialism and the panic over the failure of boys, which can result in discriminatory employment practices by some boards of trustees.

As reported earlier, the statistics indicate that women are more likely to be principals of small rural schools and low-decile schools, which bring with them special challenges. Rural schools "are the least desirable schools combining both teaching and principal responsibilities" (Brooking, 2005, p. 135). This is very hard work that often requires long hours and high levels of stress (Hodgen and Wylie, 2005). Urban schools are the larger schools and are dominated by male principals. The pay for principals is based on pupil numbers, so the larger the school the higher the salary for the principal, exacerbating the pay gap between males and females in the teaching workforce. This is reflected in the general workforce where on average women

earn just over 80% of what men earn (New Zealand Council of Trade Unions, 2005).

The lower the decile ranking of the school, the higher the proportion of Maori and Pacific students in the school. Low-decile schools are more likely to have a woman principal. As with their colleagues in schools with teaching principals, this role brings with it unique challenges, including long hours of work as principals strive to offer culturally appropriate learning opportunities. This makes the work/life balance very difficult to achieve. Recent research indicates women's family responsibilities continue to affect their professional lives (Court, 2004; Equal Employment Opportunity Trust, 2007; Fitzgerald and Moore, 2005). This is particularly so for Maori and Pacific women who have multiple roles, family and community obligations (often unpaid) that require extensive amounts of time out of (and sometimes within) working hours (Brown, Devine, Leslie, Paiti, Sila'ila'i, Umaki and Williams, 2005; Mara, 1995).

Some research findings suggest that women are uncomfortable with[9] and resist a managerial, masculinist style of leadership (Blackmore, 1993; Court, 1998; Strachan, 1999). Some women would prefer to stay in teaching or middle management positions where the managerial demands are fewer (Post Primary Teacher's Association, 2005). Others challenge and resist leading in a masculinist way and create their own feminist leadership agenda (Strachan, 1999). Others develop more democratic leadership practices such as shared leadership (Court, 2003). What this indicates is that women are not just passive observers. Rather, they are active in creating ways they can work in educational leadership that best suits them.

In the 1980s in New Zealand, there was a campaign called "Girls Can Do Anything." The purpose was to encourage girls to broaden their subject choices at school and, in doing so, their career choices. At this time, girls were academically outperformed by boys, left school earlier with fewer qualifications, and usually chose gender-stereotypical careers. The campaign was moderately successful. Girls now academically outperform boys and dominate numerically in undergraduate degrees (Ministry of Education, 2006). However, recently there has been concern about "boys' failure." With the increasing feminization of the teaching profession, some boards of trustees (who appoint principals) have expressed concern over the lack of male role models for boys and the need to redress what they see as the gender imbalance in schools. This disadvantages women applicants. Brooking (2005) comments:

Another populist discourse reported in the media and provoking moral panic, which has been taken up by many boards [Boards of Trustees], was the link between "feminized schooling" and "failing boys." This has resulted in appointment decisions based on the perceived need for male role models for boys. (p. 132)

MELANESIAN WOMEN AND EDUCATIONAL LEADERSHIP

Melanesia women's participation in decision-making is difficult to track as sex-disaggregated data are not systematically collected. However, if women's national political representation is taken as a measure of women's participation in decision-making the situation is not good. Papua New Guinea has one woman member of Parliament (Reilly and Phillpot, 2002), the Solomon Islands has none (Pollard, 2006) and Vanuatu has two (Strachan and Dalesa, 2005). Women in Melanesia and elsewhere in the developing world face barriers to accessing leadership not experienced to the same extent or in the same way by women in New Zealand.

It is particularly difficult to obtain statistical data on the representation of women in educational leadership positions in Melanesia. While statistical data are not readily available or not available at all, anecdotal evidence is plentiful. Only Vanuatu has carried out a comprehensive gender analysis of the education sector (Strachan, 2002). In Vanuatu women are grossly underrepresented in principals' positions. In the primary sector, 30.4% of principals are women, yet women are 50.1% of primary teachers. In the secondary sector, 8% of principals are women, yet women are 38.4% of secondary teachers (Strachan, 2002).

In addition, all the directors of education[10] and members of the Teaching Service Commission in Vanuatu are males (Strachan, 2002).[11] The situation is very similar in both the Solomon Islands and Papua New Guinea. Although data are not available on the representation of women in senior positions across the education sector in the Solomon Islands (Malasa, 2006), there is a large imbalance in the number of males and females employed in MEHRD (the Ministry of Education and Human Resource Development). In 2004, of the 169 positions, 45 were filled by women (26.6%) and the more senior the position, the fewer women there were (Ministry of Education and Human Resource Development, 2004).

Sex-disaggregated statistics on the teaching workforce are regularly collected in the Solomon Islands, but they do not provide information on the gender representation of principals (Ministry of Education and Human Resource Development, 2005). However,

I have had many conversations with people working in education in the Solomon Islands and Papua New Guinea who readily acknowledge that women are grossly underrepresented in educational leadership (personal communication with Donald Malasa, May 31, 2007), which reflects their representation in formal leadership in other sectors (Pollard, 2006).

When Bessie Kilavanwa was undertaking her master's research on women principals in PNG, many schools had no women teachers and only one woman was principal of a national secondary school, and PNG has a population of over four million, similar to that of New Zealand (Kilavanwa, 2004). Women do hold some leadership positions in Melanesia, but they are usually located in their communities and in their churches and often women do not perceive these as leadership roles or see themselves as leaders (Strachan and Saunders, 2007). As with Maori and Pacific students in New Zealand, Melanesian girls lack women role models in leadership positions in education, in politics and, to a lesser extent, in the community.

Although access to educational leadership remains a problem for women in New Zealand and a significant problem in Melanesia, the issues facing New Zealand women do not play out in the same way in Melanesia. Melanesians are the majority culture so most principals are Melanesian, but very, very few are women. Gender thus plays a larger role in women's underrepresentation in Melanesia than it does in New Zealand.

I now explore some of the contributing factors to women's underrepresentation such as girls' and women's access to education, the impact of culture, literacy and participation rates, and violence against women.

THE ISSUES FOR MELANESIAN WOMEN

Accessing educational leadership begins with girls and women being able to access education. In Melanesia, teaching is not feminized to the same extent as it is in New Zealand. In Melanesian countries such as PNG, the Solomon Islands and Vanuatu, where paid employment opportunities are very limited, teaching is a respected and sought-after career option for both men and women. In these Melanesian countries education is not compulsory, males' education is privileged and females access education at a lower rate than males. Accessing education can be a struggle for girls. Therefore, women are less likely to have the secondary school qualifications necessary to enter teacher education, a situation similar to that for Maori and Pacific women in New Zealand.

Educating females brings with it social and economic advantages to developing countries, including reducing levels of poverty and infant and maternal mortality rates, improved levels of reproductive health and women's participation in decision-making (United Nations Population Fund, 2004). The New Zealand Human Rights Commission recognizes the power of education in reducing poverty:

> It [education] is the primary vehicle by which economically and socially marginalized adults and children can lift themselves out of poverty and obtain the means to participate fully in their communities. Throughout the world, education is seen as one of the best financial investments that a State can make. (Human Rights Commission, 2007, paragraph 2)

However, even when women do have education and experience, women face discrimination when applying for positions. In a small-scale study of three Solomon Islands women educational leaders, the women complained that positions often were given to less experienced and less qualified men. They put this down to cultural attitudes that consider men, not women, should be leaders and the *wantok* system in which jobs are given to relatives (Akao, 2007).

Culture

Culture in Melanesia significantly affects females' ability to participate in education and decision-making at all levels, including educational leadership. Cultural attitudes such as "women belong in the home," "leadership is tough" (therefore women are not suitable) and "the time is not yet right," were identified by Solomon Islands' members of Parliament as the core barriers to women's participation in formal leadership. However, women are very well represented in positions of informal leadership, particularly in the villages and churches. According to Pollard (2006), the roles of men and women in these locations are complementary but separate.

There are many different cultures in Melanesia that sustain and enrich the lives of its people, but women's roles are tightly, culturally prescribed:

> Women are the home makers, food providers tending family plantations/food gardens and/or gathering seafood, caregivers and nurturers of children, the sick and the elderly, pillars of the family, church and village, peacemakers, informal educators. (Vaa, 2006, paragraph 4)

These cultures have evolved over many centuries. Cultural practices vary from island to island and within islands. However, culture does not stand still. It changes over time. This is the case in Melanesia. For example, over the last 150 years Christianity has become central in lives of the people of Melanesia. Douglas (2000) commented that "religion is central to Melanesian individual and collective lives and is attributed practical efficacy as well as spiritual significance" (p. 3). The role of Christianity and traditional practices as constraining and/or liberating forces for women is contested ground, posing questions for which there is no easy answer. Both are powerful and influential forces that cannot be ignored or dismissed as inconsequential. Pollard (2006) commented that Christianity has affected the traditional perspectives of women in leadership, but today it is the churches that bring women together and offer many leadership opportunities: "Women's active participation [in] the informal structure gives them an influential position as change agents" (p. 157). Some research in PNG has shown that Christianity is very influential in how men and women lead schools, including praying for guidance and wisdom and adopting a caring and nurturing approach (Malpo, 2002), which is closely aligned to servant leadership (Pollard, 2006; Sanga and Walker, 2005). Servant leadership is characterized by service to others, submission, humility and truthfulness, and fits with women's stereotypical roles within Melanesian society. It is also less likely to threaten men (Pollard, 2006; Strachan and Saunders, 2007).

From 1998 to 2003, the influential position of women and their willingness to take leadership was graphically illustrated during the civil conflict in the Solomon Islands when the Women for Peace movement negotiated between the warring factions. Although they played a significant role in brokering peace, they were left out of the formal negotiations that were attended only by men. "Clearly women demonstrated leadership as a process of influence and power to empower in this warring situation" (Pollard, 2006, p. 17).

A similar situation occurred in Vanuatu during the struggle for independence. Women played a central role in the struggle yet were shut out when it came to sharing power after independence was gained (Molisa, 2001). The culture of "big man" leadership dominates Melanesian society (Kilavanwa, 2004) as they have traditionally been the warriors, the feast providers and the priests. Pollard argues that there is such a thing as "big woman" leadership but their leadership role in the public sphere is almost invisible. Women are also feast providers and priests but, rather than warriors, they are the peacemakers (Pollard, 2006).

While it is important to preserve those aspects of culture that help sustain and enrich people it is also important to change those aspects that limit people's opportunities based on their gender. Both males and females need to be valued equally in all aspects of their lives, including education. Culture affects girls' and women's ability to access education, which affects literacy rates and their participation in education at all levels.

LITERACY AND PARTICIPATION

Although statistical data are incomplete, they do provide an indication of the situation with respect to the education of girls and women. There are data available on important indicators such as literacy rates and female participation in education. If these are low, as the data indicate, this dramatically reduces females' ability to access tertiary education and therefore their ability to become teachers and educational leaders. Lady Carol Kidu, the only woman member of Parliament in Papua New Guinea, recognized the connection between women's low literacy rate and their access to decision-making. In rural areas the literacy rate for women is particularly low (Kidu, 1997; Netine, 2000).

In PNG, the Solomon Islands and Vanuatu, girls are less likely than boys to attend school. Also, girls are less likely than boys to complete secondary education (UNICEF, 2005). Because there are not enough places for all students who want to go to secondary schools, an examination system culls out the less academically able. Advancement is based strictly on academic results. For example, in Vanuatu only 48% of all students will advance into Year 7 (at about age 13). This occurs again in later years when a similar weeding-out process takes place as students compete for fewer and fewer places in secondary schools.

Girls are as successful as boys in passing the exams but are less likely to take up those places. The reasons for this are mainly culturally embedded. Families have to pay school fees, and if there is not enough money then boys will be chosen to attend school and the girls drop out. Education for girls is not as valued as it is for boys, as girls are the homemakers and are often required to stay at home and look after younger children and the home (Strachan, 2002).

There are also organizational barriers to girls' participation in secondary education. For example, there are few secondary schools in Melanesia, so students

often have to move away from their home and live in school hostels. Fewer hostel beds are provided for girls than for boys (Ministry of Education, 2005). So even if a girl has passed the examination to be able to attend secondary school, she may not be able to because there is no hostel bed for her.

Even for those girls who finish secondary education, rates of participation in tertiary education are low. Girls are less likely to apply for and be awarded scholarships. Participation in tertiary education for citizens of PNG, the Solomon Islands and Vanuatu is dependent upon them being awarded a scholarship from either their own government or the governments of Australia and New Zealand (Strachan and Lapi, 2006). The competition for scholarships is fierce and most go to males, as they are more likely to have completed secondary school. For cultural and safety reasons, women often are discouraged from applying for scholarships by their families (Strachan, 2002).

What this rather eclectic collection of data reveals is the flow-on effect that occurs when girls are unable to access education:

> Low literacy adversely affects women's access to information and technology. Poor educational achievement limits their ability to participate in decision-making processes at the family, community and national levels. The combined resource constraint in turn impairs their capacity to work for change. (Food and Agricultural Organization of the United Nations, 2007, paragraph 2)

Initiatives to improve women's literacy can have wide-ranging benefits, as Netine (2000) describes:

> When a woman is literate there is a change in the family, which enables it to play a more active part in the community development process. Most of all, there is a change in the woman, giving her a feeling of hope and achievement. (p. 50)

VIOLENCE AGAINST WOMEN

In 2003, the United Nations Population Fund (UNFPA) conducted a global survey field enquiry that looked at gender-related issues in the Pacific. PNG, the Solomon Islands and Vanuatu commented that in their cultures "men are considered superior and women are considered subordinate to men. This cultural belief has placed limitations on women's freedoms, movement, opportunities and choices" (Robertson, 2004, pp. 13–14).

Women often face very strong opposition, particularly from men, when they try to operate outside their tightly prescribed cultural roles (Donald, Strachan and Taleo, 2002), which often results in violence against women (Kilavanwa, 2004). As is the case in New Zealand (Chamberlain, 2006; Tan, 2006), women in Melanesia experience very high levels of violence. This is a serious issue that impacts on women's ability to participate in leadership and significantly limits women's opportunities. Even though PNG, the Solomon Islands and Vanuatu have ratified the United Nations Convention on the Elimination of All Forms of Discrimination Against Women (CEDAW), there is little assistance for women who experience violence, especially for women living in rural communities (Robertson, 2004). Bride price, whereby the groom pays his bride's family with money and gifts, is still very commonly practiced and limits women's ability to leave violent relationships as this would mean the bride's family would have to return the bride price, which is often considerable (Amnesty International, 2004).

In both the Solomon Islands and PNG, tribal tensions and warfare have resulted in terrible violence against women and children. Michael Agua, a teacher and community leader in Kup[12] (PNG), commented at the Human Rights Day celebration in 2002:

> There is no law and order or justice system here in Kup. Women are raped regularly, which is taken as seriously as school children stealing pencils, or stealing *kaukau* (food) from a garden. Women are accused of sorcery and killed. Widows are abused and forced to marry and have sex against their will.... There are no women's human rights in Kup. (Garap, 2004, p. 5)

In PNG violence against women is considered normal by much of the population. The threat of rape, assault and sexual violence means women cannot freely move around or attend school, work and church. AIDS infection among women is reaching epidemic proportions, and this is exacerbated by the high levels of sexual violence. Amnesty International (2004, paragraph 1) reports, "The state's failure to enable women to become safely involved in civil and economic life severely constrains the full use of resources for national development."

The high levels of violence against women in Melanesia, including controlling behavior by male relatives and husbands (personal communication with Dulcie Paina, 28 June 2007), make it impossible for women to fully participate in leadership, deny women their basic human rights and directly contravene Article 3 of CEDAW guaranteeing women's human rights.

SOME CONCLUDING THOUGHTS

Women's underrepresentation in educational leadership is a human rights issue and a social justice issue, both in New Zealand and Melanesia. It should concern us all. Many feminist educational leaders have widened their social justice agenda to include other marginalized and disadvantaged groups, for example ethnic minorities, the disabled, and men and women of a different sexual orientation (Strachan, 1999). Those of us who claim to have social justice as a platform for our leadership work should be very concerned by the social injustices and lack of women's human rights in Melanesia. Rapp (2002) suggests:

> Leaders for social justice . . . resist, dissent, rebel, subvert, possess oppositional imaginations, and are committed to transforming oppressive and exploitive social relations in and out of schools. (p. 226)

We can resist, dissent and rebel in the local and the international arenas. While not wanting to diminish the situation for women in New Zealand (and we must continue to work to improve women's representation in educational leadership in New Zealand), the difficulties women face in Melanesia are greater. We need to look beyond women's representation in leadership to the underlying causes of that underrepresentation. Women's invisibility in formal leadership positions has its roots in violations against women, such as low participation rates in education, violence, low literacy rates, AIDS, and cultural and male hegemonic practices that deny women access to equal participation in society.

Women in both New Zealand and Melanesia have been active in working for their own liberation. In some countries this can be hard and dangerous work, as those working in the Women for Peace movement in the Solomon Islands experienced (Paina, 2000; Pollard, 2006). In New Zealand, the human and financial resources needed to support change, although never enough, are more plentiful and accessible than they are in Melanesia. New Zealand also has legislation, including employment laws that protect women to some extent. Although not easy, women can take legal action if they have been unjustly treated. Melanesian women may have some protection under the laws of their country but do not have the same access to the justice system and its services. It is expensive, women often do not know their rights and, for rural women in particular, lawyers and the courts are far away.

Melanesia is mainly reliant upon international funding to resource initiatives both within the government and the nongovernmental organization (NGO) sectors. External support is crucial. As women leaders we need to be involved in offering external support such as lobbying for appropriate legislation to protect women and for the New Zealand government to financially support the CEDAW reporting process in PNG and the Solomon Islands.

We must resist imposing Western colonial practices and solutions. Those of us who are not "of the culture" must listen to how women in Melanesia might want that support to manifest. They know how best to work within their own cultural context. The support of both men and the churches is critical and needs to be included in any strategy for change (Pollard, 2006). Men, as Michael Agua mentioned earlier, can be powerful advocates for change and are more likely to be listened to by other men. The churches offer women informal leadership opportunities and experiences that can help prepare women for more formal leadership positions. Changing deeply embedded practices, attitudes and beliefs is slow. Making visible the factors that constrain women's lives and deny them human rights is important. Silence perpetuates discrimination.

So what can we do? We can urge our education unions to be concerned about and active in working for women's human rights internationally, as well as nationally. We can support highly respected NGOs such as Amnesty International and the Association of Women's Rights in Development (AWID) that speak out about social injustices and the abuse of women's human rights, including violence against women. We can join online lobby groups such as NetAid, which works to reduce poverty and promote education for girls and women. All these organizations provide opportunities for us to join global campaigns. Through working with local NGOs, such as the National Council of Women and Volunteer Service Abroad, we can lobby the New Zealand government to increase its aid budget and give a greater focus to making the aid dollar work for women's human rights.

Using the Internet we can give support without leaving our homes. The Internet provides us with easy access to information from some highly respected sources about women globally. The Internet can bring these women into our workplaces and homes so we can better understand their lives. We can use blogs to discuss and debate the issues. The Internet provides us with the opportunity to step out from our local comfort zone and cross international borders in support of our sisters. When invited we can provide our professional expertise, either free of charge or at rates that are aligned to the Melanesian economic context. There is a huge development consultancy industry in Melanesia and elsewhere in the developing world where expatriate consultants can earn very large salaries by selling their expertise to very poor people. That is unethical. Above all, we must not remain silent and we must act.

NOTES

1. *Tangata whenua* means first people of the land.

2. Melanesia includes Papua New Guinea, the Solomon Islands, Vanuatu, Fiji and New Caledonia. In this chapter I focus on Papua New Guinea, the Solomon Islands, and Vanuatu, and I use Melanesia to refer only to these three.

3. I worked for two and a half years full-time as an adviser to the Director of Women's Affairs in Vanuatu. Currently I am directing a project to build teacher education in the Solomon Islands. Although I have not visited Papua New Guinea, I have taught a number of women from PNG and supervised their theses on women and leadership.

4. Ni Vanuatu are the indigenous people of Vanuatu.

5. Primary schools (elementary schools) and secondary schools (high schools).

6. *Kura kaupapa* and *wharekura* are primary and secondary schools in New Zealand that teach in the Maori language and have a philosophical approach based in Maori culture.

7. At this writing, the data on Maori and Pacific representation in tertiary education (staff and students) were being updated by the New Zealand Ministry of Education and so were not available.

8. Each school is given a decile ranking based on the socioeconomic status of the student population. The rankings are 1 (very low) to 10 (very high). Low-decile schools generally have a high Maori and/or Pacific Island student population. High-decile schools have a high Pakeha (European New Zealander) student population.

9. I am not suggesting here that all women are uncomfortable with a managerial, masculinist style of leadership.

10. Since the gender analysis was completed a woman has been appointed to one of the director positions.

11. The Teaching Service Commission is the authority that appoints principals.

12. Kup is a subdistrict of Simbu Province in the highlands of Papua New Guinea.

REFERENCES CITED

Akao, S. M. (2007). *Leadership in Solomon Islands schools: The experiences of Solomon Island women.* Unpublished Master of Educational Leadership Research Report. Hamilton: University of Waikato.

Amnesty International. (2004). Solomon Islands women confronting violence. Retrieved 23 June 2007 from http://web.amnesty.org/library/index/engasa430012004.

Blackmore, J. (1993). In the shadow of men: The historical construction of administration as a "masculinist" enterprise. In J. Blackmore and J. Kenway (Eds.). *Gender matters in educational administration* (pp. 27–48). London: The Falmer Press.

Brooking, K. (2005). Boards of trustees' selection of primary principals in New Zealand. *Delta, 57*(1/2), 117–140.

Brown, T., Devine, N., Leslie, E., Paiti, M., Sila'ila'i, E., and Williams, J. (2005). *Pasifika teachers in secondary education: Issues, possibilities and strategies.* Hamilton: Wilf Malcolm Research Institute, University of Waikato.

Chamberlain, J. (2006). Our shame: North and South. Retrieved 24 June 2007 from the Australia/New Zealand Reference Centre database.

Court, M. (2004). Work/life balance as a social justice issue for school principals: What can we learn from innovatory practice? *New Zealand Journal of Educational Leadership, 19,* 63–78.

———. (2003).Towards democratic leadership: Co-principal initiatives. *International Journal of Leadership in Education, 6*(2), 161–183.

———. (1998). Women challenging managerialism: Devolution dilemmas in the establishment of co-principalships in primary schools in Aotearoa/New Zealand. *School Leadership and Management, 18*(1), 35–57.

———. (1993). 1893–1993: How far have we come in women's employment in education? *New Zealand Annual Review of Education 3,* 81–128.

Donald, I., Strachan, J., and Taleo, H. (2002). Slo slo: Increasing women's participation in parliament in Vanuatu. *Development Bulletin, 59,* 54–57.

Douglas, B. (2000). Introduction: Hearing Melanesian women. In B. Douglas (Ed.). *Women and governance from the grassroots of Melanesia* pp. 3–7. Canberra: The National University of Australia.

Equal Employment Opportunities Trust. (2007). *Work-life balance, employee engagement and discretionary effort.* Auckland: Equal Employment Opportunities Trust.

Fitzgerald, T. (2003). Interrogating orthodox voices: Gender, ethnicity and educational leadership. *School Leadership and Management, 23*(4), 431–444.

Fitzgerald, T., and Moore, W. (2005). Balancing or juggling? The challenges of professional and domestic work for women principals. *New Zealand Journal of Educational Leadership, 20*(2), 59–69.

Food and Agriculture Organization of the United Nations. (2007). Asia and the Pacific region: Rural women's equality challenges. Rural women's educational status: Regional overview. Retrieved 20 May 2007 from http://www.fao.org/docrep/008/af348e/af348e06.htm.

Garap, S. (2004). Kup women for peace: Women taking action to build peace and influence community decision-making. *State Society and Governance in Melanesia.* Discussion paper. Canberra: Research School of Pacific and Asian Studies, Australian National University.

Hodgen, E., and Wylie, C. (2005). *Stress and wellbeing among New Zealand principals.* Wellington: New Zealand Council for Educational Research.

Kidu, C. (1997). Information and women in Papua New Guinea. Paper presented at the 1997 Waigani Seminar. Retrieved 20 May 2007 from http://www.pngbuai.com/600technology/information/waigani/info-women/WS97-sec12-kidu.html.

Kilavanwa, B. (2004). *Women leaders in schools in Papua New Guinea: Why do women leaders labor in the shadows?* Unpublished master's thesis. Hamilton, New Zealand: University of Waikato.

Korndorffer, W. (1992). Look like a lady, act like a man and work like a dog: Senior women and equal employment opportunities at Victoria University or Wellington. In S. Olsson (Ed.). *The gender factor,* pp. 127–138. Palmerston North: Dunmore Press.

Malasa, D. (2006). *A study to investigate the low participation of girls in Solomon Islands secondary schools.* Unpublished research report. Hamilton: University of Waikato.

Malcolm, M. (1978). The almost invisible woman. *Set, 2,* Item 12.

Malpo, K. K. (2002). The influence of cultural traditions on school principals in Papua New Guinea. In P. Ninnes (Ed.). *Internationalizing education in the Asia-Pacific region,* pp. 379–388. Armidale: University of New England.

Mara, D. (1995). *Te puai no te vahine: Pacific Islands women, education and power.* Paper presented to the New Zealand Association of Research in Education Conference, Massey University, Palmerston North, 7–10 December 1995.

Molisa, G. (2001). *Preliminary CEDAW report.* Port Vila: Department of Women's Affairs.

Netine, E. (2000). A literacy program for women in Vanuatu. In B. Douglas (Ed.). *Women and governance from the grassroots of Melanesia,* pp. 17–20. Canberra: The National University of Australia.

Neville, M. (1988). *Promoting women: Successful women in educational management.* Auckland: Longman Paul.

New Zealand Council of Trade Unions. (2005). Pay gap for women widens. Retrieved 25 May 2007 from http://www.union.org.nz/news/524.html.

New Zealand Human Rights Commission. (2007). Chapter 15: The right to education He tāpapa mātauranga, Introduction. Retrieved 23 June 2007 from http://www.hrc.co.nz/report/chapters/chapter15/education01.html.

———. (2006). New Zealand census of women's participation 2006. Wellington: Human Rights Commission.

New Zealand International Aid and Development Agency. (2007). Key NZAID measures/statistics—May 2007. Retrieved 25 June 2007 from http://www.nzaid.govt.nz/library/publications/corporate/key-measures.html.

New Zealand Ministry of Education. (2004). *Education counts.* Retrieved 4 May 2007 from http://education-counts.edcentre.govt.nz/statistics/schooling/teaching-staff-at-march04.html.

———. (2005). *Gender equity policy and action plan 2005–2015.* Port Vila: Vanuatu Ministry of Education.

———. (2006). *Education counts.* Retrieved 4 May 2007 from http://educationcounts.edcentre.govt.nz/statistics/tertiary/resources.html.

Paina, D. T. (2000). Peacemaking in the Solomon Islands: The experiences of the Guadalcanal Women for Peace Movement. *Development Bulletin, 53,* 47–48.

Pollard, A. A. (2006). *Gender and leadership in the 'Are 'Are society, the South Sea Evangelical Church and parliamentary leadership.* Unpublished doctoral thesis. Wellington: Victoria University of Wellington.

Post Primary Teacher's Association. (2005). *Annual report 2002–2005.* Wellington: Post Primary Teacher's Association.

Rapp, D. (2002). Social justice and the importance of rebellious, oppositional imaginations. *Journal of School Leadership, 12,* 226–245.

Reilly, B., and Phillpot, R. (2002). Making democracy work in Papua New Guinea. *Asian Survey, 42*(6), 906–927.

Robertson, A. S. (2004). *ICPD+10: Progress in the Pacific in gender equality, equity and the empowerment of women.* Suva: UNFPA Office for the Pacific.

Sanga, K., and Walker, K. (2005). *Apem moa Solomon Islands leadership.* Wellington: Victoria University of Wellington.

Solomon Islands Ministry of Education and Human Resource Development. (2004). *Annual Report 2004.* Honiara: Solomon Islands Government, Ministry of Education and Human Resource Development.

———. (2005). *Digest of statistics 2005.* Honiara: Solomon Islands Government Ministry of Education and Human Resource Development.

Statistics New Zealand. (2006). *QuickStats about New Zealand's population and dwellings, 2006 census.* Wellington: Statistics New Zealand.

Strachan, J. (1993). Including the personal and the professional: Researching women in educational leadership. *Gender and Education, 5*(1), 71–80.

———. (1999). Feminist educational leadership: Locating the concepts in practice. *Gender and Education, 11*(3), 309–322.

———. (2002). *A gender analysis of the education sector in Vanuatu.* Port Vila: Department of Women's Affairs.

Strachan, J., and Dalesa, S. (2005). The experiences of women political candidates in Vanuatu. *Development Bulletin, 67,* 119–123.

Strachan, J., and Lapi, G. (2006). Tertiary e-education: Is it feasible for Ni Vanuatu women? Development *Bulletin, 71,* 100–103.

Strachan, J., and Saunders, R. (2007). Ni Vanuatu women and educational leadership development. *New Zealand Journal of Educational Leadership, 22*(2), 37–48.

Tan, L. (2006, November 6). Family abuse is not acceptable, regardless of culture. *New Zealand Herald,* Retrieved 9 June 2007 from http://www.nzherald.co.nz/topic/story.cfm?c_id=178&objectid=10409260.

Thomson (now Strachan), J. (1988). *Women in education: Management training needs.* Hamilton, New Zealand: University of Waikato.

UNICEF. (2005). Country statistics. Retrieved 18 May 2007 from http://www.unicef.org/infobycountry/papuang_statistics.html#26; http://www.unicef.org/infobycountry/vanuatu.html; http://www.unicef.org/infobycountry/solomonislands_statistics.html.

United Nations Population Fund. (2004). *ICPD+10: Progress in the Pacific.* Suva: UNFPA Office for the Pacific.

Vaa, L. R. (2006). Women: The Pacific potential. Retrieved 9 June 2007 from http://www.nzfgw.org.nz/Documents/Pacific-Oct06.pdf.

Watson, H. (1989). Getting women to the top. *PPTA Journal, Term 2,* 10–12.

Whitcombe, J. (1979). Comparison of career patterns of men and women teachers. A paper presented at the first National Conference of the New Zealand Association for Research in Education, Victoria University of Wellington, 7–10 December 1979.

———. (1980). *An investigation of the position of women in primary and secondary teaching in New Zealand: Teacher career and promotion study.* Wellington: Department of Education.

———. (1995). Women in education management, 1975–1995. In N. Alcorn (Ed.). *Education and the equality of the sexes twenty years on,* pp.72–82. Conference proceedings. Hamilton: University of Waikato.

Wilson, M. (1995). Academic women in the 1990s. In N. Alcorn (Ed.), *Education and the equality of the sexes twenty years on,* pp. 61–71. Conference proceedings. Hamilton: University of Waikato.

THE DEEP INFLUENCE OF CULTURE AND PERSONAL VALUES

Greece, Bangladesh and Muslim Society

CHAPTER 14

Overview for Part IV

Eileen Zungolo

MY PARTICIPATION IN THIS conference has been an eye-opening experience. Since I am a female career administrator in higher education, I expected to join my Duquesne University colleagues in overtly sharing a great deal with the conference participants—also mostly women, and administrators in education. But that has not been the case. Let me share a personal story to document my point.

A number of years ago, I was on a whitewater rafting trip in the Pacific Northwest of the United States. Since I had experience in rafting, not necessarily considerable skill, I was placed in the front of the raft. My instructions from the guide were to follow his "commands" and help the other seven fellow rafters work together. The rafters were told to row quickly through rapid whitewater, and to do so with attention to my directions from the front of the raft. We had a successful run—we did not capsize, nor did we have any rafters fall out. In addition, everyone had a good time. As we were pulling in to shore one of the men on the raft commented to me that I had done a good job with the directions, which suggested to him that I had a number of brothers. I was taken aback by this observation, preferring to think it was my strong leadership and good people skills which had delivered the day (I knew my limits as a rafter!). I inquired as to why he thought that. He responded that in his experience women who can give direction to men have usually learned that at a young age, with brothers. I pondered that and commented, "interesting observation." However, he refused to let me off the hook and pressed on, "Well, how many brothers do you have?" I reluctantly replied, five! Five brothers I had. Now it may well be that my brothers were an influence on my development, but the relevance of that story to this conference is that very few of you ever mention men. While your descriptions of your cultures and specific circumstances have been vivid, and in many cases very moving, I have not heard any descriptions of how men function in the educational administrative roles they occupy, nor how they relate to you. In fact, the lack of attention to men in your

scholarship is extraordinary, given your attention to gender.

Your rhetoric is suffused with references to how many women occupy leadership positions in different countries and institutions, and the nature of the impediments to their progress up the administrative ladder, yet few references are made to the interface of these women with their male counterparts and the nature of the relationships that prevail between men and women in the workforce. I encourage you to look at this approach in your work and assess its impact.

I also notice comments about the skills that women bring to administration such as a strong values orientation and a commitment to collaboration that men generally do not possess. However, I have not heard any data substantiating this conclusion, or is it an assumption? I hope not, for in my experience men bring a range of talents and abilities to many positions.

My own discipline is nursing, and while it clearly is a female-dominated occupation, nurses have historically struggled to attain authority over their practice and in the design of clinical practice settings. To translate nursing experiences into those experiences that many of you have described in educational administration, nurses have often occupied positions of presumed authority but have lacked the autonomy to exercise or direct policy planning. In fact, the barriers that nurses have confronted in exerting influence on policy in health care facilities are extraordinary. Perhaps because of this experience in nursing, I am wondering why your studies direct so much attention to the numbers of females who occupy leadership positions in education, rather than assessment of the influence that females can apply within the educational setting.

The dimensions in which our professions share experiences relate to the phenomenon you have described as "invisibility" and the indignity of being "marginalized." Female nurses in the United States encounter these dimensions in professional roles on a regular basis. For example, during the tragic days surrounding September 11, 2001, in New York

113

City television cameras were posted at the emergency room of St. Vincent's Hospital in downtown Manhattan, hoping for survivors. Story lines for the TV audience came from passers-by and men and women dressed in white by the emergency room doors. Men were always identified as Dr. Smith, Dr. Brown, et cetera. Women, on the other hand, were not identified by profession, rank or name—the ultimate "invisibility."

Gender discrimination is certainly not new, nor is understood by the folks women often hold accountable for that discrimination: men. I urge you as investigators of women in educational administration to be astutely aware of the need to be inclusive of all of our colleagues, of the men in our professional worlds who hold the key to the spheres of influence, and who contribute to the fullness of our leadership. In addition, one of them might be one of my brothers!

CHAPTER 15

Leadership, Change and Gender
Reflections of Greek and U.S. Women Leaders

LINDA L. LYMAN, ANASTASIA ATHANASOULA-REPPA AND ANGELIKI LAZARIDOU

INTRODUCTION

GARDINER, ENOMOTO AND GROGAN (2000) identified shared decision making as an approach characteristic of feminist leadership. By whatever name, shared or collaborative, decision making is also one manifestation of democracy. Democratic schools require attention to democracy in the curriculum, and in the structures and processes by which the schools operate (Apple and Beane, 1995). But whether one looks for "thin" or "thick" democratic practices (Strike, 1999), in the words of Furman and Starratt (2002), "the practice of democracy in schools has been minimal" (p. 111). Traditional command and control leadership styles still thrive in bureaucratic organizational structures and tend to perpetuate the status quo. However, women leaders, in part because of their marginalized status, might be expected to do things differently, to teach us how to push the bureaucratic boundaries and bring about change.

In this chapter, we present findings about women's leadership practices from a small qualitative exploratory pilot study in Greece and compare them with findings from a larger qualitative inquiry into U.S. women's leadership practices. This larger study (Lyman, Ashby and Tripses, 2005) served as a model for our work in Greece. Our comparative discussion of the findings from the two studies embodies a variant of the *nested design*, with both studies utilizing qualitative methodology (Tashakkori and Teddlie, 1998). We specifically framed the Greek study to explore the principals' values and their experiences with bringing about change. We were also interested in the gender-related challenges women leaders encounter in the Greek educational system and their perceptions of factors that contribute to their successes. As in the U.S. study, a central concern was how women leaders, because of their values, were pushing the bureaucracy to change the status quo.

CONCEPTUAL FRAMEWORKS

Interpreting findings from the Greek study and constructing a comparison with the U.S. study involved interweaving the literature on gender differences in leadership, the role of values in leadership, and leadership of change. We chose not to interpret the Greek study or construct the comparison of the two studies from an outright feminist perspective. Our intention was to let the views of the Greek women interviewed speak for themselves (Young and Skrla, 2003). Neither the U.S. nor Greek participants were asked if they considered themselves feminists. In this section we highlight issues from selected conceptual frameworks that influenced our interpretations.

GENDER DIFFERENCES IN LEADERSHIP

Contemporary literature on gender differences in leadership supports the contention that women are inclined to approach change through democratic processes. For example, Northouse (2004) reported that a meta-analysis conducted in the past 15 years of more than 160 studies of sex-related differences in leadership style found only one difference: "Women used a more participative or democratic style and a less autocratic or directive style than men did, although this tendency declined in a highly male-dominated setting" (p. 270). Bjork (2000) also concluded that women are "perceived as being more likely to be facilitative and collaborative in their working relationships, and they tend to use democratic leadership styles and power" (p. 10). On the other hand, having completed a large-scale analysis of studies of women in leadership positions in a variety of institutions, Rhode (2003) concluded that "perceptions of gender differences in style or effectiveness remain common, although the evidence for such differences is weaker than commonly supposed" (p. 19). Whether gender differences in leadership exist or not continues to be debated, and answers to the question are perhaps ultimately a matter of perception.

VALUES AND LEADERSHIP

Alignment of leadership practices with one's values can occur at either the micro or macro level. When personal values are reflected in actions at the micro level we see a leader who has integrity and authenticity (Goleman, Boyatzis and McKee, 2002). When leadership focuses on values at a macro level we see a leader with purpose, one committed to issues such as democracy and social justice. Begley (1999) offers a macro-level definition when he defines values as "those conceptions of the desirable which motivate individuals and collective groups to act in particular ways to achieve particular ends" (p. 237). Specifically, in later work, he advocates democratic and ethical school leadership (Begley and Johansson, 2005).

Numerous scholars have been calling for leadership that is driven by moral purpose rather than compliance toward bureaucratic rules and authority (e.g., Blackmore, 2002; Fullan, 2003; Furman, 2003; Larson and Murtadha, 2002; Lyman, Ashby and Tripses, 2005; Sergiovanni, 1992). Furman (2003) claims that scholarship in the field of educational administration has shifted, "that educational leadership as a field is focusing more and more on what leadership is *for*; that it is the *moral purposes* of educational leadership that are emerging as the central focus" (p. 1). Echoing Furman are Blackmore's (2002) words: "We need to ask what we are leading for" (p. 64). Whether at the micro or macro levels, leading from values requires continuing re-examination of the status quo and pushing the bureaucratic boundaries.

LEADERSHIP OF CHANGE
No agreed upon definition of the concept of leadership or postmodern leadership exists (Chapman, Sackney and Astin, 1999; Furman, 2002; Leithwood and Duke, 1999; Willower and Forsyth, 1999). Furthermore, the societal changes that now affect many institutions have brought about changes in the way leadership is provided and conceptualized. For example, Begley (2004) recently characterized authentic leadership as "a metaphor for professionally effective, ethically sound, and consciously reflective practices in educational administration" (pp. 4–5). As we begin to define leadership in new ways, the leadership of change is understood to be the collective responsibility of an educational community rather than something that can be mandated (Fullan, 1999, 2001).

Numerous other scholars place relationships at the heart of good leadership that facilitates change (Drath, 1996, 2001; Drath and Palus, 1994; Fullan, 2001; Lambert, 2003; Lambert, Walker, Zimmerman, Cooper, Lambert, Gardner, and Szabo, 2002; Rost, 1991; Sebring and Bryk, 2000; Wheatley, 1992, 1999). Similarly, yet others posit that possibilities of change are enhanced when leaders offer respect, build relationships, and practice collaborative decision-making processes involving conversation and dialogue (Lambert, 2003; Shields and Edwards, 2005). If women because of their marginalized status are more inclined to "trouble the bureaucracy" (Blackmore, 1999), to practice creative insubordination (Lyman, Ashby and Tripses, 2005; Morris, Crowson, Porter-Gehrie and Hurwitz, 1984), to build relationships and make decisions collaboratively (Gardiner, Enomoto and Grogan, 2000), then they offer a collective example of democratic and ethical school leadership to the field of practice.

THE GREEK EDUCATIONAL CONTEXT
In Greece education is centrally controlled by the Ministry of National Education and Religious Affairs (MNERA). Practically all funding for schools is dispensed at the national level. Koulaidis (2004) explains, "The Ministry of National Education and Religious Affairs (MNERA) of Greece provides for infrastructure, books, educational material and teaching aids and necessary human resources" (p. 14). Recent reforms have brought changes, but the centralized bureaucratic structure remains in place.

Education in Greece is free to students in pre-primary, primary, secondary and higher education. Public and private preschools are available for Greek children between three and a half and five and a half years of age. Greek students enter the system at age six and compulsory schooling ends at age 15. Teachers in Greece are "selected" at the national level. Teachers at both the primary and secondary levels are appointed to public schools only after successfully taking highly competitive, state-controlled exams. Bryant (2005) reports that "while all but two of the fifty U.S. states require a state issued certification for school principals (Feistritzer, 2003), European countries typically do not (Watson, 2003)" (p. 1). No formal training in educational administration or certification process is required in order to become an educational leader in Greece.

The process of becoming a principal in Greece requires substantial teaching experience (a minimum of five years but preferably more than 20 years), submitting an application to MNERA, and going through an interview—usually with a Selection Council at the local level. The three types of criteria used for selection are training and work experience, work evaluations (performance evaluation reports) and appraisals by the Selection Council based on data in the candidate's files, resume and interview. Five members are on the

Selection Council, with two elected and three appointed by MNERA. Therefore the power dynamics are determined by the appointed members, making the process highly political (Athanasoula-Reppa, Lazaridou and Lyman, 2006).

Available figures from 1997 document that 57.9 percent of the teachers are women (Athanasoula-Reppa and Koutouzis, 2002). Women represented 56 percent of the teachers in primary education, but only 41 percent of the administrators; and in secondary education women represented 59 percent of the teachers, but only 36 percent of the administrators. Athanasoula-Reppa and Koutouzis (2002) cite three reasons for the low participation of women in managerial positions: psychological barriers, institutional barriers and social-cultural barriers such as the belief that leaders should be men.

THE GREEK STUDY

The small qualitative exploratory pilot study completed in 2005 was conceptualized as a starting point for further qualitative research on women's leadership in Greek education. Participant selection, development of the interview guide, data collection and analysis procedures, and a discussion of the findings follow.

Participants

We chose the principals for interviews through purposeful reputational sampling (Patton, 1990) and for convenience. Because we had a short time frame in which to complete the study, we were limited to participants from Thessaloniki and Athens. Faculty at Aristotle University in Thessaloniki recommended three potential participants known to be successful school leaders to Lyman, who was in residence as a Fulbright scholar. Coauthor Lazaridou, who is fluent in both English and Greek, her first language, traveled to Thessaloniki to conduct the interviews because only one of the participants spoke English. Two principals were interviewed, but the third withdrew from the project. The six Athens participants were all secondary principals known to coauthor Athanasoula-Reppa by reputation. Thus a total of eight women principals from Athens and Thessaloniki were interviewed. One interview was conducted in English and the other seven in Greek.

Six of the women interviewed were secondary principals in state schools; one was an elementary school principal in a state school; and one was a former university professor who directed a private kindergarten school. Their years of experience in education ranged from 22 to 45; their years in administration ranged from three to seven. The six secondary principals all had university degrees, but none had a specialization in education. The preschool director had three B.A. degrees as well as a Ph.D. from Ohio State University. The elementary principal also had an education degree.

Interview Guide

We developed a semistructured four-part interview guide with 25 questions adapted from the previously mentioned U.S. study (Lyman, Ashby and Tripses, 2005). The first section included introductory questions about the educational background and training of the principals and their beliefs about leadership. The questions in the second section asked about values influencing their teaching and leading. The questions in the third section probed their experiences with bringing about educational change, including the obstacles they encountered as well as their successes. The fourth section's questions focused on perceptions of the effects of gender and the role of women leaders in the Greek educational system.

The interview guide was originally written in English. Lazaridou, fluent in both Greek and English, translated the questions into Greek, and Athanasoula-Reppa submitted them for review to a number of practitioners who did not participate in the study. No language/expression problems were identified by that group or subsequently by the study's participants. We are confident that translation of the interview guide did not create issues of understanding for our participants. All interviews were completed in March 2005.

Data Collection and Analysis

We audiotaped each interview and Lazaridou translated the Greek transcripts into English. We analyzed the data inductively to find the recurring themes using a combination of content analysis and constant comparative methodology (Glaser and Strauss, 1967; Merriam, 2001). Themes were identified jointly by Athanasoula-Reppa and Lazaridou, while Lyman analyzed independently. Before finally categorizing the data into themes, we compared results of our analyses to maximize the advantage of cross-cultural perspectives. The final step in the cross-cultural analysis of the data was a consideration of how themes in the Greek pilot study compared with major themes from the Illinois project and reflected the larger context of literature on leadership in education.

Findings and Discussion

Three groups of major themes were evident in the Greek study data: the role of values in leadership, confronting power/authority to bring about change and the effects of gender on women's leadership in the Greek educational system. Major themes are those mentioned by six of the eight leaders, with minor themes mentioned by at least two.

THE ROLE OF VALUES IN LEADERSHIP Exploring the role of values, we asked the principals about their values in relation to teaching, decision making and leading. With regard to values associated with teaching, six of the eight expressed respect for students and teachers and five of the eight named justice/fairness in their treatment of all persons. For example, about respect, one woman mentioned "respect for students' and teachers' personalities." Another emphasized justice: "I'm mainly interested in justice first in the classroom and then at the office—democracy, respect for others, empathy, providing a calm and peaceful climate in the classroom and at the office." Their comments suggest that the principals were concerned with creating an environment for learning through their caring and regard for others, students as well as teachers. At the micro level of personal relationships, the values of these principals mattered. They brought presence and authenticity into their teaching and their leading (Starratt, 2006).

Responses to questions about values associated with decision making reflected similar values, including "justice," "fairness," "honesty," "equality," "reciprocity," "respect" and even "love." For all eight leaders the values of respecting others and including or collaborating with them in decision making and leadership were important. One principal said, "I respect people's points of view and I always take them into account when I make decisions. I like everyone to be involved in the decision-making process." Their comments and examples of respect and collaboration suggest that they operated from what can be called a democratic paradigm for schools (Apple and Beane, 1995). Phrases from these comments include: "making team decisions about educational matters," "including students in decision making," "democratic processes," and "considering ideas, wishes, points of view of everyone to work toward ways to achieve our goals together."

When defining leadership, six of the eight focused on people and relationships. Their definitions suggest an affinity for relational leadership practices (Drath, 1996, 2001; Fullan, 2003; Sebring and Bryk, 2000). For example, speaking of her leadership, one said, "I am very much interested in the interpersonal relationships with the staff members and I do have a very good relationship with my staff, according to what they say about me. When there is a problem we all try to solve it together." A definition from a broader perspective of relationships, including relationships with parents, was: "Leadership is a combination of abilities and capabilities one has so that he/she can organize efficiently and more effectively the relationships of those who are involved in the school community (students, teachers, parents)." A third person who emphasized relationships said, "It is not the theory that makes a leader. It is the personality and the experience and the values. . . . I made time in the school every week for several hours to share ideas and philosophy with the teachers so that we could grow to become a very successful group."

Seven of the eight leaders revealed ultimate idealistic goals they had for leadership, what their leadership was *for* (Blackmore, 2002; Fullan, 2003; Furman, 2003). One said, "I have a passion for education. I believe this is the only way to change society." Echoing that theme, another said, "I believe that school is the prime place for the betterment of society." More typical was a focus on improving the school. One stated, "I was hoping to help the school achieve higher educational goals." Still another explained, "I hoped to achieve better organization of the school environment, by introducing new programs and by bringing a different way of thinking. I am bold." Finally, a principal used these words, "I was dreaming of a utopian school where teachers would be happy to teach and students would be glad to come to school and learn." Not one valued what Starratt (2006) has called "test-fixated learning." When asked what they wanted to be remembered for, half the principals spoke of what they had given to others, including making students' lives better, the influence of their ideas and values, the good emotional climate created in the building, and changes they had brought about. Each had a sense that she was building a legacy, either for things she had accomplished or who she was as a person. Values operated in the lives of the Greek women leaders interviewed at both the micro and macro levels.

To summarize, the major themes in comments of the Greek principals about the role of values in their leadership were: (a) have a respectful presence and promote justice, authenticity and caring relationships; (b) use collaborative decision-making in support of learning; (c) define leadership in terms of relationships; (d) hold a passion for idealistic goals; and (e) build a legacy by making a difference.

CONFRONTING POWER/AUTHORITY TO BRING ABOUT CHANGE Complex cultural and systemic issues of power/authority emerged in what these Greek principals perceived as obstacles to their leadership. The Ministry of National Education and Religious Affairs (MNERA) has all the power to hand down laws, rules and regulations as well as to hand out resources. Six of the eight principals perceived the bureaucracy and lack of resources to be the main obstacles they encountered as leaders. They were critical of the centralized system, emphasizing that maintenance of the status quo seemed to be its only long-term goal. MNERA was characterized as a highly political, many-layered bureaucracy, within which they often encountered resistance and negativity, as well as different values concerning learning. In regard to divergent values, one said "huge differences" existed between her values and those reflected by actions of persons in the bureaucracy. Another woman described persons in higher administrative positions as being "mainly men, older in age, more conservative, with old-fashioned views about women and with different values about how things should be in education." Such observations seem to reflect Blackmore's (2002) thinking about women and power: "Their power is derived from their difference, their capacities as women to facilitate change" (p. 59).

Change was possible but difficult given the context of the centralized, bureaucratic and all-powerful MNERA. Half of the eight believed their authority to bring about change was constrained by the system, specifically the rules and regulations of MNERA. Three of the eight acknowledged that they had the authority to make change, but using it depended upon having good communication skills. In spite of confronting obstacles to their leadership, all of the leaders described successful changes they had accomplished, such as: improving the culture and climate for learning; building better relationships within a building; introducing new educational programs; negotiating a land purchase for a school addition; and upgrading the school with new equipment, paint and improved heating.

In every case the underlying value motivating change was to make school a better place for students and learning (Fullan, 2003; Furman, 2003). Their successes reinforce the idea that leadership of change can happen at the building level even in a highly bureaucratic centralized system. One person described the process this way, "You cannot bring any change to the decisions of the Ministry. On the other hand, in collaboration with the school's [faculty] association, a principal can create a few minor 'cracks' and develop a creative climate in the classroom." Another explained, "Because the Greek educational system is highly centralized, the principal's role is limited and subject to the central government. Nevertheless, principals can intervene and shape people's minds to perform to the best of their abilities and capabilities, whether these people are teachers or students." Another expressed the paradox of power that Greek principals live with: "In some areas like the everyday function of the school, I have enough authority to make changes. In most others, though, I have to abide by the Ministry's rules and regulations."

Their answers to why they had been successful in bringing about change fell into three broad categories, with responses from each person typically illustrating more than one of the categories.

1. Personality (examples included "intuitive," "spoke to the heart," "love for the beautiful and important," "openness" and "empathetic")
2. Style (examples included "goal-oriented," "balanced needs of school and needs of bureaucrats," "respected students and teachers," "did not hide my own mistakes" and "openness to dialogue")
3. Personal Initiative (examples included "proactive," "determination," "focused on planning" and "activity")

They did not directly attribute their successes as change agents to values or democratic leadership processes. However, implied in the illustrations for the categories of Personality and Style are both strong values and personal relationships based on respect. Six of the eight principals said they felt very comfortable with their knowledge, skills and experiences in bringing about change. Although successful at bringing about change, the other two said they did not feel comfortable with it.

In spite of the constraints of bureaucracy and their role in it, all the leaders spoke of the school itself as a place where, through positive interpersonal relationships, they were able to work toward creation of a good environment in the classroom, manage crises, develop new educational programs, and get people to work together more effectively and more efficiently. These leaders were able to successfully confront the power of the bureaucracy and accomplish change because of a sense of purpose and the power of their own individual strengths as leaders. Their values engendered discontent with the status quo and inclined them to trouble the bureaucracy (Blackmore, 1999).

To summarize, the major themes in the comments of Greek principals about confronting power/authority to bring about change were: (a) they were definitely constrained by the centralized system, the laws, a lack of resources and differences between their values and those of persons, mostly men, who had the power/authority in the highly political MNERA environment; (b) they described successful changes they had made to better their schools in spite of the constraints under which they operated; (c) they understood their successes with change to have resulted from personal strengths and were comfortable with their abilities to bring about change.

EFFECTS OF GENDER ON WOMEN'S LEADERSHIP OPPORTUNITIES AND ROLES

The participants had different perceptions about the effects of gender on leadership opportunities for women and their roles in the Greek education system. Five of the eight thought leadership opportunities for women were limited; yet only two mentioned gender specifically as a limiting factor in their own opportunities. Six admitted to having experienced obstacles to their leadership, but only three perceived these to be gender-related. One explained, "In some cases I can attribute the obstacles to the fact that I'm a woman. That mainly comes from a few men colleagues who have psychological problems and other exceptionalities and perceive women as inferior." Another observed, "Many of my men colleagues always try to find a mistake and if they don't find one, they invent it. I've also been accused of being too authoritative." Another principal lamented, "Besides experience in the classroom, the educational community requests that women have graduate education, have attended seminars, [and have] been involved in political parties. When women have families to care for and children to raise, when will they find the time to do all of the above?"

Whether they acknowledge the effects on their own careers or not, it seems Greek women do face cultural and political barriers against becoming principals. Indeed, according to a Commonwealth Council on Educational Administration and Management report (CCEAM, 2002), "social stereotypes, maternity, and family responsibilities are the major barriers constraining women from pursuing an administrative career" (p. 1). Athanasoula-Reppa and Koutouzis (2002) state, "Quite simply, educational management is considered a 'male' job, not only by society in general but also by teachers and even pupils" (p. 9). They also elaborate on

role conflict as a psychological barrier that explains the low numbers of women in administrative positions. Athanasoula-Reppa (1999) summarized the effects of these psychological and social-cultural barriers, writing, "The double shift of working in many schools of the big cities, the differentiated role of women in double career families, the pregnancy and confinement permit, as well as the absence of female role-models in the higher administration also create obstacles that work against women and for men" (p. 16). In addition to these covert barriers, the overt institutional barriers are also a factor, according to Athanasoula-Reppa and Koutouzis (2002). Such overt institutional barriers are maintained by the politicized character of the ministry. For example, committees that select principals have always been male dominated. Additionally, Athanasoula-Reppa and Koutouzis (2002) write, "The fact that in every governmental change there is also an imposed change of persons in the above-mentioned positions can only confirm the argument of political manipulation of the system and its key posts" (p. 9).

When asked whether women lead differently than men, one of our participating Greek principals asserted that women have greater flexibility. She continued, "Women are more people-oriented and always ask for the collaboration and cooperation of others." Six of the eight provided generally affirmative responses to the question. One said, "Women think differently. Intuition is a female weapon, as I said earlier. Women see things holistically, they synthesize ideas." On this subject of gender differences, Athanasoula-Reppa (1999) described research supporting the view that women lead differently:

> Surveys that concern the administration and effectiveness of schools report that the women school directors have the tendency to be more democratic than men, their way of speaking is more polite, less offensive and more hesitant. The educators working with female directors are usually more productive, have higher morale and they feel that they form a community with their colleagues. (p. 18)

The interview question asking about the role of women in educational leadership in Greece elicited a wide range of assertions that women create opportunities for themselves by being well prepared and fighting for them. For example, one person explained, "I created the opportunities for this position through my continuous efforts, my desire, my personality, my temperament, everything I had done to prepare myself for this. I always look for opportunities to improve myself so that I become competitive." Another woman said, "Because there are few women in leadership positions, [all women in leadership positions] need to always prove to others that we have the skills and abilities for the job." One principal spoke at length about how important it was to nourish the ongoing change in women's attitudes about seeking leadership positions:

> More women are now in leadership positions as opposed to a few years back when women didn't dare go for a principal's job. The highest they would go for was vice principal. If there were a woman and a man with the same years of teaching experience, the man would get the job . . . and the women thought it was all right to be put aside and give the position to a man. It was a different mentality.

Gender is a culturally constructed concept, and cultural realities for Greek women are still complicated. In a commentary for a Greek newspaper, Karaiskaki (2006) wrote, "The image of Greek women [is that they are] educated, economically independent, and unafraid of taking their lives in their own hands. However, this image does not account for the multiple roles of women, the dramatic changes they experience through their lives, and the stereotypes which affect them." Karaiskaki explained that in Greece only 40 percent of women work, that they are paid about two-thirds of what their male counterparts earn, and that only 4.9 percent of them make it into top managerial posts. Women's limited role in the leadership of education clearly reflects the larger social and cultural realities of contemporary Greece.

To summarize, the major themes in the comments of Greek principals about effects of gender on women's leadership opportunities and roles were: (a) mixed perceptions regarding effects of gender on leadership opportunities; (b) barriers to women's leadership in education are covert and overt, including psychological, socio-cultural, and institutional or political barriers; (c) differences in women and men as leaders are perceived by the majority, with women's leadership interpreted more positively than men's; and (d) women must continue proactively to support each other and to fight to create more leadership opportunities.

COMPARING AND CONTRASTING FINDINGS OF THE GREEK AND U.S. STUDIES

The U.S. research (Lyman, Ashby and Tripses, 2005) began with a desire to capture the stories of impressive women leaders in Illinois. "A central purpose of the research was to learn more about how these educational leaders have worked successfully within the boundaries of school bureaucracies" (p. 1). This was also a central purpose of the Greek research, and therefore the findings of the two studies can be productively compared.

Interviews for the U.S. study were completed during 2000–2001. The 18 women selected for interviews represented a wider range of experience than that of the Greek principals. Only one woman in the U.S. study was a principal at the time of the study, but almost all were former principals. Their years in education ranged from one to 35; their years in administration ranged from 10 to 38. All had degrees beyond the bachelor's level. Thirteen had either an Ed.D. or Ph.D. degree. All had earned teaching and administrative credentials, and they represented communities and institutions from across the state. Analysis of the data identified four major themes in the leadership practices of the participants: (a) pushing the bureaucratic boundaries, (b) claiming power through politics, (c) living and leading from values, and (d) using collaborative decision-making processes. Two themes reveal differences and two reflect similarities, when comparing findings of the two studies.

Differences

The concept of pushing the bureaucratic boundaries to create change is present in comments of several of the Greek principals, but does not have the same meaning as in the U.S. context. Claiming power through politics is not addressed by the Greek women; however several commented on the role of politics and political awareness in the Greek system. These differences between the studies seem clearly to reflect differences between the systems of education in the two countries. Pushing the bureaucratic boundaries is more difficult in Greece where MNERA is the only game in town. Probably it is their political awareness that keeps Greek women principals from pushing too far. Most are in no position to claim political power the way the women in the U.S. study have done, by being involved with political initiatives at local and state levels.

PUSHING THE BUREAUCRACY In the U.S. study Lyman, Ashby and Tripses (2005) explored the matter of pushing bureaucratic boundaries with a series of questions about the concept of creative insubordination, defined as "a counter-bureaucratic approach to decision making that bends and/or ignores rules and otherwise subverts the authority of the chain of command when such subversion is justified by the greater authority of personal values, service to students, and common sense" (p. 63). Questions in the Greek interview guide asked the principals to comment on bureaucracy rather than creative insubordination. Still, language about pushing the bureaucracy was clear in the comments of three. One Greek principal referred to solving problems on her own rather than "getting into the bureaucratic machine." She spoke of going around the bureaucracy to solve problems. At another point in the interview this same woman said, "I have to answer to the administrators at higher levels; I can't ignore them; but I try to work around them. . . . When administrators see that the work they ask you to do is done, they don't care how you did it; they leave you alone." Clearly this principal has learned how to push the boundaries in the Greek system, although she still experiences and commented on the constraints. Others were not so proactive. For example, one Greek woman expressed her total frustration with the bureaucratic system, saying "bureaucracy has affected the exercise of leadership negatively. A principal is the equivalent of a bureaucrat. That analogy is even more accentuated by the lack of support staff."

Even though they acknowledged bureaucratic constraints, two claimed the autonomy to bring about changes that mattered to them. Speaking directly to issues of autonomy, one Greek leader said, "I have autonomy when it comes to the interpersonal relationships and to helping the team achieve its goals." Another Greek principal explained, "I have enough autonomy that I don't clash with the law (even if I disagree with it) and that I don't step beyond my boundaries to the autonomy of others." This echoed declarations by the U.S. leaders that they would not break the law.

Participants in the U.S. study, partly because of their status in positions beyond the principalship, clearly experienced greater autonomy than the Greek principals. In fact, 12 of the 18 participants in the U.S. study had a high level of comfort with pushing the boundaries through creative insubordination. According to Lyman, Ashby and Tripses (2005), the U.S. subjects told numerous stories of bending the rules to make the right things happen and revealed a variety of motivations for pushing the boundaries "and a rich level of understanding about how to get things done in bureaucracies" (p. 69). Additionally, those who practiced creative insubordination "were willing to take the risks . . . when the alternative was compromise of their values. They seemed to rely on previously built relationships as well as political skill and competence to manage the risks" (p. 74).

POLITICAL AWARENESS Several of the Greek women interviewed spoke of politics, but not of "claiming power" through politics. If the political party in power changes as a result of a national election, chances are that administrators will be replaced throughout the educational system including at the university level. Whereas women leaders in the United States see themselves as consciously claiming power through politics, women leaders in Greece may in reality owe their positions to their political awareness and skill. Three of the eight Greek women commented specifically on some aspect of politics. One woman repeatedly characterized women as more politically skillful. This principal, who thinks women play the political game better than men, explained the pervasive reality of politics in Greek education in these words:

> You deal with colleagues who are educated and well qualified, but who also bring their own personalities, specific behaviors, and different characters. [Furthermore,] many belong to political parties and they bring these ideologies in school. You, as a leader, need to understand each and everyone's psychology and to act accordingly. You need to play the political game in such a way, though, that it will allow you to work keeping always in mind the result you want to achieve.

Similarities

The leadership practices of participants in the Greek and U.S. studies exhibit two major themes in common: leading from values and using collaborative decision-making processes. We are cognizant of Freeman and Bourque's (2001) warning that "few descriptions of women's leadership will hold across all cultures" (p. 5). Although we claim no cross-cultural generalizations, we highlight evidence that women leaders in both the Greek and U.S. settings lead from their values and use collaborative, democratic decision-making processes to accomplish change.

LEADING FROM VALUES Highlighting the U.S. data about values, Lyman and colleagues (2005) wrote, "In articulating values behind decision making, all 18 of the leaders in our study spoke directly to the importance of caring about people and relationships when making decisions" (p. 124). The same values are echoed in the words of the Greek women, six of whom focused on people and relationships in defining leadership. "Making decisions that benefit children/students was mentioned by 16 of the [U.S.] leaders" (Lyman, Ashby and Tripses, 2005, p. 127), and also expressed by the Greek women interviewed. Respecting others was another value emphasized by the women in both studies.

Clearly, women in both studies lead from their values and focus on what leadership is for (Blackmore, 2002; Fullan, 2003; Furman, 2003). Lyman and colleagues (2005) concluded that the leadership practices of the women in the U.S. study reflected an integration of doing and being, that their leadership practices could be said to emanate from "a constructive postmodern paradigm aimed at social reconstruction" (p. 143). Six of the eight leaders in the Greek study and 17 of the 18 leaders in the U.S. study held idealistic leadership goals that included changing society as well as changing schools, and said that their personal values differed from bureaucratic values.

COLLABORATIVE DECISION-MAKING PROCESSES Lyman and colleagues (2005) asked the U.S. women leaders to "characterize themselves as decision makers, to describe the processes they use in making decisions, the most difficult and important decisions they have made, and the values behind their decisions" (p. 38). Responses to these questions intertwined and reflected tension between commitment to collaboration on the one hand, and information-driven decision making on the other. Summarizing the data about collaborative decision making, Lyman, Ashby and Tripses (2005) wrote, "One major finding of our research is that, for 14 of the 18 leaders we interviewed, collaborative decision-making processes were the norm. In every case the commitment to collaboration grew out of the leader's values" (p. 38). In discussing their commitments to collaboration the participants explained that they used these processes as an expression of their values, including care and respect for others. Lyman and colleagues (2005) argue that "collaborative decision making integrates doing and being in a leadership practice that grows out of a constellation of values" (p. 157).

Correspondingly, as previously explained, every Greek principal interviewed said her values involved respecting others and collaborating with them in decision-making processes. Specifically mentioned by the Greek principals as examples of collaboration were "team decisions," "democratic processes," "reciprocity," "cooperation," and "recognizing the talents and abilities of others." For Greek women leaders to use collaborative decision-making processes is somewhat surprising, given their positions within the centralized hierarchical authoritarian structure of the Greek educational system. On the other hand, Greece has a longer democratic tradition, albeit an interrupted

one, than the United States. Furthermore, the contemporary literature on gender differences in leadership supports the idea that women are inclined to approach change through democratic and collaborative processes (Athanasoula-Reppa, 1999; Bjork, 2000; Gardiner, Enomoto and Grogan, 2000; Northouse, 2004).

IMPLICATIONS

We framed the Greek study to investigate challenges women leaders encounter in the bureaucratic system and their perceptions of factors that contribute to their successes. We focused on values and the experiences of Greek women principals in bringing about change. The U.S. study looked specifically at how women leaders, because of their values, were pushing the bureaucracy to change the status quo. Major similarities between the studies are that the majority of the women leaders interviewed in both countries lead from their values and use collaborative decision-making practices, both of which reflect the emerging literature on leadership in education. From this perspective, we highlight several implications for leadership theory and practice.

Implications for Theory

An important aspect of the Greek and U.S. women leaders' ability to facilitate change is their affinity for relational leadership practices. This finding supports claims in contemporary leadership theory. They demonstrated, by their use of collaborative decision-making practices, that school leadership is a collective enterprise (Fullan, 2003). Their attention to relationships and commitment to collaboration grew out of their values and may be seen as an attempt to compensate for the limitations of "one-best-way" hierarchical leadership even in the midst of bureaucratic educational systems. Relational leadership is one of the emerging leadership approaches of the postmodern era. Drath (1996) has suggested that "good sets of relationships constitute good leadership" (p. 2). Although some argue that women's leadership success comes from their sensitivity and attention to personal relationships, others argue that relational leadership approaches do not necessarily reflect gender but a new understanding that leadership can take various forms.

Persson, Andersson and Lindstrom (2004) did not note gender as a factor when they reported on what made a headmaster successful in Sweden. They identified headmasters as living in fields of tension created by the conflicts between the forces of continuity and the processes of change, and examined how the headmasters dealt with these tensions. The headmasters used a variety of strategies, but one was dominant—paying careful and sustained attention to building and nourishing a variety of alliances or formalized cooperative relationships. Relationship building created cultures where teachers experienced trust. Persson, Andersson and Lindstrom (2004) noted that "the headmaster respected the teachers' professional autonomy, showed confidence in them, and supported their development, while the teachers in general were united in giving their support to the headmaster" (p. 68). This is among the studies suggesting that successful leaders of change, whatever their gender, build relationships and trust. We hope this understanding will move all cultures closer to a gender-inclusive vision of who leaders are and what leadership is. When that happens we can begin to close the gender leadership gap, a change that is overdue in both Greece and the United States.

Relational emphases in leadership are congruent with the concept of "quantum" leadership suggested by the new sciences—in particular, chaos or complexity theory (e.g., Pascale, Millemann and Gioja, 2000; Stacey, Griffin and Shaw, 2000; Wheatley, 1992, 1999; Zohar, 1997). When applied to organizations and administration, complexity theory has us concentrate on relationships and culture more than on control and measurement techniques. As Fris and Lazaridou (2006) point out, an administrator who adopts the "quantum" perspective assumes that in complex situations prediction is impossible and accepts indeterminacy and ambiguity. In such complex situations, the leader relies on intuitive feel for situations and trusts in the character, creativity and abilities that both she/he and others bring to the organization. Leaders see their overarching task as helping to release the potential of individuals, helping them evolve through relations with others. This theoretical perspective, too, is congruent with the practices reported by the Greek and U.S. women leaders interviewed.

Implications for Practice
Implications for practice center on leadership of change. In the words of Gardiner, Enomoto and Grogan (2000), in order to be effective change agents "women also have to learn the rules and then bend them to their advantage—to be smart and have political savvy, able to change the face of educational leadership" (p. 125). Values of inclusion and connection, viewed as common for women, are important to leadership, including leadership of change (Brunner, 1999;

Dunlap and Schmuck, 1995; Gardiner, Enomoto and Grogan, 2000; Grogan, 2003; Gupton and Slick, 1996). Clear values arise from integrity, enhance a leader's credibility and contribute to bonding and shared vision in a community. Concern for community and caring, often seen as women's values, in fact are central to moral leadership in the service of all children, whatever a leader's gender.

Strong values are implied in leadership driven by moral purpose. Fullan (1999) and Sebring and Bryk (2000) both report that change requires leadership practices that combine support and pressure. In a more recent book, Fullan (2003) writes about change: "The most important thing to know is that the combination of moral purpose and relational trust generates the wherewithal to go the extra mile. It makes a complex, difficult journey worthwhile and doable" (p. 62). Democratic leadership builds the relational trust that contributes to change. In his study of insider change leadership, Miller (2002) contended:

> Those managing change processes need to recognize that the quality of the teachers' relationship with the individual introducing the change could be a significant determinant of successful implementation. . . . A view of teaching as moral activity implies that the work of the change leader is also essentially moral activity. (pp. 344, 348)

One manifestation of democracy in schools is collaborative decision making, particularly when the goal of the decision making is the common good. In the words of Furman and Starratt (2002), "Democratic community is processual and moral. It is the enactment of participatory processes of open inquiry in working for the common good in regard to both local and global concerns" (p. 116). The majority of women leaders interviewed for the Greek study articulated idealistic goals that include changing society. They lead from strong value systems and use collaborative or democratic decision-making processes. The majority of women leaders interviewed for the Greek and U.S. studies approached change through democratic leadership practices even though operating in educational systems structured quite differently.

Further comparative research is needed to explore whether the use of collaborative or democratic decision-making processes to approach change is a description of women's leadership that will hold across cultures. One book addresses women and school leadership from international perspectives, but it is not a comparative study and chapters are written by scholars from only five English-speaking countries (Reynolds, 2002). Although scholars have compared women's leadership in higher education, as well as women political leaders and women scientific leaders from different countries, a search of the Internet and library databases (ERIC, International ERIC, Academic Search Premier) turned up only a handful of articles comparing women educational leaders from different countries at the PK-12 level. Two looked at differences between women principals in Canada and the United States (Green and Manera, 1995; Wallin, 2005) and one compared women from Shaanxi Province in China with women educational managers in European countries and the United States (Haiyan, Yanping and Coleman, 1998). One conference paper (Rarieya, 2006) compared women educational leaders of Kenya and Pakistan. A broader global examination of women's leadership in education would contribute to building a more gender-inclusive understanding of leadership to enlighten both theory and practice.

CONCLUSIONS

We draw a cluster of conclusions, including that the majority of women leaders interviewed in Greece and the United States clearly demonstrate moral purpose. They lead from strong values, are politically aware, care about relationships and use democratic processes of collaboration to bring about change. Educational leaders accomplish change through a combination of moral purpose and relational trust, engendered in part through collaborative decision-making practices. In spite of bureaucratic constraints, women leaders interviewed for both the Greek and U.S. studies are pushing the boundaries, both systemic and cultural, to challenge the status quo. Collectively, they embody democratic and ethical school leadership (Begley and Johansson, 2005). Their successes suggest that women leaders can have the political savvy required to be able "to change the face of educational leadership" (Gardiner, Enomoto and Grogan, 2000, p. 125).

An extensive body of literature points to a continuing leadership gap between men and women. Often this is attributed to factors such as traditional gender stereotypes, inadequate access to mentors and support networks, and inflexible workplace structures (Athanasoula-Reppa and Koutouzis, 2002; Blount, 1998; Rhode, 2003; Wilson, 2004). Speaking specifically of Greece, Athanasoula-Reppa and Koutouzis (2002) argue,

> The fact that the teaching profession is "dominated" by women has not resulted in equal representations in positions of relatively higher status and responsibility. Such discrimination . . . is not just evidence of male-female inequality and unfair treatment. It goes far beyond that, and it is a rather clear sign of violation of democratic attitudes and practices in a democratic country. It demonstrates the exclusion (overt or covert) of a significant part of the society from certain positions and the weakening of the *social* dimension of citizenship. (p. 10)

In the final analysis, opportunities for women to obtain educational leadership positions are still limited in Greece and in the United States. Speaking of the United States, after a large-scale analysis of research on women in high-level formal leadership positions in law, politics and business, Rhode (2003) wrote that "gender inequalities in leadership opportunities are pervasive; perceptions of inequality are not. A widespread assumption is that barriers have been coming down, women have been moving up, and equal treatment is an accomplished fact" (p. 6). In fact a leadership gap exists in every major institution of Greece and the United States. Why? Because the cultural ideal in both countries is that leaders should be men. As a result, women have not had equal access to leadership roles in any institution. Remedying the situation is on one level a question of establishing full social and democratic rights.

In Greece the concept of gender equality as a legal right is fairly new, established by the Constitution of 1975 and still evolving and gaining acceptance. In fact, "it was only in 1983 that institutional and legal 'barriers' were truly removed, establishing gender equality" (Athanasoula-Reppa and Koutouzis, 2002, p. 9). Similarly, women in the United States technically experienced full citizenship beginning with the right to vote when the Nineteenth Amendment was passed by Congress in 1919. However, it took the women's movement of the 1970s to legally dismantle from both laws and policies the long-standing preference that women be relegated to private sphere roles (Blount, 1998). The situations of women in Greece and the United States are remarkably alike. Women who would lead in Greece and the United States experience cultural constraints and institutional barriers. The journey toward gender equity in educational leadership is clearly part of a larger unfinished journey toward full democracy and social justice in both countries.

REFERENCES CITED

Apple, M. W., and Beane, J. A. (1995). *Democratic schools.* Alexandria, VA: ASCD.

Athanasoula-Reppa, A. (1999). Under-representation of women in decision-making centres of school education: A view of unequal distribution of authority into school mechanisms. In the proceedings of the seventh conference of Karagiorgas Foundation/Panteion University.

Athanasoula-Reppa, A., and Koutouzis, M. (2002, January 31). Women in managerial positions in Greek education: Evidence of inequality. *Education Policy Analysis Archives, 10*(11), 1–13.

Athanasoula-Reppa, A., Lazaridou, A., and Lyman, L. L. (2006, October). Newly appointed principals in Greece and Cyprus: Comparing requirements, roles, and challenges. Paper presented at the CCEAM Conference, Lefkosia (Nicosia), Cyprus.

Begley, P. T. (1999). Value preferences, ethics and conflicts in school administration. In P. T. Begley (Ed.). *Values and educational leadership,* pp. 237–254. Albany: SUNY Press.

———. (2004). Understanding valuation processes: Exploring the linkage between motivation and action. *International Studies in Educational Administration, 32*(2), 4–17.

Begley, P. T., and Johansson, O. (2005, November). Democratic school leadership: A matter of professional values and social ethics. Paper presented at the Annual Convention of the University Council for Educational Administration, Nashville, TN.

Bjork, L. G. (2000). Introduction: Women in the superintendency—Advances in research and theory. *Educational Administration Quarterly, 36*(1), 5–17.

Blackmore, J. (1999). *Troubling women: Feminism, leadership, and educational change.* Buckingham: Open University Press.

———. (2002). Troubling women: The upsides and downsides of leadership and the new managerialism. In C. Reynolds (Ed.). *Women and school leadership: International perspectives,* pp. 49–70. Albany: SUNY Press.

Blount, J. M. (1998). *Destined to rule the schools.* Albany: State University of New York Press.

Brunner, C. C. (1999). *Sacred dreams: Women and the superintendency.* Albany: SUNY Press.

Bryant, M. (2005, Fall). Variation in school leader certification. *Teaching in Educational Administration Newsletter, 13*(1), 1–2.

CCEAM (2002). Conference report from "Women in Educational Leadership," University of Cyprus, April 5–6, 2002. Retrieved March 11, 2003, from http://www.websol.co.nz/cceam/AnnouncementView.asp?nid=46.

Chapman, J. D., Sackney, L. E., and Aspin, D. N. (1999). Internationalization in educational administration: Policy and practice, theory and research. In J. Murphy and K. S. Louis (Eds.). *Handbook of research on educational administration,* pp. 73–98. San Francisco, CA: Jossey-Bass.

Drath, W. H. (1996). Changing our minds about leadership. *Issues and Observations, 16*(1), 1–4.

———. (2001). *The deep blue sea: Rethinking the source of leadership.* San Francisco: Jossey-Bass.

Drath, W. H., and Palus, C. J. (1994). *Making common sense: Leadership as meaning-making in a community of practice.* Greensboro, NC: Center for Creative Leadership.

Dunlap, D. M., and Schmuck, P. A. (Eds.). (1995). *Women leading in education.* Albany: SUNY Press.

Freeman, S. J. M., and Bourque, S. C. (2001). Leadership and power: New conceptions. In S. J. M. Freeman, S. C. Bourque, and C. M. Shelton (Eds.). *Women on power: Leadership redefined,* pp. 3–26. Boston: Northeastern University Press.

Fris, J., and Lazaridou, A. (2006, January 5). An additional way of thinking about organizational life and leadership: The quantum perspective. *Canadian Journal of Educational Administration and Policy, 48.* Retrieved June 1, 2007, from http://www.umanitoba.ca/publications/cjeap/currentissues.html.

Fullan, M. (1999). *Change forces: The sequel.* Philadelphia: Falmer Press.

———. (2001). *Leading in a culture of change.* San Francisco, CA: Jossey-Bass.

———. (2003). *The moral imperative of school leadership.* Thousand Oaks, CA: Corwin Press.

Furman, G. C. (2002). Postmodernism and community in schools: Unraveling the paradox. In G. Furman (Ed.). *School as community: From promise to practice,* pp. 51–75. Albany: SUNY Press.

———. (2003). The 2002 UCEA presidential address. *UCEA Review, XLV*(1), 1–6.

Furman, G. C., and Starratt, R. J. (2002). Leadership for democratic community in schools. In J. Murphy (Ed.). *The educational leadership challenge: Redefining leadership for the 21st century,* pp. 105–133. Chicago: National Society for the Study of Education, University of Chicago Press.

Gardiner, M. E., Enomoto, E., and Grogan, M. (2000). *Coloring outside the lines: Mentoring women into school leadership.* Albany: SUNY Press.

Glaser, B. G., and Strauss, A. L. (1967). *The discovery of grounded theory.* Chicago: Aldine.

Goleman, D., Boyatzis, R., and McKee, A. (2002). *Primal leadership: Realizing the power of emotional intelligence.* Boston: Harvard Business School Press.

Green, V. A., and Manera, E. (1995). Educational leadership: The practice of successful women administrators in the U.S.A. and Canada. *International Studies in Educational Administration, 23*(2), 10–15.

Grogan, M. (2003). Laying the groundwork for a reconception of the superintendency from feminist postmodern perspectives. In M. D. Young and L. Skrla (Eds.), *Reconsidering feminist research in educational leadership,* pp. 9–34. Albany: SUNY Press.

Gupton, S. L., and Slick, G. A. (1996). *Highly successful women administrators and how they got there.* Thousand Oaks, CA: Corwin Press.

Haiyan, Q., Yanping, L., and Coleman, M. (1998). Women in educational management in China: Experience in Shaanxi Province. *Compare: A Journal of Comparative Education, 28*(2), 141–155.

Karaiskaki, T. (2006). Commentary: A gloomy future for Greek women. *Kathimerini* (English edition), May 21–22.

Koulaidis, V. (Ed.). (2004). *A report on education and training in Greece.* Athens: Education Research Centre of Greece.

Lambert, L. (2003). *Leadership capacity for lasting school improvement.* Alexandria, VA: Association for Supervision and Curriculum Development.

Lambert, L., Walker, D., Zimmerman, D. P., Cooper, J. E., Lambert, M. D., Gardner, M. E., and Szabo, M. (2002). *The constructivist leader* (2nd ed.). New York: Teachers College Press.

Larson, C. L., and Murtadha, K. (2002). Leadership for social justice. In J. Murphy (Ed.). *The educational leadership challenge: Redefining leadership for the 21st century,* pp. 134–161. Chicago: National Society for the Study of Education, University of Chicago Press.

Leithwood, K., and Duke, D. L. (1999). A century's quest to understand school leadership. In J. Murphy and K. S. Louis (Eds.). *Handbook of research on educational administration,* pp. 45–72. San Francisco, CA: Jossey-Bass.

Lyman, L. L., Ashby, D. E., and Tripses, J. S. (2005). *Leaders who dare: Pushing the boundaries.* Lanham, MD: Rowman and Littlefield Education.

Merriam, S. B. (2001). *Qualitative research and case study applications in education.* San Francisco: Jossey-Bass.

Miller, N. (2002). Insider change leadership in schools. *International Journal of Leadership in Education, 5*(4), 343–360.

Morris, V. C., Crowson, R. L., Porter-Gherie, C., and Hurwitz, E. (1984). *Principals in action: The reality of managing schools.* Columbus, OH: Charles E. Merrill.

Northouse, P. G. (2003). *Leadership: Theory and practice.* Thousand Oaks, CA: Sage Publications.

Pascale, R. T., Millemann, M., and Gioja, L. (2000). *Surfing the edge of chaos: The laws of nature and the new laws of business.* New York: Crown Business.

Patton, M. Q. (1990). *Qualitative evaluation methods.* Thousand Oaks, CA: Sage Publications.

Persson, A., Andersson, G., and Lindstrom, M. N. (2004). Successful Swedish headmasters in tension fields and alliances. *International Journal of Leadership in Education, 8*(1), 53–72.

Rarieya, J. F. A. (2006, February). *Women in educational leadership: A comparative study of Kenyan and Pakistani women educational leaders.* Paper presented at the Quality in Education Conference at Aga Khan University, Karachi, Pakistan.

Reynolds, C. (2002). *Women and school leadership: International perspectives.* Albany: SUNY Press.

Rhode, D. L. (2003). *The difference "difference" makes.* Stanford, CA: Stanford University Press.

Rost, J. C. (1991). *Leadership for the twenty-first century.* Westport, CT: Praeger.

Sebring, P. B., and Bryk, A. S. (2000). School leadership and the bottom line in Chicago. *Phi Delta Kappan, 81*(6), 440–443.

Sergiovanni, T. J. (1992). *Moral leadership: Getting to the heart of school improvement.* San Francisco, CA: Jossey-Bass.

Shields, C. M., and Edwards, M. M. (2005). *Dialogue is not just talk: A new ground for educational leadership.* New York: Peter Lang Publishing.

Stacey, R. D., Griffin, D., and Shaw, P. (2000). *Complexity and management: Fad or radical challenge to systems thinking?* London: Routledge.

Starratt, R. J. (2006, October). Cultivating the moral character of learning and teaching: A neglected dimension of educational leadership. Keynote address presented at the CCEAM Conference, Lefkosia (Nicosia), Cyprus.

Strike, K. A. (1999). Can schools be communities? The tension between shared values and inclusion. *Educational Administration Quarterly, 35,* 46–70.

Tashakkori, A., and Teddlie, C. (1998.) *Mixed methodology.* Thousand Oaks, CA: Sage Publications.

Wallin, D. C. (2005). Through the looking glass: A comparative analysis of the career patterns of rural female administrators in Saskatchewan and Texas. *Alberta Journal of Educational Research, 51*(2), 135–154.

Wheatley, M. J. (1992). *Leadership and the new science: Learning about organization from an orderly universe.* San Francisco, CA: Berrett-Koehler.

———. (1999). *Leadership and the new science: Discovering order in a chaotic world.* San Francisco, CA: Berrett-Koehler.

Willower, D. J., and Forsyth, P. B. (1999). A brief history of scholarship on educational administration. In J. Murphy and K. S. Louis (Eds.). *Handbook of research on educational administration,* pp. 1–24. San Francisco, CA: Jossey-Bass.

Wilson, M. C. (2004). *Closing the leadership gap: Why women can and must help run the world.* New York: Viking.

Young, M. D., and Skrla, L. (Eds.). (2003). *Reconsidering feminist research in educational leadership.* Albany: SUNY Press.

Zohar, D. (1997). *Rewiring the corporate brain: Using the new science to rethink how we structure and lead organizations.* San Francisco, CA: Berrett-Koehler.

CHAPTER 16

Women and Educational Leadership in a Muslim Society

A Study of Women College Heads in Pakistan

SAEEDA SHAH

EDUCATIONAL LEADERSHIP is being defined and theorized in multiple ways (Davies, 2005), but these conceptualizations generally exclude any recognition of gender and its implications for theory and practice. This chapter focuses on a particular Muslim society and explores educational leadership with reference to gender. Being a Muslim woman educationist with experience of work in public and voluntary sectors in two very different societies—in the conservative Muslim society of Pakistan and the liberal Western society of England—I argue that educational leadership is a situated concept (Shah, 2006b).

This chapter debates how educational leadership is conceptualized and experienced differently across the gender divide, underpinned by societal beliefs, values and knowledge sources (Shah, 2006a). It presents philosophical and theoretical underpinnings of these conceptualizations from an Islamic perspective, and highlights the interplay between belief systems, dominant discourses, gender and educational leadership. The chapter deliberates how these discourses interact to formulate "educational leadership" in a Muslim society, and explores the implications of these constructions for women leaders and for the status of women in educational leadership in that society. The discussion is premised on the observation that a study of gender is significant to seek understanding of organizational life and roles:

> Gender is a key constitutive component of the field of social, economic and political relations that make up the terrain within which ways of organizing are forged and constructed. (Halford, Savage and Witz, 1997, p. 12)

This is primarily a conceptual chapter but it also draws on direct data collected from a study of roles and practices of women heads of girls-only colleges in Pakistan. The research data consist of in-depth interviews with eleven heads of girls-only colleges, and is availed in conjunction with a wide range of international literature to explore the discourses and practices. The aim is to open a debate on women in educational leadership in a Muslim society and how they experience this role, with the intention to critique the complex and sensitive discourses, and to encourage collaborative research in a hitherto unexplored area of educational leadership.

EDUCATIONAL LEADERSHIP AND GENDER

Gender is often not confronted in different leadership theories "on the assumption that leadership styles and administrative contexts are gender neutral" (Blackmore, 1995, p. 103). Hodgkinson (1991) dismisses the use of feminine pronouns, explaining it in the preface as being "in the interests of clarity, emphasis, or literary merit." Besides such linguistic interests, it is often either a blind eye as if women are not there or tokenism when women are assumed to be there for political reasons. It is bewildering how professional experiences of women often get ignored in the mainstream literature, which may result in theoretical misconstructions.

Women's experiences are influenced by their position as women in interplay with culture-specific practices. Therefore, it is only the voices of women leaders in diverse cultural settings that "may provide insight into a variety of 'female' leadership perspectives emanating from their cultural scripts" (Oplatka and Hertz-Lazarowitz, 2006, p. 3). Ben-Habib argues, "The viewpoint of the concrete other emerges as a distinct one only as a result of self-definition" (1992, p. 168). However, like women leaders themselves, any attempts at "self-definition" by women leaders often get relegated to peripheries, making them invisible. The invisibility of women is not specific or restricted to educational leadership but reflects a wider and complex interplay of discourses over time and across societies, aimed at the marginalization and de-voicing of women. The issue of female exclusion paradoxically comprises both invisibility and visibility, underpinned by politicized discourses of public/private, nature/culture and emotional/rational dualisms which have "rendered women invisible in political and social theory and later in education" (Blackmore, 1995, pp. 107–109).

Any discussion of women in leadership roles "necessarily involves the kinds of conflicts that often accompany their ascendancy to such positions, including the questions of identity, balancing socially constructed and normalized roles and responsibilities, and the issue of marginality both in their professions and in the public mind" (Curry, 2000, p. 4). Three major sets of assumptions leading to female marginalization in educational leadership positions and subsequent absence from theoretical conceptualizations emerging from literature are:

- Sex roles
- Organizational roles
- Power relations

Sex Roles
Entrenched gendered roles have been a common feature of human societies. Patriarchal traditions have forced women into places of invisibility and immobility by "a general identification of women with the sphere of domesticity" (Afshar, 1987, p. 3), by overemphasizing the domestic role and by belittling its status, even though sex roles are scripted and experienced differently across cultures. This role socialization generally gets transferred to public and professional contexts in spite of all the claims to the contrary. When women acquire a leadership role in public, the role change poses a challenge. Al-Khalifa quotes a male teacher as saying, "It grates me to have a woman in position of authority over me," arguing that "rejection of women's leadership [is] a standpoint shared by many men" (1992, p. 101). In many societies, men find it hard to accept women in positions of authority and leadership even in professional contexts, which suggests home-to-job transferring of role relationships.

Sex-role stereotyping is reflected not only in the association of nurturing, caring or domestic roles with women but also in the unpaid domestic labor and "occupational segregation" of women (Fine, 1992, pp. 70–86). This stereotyping often consigns women to low-paid, less prestigious and less powerful positions, and then attributes it to women being less motivated and less ambitious. It is the socio-eco-historical development of the sex roles and the image of women and its dissemination through different channels throughout human history that lies behind such simplistic and misleading assumptions.

The female child is subjected to gendering of sex roles, intentional or unintentional, from a very early age, and learns the stereotyped role, which may require an unlearning when moving into leadership positions, or may result in underplaying her leadership role (Davies, 1992). Different female leaders in Shakeshaft (1991) describe women as tentative, doing more listening, avoiding questions, less assertive, conveying signals of courtesy, and more inclusive rather than exclusive. This can be the impact of role socialization processes influencing women's experiences and expectations in organizational roles.

Organizational Roles
Organizational roles are "traditionally gendered, reflecting the patterns of wider society" (Hall, 1994, p. 3). Gender-specific socialization and organizational structures favor men and disadvantage women. Identification of predominantly male traits and behavior with leadership stems primarily from the socialization processes (Davies, 1992; Hall, 1994, 1996; Kirdar, 2006; Ouston, 1993; Ozga, 1994; Shakeshaft, 1991; Strachan, 1993). Ashburner maintains that "what are termed 'male' and 'female' values are not necessarily attributable to men and women individually but form the basis of stereotyping" (1994, p. 192) through complex processes of socialization. Studies recognize other factors—such as religion, ideology, social class, economic class, race, sect, age and many others—that act as determinants for female exclusion from leadership positions (Ahmed, 1992; hooks, 1990; Ouston, 1993), but to a certain extent all these factors are influenced by gender. Youngs argues that all institutions involve the "exercise of power to the advantage of some and the disadvantage of others," and "gender is a pervasive basis for such differentiations" (2000, pp. 12–13). Women who are leaders or who wish to become leaders are "seen as being in the wrong place" (Gold, 2006).

The gendering of organizational roles is a disadvantage to women leaders (Davies, 1987; Evetts, 1994; Shakeshaft, 1993). Role socialization of women, reinforced by male cultural domination and the tendency to place more value on male tasks (Shakeshaft, 1991), subjects women to a predetermined devaluation of their contributions to work. A perceived association between theories of organizational leadership and masculinity deters women from identifying with the role of leader (Al-Khalifa, 1992). Jill Blackmore rightly argues for a deconstruction of masculine notion of leadership, and invites us "to question what is not included in the discourse as much as what is" (1995, p. 96).

Power Relations

The sex-role inscriptions and gendering of organizational roles influence power relations in professional contexts. The public/private and nature/culture divides, underpinned by histories of feudal patriarchal societies, define the complex interplay operative in relationships and practices. Cultural norms play a further role and, consequently, women leaders' professional experiences of power relations become scripted by their position as women in their microcultures.

In feudal societies, irrespective of cultural variations, a specific concept has functioned of "domestic," structured around the head of the house as the locus, possessing complete authority and the decision making powers on behalf of the "family" (Murray, 1995). Hartmann defines family as a "locus of struggle" (1981, p. 368), emphasizing its implications for women through emotional ties and ideological norms, arguing that "family . . . remains a primary arena where men exercise their patriarchal power" (p. 377). Traditionally, family has served as a convenient space for exercising control, with specific implications for gender, which Mies (1986) discusses as colonization of women, claiming male superiority in the family and then transferring it to other spheres of activity. These strategies diminish women's confidence and self-esteem—a classical colonization "technology," observes Aptheker:

> The process of colonization is not only one of limiting access, of subjugation, of political domination, of racial superiority, or of a poverty of resources, but also an internal erosion, a loss of esteem, a loss of confidence in one's knowledge, an inability to give expression to experience, to name oneself. . . . At the heart of the colonization of women is a belief in the superiority of men, in the infallibility of male judgement and authority and in the absolute priority given to achieving male approval and validation. (1989, p. 8)

Colonization of women leaves men as sole occupiers of the public space with all power over decision making, which is associated with the "powerful" and is symbolic of a right to occupy and operate in the public space:

> We have not yet succeeded in either creating a public space that women can enter, or of overcoming the dilemma of the public/private distinction that such a public space implies. (Seller, 1996, p. 120)

Occupation of public space is a political issue (Arendt, 1959), dominated by economic considerations and politics of representation. And in the case of women, economic imperatives are complicated by gender:

> Women's position is structured by a double set of determinants arising from the relations of gender and derived from the economic organization of the society. (Afshar, 1991, p. 1)

Public space is theoretically open to struggle, challenge and contestations. When women are associated with the private, their access and participation in the educational leadership positions becomes problematic. The issues in networking and relationships for women, which may vary from society to society, further influence power relations in professional contexts. The significance of gender with regard to female experiences across professions and societies makes it important to take into account "women's experiences of gendered power relations . . . as a source of knowledge" (Ramazanoglu, 1993, p. 209). It is not "privileging the significance of gender" (Alcoff, 1988) over other factors, but a recognition of the gender element and of power differentials instituted through given discourses, produced culturally and socially to exercise power:

> Discourses are, therefore, about what can be said, and thought, but also about who can speak, when, where, and with what authority. Discourses embody meaning and social relationships; they constitute both subjectivity and power relations. (Ball, 1990, p. 17)

COUNTRY CONTEXT: PAKISTAN

Any discussion of women in educational leadership or "unique leadership styles of women that ignores important factors such as cultural differences, economic and social-political divisions, race and nationality, religion and identity would not only be unrealistic but may present a distorted picture" (Oplatka and Hertz-Lazarowitz, 2006, p. 3). A complex interplay of these factors shapes women's professional lives in different ways around the world, which may in turn engender diverse leadership styles and practices. The discourse of "female leadership" is determined not simply by the biological gender (Blackmore, 1999; Oplatka, 2001;

Table 16.1. Educational Institutions in Pakistan by Gender

Institutions	Female	Male	Mixed	Total
Primary Schools	43,733	74,005	17,435	135,173
Middle Schools	6,885	7,159	565	14,609
High Schools	2,776	5,965	254	8,995
Higher Secondary Schools	332	472	32	836
Mosque Schools	105	12,184	11	12,300
Colleges	398	445	81	938
Technical/Vocational Institutions	328	388	31	747
Teacher Training Institutes	45	66	24	135
Universities	3			103
Deeni Madaris				12,654

Reay and Ball, 2000), but by the way biological gender is socially constructed in a particular society at a particular time in history.

Pakistan is an Islamic state, created specifically in the name of religion (Islam) (Jaffrelot, 2005). This religious ideology guides the discourses and practices in all fields, including education. It is explicitly stated in the constitution of Pakistan (Khan, 1973) that all the laws and policies will be formulated in conformity with the teachings of the Quran and the *Sunnah* (the Prophet's way). This confirms the role of religion in shaping the roles and practices in public and private.

The government of Pakistan has officially endorsed a global mandate on gender equity for advancing the concept of "gender mainstreaming," which promotes integration of gender-sensitive policies and programs at all levels and throughout all sectors (ESCAP, 1997). However, "statistics indicate that targets have remained unachieved except some pockets of progress" (Qureshi, 2004, p. 11), and this applies to the educational scene as well. According to the Pakistan Economic Survey (2005–2006), Pakistan's overall record in promoting and delivering gender equality has been weak. In spite of the stated aims of the Ministry of Women's Development to ensure equality of opportunity in education and employment, and active participation of women in different spheres of national life, female participation in all spheres including education is hindered by multiple barriers. In the segregated Pakistani society, where women are 47.96% of the population, the breakdown of male, female and mixed-sex institutions at different levels (presented in table 16.1) clearly indicates that women have considerably lower opportunities of education because of less educational provision for females at every level.

This has similarities with other Muslim countries, such as the Arab states where "the number of schools for boys exceeds that for girls, and not many are co-educational" (Kirdar, 2006, p. 192). These disparities

affect the number of women working in the education sector, which is significantly lower than men, as reflected in table 16.2.

Table 16.2 shows that the numbers of women teachers decrease as the level of educational institution goes up, with lowest female ratio in institutions of higher education. In universities there are only 7,962 women teachers as compared to 52,671 men, a ratio of nearly 1:7. The total numbers of women teachers in pre-university institutions are comparatively better, which can be attributed to the segregated system of education, adhered to more strictly at post-primary to pre-university levels (Shah, 1999), and thus providing spaces for women to engage professionally. In the universities, with the exception of new women-only universities (established since 2000), women are very few in numbers and generally concentrated into lower positions. However, there are some indications of change in the new universities. Data collected from three universities in Lahore, known as the educational center of Pakistan, show interesting differences between an old university, a new university, and the new Education University (see table 16.3).

The colleges are generally single-sex and fall within the remit of the Provincial Education Departments.

Table 16.2. Teachers in Pakistan by Institutions and Gender

Teachers	Female	Male	Total
Primary Schools	125,593	197,941	323,534
Middle Schools	52,834	58,425	111,263
High Schools	52,763	108,529	161,292
Higher Secondary Schools	9,729	15,141	24,870
Colleges	6,417	13,170	22,587
Technical/Vocational Institutions	1,450	5,906	7,356
Teacher Training Institutes	965	1,711	2,676
Universities	7,962	52,671	60,633
Mosque Schools	154	17,448	17,602
Deeni Madaris			63,617

Source: Pakistan Education Statistics, 2004–2005.

Table 16.3. Staff by Gender in Three Universities in Lahore, Pakistan

	University of Punjab, est. 1882	Government College University, est. 2003	Education University, est. 2003
Female admin. staff	Nil	7	7
Male admin. staff	67	40	41
Female academics	230	53	49
Male academics	485	184	58
Female deans	3	Nil	N/A
Male deans	8	3	N/A
Female HoD	13	2	3
Male HoD	65	20	8

Source: Author's personal contacts.

Table 16.4. Directors/Deputy-Directors of Colleges in Punjab

Designation	Male	Female	Total
Director of Public Instruction (DPI)	1	Nil	1
Add'l Director of Public Instruction (ADPI)	1	Nil	1
Directors	4	Nil	4
Assistant Directors	6	2	8
District Education Officers (C), DEO	37	Nil	37

Source: Office of the Director of Public Instruction (Colleges), Punjab, Pakistan, March 28, 2007.

The data collected from the most developed province of Pakistan (Punjab) illustrate that the structure responsible for managing male and female colleges is again highly male-dominated (see table 16.4).

This indicates that women have generally marginal participation in mixed-sex contexts and institutions. The positions of leadership occupied by women are either gender-specific or in women-only institutions. Sex segregation, generally critiqued by liberal Western thought, emerges as a factor supporting women in accessing educational leadership in Pakistan. However, this also raises questions regarding female participation on desegregated sites and its implications for equal opportunities. The relevant debates that need to be examined here are Islamic philosophy of education, the concept of educational leadership in Islam, and women in educational leadership and Islam, and how these shape and determine women's leadership role in this segregated context.

EDUCATION, EDUCATIONAL LEADERSHIP, GENDER AND ISLAM

The notion of educational leadership is usually linked with the aims and theory of education. "The Islamic theory of education is fundamentally based upon the Quranic concepts" (Abdullah, 1982, p. 43). The emphasis on seeking and acquiring knowledge is one of the basic teachings of Islam, making it *faraz* (incumbent) upon every Muslim male and female. Knowledge is expected to contribute to the development of *self* and society, and *self* in articulation with knowledge actualizes its own potentialities: "The self (*nafs*) owns only that which it earns and it changes through what it assimilates, good or bad" (The Quran, 74:38).

Thus the primary aim of education is an ongoing development of the *self*. Education is expected to "facilitate developing those values whose roots are in the attributes of God and which God has planted within human beings as potentialities" (Ashraf, 1995). The role of the leader is to bring out these "potentialities" and to guide the learners nearer to God. Knowledge is the source and justification of status and leadership, which operates beyond the gender divide: "God will raise in ranks those of you who believe as well as those who are given knowledge" (The Quran, 58:11). And, "If any do deeds of righteousness, be they men or women, and have faith, they will enter paradise" (The Quran, 4:124).

In Islam, women share in all the rights, duties and activities of religious, social, economic and political life. Many Muslim women excel in spiritual, intellectual and physical achievements even in the oppressive patriarchal societies. In early Islam, women were active in public (Ahmed, 1992; Mernessi, 1993), participating in the mosques and in the Prophet's discourses. There were also women like Nessiba bint Ka'ab and Khawlah bint Al-Azwar (Al-Hibri, 1982, p. 211; El-Saadawi, 1982, p. 197), who surpassed men in the battlefields in their valor and skill. The stance often adopted by the women Muslim scholars (Ahmed, 1992; Al-Hibri, 1982; El-Saadawi, 1982; 1991; Hussain, 1984), and as often supported by non-Muslim women writers (Schimmel, 1982; Stowasser, 1994), is that Islam and the Quran do not establish any inherent spiritual, intellectual or physical inferiority of women. However, various cultural, economic and sociopolitical factors have contributed to the formation of a patriarchal image of women in Islam:

> Patriarchy co-opted Islam after the death of the prophet—many passages in the Quran were interpreted by patriarchy loosely and out of context, in support of a vicious patriarchal ideology. These interpretations were then handed down to women as God's revealed words. (Al-Hibri, 1982, p. viii)

The Islamic philosophy of education or the Quranic teachings may not be gender discriminatory, but the discourses that have been produced in articulation with multiple social, economic, political and cultural factors in different Muslim societies and legitimized in the name of religion are often gendered. The remaining part of this chapter discusses women educational leaders in the Muslim society of Pakistan, with a focus on how discourses of *Muslimness*, or what counts as *Muslimness* in that context, shape the role and practices of these leaders.

GENDER AND EDUCATIONAL LEADERSHIP PRACTICES IN PAKISTAN

Pakistan is a Muslim society with feudal patriarchal structures and traditions. The patriarchal assumption that women cannot be leaders at the highest level—particularly where the followers include men—is implicit in the Constitution of Pakistan (Khan, 1973), which requires the head of the Islamic Republic of Pakistan to be male. The controversy in religious circles following the election of a woman, Benazir Bhutto, as the first female prime minister in 1988, and the efforts on the part of her party to appease the critical *Ulema* (religious scholars) by stressing the difference between the "head of the state" and the "head of the government" (legitimizing Benazir Bhutto as head of government), is an example of the oppressive force of entrenched traditions and vested interests in forming discourses and setting agendas.

In Pakistan, views about women have further been affected by the intermingling of Muslims on their arrival in the subcontinent with diverse local cultures, especially the Hindu religion and culture which at that time accorded very low status to women and at times even negated their right to education (King, 1987). At the intersections of tribal Arab cultures brought by the Muslims, local Hindu culture, regional feudal patriarchal structures, and given discourses of what it meant to be a Muslim in that context, discourses emerged which marginalized women, confining them to the domestic.

However, women's lives in Pakistan do not form a homogeneous entity. Depending on geographical location, a Pakistani woman can be "a highly qualified and self-confident professional or a modest domesticated housewife, leading an extremely isolated life cut off from all decisions and information" (Qureshi, 2004, p. 3). It is the broader social framework that is segregatory, with implications for female education and educational leadership. Single-sex schools and colleges are a common feature of this society, as in most Muslim societies. During the period of General Zia (1977–1988), segregation was imposed more strongly on educational sites in the name of Islamization (Saigol, 1993). Single-sex institutions were projected as an important feature of Muslim society that led to the development of two almost separate sectors of education—male (*mardana*), and female (*zanana*).

Segregation is observed more closely in the rural regions in Pakistan than in the urban areas, and is generally stricter at post-primary-to-pre-university levels. One reason is the age group of the students at that level, perceived as sensitive within socio-religious discourses of sex, marriage, inheritance, family and family honor (*izzat*). Nevertheless, due to pragmatics involved, this dichotomy has never been as complete as, for example, in some other Muslim countries such as Saudi Arabia (Al-Harriri, 1987; Al-Shallan, 1990), where male/female communication is completely forbidden. In female colleges in Pakistan, office support staff, some lab assistants/helpers, and many other workers are often males, adding to the complexity of educational context for women leaders.

This sex-segregated structure, premised on conflicting discourses of keeping "the intruders out" (Helms, 1995) and "the confinement of women" (Mernissi, 1985), does create a space for women to access educational leadership. However, the nature of female leadership roles and women leaders' experiences are influenced by the essential framework of the concerned social structure and its ideological basis that determines sex roles, organizational practices and power relations. The most significant influences in this regard are the concepts of family, honor (*izzat*) and sex segregation. Moreover, certain aspects of the teachings of Islam such as family, family obligations and domestic role of women further determine the discourses and practices.

RELIGION AND DISCOURSE FORMATION

In a proclaimed Islamic state like Pakistan, religion determines those power structures and social controls that regulate and legitimize discourses and practices. Different Muslim societies may develop diverse structures and discourses, but they all need to gain validation from religion. Discourses are shaped and attain power and control in societies through those "who are charged with saying what counts as true" (Foucault, 1980, p. 131). In Muslim societies, these discourses are produced and manipulated by religious scholars or groups through a self-acquired, self-appropriated power of interpretation (Shah, 1999). These interpretations are accepted by the believing followers as religious teachings, mainly because of the high status of knowledge and knowledge-givers in Islam. These discourses are constructed and disseminated in such a way that the masses are often unable to differentiate between Islamic principles and teachings, and social practices. Discussing in a different context, Basit attributes this inability of the masses to judge interpretations to their lack of knowledge: "The fact that they were religious but uneducated meant that they misinterpreted [the] Quran and the Hadith" (1995, p. 51).

A particular view of Islam has been constructed in the feudal patriarchal society of Pakistan through discourses produced by those occupying spaces for interpretation of religious teachings, which has discouraged freedom of thought and at times negated the Islamic spirit of equality and social justice. Religion is manipulated to produce a political and practical depowering of women, forcing them to submit to cultural pressures and practices through discourses of *Muslimness*. Interpretations of religious texts are used as a tool of social control centrally involved in the propagation, selective dissemination, and social appropriation of discourses (Ball, 1990; Talbani, 1996), and aimed at perpetuating gender inequality and discrimination.

The power of these discourses is so strong that women leaders are seduced into compliance. My research participants[1] were explicit in their allegiance to religion and they believed that it was their duty as Muslim women to follow "Islamic traditions." What they appeared to understand as "Islamic traditions" was uncritical acceptance of dominating discourses. For example, they explained their dress code, demeanor and observance of segregation as "Islamic." The head of a large girls-only college argued:

> We are Muslims and we must observe our values . . . not shaking hands with men, not walking on the road without covering our heads . . . this is what I teach my students also.

In spite of admitted problems in performing in a segregated society, these Muslim educational leaders not only followed the prescribed discourses but imposed them on the female students as well, contributing to a process of "social reproduction" (Giddens, 2006). Their response is similar to that of the Orthodox Jewish principal in Karnieli (2006) who "adheres strictly to all of her society's regulations and conventions; [and] of teachers, she demands circumspect, responsible conduct, with no compromises" (pp. 116–117).

FAMILY AND FEMALE ROLE: DEPLOYING THE DISCOURSES

Family, as an institution, generally reflects the relationships among people in a specific society. However, interpretations of the notion of family in diverse cultures and societies have been constructed to suit the exploiting groups. Family has been used as "an ideological and economic site of oppression which is protected from scrutiny by the very privacy that 'family life' celebrates" (Fine, 1992, p. 10). Mies proclaims that women emerge as "a sociological minority; . . . discriminated against everywhere—in politics, employment, and education, in the family and by the institution of the family" (1986, p. 21). The authority rests with male members of the family, creating unequal power structures. Although Islam does not legitimize unequal power structures, religious texts have always been availed for these purposes.

In Islam, family is the basic unit of social existence, which serves as a reference for rights and duties. The Quran proposes different role priorities in different relationships, expounding a network of rights and duties within the family and wider community:

> O people! Be careful of your duty to your lord, Who created you from a single soul and created its mate of the same and spread from these two a multitude of men and women. (4:1)

Women in Islam have a nurturing responsibility toward the "family," and men are the "maintainers." This has encouraged prioritizing of women's domestic role in the Muslim societies to the extent of making women invisible through given interpretations of the notions of motherhood and family (Brock, Dada and Jatta, 2006). It is often ignored that if there were no professional roles for women, the Quran would not be explicit about women being masters of their own possessions and earnings (Afshar, 1994, p. 131). According to a participating college head, this prioritizing of family role constrains women educational leaders:

> I am planning to give up principalship. Government is transferring me to another town, and my husband and in-laws don't agree with the move. It will affect children also. My father-in-law is old and I have to look after him as well. The in-laws and even other relatives will criticize that I am after career and do not care for family responsibilities. Family comes first—how can I choose to continue? (PF 6)

Family emerges as a doubly emphasized phenomenon, deeply embedded both in ideology and culture, creating a network of relationships that is complex and challenging in its impact on roles and practices of women educational leaders. Not only does it impose restrictions on physical and professional mobility, but it also puts women leaders under pressure in decision-making, as explained by one principal:

> You are not free to make even professional decisions. It is always somebody either related to you, or a member of the *baradari* (extended family), or a friend of a member of the *baradari*—and you are caught in this! You have to oblige them—particularly if it happens to be somebody approaching through a male member of the family.

The depowering enacted through "family" and through "male" members of the family is challenging. The intricate networks of relationships and obligations in the family make women leaders vulnerable in the professional domain. Professional decision-making becomes subservient to family obligations. By deploying sociocultural discourses and practices, family is converted into a space of oppression. Second, a difference in the responsibilities within the institution of family is constructed as a gender-specific phenomenon and extended to the public, which depowers women leaders in the performance of their professional responsibilities.

For the women college heads, family obligations required attending to family and extended family priorities and wishes, and trying to be successful leaders as well in the face of all the challenges posed in a feudal, patriarchal, segregatory society. However, paradoxically, the dilemma of a public activity such as educational leadership in a segregated society is resolved to some extent in the case of women college heads by reinventing the site as "family" and relocating it within the domestic: "The college is a family, an extended family. The head has to manage the same way as a family head, treating each one according to one's positioning" (PF3).

This reinvention is aimed at appropriating power through the discourses of family and motherhood. Ali explains the "patterns of female control, dominance and decision-making" among Asians, where "domestic content is predominantly female-controlled" (1996, p. 453). Also, within the context of relationships in Islam, certain positions have claims to higher respect and authority, with particular emphasis on the status of

mother (Abdalti, 1994; Badawi, 1994). By constructing colleges as "family," the "excluded," "segregated" women college heads moved into a discourse where they could lay claims to power and authority as mothers, sanctified by the religion. In addition to that, family also emerges as a strong network and source of protection:

> You know how difficult it is for women to work in positions like this. You have to communicate with men and influential people, who are men generally. And what our society is like! Having a strong family helps—people are careful in talking about you, and listen to what you have got to say even though you are a woman. (PF 2)

Apparently the women leaders felt safer and stronger in managing the institutions, students and staff from a position of status and authority within the religious discourse. Schrijvers discusses the "paradox of powerlessness and power" of women in Sri Lanka, arguing that "one-sided portrayal of these 'others' as passive victims of colonialism, patriarchy and capitalism was not correct. . . . I had seen motherhood and sexuality as source of women's power" (1993, p. 155). The integration of religious and social discourses invested women with a status and authority where gender discrimination could be resisted. Whether or not they experienced balancing of different roles as "a source of pressure" (Al-Khalifa, 1992, p. 96) assumes secondary significance in view of the empowerment achieved through fusion of personal and professional:

> The head's role is like a parent. S/he should manage the institution as head of the family. S/he should be flexible but firm. (PF3)

In many Muslim societies, women have been deprived of many of the Quranic rights in the name of family peace and interest (Afshar, 1987, p. 132), but there seem to be certain advantages, ideological as well as practical, associated with the institution of family. In a Western context, women's career mapping appears to be affected by the motherhood issue and responsibilities of looking after a family (Ozga, 1994; Shakeshaft, 1993). However, in Pakistan, and maybe in many other countries that have extended family networks, women do not have to take themselves off work for child rearing. They get child care and even sharing of domestic work from within the family, and thus child rearing and family duties do not emerge as a strong barrier to professional roles.

Roles are socially constructed, whether domestic or public. In this research context, social was further enmeshed with religious to the extent that to disentangle and identify the discourses was problematic. Women-only colleges offered aspiring women an opening of space in public. However, the structural denominations inscribed the roles and practices, reinforced by the sociocultural practices where "traditional patterns of behaviors prescribe certain roles to which individuals, males and females, partially conform to differing degrees" (Blackmore, 1995, p. 121). What Valerie Hall observes regarding educational managers in a British context holds true of women leaders in this context as well, that:

> As individuals, they cannot be separated from the society and culture in which they work and in which assumptions about men and women in public and private, in work or at family, prevail. (1996, p. 12)

The roles of women leaders reflected these "assumptions." The leadership practices often conformed to the gender stereotypes in the wider social order. The roles of female college heads were discursively constructed through historically inscribed discourses of what it was to be a Muslim, a woman, and in the "domestic/public," according to given interpretations of religion in that culture. This meant that not only the site of activity got dislocated from the public to the private, as suggested by the pervasive metaphorical use of family for the colleges, but also that the female colleges became defined as female space within the "family."

The female colleges are officially termed in Pakistan as *zanana* (for women) colleges, which reflects the marked boundaries of family space on the cultural scene with associated connotations of rights and duties, positions, norms, movements and access. Such cultural norms reinforce a gendered notion of authority which does not allow women to be mobile in public or be in immediate authority above men. Women bring their femaleness with its connotations and status in society with them when they enter organizations. Even in the professional capacity, women college heads were expected not to move out of *zanana* except strictly in accordance with the notion of "family" and norms of *izzat*.

HONOR (*IZZAT*): PLYING THE PARADOX

Izzat is a powerful discourse that determines women leaders' professional practices and roles in Pakistan.

Females are perceived bearers of *izzat*, whether publicly or domestically (Shah, 1998). The term embodies enormously powerful cultural judgments that transcend linguistic interpretation. Females are expected to uphold the honor of the family, community and almost everyone else through a strict maintenance of an honor code defined often by males. These honor codes are without exception gender-discriminatory and highly marginalizing for women. Women become subjects of *izzat* through no personal choice or act, but simply because they are females. This may imply females being bartered in feuds, used for settling disputes, and becoming targets of vengeance in conflicts (Mukhtar Mai, online).

The notion of *izzat* for women educational leaders indirectly implies acceptance of prevailing social norms (Shah, 1999) and submission to the male head of the family—if not husband or father then the next male in hierarchy (Weiss, 1994)—in all matters concerning personal, marital, professional, social, economic and others; capitulation to restricted/proscribed mobility; observance of sex segregation; and even withdrawal from the public. This promotes male control by subjecting women to "surveillance" and "disciplining" (Foucault, 1980). Double moral standards for men and women (Afshar, 1994) and a politically constructed notion of *izzat* control women in public. The discourse was manipulated and misappropriated to "blackmail" women into silence and invisibility, subjecting them to a close surveillance, as remonstrated by many women participants. However, women leaders also admitted higher pertinence of *izzat* for females:

> We and our girls are responsible for family *izzat*. A breath of scandal and that not only ruins your professional future and career but also upsets family life—even destroys it. That is a stigma, and a woman with this stigma gets sidelined in the professional field as well. You become excluded at home and in the profession. Better play it safe—keep your head bowed and protect your *izzat*.

Women leaders perform under high pressures because of the social norms and the associated fear of "gossip," "scandal" and "social victimization." In view of the perceived threats to their careers, reputation and family setups, they often try to underplay their leadership roles. They prefer to remain "invisible in the interest of family *izzat*" (PF3), and often leave mainstream leadership positions for men. Threatened by the patriarchal norms and surveillance dominating in the public, women college heads appeared to feel secure in the reconstruction of colleges as "family" as discussed earlier. However, the tensions between the Islamic and the patriarchal notions surfaced when "religious content" (Sharma, 1980, pp. 3–7) was replaced by patriarchal content and disseminated under religious cover. For example, Islamic injunctions regarding rights and status of a wife and mother were reconstructed as "discourse of motherhood and wifely duty to household for honorable, implying otherwise who extend the sphere of activities" (Afshar, 1987, p. 73), thus effectively confining women and curtailing their mobility.

A mobile woman posed the threat of putting the family *izzat* at risk. Women leaders were the subjects and objects of family *izzat* and as such were in an extremely vulnerable position. They were culturally constructed as "site of familial honor" (Afshar, 1994, p. 129), and if anything unseemly, to say the least, happened to a woman outside the family bounds it was to be viewed by how it affected the social family, rather than the woman as a person. Thus the women became subject to "surveillance" and manipulations. Foucault (1977), discussing the effect of constant surveillance on prisoners, argues that it instills anxiety so that the inmates come to scrutinize their own behavior and eventually adopt the norms of conduct desired by the disciplinary institution, forming them into obedient subjects. By being constructed as "the guarded," the women subjected to surveillance gradually lose their agency and subject position. They are disciplined into compliance in anticipation of the possible social threats:

> No one is interested in going [away from family home] as a principal. Whoever wishes can publish anything against you in the [news-]chapters . . . anything false or completely baseless, which not only affects you professionally but makes social life difficult in our society. You can't put family *izzat* at stake!(PF1)

Izzat emerges as a socioculturally constructed discourse to "control" women. The women leaders mentioned the gender-discriminatory nature of *izzat* but there was no indication of resistance to discourse in spite of the fact that the ethical charter of conduct/character laid down by Islam in the Quran provides an identical framework for men and women. The Quran says to both "believing men to lower their gaze" (24:30), and to women to "cover their bodies when they go out" (24:31). However, in practice, this code is often completely relaxed for men and magnified for women in the name of *izzat*.

The skewed codes of conduct constructed by male authority posed threats to women leaders who might choose to move in the positions of visibility. Participation in the public was made into a challenge as attributes like "seditious, corrupt or prostitution" were "granted freely to women but not to their male 'accomplices'" (Afshar, 1987, p. 74). By associating disparate notions of *izzat* with women and men and making women solely responsible for it (Weiss, 1994), the concept is given a gendered description that has serious implications for women leaders operating in the public. The tradition of sex segregation in Pakistani society provided spaces for women to access leadership positions in single-sex institutions, but their leadership role was effectively curtailed by the threat of possible risks and social hazards in moving across the boundaries:

> You cannot travel alone or meet male colleagues alone. If you are a woman, you would be immediately labelled as immoral. (PF1)

According to the respondents, localized social and behavioral norms marginalized women. A fear of interpretations and consequences effectively discouraged communication and movement across the boundaries, with quite explicit demarcations of the sites of activity. Norms of conversation and behavior across genders further disciplined behavior and communication. A female interviewee stated:

> Being a woman principal, I occasionally do face problems. Then I talk to the concerned male personnel on the phone. If the problem is not solved I have to make a second call; but there would be hesitation this time! I intentionally try to avoid the situation. (PF4)

Stronger claims to the discourse of *izzat*, linked with the leadership role, required close observation of religious values and what it meant to be a Muslim woman in that context. An effective leadership role was premised on being perceived as a good Muslim woman of moral values and character. A genuine emphasis on conduct and character can be traced back to the Islamic concept of a teacher who has the dual role of a knowledge giver and moral role model to be emulated. But there can be another aspect to it: an honorable family could be destroyed through the character assassination of a woman member of the house, encouraging immobilization and invisibility of women. Then it becomes a "power technology" linked with sex segregation, posing challenges to women leaders.

SEX SEGREGATION: ENABLING OR DISABLING?

Sex segregation emerges as a political technology for ordering roles and practices. The rhetoric emphasizes it as an Islamic injunction, but in Islam, segregation is not to constrain women, but to restrain men *and* women in accordance with the Quranic values and code of conduct. Sex segregation as defined by the Quran is a part of a particular educative program, which aims at a nonthreatening environment to ensure equal participation of women in the public, in which aspect it has certain similarities with the feminist approach. In the first Muslim society of Medina, during the Prophet's lifetime, two major public sites were the mosque and the battlefield. Muslim women participated in both, which shows that the practice of excluding women from the public was not the intent of the Prophet (Ahmed, 1992; Fernea and Bezirgan, 1977; Mernissi, 1991). Segregation derives from the concept of veiling, which is political and situation specific. For example, the Quran says:

O Prophet! Tell thy wives and thy daughters and the women of thy believers to draw their cloaks close around them (when they go out/abroad). That will be better, *so that they may be recognised and not annoyed.* [emphasis added] (33:59)

Here, the recommendation of "veiling" emerges as a sociopolitical strategy to make Muslim women "visible" as distinct from non-Muslim women. Making situated commands a basis for sex segregation has served as a mode for ordering power relations in Muslim societies. There is a huge literature on veiling, discussing it as a quasi-religious, politically charged cultural phenomenon generating norms and practices oppressive for Muslim women (Zein-Ed-Din, 1982). In the Pakistani context, veiling and associated discourses are used to impose and perpetuate segregation. Women principals admitted of advantages of sex segregation in education, but also recognized constraints and barriers imposed by it.

Contending discourses of advantages/disadvantages of this segregated site make the analysis complex. Data say that women's colleges in general perform better than male colleges, which was emphasized by the participating heads and supported by evidence from national examination results at that level. The interviewees ascribed this to the ethos and norms of the *zanana*: female population, both staff and students, being more cooperative, obedient, hardworking and disciplined, who concentrated on work in the absence of any distractions or diversions. This approach, to underplay hard work and underestimate great effort to achieve success in that context, hints at the disciplining effects of the prevailing discourses where male heads must prevail and women should not appear to outperform males.

Furthermore, the construction of colleges as "domestic" shifted the site from the public to the familial/private with all the associated connotations of power differential with control over finances emerging as another issue. In the absence of higher male authority, the control of money practically went into the hands of the senior male figure on the site, even when "lower in authority," in this case an accountant/clerk. The accountants in most female colleges in Pakistan happen to be men, who operate in the male domain of finance. The participating women in powerful leadership positions continued to feel powerless because of the cultural "gendered ideological foundation of authority" (Luke, 1996, p. 289). The mother figure was rendered a *bechari* (helpless dependent), often little more than a signing robot. Finances were centrally controlled by the education department, with fixed budgets allocated to the colleges. The principals officially had powers as "drawing/dispersing officers," but in practice, all matters related to purchases, invoicing, bills and payment were delegated to the accountants because finance offices and banks were "male domains" (*mardana*). For a woman it would be a violation of family *izzat* to move into "male domains," and here *izzat* as a technology of power serves a double purpose: control of women and control of finances/resources.

A woman principal had to think twice before even deciding to visit a male-dominated public space on her own. Some did mention that they went to male offices occasionally but accompanied by a male member of the immediate family for the sake of appropriateness. Valerie Hall's observation in the British context has relevance here: that organizational roles reflect the patterns of wider society and that expectations of men's and women's behavior outside the workplace influence expectations at work (1994, p. 3). A female participant (PF11) remarked that for a woman "going to the accounts office is itself a problem." The women's restricted and proscribed mobility not only caused delays and malpractice in performance of professional tasks, but also subjected women to exploitation: "Many years back, my clerk asked for 500 [Pakistani] rupees to get my bill passed. I refused and the bill did not pass. Much later, I got it done through personal influence" (PF6).

Power differentials and gender demarcations had implications for the leadership of women-only colleges regarding roles and practices of women leaders in a society that prioritized and approved sex segregation. Women in this specific Islamic society were subject to a complicated multidimensional power play. The depowering of women college heads by subordinate finance staff, who predominantly happened to be males at this women-only site, reinforced patriarchal power, aiming at women's exclusion from positions of power, or at least restraining the exercise of power through weakening their hold over money/finances, which has great significance in that society as a power marker. Structural constraints such as all-male offices and male support staff, cultural traditions of male supremacy, and the notion of sex segregation appear to be exploited to restrain women in role performance, and ultimately limit the opportunities of career progression:

> Men get angry if a woman is appointed in a senior position. Their stand is that women should be selected for women-only posts but not for open-to-both ones. . . . As long as we are in subordinate positions, there is no problem . . . otherwise there would be even attempts at character assassination. (PF9)

Policy-making was another area from which women were excluded by default. They often chose to be low profile, self-effacing and compliant, acting upon the policies rather than generating the policies by actively engaging in the debates. The discipline in the performing *zanana*, where women are "seen but never heard" (Belenky, 1986, p. 32), feeling "deaf and dumb" (1986, p. 24), a consequence of self-policing or social gaze or both gets transferred to the professional context. Although women leaders appear to have different ways of coping with powerlessness (Lamphere, 1994, p. 220), that does not mitigate the issues of de-voicing and silencing. The following quotation from one female college head illuminates the point:

> In general, attention is not paid to women's words. Their opinion regarding any official matter is not given that weight as a man's word. Then, being a woman, it does not seem appropriate to argue with men. (PF3)

Paradoxically, women heads of *zanana* colleges also felt protected by the "walls and veils," which kept the intruders out. Unlike *mardana* (men-only) colleges, *zanana* colleges were closed to the "public" and a violation of the bounds by the males, unless prescribed,

was culturally inappropriate and liable to social censure. This provided women leaders a space in which to maneuver without the threat of open interference and blatant pressures. In spite of the obvious disadvantages such as issues of mobility, socio-professional networking, barriers to career progression and many others, the women leaders felt advantaged by the comparative protection of the *zanana*.

CONCLUSIONS

Educational leadership for women in Pakistan is framed in a discourse of *Muslimness*. What is empowerment or development for a Muslim female leader cannot be delinked from their *Muslimness*. The tradition of sex segregation in Pakistani society provided spaces for women to perform in the single-sex institutions, but the confinement continued to prevail by reconstructing those as "family" and/or "private." Outside these institutions, at the top leadership level, women were effectively kept out or frightened away through the threat of social hazards.

The management practices of the college heads appeared to draw on the religious, sociocultural and professional discourses, moving from one to the other according to the situational demands. The women educational leaders in this context performed within the gender discourse which, in this case, had its roots in interpretations of religion and the status of women in Islam. These appeared to be deliberately wielded by women and men to perpetuate certain regimes and indicated "how truth is implicated and deployed in social practices and how 'regimes of truth' can have profound social and cultural consequences" (Beechy and Donald, 1985, p. xiv). These discourses opened discursive fields to the Muslim women college heads to position and redefine themselves. The discourse of equality encouraged women to enhance economic independence, some career progression and social mobility, but a counter-discourse of gender difference imposed constraints. Movements within and across the discourses of gender, culture and religion were situation-determined, and continuously changed priorities. This suggests that any analysis and theorizing of roles and practices needs to be debated within the parameters of these discourses, particularly the religious ones because of the Quran being the accepted ultimate validating authority in that context.

NOTE

1. The study included male and female heads of single-sex colleges in the region. Each was given a code, PF for

Participating Female and PM for Participating Male, and a number. Only data collected from women college heads are used in this chapter.

REFERENCES CITED

Abdal'ati, H. (1994). *Islam in focus.* Doha-Qatar: The Ministry of Awqaf and Islamic Affairs.

Abdullah, A. S. (1982). *Educational theory: A Quranic outlook.* Makkah, Saudi Arabia: Umm-Al-Qura University.

Afshar, H. (Ed.). (1987). Women, marriage and the state in Iran. In H. Afshar (Ed.). *Women, state and ideology,* pp. 70–86. London: Macmillan Press.

———. (1991). *Women, development and survival in the Third World.* London: Longman.

———. (1994). Muslim women in West Yorkshire. In H. Afshar and M. Maynard (Eds.). *The dynamics of race and gender: Some feminist interventions,* pp. 127–147. London: Taylor and Francis.

Ahmed, A. S., and Hastings, D. (Eds.). (1992). *Post-modernism and Islam: Predicament and promise.* London: Routledge.

Ahmed, L. (1992). *Women and gender in Islam: Historical roots of a modern debate.* New Haven CT: Yale University Press.

Al-Rawaf, H. S., and Simmons, C. (1991). Religion, tradition and the education of Muslim women in Saudi Arabia. *Muslim Education Quarterly,* 9(1), pp. 24–33.

Alcoff, L. (1988). Cultural feminism vs. post-structuralism: The identity crisis in feminism. *Signs, 13*(3), pp. 405–436.

Al-Harriri, R. (1987). Islam's point of view on women's education. *Comparative Education, 23*(1), pp. 51–57.

Al-Hibri, A. (Ed.). (1982). *Women and Islam.* Oxford: Pergamon Press. Special issue of *Women's Studies International Forum,* 5(2).

Ali, R. E. (1996). The youth service and the young Asians in Peterborough. Unpublished Ph.D. thesis, University of Nottingham.

Al-Khalifa, E. (1992). Management by halves: Women teachers and school management. In N. Bennett, M. Crawford, and C. Riches (Eds.). *Managing change in education,* pp. 95–106. London: Paul Chapman and Oxford University Press.

Al-Shallan. (1990). The duties and responsibilities of primary school head-mistress in Riyadh, Saudi Arabia. Unpublished Ph.D. thesis. University of Cardiff.

Aptheker, B. (1989). How to do meaningful work in women's studies. In E. Abel and M. Pearson (Eds.). *The spectrum of women's lives,* pp. 5–16. New York: Gordon and Breach.

Arendt, H. (1959). *The human condition.* New York: Doubleday.

Ashburner, L. (1994). Women in management careers: Opportunities and outcomes. In J. Evetts (Ed.). *Women and career: Themes and issues in advanced industrial societies,* pp. 188–202. London and New York: Longman.

Ashraf, S. A. (1995). Basic principles in the formulation of curriculum for tertiary education with specific reference to humanities. *Muslim Education Quarterly, 13*(1), pp. 5–11.

Badawi, L. (1994). Islam. In J. Holm and J. Bowker (Eds.). *Women in religion,* pp. 84–112. London, New York: Pinter Publishers.

Ball, S. J. (1990). *Politics and policy making in education: Explorations in policy sociology.* London: Routledge.

Basit, T. N. (1995). "I want to go to college": British Muslim girls and the academic dimension of schooling. *Muslim Education Quarterly, 12*(3), pp. 36–54.

Belenky, F. M., et al. (1986). *Women's ways of knowing: The development of self, voice, and mind.* New York: Basic Books.

Beechy, V., and Donald, J. (Eds.). (1985). *Subjectivity and social relations: A reader.* Milton Keynes: Oxford University Press.

Ben-Habib, S. (1992). *Situating the self: Gender, community and post-modernism in contemporary ethics.* Cambridge: Polity Press.

Blackmore, G. (1995). Educational leadership: A feminist critique and reconstruction. In J. Smyth (Ed.). *Critical discourses on teacher development,* pp. 93–129. London: Cassell.

Blackmore, J. (1999). *Troubling women: Feminism, leadership and educational change.* Buckingham: Open University Press.

Brock, C., Dada, J., and Jatta, T. (2006). Selected perspectives on education in West Africa, with special reference to gender and religion. In R. Griffin, *Education in the Muslim world: Different Perspectives.* Oxford: Symposium Books, pp. 211–238.

Curry, B. K. (2000). *Women in power: Pathways to leadership in education.* New York: Teachers College Press (Athene Series).

Davies, B. (2005). *The essentials of school leadership.* London: Chapman.

Davies, L. (1987). Gender and the management of education in the Third World countries. *Comparative Education, 23*(1), pp. 85–94.

Davies, L., and Gunawardena, C. (1992). *Women and men in educational management: An international enquiry.* Paris: IIEP.

El-Saadawi, N. (1982). Women and Islam. In A. Al-Hibri (Ed.). *Women and Islam.* Oxford: Pergamon Press. Special issue of *Women's Studies International Forum,* 5(2), pp. 193–206.

ESCAP (1997). *Women in Pakistan: A country profile.* New York: United Nations.

Evetts, J. (1994). Gender and secondary headship. In J. Evetts (Ed.). *Women and career: Themes and issues in advanced industrial societies,* pp. 157–169. London and New York: Longman.

Fernea, E. W., and Bezirgan, B. Q. (Eds.). (1977). *Middle Eastern Muslim women speak.* Austin and London: University of Texas Press.

Fine, B. (1992). *Women's employment and the capitalist family*. London: Routledge.

Foucault, M. (1977). *Discipline and punish: The birth of the prison*. London: Allen Lane.

———. (1980). *Power/knowledge: Selected interviews and other writings, 1972–1977*. Brighton: Harvester Press.

Giddens, A. (2006). *Sociology*. (5th ed.). Cambridge: Polity Press.

Gold, A. (2006). Women, leadership and values. In *Proceedings of International Conference on Social Sciences: Endangered and Engendered*, FJWU (Fatima Jinnah Women University: Pakistan). December, 2004, pp. 17–39.

Halford, S., Savage, M., and Witz, A. (1997). *Gender, career and organizations*. London: Macmillan Press.

Hall, V. (1994). Making it happen: A study of women head teachers. Chapter presented at American Educational Research Association Annual Meeting, New Orleans, April.

———. (1996). *Dancing on the ceiling: A study of women managers in education*. London: Paul Chapman Publishing.

Hartmann, I. H. (1981). Family as the locus of gender, class and politics. *Signs, 6*, pp. 366–394.

Helms, L. M. (1995). The haram as a sacred space for Muslim women. *Muslim Education Quarterly, 12*(3), pp. 62–72.

Hodgkinson, C. (1991). *Educational leadership: The moral art*. Albany: State University of New York Press.

Holm, J., and Bowker, J. (Eds.). (1994). *Women in religion*. London, New York: Pinter Publishers.

hooks, b. (1990). *Yearning: Race, gender, and cultural politics*. Boston: South End Press.

Hussain, F. (1984). *Muslim women*. New York: St. Martin's Press.

Jaffrelot, C. (Ed.). (2005). *A history of Pakistan and its origins*. London: Anthem Press.

Jones, A. (1993). Becoming a "girl": Poststructuralist suggestions for educational research. *Gender and Education, 5*(2), pp. 157–166.

Karnieli, M. (2006). The diamond workshop: A story of an ultra-orthodox female principal. In I. Oplatka and R. Hertz-Lazarowitz (Eds.). *Women principals in a multicultural society: New insights into feminist educational leadership*, pp. 103–121. Sense Publishers.

Kelly, G. P., and Elliot, C. M. (1982). *Women's education in the Third World: Comparative perspectives*. Albany: State University of New York Press.

Khan, S. M. I. (1973). *The constitution of the Islamic Republic of Pakistan*. Khyber Law Publishers.

King, U. (1987). World religions, women, and education. *Comparative Education, 23*(1), pp. 35–49.

Kirdar, S. (2006). The development of women's education in the Arab world. In R. Griffin (Ed.). *Education in the Muslim world: Different perspectives*, pp. 191–210. Symposium Books.

Lamphere, L. (1994). (Response). Expanding our notions of "critical qualitative methodology": Bringing race, class, and gender into the discussion. In A. Giltin (Ed.). *Power and method: Political activism and educational research*, pp. 217–224. New York and London: Routledge.

Luke, C. (1996). Feminist pedagogy theory: Reflections on power and authority. *Educational Theory, 46*(3), pp. 283–302.

Mernissi, F. (1985). *Beyond the veil: Male-female dynamics in modern Muslim society*. London: Al Saqi.

———. (1991). *Women and Islam: A historical enquiry*. Oxford: Basil Blackwell.

Mies, M. (1986). *Patriarchy and accumulation on a world scale: Women in the international division of labour*. London: Zed Books.

Mukhtar Mai (online). http://en.wikipedia.org/wiki/Mukhtaran_Bibi.

Murray, M. (1995). *The law of the father*. London and New York: Routledge.

Oplatka, I. (2001). I changed my management style: The cross-gender transition of women head teachers in mid-career. *School Leadership and Management, 21*(2), 219–233.

Oplatka, I., and Hertz-Lazarowitz, R. (Eds.). (2006). *Women principals in a multicultural society: New insights into feminist educational leadership*. Sense Publishers.

Ouston, J. (Ed.). (1993). *Women in education management*. Harlow, U.K.: Longman.

Ozga, J. (Ed.). (1994). *Women in educational management*. Buckingham: Routledge.

Pakistan Economic Survey (2005–2006). Finance Division, Economic Advisor's Wing. Government of Pakistan. Islamabad.

Pakistan Education Statistics (2004–2005). National Education Management Information System, Academy of Educational Planning and Management, Ministry of Education (Nemis Project), Islamabad.

Qureshi, S. (2004). *Pakistan education and gender policy: Girls' education: A lifeline to development*. Research chapter by Sabina Qureshi, IPF Fellow (2003–2004). Online. http://www.policy.hu/qureshi/Reschapter.pdf.

Ramazanoglu, C. (Ed.). (1993). *Up against Foucault: Explorations of some tensions between Foucault and feminism*. London: Routledge.

Reay, D., and Ball, S. J. (2000). Essentials of female management. *Educational Management and Administration, 28*(2), pp. 145–159.

Saigol, R. (1993). *Education: Critical perspectives*. Lahore, Pakistan: Progressive Publishers.

Schimmel, A. (1982). Women in mystical Islam. In Al-Hibri (Ed.). *Women and Islam*. Oxford: Pergamon Press. Special issue of *Women's Studies International Forum, 5*(2), pp. 145–152.

Schrijvers, J. (1993). Motherhood experienced and conceptualized. In D. Bell, P. Caplan and W. J. Karim (Eds.). *Gendered fields: Women, men and ethnography*. London: Routledge.

Seller, A. (1996). Hannah Arendt's politics of difference. In *Women Review Philosophy* (special issue). Edited by M. Griffiths and M. Whitford. University of Nottingham.

Shah, S. (1993). Women in educational management in the United States. In J. Ouston (Ed.). *Women in education management,* pp. 47–63, Harlow, U.K.: Longman.

———. (1998). Flash-backs-and-forth: Researching the roots, and A muddled maze: Reworking the routes. In K. Haw and S. Shah, *Educating Muslim girls: Shifting discourses.* Buckingham: Open University Press.

———. (1999). *Education management: Braving boundaries.* Islamabad, Pakistan: National Book Foundation.

———. (2006a). Leading multiethnic schools: A new understanding of Muslim youth identity. *Journal of Educational Management, Administration and Leadership.* Special Edition on Leadership and Diversity, April 2006; 34(2), 215–237.

———. (2006b). Educational leadership: An Islamic perspective. *British Educational Research Journal, 32*(3), 363–385.

Shakeshaft, C. (Ed.). (1991). *Women in educational administration.* Thousand Oaks, CA: Sage Publications.

———. (1993). Women in educational management in the United States. In J. Ouston (Ed.). *Women in education management,* pp. 47–63, Harlow, U.K.: Longman.

Sharma, U. (1980). *Women, work and property in North-West India.* London: Tavistock Publications.

Stowasser, B. F. (1994). *Women in the Quran: Tradition and interpretation.* New York: Oxford University Press.

Strachan, J. (1993). Searching women in educational leadership. In *Gender and Education, 5*(1), pp. 71–80.

Talbani, A. (1996). Pedagogy, power, and discourse: Transformation of Islamic education. *Comparative Education Review, 40*(1), pp. 66–82.

The World Factbook. (2007). Online. https://www.cia.gov/library/publications/the-world-factbook/print/pk.html. Last updated on 19 June 2007.

Weiss, A. M. (1992). Challenges for a Muslim woman in a postmodern world. In A. S. Ahmed and D. Hastings (Eds.). *Post-modernism and Islam: Predicament and promise,* pp. 127–140. London: Routledge.

Women's Organizations, Pakistan (online). http://www.distel.ca/womlist/countries/pakistan.html.

Youngs, G. (2000). Embodied political economy or an escape from disembodied knowledge. In G. Youngs, *Political Economy, Power and the body: Global perspectives.* Houndmills, U.K.: Macmillan Press.

Zein-Ed-Din, N. (1982). Removing the veil and veiling. In Al-Hibri, A.(Ed.). *Women and Islam.* Oxford: Pergamon Press. Special issue of *Women's Studies International Forum, 5*(2), pp. 221–226.

CHAPTER 17

Preparing Women for Educational Leadership

Opportunities in Nonformal Education in Bangladesh

Jill Sperandio

INTRODUCTION

THERE ARE FEW AREAS OF the world where women have an easy journey to educational leadership. The road to school headships, district management and national educational policy-making at the state and national level continues to present many barriers. These barriers have proved difficult to dismantle despite the growing acknowledgment by governments of the need for gender equity in educational leadership. Women must find new paths to reach their goals, routes that can be navigated by women who may lack traditional educational and experiential requirements, but who have the dedication, ingenuity and enthusiasm to transform teaching and learning by their leadership.

Developed countries, such as the UK and United States, seek to address the issue of underrepresentation of women in educational leadership through preparation programs grounded in the social and contextual understandings of their educational systems. Most developing countries, as defined by low gross national product and limited educational opportunities for children, are unlikely to be able to afford the luxury of such programs. In many of these countries, of which Bangladesh is representative, there has been a rapid expansion of the education system in response to attempts to meet international goals to provide elementary and secondary education for all children. This expansion has included the growth of nonformal and private education initiatives, creating an additional need for informed and capable school leaders and policy makers.

Women, often poorly positioned or facing discriminatory hiring and promotion practices in the formal education structure, may find opportunities to learn and practice leadership skills in new initiatives in the nonformal sector. Following the journeys of women who take these paths, describing the roles they fill, measuring their achievements and assessing the impact on those they serve, is an important step toward understanding the global location, activities and needs of women who hold positions in, or who aspire to, educational leadership. Knowledge gained from the experiences of these women can inform initiatives to develop nontraditional educational leadership preparation in a variety of different cultures and contexts.

CHAPTER OUTLINE

This chapter will focus on Bangladesh, one of the world's poorest countries and a country with a large and growing nonformal education sector. Like many developing countries in South Asia, where teaching has traditionally been overwhelmingly male-dominated (Haq and Haq, 1998), women are poorly represented at all levels in the formal educational administrative and leadership structure. National attention has been focused on the provision of basic education for all rather than the quality of existing educational leadership or the provision of innovative leadership models.

The chapter begins with a description of the current distribution patterns of women in roles of management and decision making in the formal, nonformal and private education systems in Bangladesh, and the historical, social and institutional contexts that have contributed to the formation of these patterns. The chapter continues with an examination of current initiatives taking place within the education system to expand educational opportunities for school-age children, and the increase in demand for school leadership this expansion has created. Nonformal education provision is examined in the context of the education program of the Bangladesh Rural Advancement Committee (BRAC), the largest provider of nonformal education in Bangladesh. The chapter concludes with a discussion of how understandings gained from a study of nonformal educational leadership, and the distributed leadership model it encompasses, can be applied to the development of education leadership training that is accessible to women and encourages them to be innovative and to place their own stamp on developing education systems worldwide.

THE BANGLADESH EDUCATION SYSTEM

Historical and Social Context

The People's Republic of Bangladesh is one of the poorest and most densely populated countries in the world. The country has an estimated population of 147.4 million, which is predicted to double in the next twenty years (Bangladesh Bureau of Statistics, 2006; Central Intelligence Agency, 2007). Seventy-seven percent of the population lives in rural areas and practices an agriculture based on rice production in the delta areas of the River Ganges as it enters the Bay of Bengal. Per capita income is approximately US$411 a year. Education has always been a luxury for the majority of the rural population. The literacy rate for both sexes for those 15 years and older is 43% and for females 31.8% (Bangladesh Bureau of Educational Statistics [BANBEIS], 2006). Bangladesh is a predominantly Islamic country with a small population (less than 10%) of Hindus. The national language is Bangla (Bengali), although English is widely spoken and understood and was the language of instruction in public secondary schools until 1970, a heritage of Bangladesh's colonial past.

Rapid population growth and limited economic development have led to massive unemployment. They have also led to a breakdown in traditional gender roles, forcing large numbers of women to enter the labor market for survival. Chowdhury (1998) describes the position of women in Bangladesh society:

> The overwhelming majority of women in Bangladesh are not only poor but also caught between two vastly different worlds—the world determined by culture and tradition that confines their activities inside family homesteads and the world shaped by increasing landlessness and poverty that drives them outside into wage employment for economic survival. (p. 1)

She notes that in traditional male-dominated Bangladesh society the *purdah* system of confining women to the home, and personal laws relating to marriage, divorce, custody of children and inheritance all traditionally discriminated against women.

In Bangladesh, as in many South Asian countries, the traditional practice of confining women to the home has resulted in teaching being overwhelmingly male-dominated. Only those women from families with high socioeconomic status and adopting "Western" attitudes have been willing to educate their daughters to the college and university level necessary to become a government schoolteacher, and accept their employment outside the home in elitist educational settings.

While the 1997 adoption of a National Women's Development Policy designed to create an environment for the empowerment of women through clear-cut national guidelines has encouraged women into the workforce, women are still underrepresented in education, which remains a gender-biased profession.

Formal and Private Education

Formal education in Bangladesh, defined as that controlled directly by the national government through the Ministry of Education (MOE), retains many characteristics inherited from the British system established when the country was part of British India. There is a three-part education system that consists of five years of primary or elementary education, three years of lower or junior secondary, and two years of secondary schooling leading to the matriculation examination. Two years of higher secondary education follow, leading to university entrance. When Bangladesh became an independent state in 1970, the language of instruction changed to Bangla (Ahmed and Ahmed, 2002).

Policy making and implementation for education takes place in two ministries and their associated directorates, the Ministry of Secondary and Higher Secondary Education, and the Ministry of Primary Education. In addition, there is a National Academy for Educational Management (NAEM) and National Curriculum and Text Book Board (NCTB).

Over 50% of the 86,737 elementary schools and 97% of the 17,386 secondary schools are nongovernment or privately owned, and the majority of these follow the government program of studies and national examinations (BANBEIS, 2004). Nongovernment schools that are community operated can opt to take the 90% salary subvention paid by the government to teachers. If schools choose this option, they must also accept a high degree of control by the government. These schools are operated by managing committees whose composition is determined by MOE regulations developed in 1977. The committees are composed of 11 members—the school's director, two teacher representatives, four elected student guardians, a prominent educationalist, a member representing principal donors to the school and a member representing the founders of the school. Over the years, modification of regulations regarding committee membership has allowed them to become increasingly politicized. It is common practice to fill the position of the chair with the advice and consent of the local member of Parliament (MP), especially if the MP belongs to the ruling party (Campaign for Popular Education [CAMPE], 2005).

A very visible group of schools in the private sector are English-medium, and at the secondary level these schools prepare students for the British Ordinary and Advanced level examinations that are administered by the British Council in Dhaka and externally graded. Three additional schools offer the International Baccalaureate Organization's programs. Bangladesh had 21 government-operated universities and 52 private universities in 2005, most modeled after higher education institutions in the United States in that they offer four-year bachelor's degrees programs, use a credit hour system and follow the U.S. academic calendar year (BANBEIS, 2006).

A large group of religious schools, the *madrasahs*, some of which are private and some government supported, are generally linked to mosques and rely on public donations to the mosques. The madrasahs provide a basic Muslim religious education and literacy to over 3 million children. Of these children, 46% are girls (BANBEIS, 2006).

Nonformal Education

A very different situation exists in the nonformal education sector consisting of donor-funded schooling initiatives, wherein the donors range from individual social entrepreneurs to large charities such as World Vision and Christian Aid to nongovernment organizations funded through international aid agencies.

In 1990, the government of Bangladesh issued a primary education development program appraisal document, the Fourth Five-Year Plan for Universal Primary Education. In this document the government acknowledged that although efforts to increase enrollment in primary school, particularly for girls, had led to improvements, the government was unable to deliver primary education to all school-age children (Jalaluddin and Chowdhury, 1997). It therefore formally recognized the importance of nonformal education and repeated its appeal for a multifront attack on illiteracy by expanding nonformal primary education, strengthening the government mass literacy centers and mobilizing nongovernmental organizations (NGOs) (Government of Bangladesh, 1990).

Notable among the providers of nonformal education has been the Bangladesh Rural Advancement Committee (BRAC), which operates the Nonformal Primary Education Program (NFPE) that controls over 34,000 schools in predominantly rural areas catering to more than a million students (BRAC, 2004). The schools have been tailored to meet the needs of the poor who cannot afford even the low costs associated

with government schooling, either due to monetary or opportunity costs. Over 70% of the students enrolled in the schools are girls.

WHERE ARE THE WOMEN IN EDUCATION LEADERSHIP IN BANGLADESH?

Women Leading in Formal Education

Women are currently underrepresented in all areas of the education system in Bangladesh as they are in other Asian countries (Azoo, 2003). They occupy few top-level positions at the policy making and implementation levels in the Ministry of Education and the Directorates with the exception of the position of Minister of Primary Education (see table 17.1). In the government schools and colleges, women's representation at head and assistant head levels is low in comparison with men despite the fact that a number of these schools and colleges are girls' institutions where female head teachers and assistant heads are mandatory (see tables 17.2 and 17.3). In the government *madrasahs*, none of the three superintendent positions are held by women, despite the large numbers of girls in these schools (see table 17.4).

Women leading in nonformal education

Women have much higher representation in both school leadership and policy making and implementation in the nonformal education sector, although no aggregated data are available. This has been in response to the deliberate policies of international organizations and charities to implement gender equity in their hiring. Motivated both by philosophical considerations and the practical need to qualify for external funding of their projects, Bangladeshi NGOs also have adopted internationally recognized gender equity standards. Outstanding in the development of nonformal educational facilities that both serve girls and promote female leadership is the BRAC Educational Program (BEP), started in 1985 to provide education to children too poor or too distant to attend primary schools, either formal or private.

A BRAC school is a one-room schoolhouse with a floor space of approximately 336 square feet. Each school has 33 students, of which two-thirds are typically girls. The same teacher teaches the group of students throughout the course of five academic years. Over 30,000 schools currently exist countrywide.

The BEP has an organizational structure with levels of entry defined by educational attainment and a gender equity policy that requires a minimum of one-third of its employees to be women. Organizational levels include teacher/head teacher of the one-room village schools, program organizers (POs) and resource teachers (RTs), district organizers, and program directors. While BRAC has actively encouraged the recruitment of women into the organizational structure, it has had most success at the school teacher/leader level (see table 17.6).

In the BEP schools more than 90% of head teachers are women who are married and live within the local community. A Secondary School Certificate (SSC) is required to become a BEP school leader. The academic qualification may be relaxed for exceptional candidates but ten years of schooling is a minimum requirement. The teacher must be prepared to complete the teacher training course of at least 15 days at any of the BRAC training centers within the first year of employment. She must be a permanent resident of the village in which the school is located, be accepted by the community, be married, and have another source of income for her family (as this is regarded as a part-time job). Additionally, she cannot bring her children to school during school time and cannot have family restrictions or social barriers for conducting co-curricular activities.

The selection process involves a panel of regional managers, quality assurance specialists and area education managers, who short-list three to five qualified women. The short-listed candidates are interviewed and take a written test to establish their mastery of mother tongue, mathematics, English and general knowledge. Two successful candidates are selected for each school position, one of whom goes on for training, while the other serves as a backup in case of sickness or dropout on the part of the selected applicant (personal communication with A. Tapan, July 2, 2006).

At the trainer and administrative level, women now hold approximately one-third of available positions in the BEP, which has actively promoted female leadership at its PO level, tailoring recruitment to women in isolated rural areas. A PO must have a minimum qualification of a Higher Secondary School Certificate (HSSC). Each PO supervises 12 to 16 schools, and the work covers three areas of leadership and management. The first concerns the opening of new schools. This involves meetings with local communities, site selection, teacher and student recruitment, communication with local government, school budget development, supplying the school and parent contacts. The second group of activities concerns the operation of

new and reopened schools, involving biweekly school supervision visits, monthly refresher training for teachers, attending and coordinating monthly parent meetings, organizing school committee meetings, maintaining contact with local government and others influential in the community, transferring students to formal education, school repair and parent contact. The third area in which POs are active is that of office management, including writing school supervision reports, weekly meetings with area officials, maintaining documents and stock registers and monitoring teacher attendance and leave.

Resource teachers are recruited from among the teachers. Teachers who complete at least two cycles of a BEP school program and have demonstrated understanding and management skills in their teaching life are eligible to apply. They must have at least ten years of education.

The positions of school teacher/head of school and of PO and RT provided a large number of secondary-school-educated women in rural areas with work outside the home, training and an opportunity to use both their education and leadership and management skills. They also have revolutionized Bangladeshi village communities. The leadership of village schools by women has done away with the stereotypical role of the male teacher or *master*. It has provided these women teachers with status in society, financial independence and also political recognition. Over 400 female teachers were elected as community representatives in local union-level elections in 2002 (BRAC, 2004). Women program organizers also defy norms regarding women's seclusion and limited physical space by bicycling or motorcycling from school to school across the countryside. In doing so they provide important role models for the female students in the schools they serve.

A Distributive Leadership Model
As can be inferred from the information given above, the BEP leadership model at the village level differs markedly from that of the formal and private schools in that leadership is shared between the schoolteacher, the PO and the RT serving the school. In some situations all three people will be women, in others they form a team of men and women. This team of three between them undertakes all the roles assigned to the head teacher in a formal or private school situation (Nath and Chowdhury, 2000).

The teacher leads in the classroom and offers daily contact with students and community. The PO and RT visit the school once a week, during which time they observe the classroom, assess performance of students and provide feedback to the teacher on the teaching-learning process. They take care of any personnel issues including the recruitment of new teachers and arrangements for leave and training for the teacher. They develop and deliver training to the group of 12 to 15 teachers they service for a monthly refresher course, and take teacher suggestions for curriculum improvement and materials to the Education Development Unit. They will also collect school fees and distribute teacher salaries, and manage resources in conjunction with the teachers, particularly the replacement of teaching materials. The teacher, PO and RT are responsible for linking the school activities to the community by attending meetings of the school management committee and the parent teacher associations, which the PO and RT facilitate.

This model is highly supportive of the teacher and of maintaining the quality of teaching and learning across a district. The teacher, far from the isolation experienced by head teachers in formal and nonformal schools, is kept informed of events and gains weekly feedback from the visits of the PO and RT as well as having an opportunity to meet with other teachers in the district at the monthly refresher trainings. The PO and RT visit a number of schools and their communities each week, so they have an excellent overview of district-wide problems and standards in the schools. Their connections with a district office and team, which oversees 70 schools, further aid dissemination of information up and down the organization.

BED Teacher Profile
Naseema is a 30-year-old teacher educated to high school level, with two children aged four and ten and a husband who is a farmer. Previous to her employment in BRAC, she had held no positions of responsibility. She was encouraged to apply for the position at BRAC by one of the village officials. This is her description of her experiences as a result of becoming the teacher-leader of a village school:

> I love working with children and I want to share my knowledge with them. I also want to continue to practice my education besides my housework. I benefit from the money I receive and the village children benefit from the education. Everyone in my family supported my application—both my husband and I thought since there will be extra income in the household and no one in the family had ever been in this profession before. I can now provide whatever things I want for my children and I do not have to ask for money from my husband. And everyone treats me differently now. My husband values my thoughts and views and I also get tremendous respect from the children's parents as well as my relatives. People greet me when I'm out walking. Some of them even come to me with their problems, and the people with authority and respect in the village also love me a lot. (BRAC teacher, 2007)

FACTORS INFLUENCING THE REPRESENTATION AND RECRUITMENT OF WOMEN IN EDUCATIONAL LEADERSHIP IN BANGLADESH

Commonalities with Other Cultures
The pattern of low representation of women in the formal system as heads of schools, colleges and universities, within government ministries and directorates, and in the private sector as heads of schools and members of the school managing committees, needs explanation. One way to approach this is to consider the question posed by Jensen (2003), who asks, "To what extent are women actively encouraged or discouraged from applying for management and leadership positions?" (p. 5). Cultural considerations must play an important part in answering this question for any given group of women. A number of researchers have explored this issue.

Cubillo and Brown (2003) examined how the "glass ceilings and glass walls" (p. 278) that face women aspiring to leadership positions vary from culture to culture. They concluded that successful negotiation of these barriers had commonalities across cultures. Many women in different cultures attribute their success to familial support and encouragement, for example. Norris and Inglehart (2000), discussing the larger issue of women assuming societal leadership roles in a worldwide study, noted that "culture matters" (p. 14) and that available opportunities and favorable attitudes toward women's leadership, by themselves "are not sufficient to produce effective breakthroughs in the structural and institutional barriers, especially in the short term" (p. 14).

Shakeshaft (1989), building on models explaining women's lack of achievement in obtaining educational management positions in the United States such as those of Hansot and Tyack (1981), proposed that women's internal barriers to success, such as low self-image, lack of confidence and lack of motivation or aspiration resulted from the social context of men holding power and privilege over women in society at large. A study of barriers to women managers' advancement in education in Uganda (Brown and Ralph, 1996) also noted the effects of reduced access of women to education, the experiences that females have in education (which are different from the experiences of males) and the additional social responsibilities that the majority of girls and women hold. All these factors have applications to the situation in Bangladesh.

A study of the problems faced by women aspiring to leadership positions in Pakistan (Memon, 2003), a country with a similar social and religious structure to Bangladesh, suggested other aspects of South Asian patriarchal Muslim cultures that discourage women moving into leadership positions. Women from middle and low socioeconomic backgrounds face competition not only from males, but also from women of elite backgrounds with access to information, resources and mobility, and who may use the "Queen Bee Syndrome" (Edson, 1988) to discourage, rather than encourage, other women. Memon also discussed the culture of male-dominated management in which women managers do not challenge their male counterparts' views in professional settings. Women become passive participants and do not learn skills or advance up the career ladder as a result.

Other factors limiting women's movement into educational leadership noted by Memon include the multilevel social responsibilities women are expected to shoulder. Women also are cautious about seeking promotion if this would mean a move away from their home. In more traditional households in a patriarchal society, issues of *purdah* or seclusion, dependence on men due to lack of personal assets, and the lack of female support groups militate against women pursuing careers. Women do not conform to the tough and authoritarian style that males in the profession adopt, and they are therefore seen as too weak to operate effectively in large schools and educational organizations. Traditional hiring and promotion procedures and requirements discourage or disadvantage women, especially when they require many years of experience in the educational labor force and previous leadership experience, or involve recommendations or interviews with predominantly male superiors. Women may face harassment from their male peers or superiors in the workplace that discourages them from pursuing a career.

ISSUES SPECIFIC TO BANGLADESH

While there is little research on the experiences of Bangladeshi women who seek careers in education and aspire to management and leadership positions, stud-

ies of the effects of promoting girls' secondary education in Bangladesh by subsidizing school fees suggest that traditional attitudes toward women could well discourage them from seeking such positions. Sarker, Chowdhury and Tariq (1995) concluded that education for girls is mostly perceived as a domestic benefit, enabling them to get better husbands, to help their husbands, or to teach and better look after their own children. Sweetser (1999), in a report exploring gender relations, nonformal education and social change in Bangladesh, discussed the marked generational difference in attitudes toward women. She described the attitudes of older men, which included their disapproval of modern trends of women or girls going to school, working in the fields, arranging their own marriages, riding bicycles and motorcycles, taking up seats on buses and being served in a shop first.

Sweetser also noted that "typically, the first benefit of girls' education cited by villagers pertains to their future roles managing the home economy" (p. 19). She quotes one man's observation that it was pointless to send girls to secondary school because they would still have to bribe someone to get a job: "What they really need . . . is a husband" (p. 18). However, Raynor (2004), in her study of girls' access to education in Bangladesh, observed that "most people linked girls' education to employment, but for the men and boys interviewed the stated reason was almost exclusively financial, whereas women and girls linked employment to such things as 'independence, confidence and worth'" (p. 95).

Raynor (2004) also noted that Bangladesh government support of gender equity has a chequered history. Bangladesh ranks 76th out of 78 countries on the United Nations Development Programme Gender Empowerment measure. When the government ratified the 1979 Convention on the Elimination of All Forms of Discrimination against Women (CEDAW), it maintained reservations on all articles calling for women's equal rights in the family (Jahan, 1995).

The lack of expansion in the formal government secondary school system resulting from financial constraints also contributes to a lack of opportunity for women to move into administrative positions. Positions become available only on the retirement or resignation of incumbents, with a group of highly qualified and long-serving practitioners waiting their turn. In situations such as this, the only women who have the formal qualifications required which include a number of years in school employment, are employed in girls' schools. These women would have to seek and be appointed to secondary school administration in coeducational schools, leaving vacancies in single sex girls' schools, before less qualified women could join the pool of female school leaders. Given traditional attitudes to women in Bangladeshi society, selection committees staffed by older males are unlikely to look favorably on women applying for leadership positions.

It is important to note that women are underrepresented in the teaching profession in general, forming only 31% of the teachers in government secondary schools, 19.1% of the teachers in nonformal and private schools and 36% of the teachers in primary schools, both government and private. Overall, less than 6.5% of all teachers and administrators in the government and private schools are women. Of those students currently training to become teachers, only one-quarter are female, and women trainers in these teacher training institutions account for one-fifth of the teaching faculty (BANBEIS, 2006).

Thus women's underrepresentation in educational leadership appears to have many causes. These range from traditional attitudes linked to patriarchy and religion, to the lack of a pool of qualified women due to limitations in access to secondary education for girls, to a failure of the government to adopt measures that would open up leadership positions to women. While some of these factors are specific to Bangladesh, others are common to cultures worldwide.

DISCUSSION

The evidence from the nonformal education sector in Bangladesh suggests that this is the area of education where women have most opportunity to obtain leadership appointments, training and experience. This is the result of two factors. The first is pressure on NGOs involved in nonformal education and health care to conform to worldwide gender equity standards if they are to qualify for donor funding.

The second encouraging factor for women's opportunities in nonformal educational leadership is the recognition by NGOs of an untapped pool of female talent, particularly in the rural areas of the country, which can be employed to good effect in developing and sustaining projects in health and education that have significant effects on the lives of both rural and urban poor. Coombs (1976), assessing the potential of nonformal education, noted, "To get a new, nonformal education program organized and off the ground, and then keep it going well, requires dedicated, ingenious, and enthusiastic leadership—especially at the local level. There is never enough such leadership to go

around"(p. 285). Recognizing this fact, organizations such as BRAC have not only instituted affirmative action programs that give women preference in hiring over men with more education and experience, but have used their own short and intensive training programs as a substitute for formal qualifications.

Thus, in the distributive leadership model that BRAC operates at the village school level, newly recruited POs receive a pre-service training in a residential course that lasts 18 days. This course includes discussions about the organizational theory, vision, values, culture and history of BRAC and its place in Bangladesh, an overview of the different development programs operated by BRAC, and rules of service. For the next 15 days the trainees accompany an experienced PO for practical learning. During this period the trainee observes BRAC schools, teaching-learning activities, the way in which student and teacher supervision is carried out, the organization of monthly refresher courses when teachers, POs and RTs in a district meet to develop their skills, and the work done at the team office level. The trainee is also taken through the different training manuals and research reports available in the organization.

After a period of service, POs can take an additional 13-day course in basic teacher training that includes teaching techniques, child psychology, techniques of continuous and summative evaluations, classroom discipline and management, community relations and office and committee management. Other advanced training modules include a 12-day operation management course devoted to better school management through academic and administrative supervision techniques, continuous assessment and different survey techniques that can be used to assess the needs of the school's community. A Master Trainer module, a two-part, six-day course developing specific knowledge in one school subject such as environmental science, and five days of training on techniques for conducting training, communication skills, and training module development to train teachers in this subject area, are also available to POs seeking to broaden their skills (Nath, Mushtaque and Chowdhury, 2000).

Although the PO has no direct experience in teaching, the teacher leader of the school and the RT, who have been recruited from the ranks of the teachers, have both the basic teacher training and teaching experience but no administrative training. So the team together has all the skills required of a head teacher in the formal or private school system. They do not operate in isolation, but attend meetings and work in the classroom, as well as share the experiences brought from other schools visited by the PO and RT. In this way, all are steadily increasing their skill levels in all areas of school operation. Monthly refresher courses reinforce this learning.

This reliance on short, intensive courses, on-the-job training, shared learning and frequent in-service and refresher courses, all focused on the needs of a particular community or district, prepares women for highly visible leadership quickly and efficiently. The BRAC model targets women for leadership positions, providing training and a work environment sensitive to women's needs, which include the ability to work near home, to have the support of the community, and an opportunity to advance up a scale of increasing responsibility. The evidence from BRAC suggests that not only do individual women benefit from such leadership opportunities, but also that once gained, women employ their leadership skills in many other spheres to the enrichment of society at large (Sperandio, 2005, 2007).

RESEARCH AGENDA

The preceding overview of Bangladeshi women's experiences in the field of educational leadership raises many questions. What can be done to draw women into school leadership in countries where training for teachers, and the promotion process from teacher to school leader, favor men? What training and leadership preparation is needed to equip women to teach in and lead schools in the rural areas where they live and where there is a need for good schools? How can teacher training and leadership preparation be provided for women who do not have the resources or freedom from domestic responsibility or social constraints to attend training or work away from home? In those areas where nonformal teacher training can be provided, what should it involve and how can women use it as a first step to entering the formal educational system and gain promotion to leadership and decision-making positions? And finally, how can our knowledge of effective leadership preparation in a variety of different contexts be shared and adapted for use in nonformal teacher training and leadership preparation in both developed and developing countries?

In the specific area of formal and private education in Bangladesh, there is clearly a need to explore ways of increasing both the pool of women qualified to move into leadership positions and ways to ensure that positions are made available to them. Raynor (2004) points out that many of the education programs operating in Bangladesh to improve girls' access to secondary education have as an objective "the channeling of girls into teaching, partly to ensure that girls have female role-models in schools, partly because teaching is seen as an 'appropriate' job for women, but also to meet the needs of the ever-expanding education system" (p. 90). While increasing girls' access to secondary education and increasing the pool of women teachers in a traditionally male-dominated profession is clearly an important first step for the government, research is needed to establish how women can be encouraged to develop aspirations and expectations of leadership experience, and to counter traditional male expectations that education will simply be used to enhance family well-being, with teaching as an end in itself.

Research is needed to gain a clearer understanding of the reasons why so few women are found in the higher levels of decision- and policy-making at the ministries and directorates. This should include an examination of current recruitment, interview and promotion practices for gender bias they may contain. A review of the qualifications needed to obtain these positions, particularly to those relating to length of service in the teaching profession, is necessary in recognition of the limited opportunities women have had to obtain a secondary education and tertiary training, and subsequent opportunities to teach.

In the private sector, women entrepreneurs are currently limited to an elite group of well-educated women who enjoy the backing and resources of their families. But the opportunities for individual women to undertake this type of entrepreneurship, to obtain the financing to do it and to gain the understanding of the ways in which schools can be made cost effective while delivering high quality education are missing. Governments, NGOs and other related agencies are providing many opportunities to promote entrepreneurial skills among women (Chowdhury and Naher, 1993; Chowdhury, 1998). A study of private schooling in India noted its potential for providing an income flow for lower socioeconomic families and individuals (Tooley and Dixon, 2003).

Research is needed into the feasibility of promoting school ownership among women, including the provision of loans and training, given that the need for schools clearly exists and that such schools could both increase the well-being of women and their families and provide an important service to the communities in which they live.

Women's participation on school management committees of community schools also warrants further research. With the expanding numbers of these schools, this is an area where women can have considerable input into improving the teaching and learning that takes place in individual schools. What training do women need, and what measures must be taken, to give them increased access to these committees, and to the positions on them where power to make decisions and allocate resources lies?

Underlying all these particular research needs relating to the ability of women to assume leadership and management roles in all areas of education in Bangladesh is a need to understand what skills and motivation women require to consider a career in educational leadership. How can training be developed that is appropriate, accessible and efficient for them? In this respect, the success of women who have moved into leadership roles in nonformal education is particularly important as an area of research. What these women can tell us about their experiences, the skills they have acquired, their perceptions of themselves as leaders, the leadership styles that work for them, and how they are perceived by those they serve, is crucial. Importing leadership training from other countries and contexts without this understanding of what has already proved successful is an unacceptable imposition. Attitudes and traditional community structures are changing. We must listen to the voices of the women who have taken the road and made the journey to educational leadership to help others position themselves to take advantage of developing opportunities.

Table 17.1.   Percentage of Females in Positions in the Ministry of Education in Bangladesh

Position	Total Positions	Females	%
Ministers, Secretaries, Directors	27	4	14.8
Deputy and Assistant Secretaries and Directors	111	27	24.3
Research and Education Officers and Trainers	61	33	54.0

Source: Arzoo, 2003.

Table 17.2.   Percentage of Females in Positions of Head and Assistant Head Teachers in Government-Funded Colleges in Bangladesh

Position	Total Positions	Females	%
College Heads	242	42	17.4

Table 17.3.   Percentage of Females in Positions of Head and Assistant Head Teacher in Government-Controlled Primary and Secondary Schools in Bangladesh

Position	Total Positions	Females	%
Secondary Head	313	71	22.7
Assistant Secondary Head	343	92	26.8
Primary Head	37,672	7,765	
Assistant Primary Head	37,672	63,956	

Source: BANBEIS, 2006.

Table 17.4.   Percentage of Females in Positions of Head and Assistant Head Teacher in Government-Funded or Licensed Madrasahs

Position	Total Positions	Females	%
Head	8,316	236	2.8
Assistant Head	6,565	113	1.7

Source: BANBEIS, 2006.

Table 17.5.   Women in Educational Leadership in the Private Secondary Education Sector

Position	Total positions	Females	%
College Heads	2,368	135	5.7
Assistant Head	419	31	7.4
Registered Secondary School Head	16,664	1,079	6.5
Registered Secondary Assistant School Head	12,888	1,067	8.3
Registered Primary School Head	18,365	1,538	8.4

Source: BANBEIS, 2006.

Table 17.6.   BRAC Educational Program Personnel by Gender

Position	Total Numbers	Females	%
Teacher	52,205	52,129	99.8
Program Organizer	6,244	2,382	38.1
Regional Manager	141	20	14.2
Director	1	1	0

Source: BRAC Human Resource Department, Dhaka, 2007.

REFERENCES CITED

Ahmed, M., and Ahmed, M. (2002, March). Bangladesh education sector overview: Final report. Retrieved June 21, 2006, from the Japan Bank for International Cooperation Web site: www.jbic.go.jp/english/oec/environ/report/pdf/eban.pdf.

Ali, M., and Choudhury, R. A. (2000). Educational Administration and Management. Secondary Education Development Project (SEDP). Ministry of Education, Dhaka.

Arends-Kuenning, M., and Amin, S. (2001). Women's capabilities and the right to Education. *International Journal of Politics, Culture, and Society, 15*(1), 125–142.

Azoo, J. (2003, July–December). Role of women in educational management in Bangladesh. *Asian Network of Training and Research Institutions in Educational Planning (ANTRIEP) Newsletter, 8*(2), 16–17.

Asian Network of Training and Research Institutions in Educational Planning [ANTRIEP]. (2007). Research proposal for a research project: Case studies in successful school management. Retrieved from http://www/antriep.net/html/school.htm. May 2007.

Bangladesh Bureau of Educational Information and Statistics [BANBEIS] (2006). *Pocket book on educational statistics.* Bangladesh: Government of Bangladesh.

Bangladesh Bureau of Statistics. (2006). *Statistical Year Book of Bangladesh, 2006.* Dhaka, Bangladesh.

Bangladesh Rural Advancement Committee. (2004). *Nonformal primary education (NFPE) report: 1997, 1999.* Dhaka, Bangladesh: Author.

Begum, H. A., and Hossain, M. Z. (1998). Educational administration and management. Institute of Education and Research, Dhaka.

Brown, M., and Ralph, S. (1996). Barriers to women managers: Advancement in education in Uganda. *International Journal of Educational Management, 10*(6), 18–23.

Campaign for Popular Education (CAMPE), Bangladesh. (1999). Education watch: Hope, not complacency: The state of primary education in Bangladesh. Dhaka, Bangladesh.

———. (2005). Education Watch: The state of secondary education: Progress and challenges. Dhaka, Bangladesh.

———. (2006). *Secondary School Management Training.* Retrieved from http://www/campebd.org. January, 2007.

Central Intelligence Agency. (2007). The world factbook: Bangladesh. Retrieved September 28, 2006, from http//www/cia.gov/cia/publications/factbook/geos/bg.html.

Chowdhury, P. K. (1998). Women entrepreneurs: Emerging leaders of rural Bangladesh. *Dhaka University Studies, 55*(1).

Chowdhury, P. K., and Naher, B. N. (1993). *Women entrepreneurs of rural industries in some selected areas.* BARD, Comilla, Bangladesh.

Coombs, P. H. (1976). Nonformal education: Myths, realities, and opportunities. *Comparative Education Review, 20*(3), 281–293.

Cubillo, L., and Brown, M. (2003). Women into educational leadership and management: International differences? *Journal of Educational Administration, 41*(3), 278–291.

Edson, S. (1988). *Pushing the limits: The female administrative aspirant.* Albany: State University of New York Press.

Directorate of Primary Education (DPE). (1997). Manual for school management training for head teachers. DPE supported by UNICEF, Dhaka.

DPE (2000). Sub-cluster training manual. DPE, Dhaka.

Government of Bangladesh. (1990). *The fourth five-year plan (1990–1995).* Dhaka, Bangladesh.

Haq, M. U., and Haq, K. (1998). *Human development in South Asia: The education challenge.* Dhaka, Bangladesh: University Press.

Jahan, R. (1995). *The elusive agenda: Mainstreaming women in development.* London: Zed.

Jalaluddin, A., and Chowdhury, M. R. (Eds.). (1997). *Getting Started: Universalizing quality primary education in Bangladesh.* Dhaka, Bangladesh: University Press.

Jensen. V. (2003, July–December). Women in educational management in South Asia. *Asian Network of Training and Research Institutions in Educational Planning (ANTRIEP) Newsletter, 8*(2), 3–6.

Memon, M. (2003). School leadership in Pakistan: Prospects and challenges. *School Head-teachers Association for Development of Education (SHADE) Newsletter, 4/5,* 1–4.

Ministry of Education, Government of the People's Republic of Bangladesh. (2005–2006). Bangladesh National Commission of UNESCO. Retrieved June 18, 2006, from www.moedu.gov.bd.about_moe-organizations_bncu.htm.

Nath, S. R., Mushtaque, A. and Chowdhury, R. (2000). School without a head teacher: One-teacher primary schools in Bangladesh. Paper presented at the Asian Network of Training and Research Institutions in Educational Planning (ANTRIEP), Dhaka, Bangladesh, 2000.

Norris, P., and Inglehart, R. (2000, August). Cultural barriers to women's leadership: A worldwide comparison. Paper presented at the International Political Science Association World Congress, Quebec City, Quebec.

Raynor, J. (2005). Educating girls in Bangladesh: Watering a neighbour's tree? In S. Aikman and E. Unterhalter (Eds.). *Beyond access: Transforming policy and practice for gender equality in education,* pp. 83–105. Retrieved June 2, 2006, from http://www.ungei.org/resources/files/oxfam_BA_17.pdf.

Sarker, P. C., Chowdhury, J. H., and Tariq, T. (1995). *Evaluation of BACE Secondary School Girls' Scholarship Project.* Dhaka, Bangladesh: Associates for Community and Population Research.

Shakeshaft, C. (1989). *Women in educational management.* New York: Sage.

Sperandio, J. (2005). Social entrepreneurs and educational leadership in Bangladesh. *Current Issues in Comparative Education, 8*(1).

———. (2007). Women leading and owing schools in Bangladesh: Opportunities in public, nonformal and private education. *Journal of Women in Educational Leadership, 5*(1), 7–20.

Sweetser, A. T. (1999). *Bangladesh Rural Advancement Committee: Lessons from the BRAC Nonformal Primary Education Program.* Academy for Educational Development/ABEL Clearing House for Basic Education.

Tooley, J., and Dixon, P. (2003). *Private schools for the poor: A case study from India.* Reading, U.K.: The Center for British Teachers.

MUST SOCIETY, POLITICS AND/OR EDUCATION ITSELF CHANGE?

Barriers and Catalysts in Turkey and Germany

CHAPTER 18

Overview for Part V

MARILYN L. GRADY AND BETTIE BERTRAM

INTRODUCTION

THE FOLLOWING SYNTHESIS is intended for those who study and write about women in leadership. The focus is research, writing and international issues. It is derived from attendance at the UCEA International Women's Leadership Conference in Rome in 2007, reading conference manuscripts, and our work, research and editorial experiences related to women in leadership.

RESEARCH AND WRITING:
THE DISCOVERY METHOD

One method of social studies instruction taught in undergraduate teacher preparation programs was called the discovery method. It was a marvelous approach to teaching social studies. New social studies teachers referred to the method frequently in their early classroom days. However, they "discovered" that the method was very effective in the university teaching laboratory but sorely lacking in the social studies classroom. For instance, it became apparent that students would never "discover" the Magna Carta no matter how long the teacher waited. Teachers soon abandoned this instructional method and, fortunately, so did undergraduate social studies methods instructors. Nevertheless, from time to time, instances of the discovery method emerge in other aspects of education (Grady, 1993).

Occasionally research about women in leadership appears to use a version of the discovery method. This practice is evident when manuscripts are prepared as though they are the first studies on a topic. In this process, each scholar "discovers" the topic and approaches the subject in the manner of an explorer new to a territory. The approach begins with the reporting of the status of women in "whatever" setting. The accounting includes a delineation of the challenges encountered by women and a lament on the paucity of women in "whatever" setting. By repeating this pattern of "discovery" research, it is unlikely that scholars will persist long enough to discover the Magna Carta or a statement of basic rights for women in leadership.

The conference manuscripts reflected a range of perspectives and approaches to the study of women in leadership. The researchers' stages of understanding of the underrepresentation of women in leadership were illuminated.

Recounting the dismal chronicle of women's disenfranchisement does not advance the scholarship in this area. Reproducing the same research in different contexts with similar results does not extend or enrich the scholarship on women in leadership.

The questions that frame future research studies should move beyond baseline reporting and explore the successes of women as leaders. This approach will move the discussion from descriptions of pathology to identification of women who have succeeded and the strategies they have employed to achieve their successes. Perhaps by moving in this direction, we can begin to identify practices that lead to greater leadership success for women. Scholars need to build or nest their research in the works of their predecessors. A bibliography on gender equity should be developed to serve as a resource to all scholars and policy makers.

SOLO STUDIES

A number of individuals have studied women in leadership and reported the findings of a single research study or a dissertation. Other individuals have committed their scholarly careers to the study of women in leadership.

The single-study events provide the authors with an "entry level" understanding of women in leadership, or a baseline understanding. It is unfortunate that these individuals do not pursue the topic in further studies. Often these single studies can be classified as Stage 1 according to Shakeshaft's Stages of Research on Women in Administration (1989, p. 13).

Senior scholars who have contributed a body of research on the topic of women in leadership reflect the later stages of research described by Shakeshaft (1989). As their inquiries continue, the insights they offer and the research questions they pose expand the understanding of women in leadership. Emerging scholars should be encouraged to dedicate long-term, focused attention to the study of women in educational leadership. Senior scholars who have established credentials in this field need to nurture the next generation of scholars.

A frequent lament of those who have championed women's educational equity is that younger women do not perceive equity issues to be an important area of concern. The assumption that gender equity has been achieved may be inaccurate. Thus, the challenge may rest with senior scholars to continue to advocate for more attention to equity issues. The prominent voices on the topic of women in leadership are usually senior scholars. The corollary to this is: Who are the junior scholars who will move into the senior scholar roles? How are these individuals nurtured? We must invite the junior scholars to the discussion. If we are to break the cycle of repetition and discovery, we must have junior participants at the table. Each senior scholar should be challenged to identify junior participants to bring into the discussion. Each person must be an advocate for those in junior scholar roles.

THE NEXT GENERATION OF STUDIES

There is a pernicious habit, practiced by some, of writing without acknowledging that "some of this territory was covered a long time ago." An analogy that may apply is the idea of research being reported as a droplet sprayed into the air from a fountain. Once the droplet flies into the air, it drops into the pool of water and is neither remembered nor noted. Scholars must acknowledge the work completed by others and move beyond the acknowledgment to explore new areas of inquiry. This would result in a new generation of research that is essential to the advancement of the research agenda. Scholar isolation from the major works of other scholars does not advance the study of women in leadership. Individuals who initiate studies of women in leadership should be responsible for reading the literature that precedes their inquiry. The works of Schuster and Van Dyne (1984) and Shakeshaft (1989) are essential frameworks for these studies.

Doctoral advisers should insist that emerging scholars move beyond recitations of the demographics and litany of barriers women encounter, the "pathology," as Lightfoot (1988) would term it, to the chronicle of excellence that women have demonstrated. Through a focus on the successes, the promising practices, the heroines, the accomplishments and the skills and

abilities, the status of women will be elevated and enhanced by this spotlighting, highlighting process.

GENERATIONS OF SCHOLARS

One of the "Aha!" moments of the conference was the reminder of "generations of scholars." The question becomes: Must every generation of scholars discover or rediscover the history of women? Must every generation discover equity? Must every generation discover gender issues? Is this a cycle that must repeat with each generation of scholars? Can nothing be learned from previous generations? A handbook on the progress of women in leadership should be developed and widely distributed. It should include a chronology of the research on gender equity and the history of women in leadership. The handbook would provide a foundation in scholarship on women in leadership for the next generation of scholars. It would provide tangible evidence of the progress women have made as scholars and leaders. Aleman, Martinz and Renn's *Women in Higher Education: An Encyclopedia* (2002) and Franck and Brownstone's *Women's World* are examples of compendiums or handbooks that could serve as models for a handbook on women in leadership.

INTERNATIONAL ISSUES

Clock—Timeline
Listening to the conference presentations and reading the accompanying manuscripts, the similarities of experiences of women in each of the represented countries were evident. In each country and in each setting, it is possible to acknowledge the lack of women in leadership roles. Through the various manuscripts, authors chronicle the struggles of women in their quests to achieve leadership roles. It would be helpful to create a "world clock" and identify on the clock the status of women in each country of the world. The extant scholarship on women in leadership would provide baseline data for this endeavor. The criteria for placement on the time increments of the clock could be derived from Shakeshaft's stages of research on women in educational leadership. Symbolically, the clock would suggest the hours that must be spent to advance the status of women in educational leadership in each of the countries.

Scholars would be challenged to identify the status of women in their countries. A discussion of the methods for uniform data collection could be instrumental in the development of an accurate international portrait of the status of women.

Invisibility of Women Scholars

At one time women assumed men's names in order to have works published. John Sedges and others found that using a man's name could open publishing doors that were closed to women authors. The style manual of the American Psychological Association (APA) requires that first names of authors not be cited in references. Gender designations must be eliminated from manuscripts. These requirements diminish potential bias against women in the referee process.

Perhaps these safeguards are still necessary to mitigate women's exclusion from scholarly journals. However, a shortcoming occurs because of this gender neutrality. Through this process, women are invisible in the scholarly world. Creating a bibliography of the writings of women scholars on the topic of women in leadership would draw attention to their contributions to the scholarly discourse (Grady, 1989; Grady and O'Connell, 1993; Grady, Udey and Carlson, 1991). The invisibility of women scholars would be reduced. The compendium of writings would be an excellent resource for other scholars. Additionally, the bibliography would be a testament to the accomplishments of women scholars and would document the progress made.

International Scholars Academy

One of the many useful aspects of the manuscripts prepared for the international conference was the reference lists that accompanied the papers. The reference lists provide an opportunity to recognize the work accomplished by other scholars. Establishing an international academy of scholars on women in educational leadership would provide a prominent focus in this scholarly field. By acknowledging the recognized scholars, it would be possible to build a repository of the writings and initiatives that have occurred in an international context. Providing a catalogue of the accomplishments of prominent women leaders would assist others involved in similar initiatives as well as drawing attention to the significance of these accomplishments.

This focus would assist emerging scholars in noting the work and individuals who have preceded them and would stem the discovery approach to this field of scholarship. An academy would guide other individuals and organizations in their initiatives and would provide leadership in the development of a future orientation and vision for research on women in educational leadership.

Religion

One prominent factor noted in the discussions and manuscripts—the exclusion of women from religious discourse and interpretation—is a factor that needs further acknowledgment in the scholarship on women in leadership. The religions of the world and their influence on customs and practices are significant forces in the access women have to leadership positions. Religious groups often determine access to positions of power, access to education, freedom of movement, and freedom of dress and have an impact on the status of women.

The conference discussions and manuscripts were an important reminder of the variety of religious adherents in the world. Figure 18.1 provides a visual example of the religions of the world. The scholarship on women in leadership should continue to examine the role of world religions and its impact on the status of women. Because religion is deeply embedded in culture, this factor and its impact may need to be brought to a more prominent place in the discourse. Perhaps we should examine and strengthen our ties with leaders of the major religious bodies who often articulate the role of women in society.

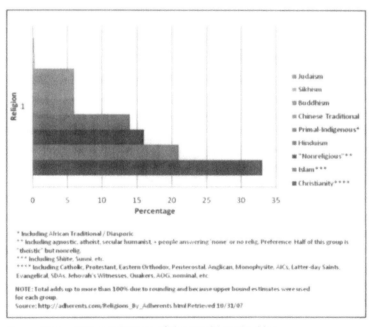

Figure 18.1.   Major Religions of the World Ranked by Number of Adherents

Hospitality and Place: The Sisters of the Holy Family of Nazareth

The international conference was held on the Rome campus of Duquesne University. The Sisters of the Holy Family of Nazareth provided hospitality for the conference. The primary meeting space was the convent's assembly room. In conversations with the sisters, they repeatedly emphasized that their involvement in this groundbreaking initiative was an important role for their religious order. Their support of the conference was clear and their enjoyment of their work and role permeated the facility and their hospitality.

The Sisters of the Holy Family of Nazareth remember 11 of their order as martyrs of World War II. Eleven sisters in Nowogrodek, Poland, offered their lives in place of local "family men" who were to be executed. The Nazis executed the sisters on August 1, 1943 (Starzynska, 1992). Their model of heroism is an inspiration for all who study leadership. This model of "servant leadership" was an important backdrop to the location of the conference.

Future meetings would benefit from careful selection of location. In 2007, the setting was an ideal retreat location for the participants. Unlike meetings held in hotels in busy urban areas, the setting for the Rome conference allowed the participants to focus exclusively on the agenda. Distractions were minimal. The sisters' hospitality was supportive of the initiative. These facilitative aspects should be sought in future meetings.

Country Distinctions

An interesting feature of the manuscripts and presentations was the limited emphasis on country distinctions. In fact, unless the country name was used or the religious aspect was cited, the manuscripts and presentations were indistinguishable by factors that pointed to a specific geographic location. This was a stunning reinforcement of the importance of the international initiative. It is important to examine the status of women in leadership throughout the world in a carefully planned review. The review would verify the common features and experiences of women in leadership. It would lead to a delineation of the unique, distinguishing features of women in leadership based on country of origin. The information would enrich the knowledge base and strengthen research and discussion on women in leadership in an international context.

AN ALMANAC OF WOMEN IN LEADERSHIP

An obligatory part of a manuscript on women in educational leadership is to provide demographics on the status of women in various roles. Often this is a discouraging way to begin a manuscript. For the author, gathering the demographic data is a labor-intensive activity since this information is often not readily available. Scholars and policy makers would be served by a world almanac on women in leadership. To develop the almanac, a census in each country using the same identifiers for women in leadership roles would be required. The almanac would necessitate an annual revision. Professional associations may be uniquely positioned to assist with this endeavor. The almanac would provide support to researchers, policy makers and the media as they address topics of gender equity. The almanac would elevate the issue of women in leadership as a visible tribute to the work of women.

If a foundation of knowledge is not established, the progress on issues of gender equity will continue to be slow, incremental and invisible. An ideal sponsor for such an initiative would be the professional associations that may have the resources and networks to sponsor and to distribute such a handbook.

THE VOICES OF WOMEN AND MEN

One of the often noted provisos in research is that White researchers are not qualified to study topics related to Black people, Anglos cannot study Hispanic issues, Whites cannot study Native issues, or men cannot study women's issues. The international conference and accompanying manuscripts debunked the myth that men cannot conduct research about women in educational leadership. Celikten (2007a; 2007b) reported research on women in leadership in Turkey. Bauer and Gruber (2007) reported the German initiative on gender mainstreaming. Macha and Handschuh-Heiss (2007a; 2007b) reported the German project that reflects gender as a men's and women's initiative. Gender equity is an issue for all.

The low status of women is often a product of intentional and unintentional actions of men and the acceptance of these actions by women; or the status of women is ascribed by men and accepted by women. To eradicate aspects of the status of women that are unsatisfactory, both women and men must participate in the process. As demonstrated at the international conference, both women and men participated as scholars in this important work. Other initiatives should foster similar involvement. The voices of women and the voices of men are critical to the conversation.

NARROWING THE FOCUS VERSUS BROADENING THE FOCUS: SIMPLICITY VERSUS COMPLEXITY

An emerging issue during the conference was the divergent views or directions in the discussions. As individuals made presentations, the conversations expanded to include many companion topics. Social justice, segregation, discrimination, poverty and world health issues such as HIV-AIDS surfaced as significant concerns for women. These are critical concerns that affect women as well as men. Should these issues be incorporated in the discussion of women in leadership? These broader issues are significant to people throughout the world. The sponsoring organizations, the American Association of School Administrators, the University Council for Educational Administration, and Duquesne University, may have initiatives in place to address these broader issues. Efforts should be made to identify and display the commitments of the sponsoring organizations to these international topics.

The topic of women in educational leadership is a broad field. Expanding the focus beyond this topic may diminish the possibility of achieving the goals identified by the group during the meeting. Identifying the goals and developing the platform are critical to goal accomplishment. The Beijing Declaration (1996) provides a platform model that should be considered.

SUPPORTS AND DEMANDS OR POWER BASES

The power bases that exist in each country need to be identified. Some of the power bases include government offices and officials, major corporations, professional associations, media outlets, and colleges and universities. Important sources of support were evident at the international conference in the sponsorship by the University Council for Educational Administration (UCEA), the American Association of School Administrators (AASA), Duquesne University, and the assembled scholars. Coalescing these support sources provided the synergy to accomplish the meeting.

An environmental scan in each country would assist advocates of women in leadership to identify power bases and sources of support for future initiatives. The scan could identify advocates, resources, public opinion shapers, collaborators, as well as sources of resistance to future initiatives.

REFERENCES CITED

Aleman, A., Martinez, M., and Renn, K. A. (Eds.). (2002). *Women in higher education: An encyclopedia.* Santa Barbara, CA: ABC-CLIO.

Bauer, Q., and Gruber, S. (2007). Must society, politics and/or education itself change? Barriers and analysts in Turkey and Germany. Paper presented at the UCEA International Women's Leadership Conference, Rome, July 24–27, 2007.

Celikten, M. (2007a). Portraying women administrators: Turkish cases. Paper presented at the UCEA International Women's Leadership Conference, Rome, July 24–27, 2007.

———. (2007b). Women school administrators in Turkey. Unpublished manuscript.

Franck, I. M., and Brownstone, D. M. (1995). *Women's World: A Timeline of Women in History.* New York: Harper Perennial.

Grady, M. L. (1993). The medical model and the preparation of education professionals. *Journal of School Leadership, 3*(3), 288–302.

———. (1995). Alert...Alert...Alert...Alert...Alert....Vaccine Failure. *Leadership Nebraska, 5*(1), 20–22.

Grady, M. L., and O'Connell, P. A. (1993). Women in K-12 educational administration: A synthesis of dissertation research. *Journal of School Leadership, 3*(4), 449–460.

Grady, M. L., Udey, S. S., and Carlson, K. J. (1991). *Women in educational administration: A selected bibliography, 1965–1990.* University Park, PA: The University Council for Educational Administration.

Lightfoot, S. L. (1988). *A world of ideas with Bill Moyers: Sara Lightfoot.* New York: Public Broadcasting Service.

Macha, H., and Handschuh-Heiß. (2007). Gender mainstreaming as an instrument of organizational development at universities. Unpublished manuscript.

———. (2007). Gender mainstreaming: Women in leadership and "the physics of calamities." Paper presented at the UCEA International Women's Leadership Conference, Rome, July 24–27, 2007.

Schuster, M., and Van Dyne, S. (1984). Placing women in the liberal arts: Stages of curriculum transformation. *Harvard Educational Review, 54*(4), 413–428.

Shakeshaft, C. (1989). *Women in Educational Administration.* Newbury Park, CA: Sage.

Starzynska, M. (1992). Eleven prie-dieux. Rome: Tipografia poliglotta della pontificia. Universita Gregoriana.

United Nations. Department of Public Information. (1996). *The Beijing declaration and the platform for action: Fourth world conference on women. Beijing, China, 4–15 September 1995.* New York: United Nations.

CHAPTER 19

Gender Mainstreaming at German Universities

Successful Strategies of Implementation

QUIRIN JOHANNES BAUER AND SUSANNE GRUBER

GOALS

IT IS THE GOAL OF THE PROJECT "Gender Mainstreaming at German Universities—Balance and Optimization" to reflect on the implementation of gender mainstreaming at universities. It will give information about how a university is organized and structured in a way that provides gender equity by using the gender mainstreaming strategy. The medium and long-term results are the achievement of optimization of gender mainstreaming—implementation strategies by network, consistency in exchange of information as well as the use of the resulting synergy effects resulting from it. Furthermore, the responsible parties in the fields of politics, science and university management will be given a basis for making decisions by "good practice" examples. Based on the empirical results and analysis, the need for further steps in the process of gender mainstreaming at each university can be coordinated and planned together with other German universities. Successful strategies and measures that have been performed and can be carried over to other universities will be discussed. When experiences are coordinated with one another, practical problems and solutions can be reflected and discussed immediately.

UNDERSTANDING AND METHODS

The goal of the Augsburg project is to take account of the present status quo of gender mainstreaming activities at selected German universities as well as to optimize the various implementation strategies. Corresponding to these goals, the empirical survey is built as a "triangulation of methods" (Flick, 2004). The subject of the research is illuminated, analyzed and interpreted from various quantitative and qualitative methodological perspectives. As every method of research has specific strengths and weaknesses and therefore only illustrates certain sections of the examined subject, the combination of different methods serves to systematically strengthen the achieved results. In this way, a more objective description of the subject is guaranteed (Denzin, 1977).

Therefore, in this case the analysis of various documents and sources (promotion plans for women, legal basis, university's guidelines in written form, etc.) is combined with the examination of both quantitative (survey by questionnaire) and qualitative (episodic interviews based on guidelines with experts of the various universities) data. Thus the heterogeneity of the elucidation of the gender mainstreaming concept at the 15 universities involved can be understood, analyzed, interpreted and optimized adequately.

In the context of triangulation by episodic interviews with experts and vice chancellors of the subject universities, a method-internal triangulation is produced. As an enlargement of the narrative interview, the episodic interview illuminates the close-to-experience narrative as well as abstract semantic knowledge (Flick, 2004). Only the method-internal symbiosis of situative, context-oriented stories of the experts and chancellors, plus precise inquiries about arguments, ideas and definitions makes a multidimensional overview, elucidation and consolidation of the questionnaire data possible. The survey is divided into six thematic fields which are represented in figure 19.1.

BASICS AND DESIGN OF THE EMPIRICAL SURVEY AND ANALYSIS

In order to form the reconstruction of the individual conditions at universities in an optimal way within the short time the project took place, the analysis of the contents of various data sources has been integrated into the survey's design. This includes an analysis of how the involved universities appear on the world wide web when it comes to the question of gender equity, of the legal framework for the implementation of the process, of the dialectic between "traditional" promotion of women and the top-down strategy of gender mainstreaming, guidelines for gender equity, preambles of the universities, and promotion plans for women. The results of these tests are key points in the main analysis and can furthermore be used as beneficial or nonbeneficial frameworks for the implementation of gender-equal structures at other universities.

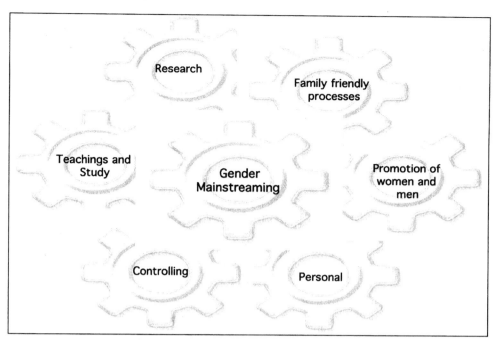

Figure 19.1.   The Survey's Six Fields
Source: Project team "Gender Mainstreaming—Balance and Optimization"

The basis of the project data is set up by an extensive questionnaire. This questionnaire consists of both statistical figures and detailed experts' estimates and is supplemented by each single university with material in the form of reports, brochures, and the like. As far as the data were available, they have been identified at all universities. Some items serve to compare—not to rank—the universities with one another in order to represent the effects of gender mainstreaming strategy relative to size, subject culture or legal frameworks.

A special focus when it comes to surveying and analyzing the data is aimed at the subject cultures of the universities. In order to achieve this, at all universities four faculties have been selected based on fixed criteria and on subject cultures in common. Thus distortions within the universities are avoidable. At every university, two faculties of the natural science–technical fields and two of the social sciences, humanities and law, respectively, are being integrated. Moreover, at one of the four faculties more than 60% of the students have to be registered properly. The data raised right at the universities are supplemented with a secondary analysis of the data of the Federal Bureau of Statistics, so that a description is made possible for each single university and can be verified throughout the Federal Republic.

The data analysis aims at optimization possibilities. Rankings are neither sought nor made possible. The results of all surveys are summarized in the form of an "ideal university." In this "ideal university," beneficial and successful structures and processes as well as "good practice" examples of the gender mainstreaming transposition are pointed out. The frameworks of a promising implementation of the gender mainstreaming strategy are also described. This form of analysis enables universities to remain anonymous when it comes to their data and simultaneously to compare themselves with successful structures and measures. In addition, the structures and measures resulting from the analysis are supplemented and contrasted, for example, by means of proceedings described in the literature.

RESULTS OF THE SURVEY: SUCCESSFUL STRATEGIES AT UNIVERSITIES

The Current Level of Research of Gender Mainstreaming at Universities

At present gender mainstreaming is implemented at several universities in Germany. The topic is highly up to date, as is shown in a series of publications edited in the recent past. Apart from the monograph of Kahlert (2003), countless essays dealing with theory and practice of gender mainstreaming at universities have been published in periodicals (e.g., "Zeitschrift für Frauenforschung und Geschlechterstudien") and collections, for example, Baaken and Plöger, 2002; Bothfeld, Gronbach and Riedmüller, 2002; Nohr and Veth, 2002; and Roloff, 2002. Examples of the practical application of gender mainstreaming at universities, the United University Duisburg-Essen (see Kahlert, 2003, p. 139ff.) as well as the Johannes Gutenberg–University Mainz (see Köhler-Raithelhuber, 2004) are particularly well described. So also is the project "QueR" ("Quality and innovation—gender equity as a strategy of reform") performed by the University of Dortmund (Roloff, 2002, 2004).

Gender mainstreaming, which turns "gender equity into a main subject" (Kirsch-Auwärter, 2002), on the one hand is a "cross-section task" of organizational development and, on the other hand, a "top-down strategy," which means that the management of the organization has to perform each step of the process. A cause can be furthered by a woman representative or a project group, yet the responsibility to use the principle of gender mainstreaming has to be taken by the head of the organization. Thus no special person such as a women's representative is responsible, but rather all the actors who plan, perform and control decision-making processes must be competent to use the gender mainstreaming principle, and they are obliged to that principle. Analogies with regard to strategic use refer to the idea of gender mainstreaming as "quality management concerning the politics of equity."

A change of perspective as well as a new philosophy is closely linked to gender mainstreaming. This means that groups in which both genders act together in order to achieve a goal, as for example the "collective actors" at the university of Augsburg, are moving the process forward. The organization identifies with the process which, in turn, allows for the changing of structures with respect to a new gender contract. Together women and men take responsibility in favor of more gender equity. If gender equity has to be achieved, in principle *every* task and action within the university has to be considered under the aspect of gender.

If one looks at such decision-making processes, it becomes clear that they can concern laws, regulations and norms, as well as politics concerning personnel, faculty goal agreements, organization studies, examination regulations, teaching contents/methods and research, as well as the distribution of resources.

These manifold tasks and acts have been systematized by Kahlert (2003). Accordingly, when it comes to gender mainstreaming at universities there are five relevant fields of acting: (1) university management; (2) development of personnel and promotion of a new generation; (3) research; (4) teaching and studies; and (5) social frameworks. These fields, as a reminder, served as orientation for the survey in the gender mainstreaming project.

WOMEN AT GERMAN UNIVERSITIES: COMPARISON OF FEDERAL STATES

At German universities women are clearly underrepresented at all levels of leading positions. This can be shown for both the field of university management as well as the scientific career and the presence of women in nonscientific fields of the universities. The facts are both clear and alarming. Among chancellors and presidents only about 8% are women (BLK, 2006). At the level of pro-chancellors, vice presidents and chancellors, the share of women in such positions is 18.3%, clearly higher but still far from a status of equity.

When it comes to the fields of scientific personnel and scientific qualifications the small number of women is obvious too. Indeed, the number of females at the beginning of the study since the mid-1990s is higher than the number of male beginners. Nevertheless, women's share of a scientific career clearly decreases. In 2006 professorships in Germany are occupied by women at 15% (Federal Bureau of Statistics, 2007). Figure 19.2 elucidates the decline in female representation in the course of scientific careers in all of Germany. It also shows that the share of women until the end of the studies remains constant, but in the transition to a doctorate, a state doctorate and to a professorship is declining rapidly. This decrease, the so-called leaky pipeline, is distinctive in the different German federal states, as is shown in figure 19.3. Figure 19.3 shows how the share of women in the different levels of scientific career and qualification compares among the German federal states. In this way, the figure shows the current level of the participation of women all over Germany.

A further analysis of the data illustrates women's situation with regard to their participation as scientific personnel. Figure 19.4 shows the proportion of women among professional scientific personnel in Germany. Women's share in all categories of scientific personnel is relatively high, about 28%. Yet a closer look at the data shows it is not really positive since the less the qualification and career level respectively, the higher the women's share. The highest share (43.5%) is found at the level of scientific assistants. This trend, in spite of permanent efforts to improve the situation, has not changed even in recent years. To the contrary, the trend has proved to be resistant.

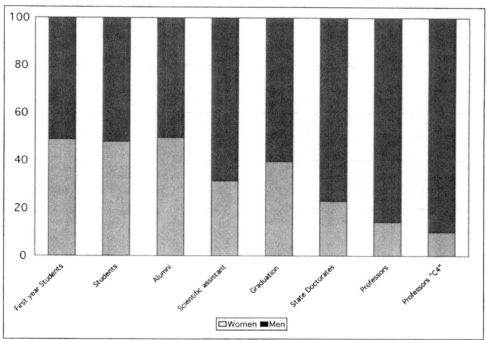

Figure 19.2. The So-Called Leaky Pipeline in Germany

Source: Project team "Gender Mainstreaming—Balance and Optimization," according to data from the Federal Bureau of Statistics (Federal Bureau of Statistics, 2007)

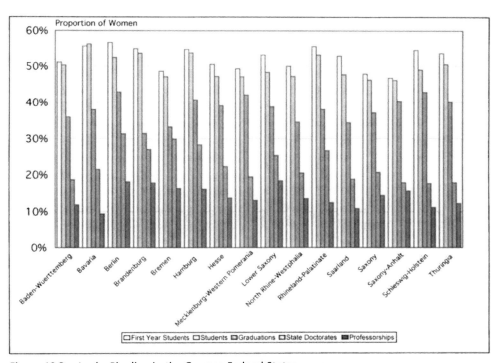

Figure 19.3. Leaky Pipeline in the German Federal States

Source: Project team "Gender Mainstreaming—Balance and Optimization," according to data from the Federal Bureau of Statistics (2006–2007)

Gender mainstreaming and women's promotion are strategies created to work against these conditions. In the long term, it is their aim to increase the share of women in all qualification levels in order to suit the legally guaranteed equity and the principle of equality of opportunity at the same time. In the following situations three of the universities in our project are compared as an example for the entire German analysis.

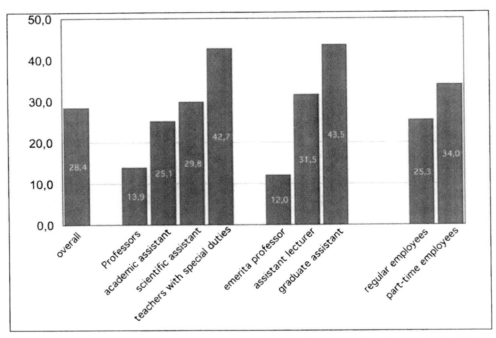

Figure 19.4. Share of Women at Different Levels of Scientific Personnel at German Universities

Source: Project team "Gender Mainstreaming—Balance and Optimization," according to data from the Federal Bureau of Statistics (2007)

WOMEN AT GERMAN UNIVERSITIES: PROJECT ANALYSIS

Never before have women in Germany been as well educated as they are today. At the beginning of university studies, women's share is higher than that of men. In the German winter term of 2003–2004, the share of female beginners was about 50%. Female students plan their studies more efficiently than their male colleagues. Consequently, there is a lower quota of dropouts as well as accelerated studies (BMBF, 2005). These are the first outcomes of strict politics aimed at the equality of opportunity for both men and women. There is a continual effort to gain more women for top positions in science and research. Female students demand better fostering and better mediation concerning the job market. The reasons for the beginning of studies are clear: female students hope to get a good university education in both natural science and engineering, which later leads to better job opportunities.

Apart from these gratifying developments there are still some issues for female students. For instance, the choice of the subject is still traditional. The share of female students choosing humanities remains very high, whereas the quota of female students in various natural and engineering sciences remains the same.

When it comes to the promotion of the new scientific generation, there is also progress to be made.

Although female students seek a doctorate as often as male students (BMBF, 2005), only 39% of doctorates are currently attained by women.

Concerning professorship, the following picture emerges: across all subjects, almost 23% of those awarded a state doctorate are female. The share of women in engineering sciences is 15.5%, which is the lowest, and in veterinary medicine 38.1%, which is the highest (BLK, 2007). The number of female professors at German universities has clearly increased: in 2006 about 5,700 women occupied a professorship, which is a share of 15%. In 1995 the share was only 8%.

So altogether there is an increasing tendency for women to enter scientific professions, but still women are underrepresented. This situation becomes even more clear by means of our examination. The number of women within the university system of the project's cooperating universities has indeed increased during recent years. Nevertheless they are far beyond the 50% mark when it comes to the qualification level. Two universities provide an illustration. The figure shows the share of the female students, those with doctorates, those who have been awarded a postdoctoral lecture qualification, and professors when comparing the university (called university "B" for reasons of anonymity) with the federal state. In favor of that comparison, the relation between the situation at the university and the situation of the federal state has been generated by means of a calculation (share of the university minus share of federal state).

Figure 19.5 shows a clearly lower share of female students compared to average figures of the federal state. This is a natural-technical university in which the number of female students traditionally is very low. However, the distance to the figures of the federal state decreases clearly when it comes to an increasing quality level. Thus one can speak of a plainly less distinctive leaky pipeline. Figure 19.6 shows (apart from the numbers of doctorates) the typical course of qualification levels with a decreasing share of women.

SUCCESSFUL STRATEGIES OF IMPLEMENTATION: MEASURES OF GENDER MAINSTREAMING

The following measures, completed in the collaborating universities, try to motivate female pupils toward natural scientific studies. They foster female students and support them through far-reaching measures. Goals of the measures are a gender-equal participation of women when it comes to the natural-technical field in both university studies and occupation. The latter promotes gender equity in the business world.

Measure A

Measure A promotes the interests and positive attitude of girls, who within natural-technical education are receiving more attention. The reason for this focus originates from growing social significance: competencies are a necessary precondition for successful work with natural and technical sciences, in which social significance is increasing steadily. In order to let girls and women participate equally, comprehensively and competently in social

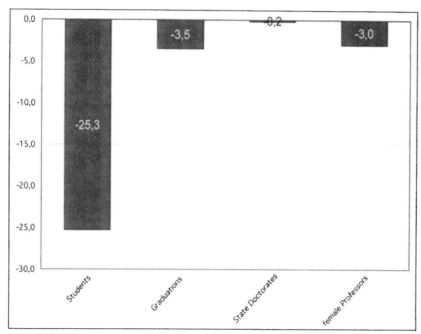

Figure 19.5.   Comparing the Federal State with "University B"
Source: Project team "Gender Mainstreaming—Balance and Optimization," according to data from the Federal Bureau of Statistics (2007)

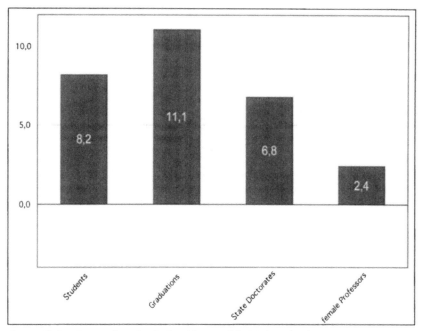

Figure 19.6.   Comparing the Federal State with "University C"
Source: Project team "Gender Mainstreaming—Balance and Optimization," according to data from the Federal Bureau of Statistics (2007)

and democratic processes of development and decision, they have to have natural scientific competencies and have to be able to discuss natural scientific applications critically. Furthermore, the highest goal of the project remains making promotion measures for girls in subjects like mathematics, computer science, natural sciences and technology more visible and widespread with a special focus on stimulating independent learning.

The goal of every measure is to increase the share of female students in the field of engineering sciences. The measures have not been precisely evaluated at any university, nevertheless the comparison of statistical reference numbers with nationwide figures shows a higher share of female students, which probably can be connected with the measures installed.

MEASURES AFTER STUDIES

Only a few women are making a career. Although more than half of the students in Germany are women, the share of women in science and research decreases dramatically the higher the level of qualification. Obviously, as a woman it is not standard but still completely possible to enter a top position in science. The following measures turn to female students who are awarded a doctorate or a state doctorate. The goal is to follow women who consider a scientific career or who have done that already, and to support women who come back to science as well as young scientists. It is also important to offer nonsubject competencies for their career. The duration of the measure is therefore always limited to about twelve months.

Measure A

Through Measure A female students, doctorates and post-doctorates, and those who want to meet the challenge of making a scientific career, are being supported. An information and qualification program suitable for the target group as a career-relevant network is offered. The female participants profit during 12 months from networking and exchange possibilities as well as a selected supply of tutorial groups, trainings and workshops. Concerning the field of strategy, the participants receive qualification-relevant studies as rhetoric, communication and time management, techniques for presentation, discussion and negotiation about dealing with the perspective of successful application to the field of science. Moreover, they are supported by means of individual coaching. Female students visit companies and gain information about the possibility of a scholarship, about the acquisition of EU funding, other public means and careers in sciences, informal rules in the field of sciences, formal rules in favor of a scientific career and financing of research plans.

Figure 19.7 shows the share of women in all doctorates of the university, the federal state and nationwide. Here it becomes clear that the share of the female doctorates on average in the years 1998–2000 has been far below the federal state and Germany. The increased

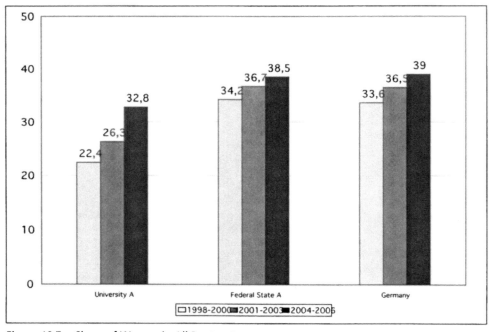

Figure 19.7. Share of Women in All Doctorates
Source: Project team "Gender Mainstreaming—Balance and Optimization," according to data from the Federal Bureau of Statistics (2007)

rate of that share is indeed remarkable. Since the measure is relatively young, we anticipate that the success will be stronger in future statistics.

Women in natural sciences, in technology and economics are usually well qualified, accomplish their work competently, and are socially adept. Nevertheless, women in attractive occupations and leading positions are still an exception. Too often, good work and diligence are not enough for working women to gain leading positions. Mostly they lack contacts, individual promotion and positive female role models. The presented measures accompany and promote women in education and after studies on the different qualification levels. They motivate toward female success as students, doctorates and state doctorates.

The goal is to follow women who start a scientific career or who have already done that, to support women who come back to science as well as young scientists. It is also very important for their careers to offer nonsubject competency. The duration of the measure is therefore always limited to about 12 months. Statistical figures show signs of first success, especially in the growing number of females earning doctorates.

SUMMARY

Gender mainstreaming is a task with high scientific requirements and which presents researchers with different dilemmas. In our view and experience, such a balance is both possible and meaningful. The research process itself intervenes positively in the gender mainstreaming processes of our cooperating universities, and the results, which we can provide to the universities, can be integrated by them profitably in their everyday work. The comparison of the universities becomes possible by statistics and numbers of comparable faculties and other universities, but without needless rankings and the associated problems such "blame" comparisons bring.

REFERENCES CITED

BMBF. (2005). Women and studies: Long-term study, 1983–2004, Berlin.

BLK (Commission for Educational Planning and Research Promotion). (2006). Women in leadership positions at universities and non-academic research establishments: Materials for educational planning and research promotion. Edition 136, Bonn.

Denzin, N. K. (1978). *The research act: A theoretical instruction to sociological methods* (2nd ed.). New York: McGraw-Hill.

Federal Bureau of Statistics. (2007). Education and culture: Non-monetary academic-statistic key data, 1980–2005. Wiesbaden.

Flick, U. (2004): *Triangulation: An introduction.* Wiesbaden, S. 158–167.

Haubrich, K. (2001). Cluster evaluation: A model for a prickly evaluation. DeGEval-Annual Conference, Block 16 Models of Evaluation. Speyer.

Kahlert, H. (2003). Gender mainstreaming at universities: Guideline for a quality-conscious acting. Opladen.

Kirsch-Auwärter (Ed.). (2003). Indicator for the success. *Un/in/form, 2*(2). Georg-August-University of Göttingen, A. A. o. S.

Macha, H., and Handschuh-Heiss, S. (2007). Gender mainstreaming: Instrument for the organizational development. In H. Macha and C. Fahrenwald, *Gender mainstreaming and further education—organizational development with potential development.* Opladen. S. 29ff.

Muckel, P. (2000). Grounded theory in the tradition of the Münsteraner School. Source: www.qualitative-sozialforschung.de%einfuehrung.htm. Retrieved April 24, 2007.

Stiegler, B. (2000). How gender came into the mainstream. Bonn, S. 7ff.

Strauss, A., and Corbin, J. (1996). Grounded theory: Basics of qualitative social research. Weinheim.

Struthmann, S. (2006). Theories and practice of gender mainstreaming. Unpublished diploma thesis. Augsburg, S. 44f.

University of Augsburg. (2006). Gender mainstreaming in the University of Augsburg. *German Society of Educational Science, 17*(32), 131–133.

CHAPTER 20

Portraying Women Administrators

Turkish Cases

Mustafa Celikten

INTRODUCTION

EMPLOYMENT IN TURKEY has always been an important political issue. Yet women have been disadvantaged in terms of employment compared to men. In the Republican period when more women became more educated, their participation in the workforce also increased. Yet there remained significant inequalities between men and women in the areas of education and employment (KSSGM, 2000). This is despite the egalitarian provisions in Turkish law. It has been due to social, cultural and economic barriers that women's participation in the workforce is lower than that of men.

Many research studies have shown that since the 1970s there has been an increase in the number of women in administrative and professional careers. This shows that women want to work together with men in the same conditions, but in recent years women have not gained the same amount of work experience and have remained behind in their career development (Morrison and Von Glow, 1990). As in many places in the world, we find that the majority of teachers in elementary education are women. However, for higher levels of education, we see that the participation of women teachers decreases. Gerni (2001) found that the proportion of women principals in underdeveloped countries and teaching at higher levels of education was significantly lower when compared with both developed countries and with lower levels of education. Tan (1996) found that, despite the fact that the teaching profession is very popular among women in Turkey, they are a strong minority among principals. Historical narratives and data reveal that this is not a new phenomenon, but a process that has occurred over a significant period of time. Both quantitative and qualitative research shows us historical aspects of the shortage of women in educational administration. They support the conclusion that the main reason Turkish women have not been equitably represented in educational administrative positions within Turkish schools has been because of how Turkish culture rigidly defined gender roles and behaviors and placed Turkish women in secondary and subordinate roles to men.

A RESTATEMENT OF THE PROBLEM

In every phase of life women and men have always worked together. However, the contributions of women to society have not been valued as much as that of men. Women are expected to work in lower-status jobs. It is difficult for them to enter higher-status occupations and to get promotions in these professions (Bayrak and Mohan, 2001). Especially when it comes to promotion to higher-level administrative positions, women face a glass ceiling and are often prevented from acquiring greater responsibilities (Arikan, 2003). And so, even though women in Turkey started to go beyond traditions they are still underrepresented in administrative positions (Acuner and Sallan, 1993). This failure to reform its traditions may hurt Turkey's ability to keep up with globalization.

A global perspective on the matter is shown in Berberoglu's (1989) research on the problems of working women worldwide. Berberoglu's research shows that 15% of middle administrative positions are held by women. This may seem very low, but in Turkey the proportion is lower. According to Soyuturk (2001), in Turkey, while overall 30% of employed people are women, the proportion of women in middle and higher levels of administration is only 10%.

It gets even worse with respect to the percentage of women administrators in basic and secondary levels of education. It is ironic that there is far more current research done collecting and analyzing accurate statistical information about the number of goats in geographical regions of Turkey (Akcapinar, 2000) than on the school principals who are responsible for the effectiveness of education (Balci, 2002; Celik, 2004, Celikten, 2001; Wootton, 2006). The Research Planning and Coordination Board, a branch of the National Ministry of Education, recently announced the number of teachers across Turkey in a booklet entitled *National Education: Numerical Data*, but there has been no similar information collected about the number of school principals. It was not until the current century that a visible effort was undertaken in regard to the underrepresentation of women in the principal position. According to the data obtained in the 2005–2006 academic year, in the city of Kayseri only 1% of the primary and secondary education administrators were women.

THE PURPOSE OF STUDY

The purpose of this research paper is to inquire as to why Turkey has such a low proportion of women principals, even though there are no legal obstacles for women being appointed and promoted into administrative positions and their education levels are similar to that of men. This study aims to call to the attention of researchers the need to scrutinize scientifically what can be done to increase the proportion of women school principals. The researcher hopes that the results of this study will be beneficial for potential female candidates for school principal positions within the education system.

SIGNIFICANCE OF STUDY

Developing women's leadership matters for a whole community so as to evaluate fairly and not neglect the abilities of the female half of the society. It is expected that this study will be useful because there is so little research on problem-solving abilities, communication skills, and time management methods of women school principals. Besides, men and women from all disciplines will benefit from the study because its findings will likely transfer to other fields of study or employment. By encouraging and promoting more women to pursue top administrative positions, we help to increase gender equity and improve school administration so they are better equipped to meet the needs of society.

LIMITATIONS

In this research, only female school principals are studied, with a sample of only 48 schools. This makes it difficult to reach conclusions that can be readily generalized to other settings. Although the results are meaningful for the city in which the study was done, they may not be valid for Turkey in general. Nevertheless, I feel confident that this is a very important line of research, one that needs to be expanded to more cases in more locales, because the improvement in the educational opportunities of women teaching in Turkish communities is too significant to ignore.

SCHOOL PRINCIPALS IN TURKEY

Turkey has a strong centralized education system in which all decision-making is done by the Ministry of National Education. At the national level, the ministry prepares budgets, drafts educational legislation and formulates educational policy. It is also responsible for the control, coordination and revision of education at all levels up to higher education, including the provision of technical and vocational education. The state assumes the leading role in aggregating the resources and hiring the technical experts to help plan, regulate and manage the educational process.

Formal education programs at the primary and secondary level are the responsibility of the Ministry of Education. Formal schooling at the primary and secondary levels comprises an eight-year basic education, including a five-year primary cycle and a three-year middle school cycle. Finally, there is a three- or four-year secondary education cycle. Formal education in training institutes at the primary and secondary levels cannot be established without the approval of the Ministry of Education.

In Turkey the curriculum is designed by the Ministry of Education, and the same curriculum is used in every school for the entire country. The Ministry of Education has the authority to decide who will teach in different communities, as well as to designate the curriculum. It is mandated that all education must be in Turkish. Using the same curriculum and instructional strategies in every school is a limitation when one considers the different learning styles of students. All teachers use similar processing and teaching requirements regardless of the learners. Eight years of elementary education is obligatory for all girls and boys (Bayram and Seels, 1997). The education is mostly based on a traditional classroom system with teacher-based learning. Memorization is encouraged, rather than analytical or critical thinking.

Turkish school principals are appointed. They are usually those who are successful in their duties as a teacher or vice principal according to given criteria (Taymaz, 2004). School administrators are the ones who organize, impress, guide, coordinate and inspect the staff in order to achieve the goals. Because of this, school administrators have to show some specific qualifications to fulfill their duties in line with the educational policies of the Ministry of Education (Gursel, 2006). In addition, educational scholars believe that principals play an important role in the organization and operation of schools. As mentioned earlier, most experts consider principals the main driving force for the organizational development and academic growth of students (Peterson, 1994; Bredeson, 1995). On the one hand, principals combine their administrative leadership with teaching, although the proportion of time spent on either role or duty depends on student and staff numbers at their schools. When principals resign, they are immediately reassigned to teaching roles, with the same duties and rights as other teachers.

In the last several years, the field of education in Turkey has been the subject of nationwide reform movements. Principals are a crucial part of school improvement, for without effective principals, highly skilled teachers become frustrated, ineffective teachers whose skills stagnate while the resources of parents and community members go unused (Jones, 1995). As a result, the principals of today must be able to lead and instruct with veracity and quickness as they deal with the never-ending tasks and interactions that come with the role (DePaola and Tschanned-Moran, 2003).

Principalship Examination
In 1998, the Ministry of Education carried out a competitive examination and put out formal educational criteria for educational administrators for the first time. With the aim of preparing modern and qualified educational administrators, it began a training course for those who succeeded at the examination (Bakioglu and Ozcan, 2002). The *Regulation of Ministry of Education on Administrator Appointment, Evaluation, Promotion and Location Change* was published on April 30, 1999, in Official Gazette number 23681. It was the first regulation to establish the preparatory training of educational managers and set out definite criteria for all of their promotions and appointments. The results of the examination applied after the regulation and observations are shown in table 20.1.

While the percentage of female primary and secondary teachers in Turkey is approximately 50%, the percentage is less for females who apply for administrative examinations. As seen in table 20.1, only 8% of the examination participants were female. The number of female participants for the exams remained low for the years 1999 and 2000. These results show that female teachers persistently do not seek to become principals.

The results are supported by additional literature. Arat's (1999) research regarding primary and secondary teachers' desire to become administrators demonstrated that overall only 23.1%, less than a quarter of them, wanted to become administrators. Not surprisingly, this percentage changes dramatically when we look at gender. While just short of two-thirds (64.4%) of male teachers wanted to become administrators, only about one out of eight (13.3%) of female teachers wanted to be an administrator. As a result, we are faced with the reality that fewer female teachers desire to become administrators compared to male teachers.

METHODOLOGY
As stated earlier, the aim of this research is to draw the attention of researchers to the issue of female school administrators and to help them to seek ways of increasing the number of female administrators at schools. For this purpose the following questions were asked:

* Would you tell us the processes you went through to become an administrator?
* What were the personal characteristics that helped you to be an administrator?
* What can you tell us about your strengths and weaknesses as a woman principal?
* Can you share with us the problems you face in this profession?
* Have you ever witnessed any discriminatory behaviors because of your gender?
* What are the reasons for a low proportion of women being school principals in Turkey?

Population and Sample
The population of the study includes all female school principals who officiate in public basic education and secondary schools in Kayseri. Due to the limited

Table 20.1. Results of the Administrative Examination Applied between 1998 and 2001

Years	Participants					Achievers				
	Total	male	%	female	%	Total	male	%	female	%
1998	30,880	28,531	92	2,349	7.6	1,558	1,470	94	88	5.6
1999	24,551	22,606	92	1,945	7.9	5,199	4,840	93	359	6.9
2001	30,214	26,528	87	3,686	12	5,922	5,459	92	463	7.8

Source: Ministry of Education, General Directorship of Educational Technologies.

number of principals in the population, women assistant principals and teachers in leadership positions were also included in the research. In the literature, although there is sufficient information about the number of teachers in Turkey, their gender, subject area and rank, there is not yet enough information about the school principals. However, "despite the lack of accessible, organized and quality data about school administrators in Turkey" (Turan and Ebiciloglu, 2002), some numerical data were obtained for this paper, using table 20.2.

As can be seen in table 20.2, while women comprise 50% of teachers in the basic and secondary education levels, only 7% of principals are female. Of this 7%, 75% are teachers who were serving only as acting principals. In 550 basic education schools, there are 23 women principals, yet only one was appointed as principal. Also, in 99 secondary schools only five women were appointed principals and the majority of them were in girls-only vocational schools.

Data Collection

The survey questions were prepared in two phases. In the first phase, the national and international literatures were reviewed. In the second phase, findings were discussed with experts in the field and people with administrative experience. Finally, the questions were written only after the theoretical basis of the topic and detailed information about the subject had been clearly identified.

Data Analysis

I transcribed tape-recorded interviews verbatim. I used a content-analysis technique to determine areas of emphasis in the data (Marshall and Rossman, 1999).

Table 20.2. State Schools and Administrators in 2005–2006 School Year in Kayseri

Levels	Number of schools	Men			Women		
		A[1]	B[2]	C[3]	D[1]	E[2]	F[3]
Kindergartens	12	0	1	0	6	5	0
Elementary	541	205	114	194	1	4	23
High schools	103	70	24	0	5	4	0
Total	656	275	139	194	12	13	23

1. A tenured principal who is the chief administrator in an elementary, middle, or high school.
2. A deputy principal who is the head administrator of a school and is expected to stay at the position until a tenured principal is appointed.
3. Principal authorized teacher is generally an inexperienced teacher who is assigned to work at a small school or most likely a village school in which s/he is expected to teach to grades 1 to 5 in one classroom.

The information was broken down into manageable categories and results were presented as emerging themes. Parallel to the diagnosis above, postgraduate studies which were performed between 1997 and 2006 and sent to the Turkish Council of Higher Education Documentation Center were examined against the aim of the study. Thirty-two studies were on women principals/administrators.

As shown in table 20.3, four of the graduate studies were conducted by male researchers and 24 of them were conducted by female researchers. Seventy-five percent of the completed doctorate-level studies were done by men. Considering that there is an inequality against women in Turkey, why haven't female university lecturers made more of an effort to research women's issues? Between the dates considered, a total of 3,033 graduate theses were conducted in the area of education. This illustrates clearly the extent to which the study of women principals has been neglected as a topic.

FINDINGS

The first question in the interview schedule sought some demographic information about the participants, whose age ranged from 25 to 46. The demographic information also showed that 65% of women administrators were married and 73 of them had at least one child.

The participants were asked to state *the processes they went through to become administrators*. Their answers showed that most of them were brought to the profession against their own free will and had to stay in the profession. When we remember the fact that school success depends on successful leadership, this situation may bring negative consequences for school effectiveness.

For some school principals these processes developed differently. One woman who was an acting principal stated: "I started to serve as a school principal before I learned how to be a teacher. When I was appointed in the village school, there was no teacher and because I was the only one who came there first I

Table 20.3 Graduate Theses on Women Principals Performed as of 2006

Level	Performers of Theses				Advisers			
	Male	%	Female	%	Male	%	Female	%
Master	4	14	24	86	12	43	16	57
Doctorate	0	0	4	100	3	75	1	25
Total	4		28		15		17	

Source: http//www.yok.gov.tr/tez/istatistik/ist_konu.htm.

became an administrator, and I have been serving as a principal for five years."

The answers to the question *"What are the personal characteristics that have helped you be an administrator?"* can be grouped under two main headings: communication and human relations. The theme of communication was emphasized in almost all of the interviews. One participant emphasized that one of the most difficult aspects of the profession is "to develop effective communication with the employees." She added that "administrators should develop effective communication with the employees because administrators are held responsible for all the problems occurring both in and outside the school building, and therefore they should not act emotionally in dealing with them." In a similar vein, one respondent commented that "being systematic, knowledgeable and hardworking are the most important characteristics administrators must have."

When the participants were asked *"to state what strong and weak characteristics they had,"* most of them did not mention any weak characteristics; however, a younger principal commented that "she was so emotional, tried not to break people's hearts, acted too democratically, neglected her family and eventually felt exhausted."

The researcher further asked the respondents to comment on *"the problems they faced in their profession."* Although the participants stated a number of different problems, some of the most frequently experienced problems were: social perspective, tradition, domestic responsibility, burden of marriage and children, fear of being unsuccessful, and negative attitudes of other female teachers toward female administrators.

When the same question was posed of a middle-aged female principal, she made the following comment: "Because of social and cultural norms, women administrators are not much favored." An experienced interviewee added that: "Parents who visited the school wanted to see male principals in front of them."

A few of the women principals responded that one of the challenges they face is the lack of respect they receive from fathers of students. One respondent complained, "There are times when women do not seem to get the respect of parents when conferencing with them about school issues," while another added, "A specific challenge women face is dealing with certain parents, particularly men, who place little or no value on women."

In addition to the role itself being perceived as a barrier, participants believed that they needed to be better at all the job requirements of a principal, and that they needed to exceed expectations. An overwhelming task thus becomes even more daunting. One respondent complained, "Women who are often more qualified for positions have to work twice as hard as their male counterparts to prove themselves. For Turkish women there may be an additional layer added—to prove their abilities and stamina under pressure."

The majority of the participants noted that one of the barriers that prevented women from advancing was their leadership style. Hackney (2003) stated that women leaders who are more relaxed in their leading are often perceived as soft, weak and incompetent. He further commented that, on the other hand, women who exhibit an intensity of professionalism are often seen as cold or too distant. One participant shared that a parent made a comment that she would be a good elementary teacher, but not a school principal because she was too kind, too nice. On the other hand, one participant commented, "At the elementary level women do not have to take on male characteristics, because they are allowed to be nurturing." Another interviewee added, "Women are often seen as nurturers, therefore, not having the image of being 'tough enough' or being able to make 'tough decisions' like a male principal."

Most of the participants stated that "women administrators could not join the group meetings where the majority of the group members were men." One woman principal stated, "Although women successfully managed to build effective communication in the work environment, they did not feel comfortable attending dinners and meetings organized outside work." Discussing the problems women principals face, one respondent complained, "Male administrators come together outside work and even make decisions. Yet I as a woman cannot partake in these occasions and therefore learn about the decisions much later."

Another woman principal said that "most of the administrators are men and because of their way of looking at women, they [the women] had difficulty in expressing themselves to men." She further said, "Men are always distant to me in meetings. I feel lonely. In society there is a common view that women principals cannot be successful. When we are successful, they look for some hidden reasons for our success."

Another interviewee told us that when she was appointed as school principal, the custodian at the same school wanted to transfer to another school, giving the excuse of not wanting to receive orders from a woman.

This statement clearly shows how people are prejudiced about female administrators in Turkish culture.

Another problem mentioned by a woman principal was that women teachers were jealous of women administrators. One interviewee made the following comment: "Women teachers are very capricious and egotistical; they act emotional and are not collaborative. Men are more collaborative and understanding." The same participant added that, "Women teachers prefer to see men in higher administrative positions rather than seeing women administrators."

Not all of the participants believed that they had experienced problems as women. One interviewee made the following comment that she did not believe she faced many obstacles because of her gender and, in fact, had benefited from the fact that she was one of the few women administrators in Kayseri. Discussing problems, this woman principal commented:

> I don't believe I have faced any barriers as a woman. To the contrary, I believe that being a woman may have given me a slight advantage because women are better listeners, better problem-solvers, more creative, can multi-task better and tend to be more objective, and less reactive. But, I may be a little biased.

When the participants were asked *to state if they witnessed any discriminatory behavior because of their gender*, it was observed that the participants did not feel comfortable in answering this question. For example, one respondent acknowledged, "I was not exposed to such behaviors but I heard that others were," or "Sometimes it happens but I cannot tell you exactly what it is."

It is fascinating, yet perhaps not surprising, that a profession in which the majority of workers are women is mostly managed by men. The shortage of women principals in education has developed over a long period of time. It was not until the 2000s that visible efforts were made in regard to the underrepresentation of women in the principal position. Unfortunately, the increased presence of women principals has remained disproportionately low in secondary administrative positions. As women became more visible in elementary principal positions, the gap in the numbers of women afforded secondary leadership opportunities becomes even more apparent.

CONCLUSION

The aim of this research was to investigate why the proportion of female administrators is very low compared with female teachers at basic and secondary schools. Although the findings cannot be generalized to all of Turkey, I believe that if similar research studies are carried out in other regions, they will possibly give similar results. The results of the study showed that most interviewed women became administrators unwillingly. The participants said that although they had the requisite communication skills, they had many problems in the profession because of stereotypes, including that of their emotionality. They added that because administration was seen as a male profession, women administrators were not welcomed at schools and this caused many problems for these women.

It can be argued that these challenges stem from the patriarchal structure of the Turkish society, which has sharp gender discrimination. Men are seen as authority figures that bring money home, while women are seen in domestic responsibilities such as cleaning, child rearing, cooking and the like (Sakalli and Beydogan, 2001). Women are thus thought to prefer the teaching profession, which they see as the continuation of motherhood and name it as an "easy and feminine profession," and therefore do not prefer administrative positions.

In conclusion, the equality of education should be ensured by the Turkish society in order to adapt to globalization. Women who have significant roles in society should be educated; their status should be improved and they should be given the opportunity to contribute to the development of society (KSSGM, 2000). Yet although women in Turkey have started to go beyond traditions, they are still underrepresented in the administrative positions. There are still significant differences between the roles of women and men. The Turkish cultural heritage of rigidly defined gender roles and behaviors places Turkish women in secondary and subordinate roles to men. Traditionally, women have not been equitably represented in educational administrative positions within Turkish schools. Unfortunately, women still remain underrepresented in educational leadership, and especially in secondary and district-level positions. This research is a positive step in the right direction because it provides a guideline for further research to be conducted on this issue.

RECOMMENDATIONS

Being assertive and diligent is not enough for women to break barriers to entry into administrative positions. In order to overcome the handicaps that face woman principals, sociocultural values have to adapt to change. Laws and especially civilian society need to better support women leaders.

One possible goal would be one woman vice principal in every school. This could become a government-sanctioned law. It would be justifiable since women school principals are important mentors for female students and teachers, as well as role models for other females. This is an important need because young females need guidance and authority figures who are better able to understand their problems.

One of the findings of this study is that there are more men with advanced degrees than women. It is, therefore, recommended that management should encourage women to pursue advanced degrees by offering scholarships, grants, work release programs, and study leave with full pay and benefits. This would help women to move up to the middle and top management positions in educational administration at all levels.

REFERENCES CITED

Acuner, S., and Sallan, S. (1993). Women in public administration. *Turkish Public Administration Journal, 26*(3), 77–92.

Akcapinar, H. (2000). *Sheep breeding.* Ankara: Ismet Publishing.

Arat, N. (1999). Milli egitimin burokratik yapilanmasinda Cinsiyetcilik, Istanbul Universitesi Sosyal Bilimler Enstitusu.

Arikan, S. (2003). Leadership behaviors of women managers in banking sector: Turkish case. *Gazi University Journal, 5*(1), 1–19.

Bakioglu, A., and Ozcan, K. (2002). Okul Yoneticilerinin mentor yoluyla yetistirilme ihtiyaci. *Yuzyilda Egitim Yoneticilerinin Yetistirilmesi Sempozyumu, 21.*

Balci, A. (2002). Introduction, Symposium of Educating Education Managers of the 21st Century. Ankara University, Faculty of Educational Science, No. 191.

Bayrak, S., and Mohan, Y. (2001). The perception styles of men towards women managers in terms of working Life. *Turkish Public Administration Journal, 34*(2), 89–114.

Bayram, S., and Seels, B. (1997). The utilization of instructional technology in Turkey. *Educational Technology Research and Development, 45*(1), 112–121.

Berberoglu, G. N. (1989). Women managers. *Anadolu University Journal, 7*(1), 289.

Bredeson, P. V. (1995). An analysis of the metaphorical perspectives of school principals. *Education Administration Quarterly, 21,* 29–50.

Celik, V. (2004). The policy of educational administrators. Symposium of Educating Education Managers of the 21st Century. Ankara University, The Publications of Faculty of Educational Science, No. 191.

Celikten, M. (2001). Problem solving skills of school administrators. *Journal of Educational Administration, 7*(27), 297–309.

DePaola, M., and Tschanned-Moran, M. (2003). The principalship at a crossroads: A study of the conditions and concerns of principals. *Bulletin, 87*(634), 43–65.

Gerni, M. (2001). *Women in Management.* Istanbul: Beta Edition.

Gursel, M. (2006). *School Administration.* Konya: Inci Publishing.

Hackney, C. (2003, Summer). Voices of women at entry level positions of educational administration. Retrieved November 11, 2003, from http://www.advancingwomen.com/awl/summer2003/HACK.html.

Jones, R. (1995). Picturing your perfect principal. *The Executive Educator, 17*(2), 516–521.

KSSGM. (2000).Women administrators' lived experiences with power. Head Office of Women's Statute, Ankara.

Marshall, C., and Rossman, G. B. (1999). Designing qualitative research (3rd ed.). Thousand Oaks, CA: Sage Publications.

Morrison, A., and Von Glinow, M. A. (1990). Women and minorities in management. *American Psychologist, 45*(2), 200–208.

Peterson, K. D. (1994). *The Leadership Paradox: Balancing Leadership and Artistry in Schools.* San Francisco: Jossey-Bass.

Sakalli, N., and Beydogan, B. (2001, July 7–11). Stereotypes about women and men managers in Turkish culture. International Association of Cross-Cultural Regional Congress, Winchester, UK.

Soyuturk, M. (2001). Women in management. Master's thesis, Hacettepe University, Ankara.

Tan, M. (1996). Women minority in educational administration. *Journal of Turkish Public Administration, 29*(4), 33–42.

Taymaz, H. (2004). *School administration.* Ankara: Saypa.

Turan, S., and Ebiclioglu, N. (2002). A study of gender differences and leadership characteristics of elementary school principals. *Educational Administration in Theory and Practice, 31,* 444–458.

Wootton, P. A. (2006). The few who succeed: Women administrators in higher education. Unpublished dissertation, University of Oklahoma Graduate School.

CHAPTER 21

Gender Mainstreaming

Women in Leadership and "The Physics of Calamities"

HILDEGARD MACHA AND STEPHANIE HANDSCHUH-HEISS
TRANSLATED BY ELISABETH ASAM-VAN-DEN BOOGAART

INTRODUCTION

Gender mainstreaming is an instrument of organizational development and universities are a specific field for the application of this instrument. Universities have a special structure due to staff hierarchies. That is why planning and organizing a gender mainstreaming (GM) process is a challenge to all. Staff, students, scientists, professors, administrators and facilities such as the library and student union are involved in a complex hierarchical structure but have different specific interests. If a GM process is to be effective, at least a rudimentary movement toward equality of chances for both sexes in all hierarchy groups must take place.

GM is a political strategy that challenges feminist theory: the traditional strategy of fostering women by a bottom-up approach through women's representatives is replaced by a top-down strategy in which the university's leadership and others make decisions together with faculty representatives. In the beginning this provoked negative reactions from feminist authors (see Metz-Göckel, 2007; Stiegler, 2007; and Süßmuth, 2007). Yet we are convinced that by following this political strategy, universities can achieve many goals that could not be reached with traditional means of fostering women. This contribution focuses on necessary premises and our positive experience.

Aiming at equality of chance for both sexes through GM means initializing a process with emancipatory goals for both sexes and the university. This implies a need for ongoing reflection on changes in order to correct processes if necessary.

Gender mainstreaming is defined as women and men of all groups at a university getting to know gender-sensitive perspectives, issues at the university being viewed as gender relevant and analyzed for injustice, and continually collecting/analyzing relevant data. Furthermore, faculty, facility and university leadership agree on objectives including the gender-relevant application of funds to certain purposes. Gender is viewed as a structuring category which cannot lead to hidden discriminations, but rather becomes an inducement to organizational changes. This new approach must be evaluated concerning its effectiveness.

In this chapter first the theoretical base is given. The principle of GM and its meaning for an organization is placed into perspective against the background of the theoretical gender discourse. Finally, the GM concept is described at the University of Augsburg.

GENDER MAINSTREAMING AT THE UNIVERSITY—THEORIES AND TERMS

Gender mainstreaming is a concept that has been fixed in the European Union for approximately 10 years. It takes gender perspective into account in all decisions. The official definition of the Council of Europe (1998) states: "Gender Mainstreaming is the (re)organization, improvement, development and evaluation of policy processes, so that a gender equality perspective is incorporated in all policies at all levels and at all stages, by the actors normally involved in policy-making" (Krell, Mückenberger and Tondorf, 2001).

In this definition, the term "equalization" is central and the phrase "policy processes" focuses on organizations and organizational development. Therefore, GM is a controlling instrument of equalization politics and human resource development.

Applied to the university, GM can accordingly be defined as a controlling instrument of the university's organizational and human resource development. A social and cultural change at the university is initiated, sensitizing for equality, enhancing work and life quality of employees, and increasing the chances of women to get an equal share in high positions and decision processes. Judicial, economic, social, organizational, structural as well as ethical reasons can be given for GM:

- *Judicial:* The phrase "equality of chances" for both sexes is installed in international, European and German law
- *Economic:* The human resources of women are still underutilized, which marks a dissipation of human resources. Society invests in the "human capital" of

women by sponsoring their education and undergoes a loss of investment if these resources are not used adequately
- *Social:* Justice and equality of chance foster higher contentment at work
- *Organizational:* The optimal use of human capital raises efficiency and effectiveness and therefore the organization's output
- *Structural:* Seen through the gender perspective, university structures lead to injustice and discrimination caused by multiple processes of segregation. Women are disadvantaged within the organization, men are disadvantaged in the female-dominated education sector, and parents are disadvantaged due to lack of child-care institutions
- *Ethical:* Justice is established as a value in society and its realization is desirable

Universities should become places where work and life, each following a different set of rules, can be continually integrated. That is how employees can be invigorated. The gender perspective is taken into consideration in all university decisions. As a top-down process, GM is compatible with other approaches to reform the university, manifested in new German university law, reform of the payment structure, and administrative modernization.

CHANGING FROM WOMEN'S ADVANCEMENT TO GENDER MAINSTREAMING

Measures of women's advancement have not yet borne the desired fruit. This is seen clearly in the decreasing numbers of highly qualified women from one career level to the next at universities. Recent statistics show that at German universities about 14% of the professors and 9% of the senior professors are female. Lind (2004) reviews reasons, based on empirical data (Engler, 2001; Krais, 2000; Zimmermann, 2000). The sad results of long-term women's advancement politics suggest giving GM a chance.

These are the specifics of gender mainstreaming. On one hand GM is a cross-section task of organizational development, and on the other hand it is a top-down strategy, meaning the organization's leadership must conduct the process. Leadership can be motivated by a women's representative or a project team; the responsibility for applying the GM principle remains nonetheless with the organization's leadership. All participants are part of decision-making. The strategic realization is that Gender Mainstreaming is quality management concerning equality.

A change of perspective and new philosophy are connected to GM. "Collective actors" (Coleman, 1990), meaning groups in which men and women act according to set goals, enhance the process. They can clarify the organization's profile concerning equality. They move the organization toward identifying with a new gender contract. Women *and* men take on responsibility for more equality. Traditional feminist political perspectives are replaced by GM perspectives. Women are no longer a random group trying to solve their specific problems by pleading and petitioning as outsiders. Centers of decision-making commit themselves to the GM principle, and women and men together are responsible for changes in gender structures (Stiegler, 2002). As Woodward (2004) states, "Women are not portrayed as an oppressed group, but as equal partners in an unequal gender contract which must be revised" (p. 89). By these means the issues of men, for instance their role as fathers, can be revised as well.

Nohr and Veth conclude that the new term "gender mainstreaming" revived the difficult debate about public interest in equalization (2002, p. 7). "Concerning equalization, universities in Germany are a developing country. Can the GM strategy promote their development? Research answers this question positively" (Färber, 2002, p. 107). This "yes" has certain conditions which make GM a promising tool. Generally, the relationship of gender mainstreaming and classical forms of feminist politics have to be taken into consideration. GM can be abused by directing it as a new strategy against the old ones (Stiegler, 2002). On the contrary, GM must be a double strategy, combining approved strategies of fostering women with a gender-sensitive evaluation of decisions and measures on equity (Färber, 2002).

All tasks and fields in the university organization must be viewed under the gender lens. Kahlert (2003) systematized those multiple tasks and fields, finding six relevant for GM at universities: the governing of the university; human resource development; encouraging young talents; research; lecturing and studies; and basic social issues.

At the University of Augsburg a special concept for implementing gender mainstreaming was developed and applied based on theory outlined in the following section.

THEORETICAL BACKGROUND OF THE CONCEPT "GENDER MAINSTREAMING"

Gender is the main component of GM, yet it is seldom mentioned in texts concerning GM. If it is mentioned, it is mostly as "gender role," disguising an approximately 40-year-old scientific discourse about the difference between sex and gender, including the deconstruction of sex which leads to the negation of the categories "woman" and "man." Even if the scientific discourse has reached the deconstruction of identity and points of view, not so the political practice. It is in need of a quasi-nondeconstructive strategy. Politics centered around sex and gender is bound to define and limit. So at least a temporary fixation is obligatory and must be used strategically, which means knowing about the fixation while reflecting upon its limits. Heath translates this as, "I must act as if I exist as a man, since I do" (1992).

The Utopia of a "world without gender" (Rubin, 1975, in Hark, 2005, p. 44f.), seems only realized through the injustice of gender. Thus one is confronted with the "gender paradox" (Lorber, 1999): the vision of overcoming the existing gender arrangement relies on the analysis of existing gender structures. The effect of this "gender paradox" is that those who want to foster women and overcome categories often are accused of fostering gender categories (Gildemeister and Wetterer, 1992).

It is clear that using the term "gender" leads to its trivialization in everyday life. Gender politics must be based on real people's understandings concerning gender in everyday life in order to be relevant, realized by men and women without ignoring their experiences (Meuser, 2004, p. 333). If this means reverting to simple gender concepts (e.g., there are men and women), this is helpful for organizations. Implementing GM changes self-evaluation. Organizations are functionally differentiated, therefore it seems they have to be gender blind. In fact, they have a gendered substructure (Acker, 1991). By orienting the working culture on the typical male biography (Meuser, 2004), male groups (Rastetter, 1994) segregate the substructure by the category gender ("glass ceiling", "glass walls"). The division of work in organizations not only follows but also constructs gender (Wetterer, 2002). With gender as a category of self-evaluation this substructure becomes evident. The question is which understanding of gender is implemented in the context of GM.

It may be assumed that through self-evaluation and development of a learning organization, knowledge about gender increases and changes continuously as an effect of GM. The knowledge transfer contains new knowledge about gender from outside the organization (Frey and Kuhl, 2003), as well as knowledge won

and communicated within the organization (Macha and Handschuh-Heiß, 2005a).

Yet there are critical opinions opposed to GM's focus on gender. Since gender is GM's only category of evaluation in all fields, gender differences are cemented. "The possibility of social fields where gender differences are not relevant does not occur in the concept GM" (Meuser, 2004, p. 330). Meuser does not view GM as deconstructive, aiming at neglecting the differences between men and women. On one hand, focusing on sex and gender is plausible and necessary, and on the other hand GM makes it a dominant factor that may hide other differentiating factors.

If one draws a conclusion from the current state of research, one finds literature that does not yet adequately focus on the transfer problem between theory and practice (Färber, 2002; Lind, 2004; Löther, 2004; Stiegler, 2002). The contribution of Kahlert (2003) is an exception, basing an empirical analysis on a solid theoretical foundation. The works relevant for our field are both theoretical (Wetterer, 2000) and practical, reflecting practical experiences of implementing GM at universities (Köhler-Raithelhuber, 2004).

In our realization of GM we use three relevant strings of theory:

- Gender Relations (Gildemeister and Wetterer, 1992; Kessler and McKenna, 1978; Rendtorff, 2006; Winterhager-Schmid, 1998). They focus on attitudes of men and women toward leading positions in science, power, success and income (Babcock and Laschever, 2003; Mayrhofer, 2005).
- Organizations and Gender (Nentwich, 2004; Rastetter, 1994). They deal with the construction of gender in organizations and the connection between job and gender-specific tasks (Macha, 2000; Wetterer, 2002).
- Systemic organizational research and development (French and Bell, 1994; Schreyögg, 1999). They enable well-grounded analyses of the changes fostered by GM. Gender-sensitive analyses of organizations' data may prove theoretical assumptions.

In order to substantiate the relation between theory and practice GM needs to connect with theoretical discourses. The connection can happen at universities. The construction of gender in professional milieus appears at the university in structures like insecure jobs for women (Allmendinger, 2003). These processes of segregation construct a gender relation signaling that women are not wanted in permanent positions with a higher responsibility. Consequently women are excluded from the university and science, as demonstrated through the lower number of female professors. Gender is constructed through segregation at the university and its "gender constructing division of work" (Wetterer, 2002, p. 20). Openly identifying, honoring and fostering talented women in all status groups as part of GM works against these structures.

The task of combining job and family life, historically the responsibility of female university staff, is another example. By establishing day care for youngsters near the University of Augsburg, which also takes care of children of fathers working at the university, the responsibility of both sexes is proclaimed.

The evaluation of GM measures at universities is just beginning. Until now individual tools have been evaluated, for example, mentoring programs, child care programs, affirmative action programs for women, or measures of modernizing the administration (e.g., at the University of Mainz). Entire concepts have not yet been evaluated. A new standard is connected to this design: realizing a new concept based on theory and data measures that are planned and a process that is evaluated immediately.

GENDER MAINSTREAMING AT THE UNIVERSITY OF AUGSBURG

The project Gender Mainstreaming at the University of Augsburg was designed on theoretical foundations and works to realize theoretically based practice. The project's goals were derived from noted theories and formulated for the university. They are:

- Changing the university according to more gender equity
- Identifying and fostering talented women in all status groups
- Data-based analysis to demonstrate injustice for both sexes
- Abolishing injustice through political measures

The project's structure is connected to the goals. The structure is theory based, goal-oriented and characterized by: (1) an organizational structure of five "collective actors," new or already existing groups at the university for planning and implementing equalization measures; (2) a complex system of modules that realizes the project's goals; and (3) a new economic incentive system for fostering women's careers.

GM's practical work within the measures at Augsburg is structured according to the following principles:

1. Implementation of decision and controlling structures (the five "collective actors")
2. Strategic and operative controlling of university governing and organizational development (objectives formed with faculty)
3. Empowerment (identification and fostering of women in all status groups on all hierarchy levels)
4. Networking in communities (developing the potential of individuals through supportive groups)
5. Family-oriented university (work-life balance for women and men)
6. Scientific evaluation of the GM process and its results

These principles stand on the following theoretical considerations.

Principle 1—Implementation of Decision and Controlling Structures: Five "Collective Actors"

At Augsburg the installation and cooperation of five connected collective actors at different levels of the university was regarded as reasonable. They guide and control the GM process, since guidance appears to be central for GM's success (Jung, 2005). While two of five groups are part of the GM process, namely the GM project team and the GM supervision team, the other three previously existed as elements of the university's organizational culture—the university's executive team, the standing committee for gender equality questions, and the advisory committee on women's concerns. The university's executive team, the faculties' women's representatives, the faculties, the equal opportunity commissioner (responsible for nonscientific staff) and representatives of all status groups are involved.

The GM supervision team is led by one of the vice presidents and is accountable for guiding and controlling the GM processes. Elected representatives of all status groups are involved, so there is connection with the senate, the university's leadership and the university's advisory board. By this structure, a dissemination of all information concerning GM into all parts of the university is guaranteed and the cooperation of all parties on all levels is fostered.

The university's executive team absorbed the university's women's representative and she informs them about progress of GM. The women's representative advises the guidance group in all questions and initiates the GM process.

The standing committee for gender equality questions is appointed by the senate and consists of a representative of each faculty's professorial staff (the so-called gender agent). Committee members further GM in the faculties, and include two elected student representatives, two representatives of the scientific assistants, one representative of the nonacademic staff, the university's women's representative and the equal opportunity commissioner. In addition, a representative of the staff board and the commissioner for equalization are present as advisers.

The advisory committee on women's concerns consists of the elected faculties' women's representatives, student representatives and representatives of scientific assistants and other staff. The university's women's representative functions as the board's adviser. The advisory committee on women's concerns suggests and implements measures.

The GM project team consists of the university's women's representative, the women's commissioner and project associates. It leads the project, gives input, registers and controls the steps of implementation. The project group is advised by an independent external socio-scientific institute.

The GM supervision team, the standing committee for gender equality questions, and the advisory committee on women's concerns meet once or twice each semester. If necessary, combined meetings take place so that information can be shared in an optimal way and a "politics of short distances" can be used. This makes quick actions and reactions possible, which is especially important when ideal results have to be brought forth within a short span of time. The project group meets more often, depending on necessity. It links the work of actors within and outside the university that realize GM goals.

Communicating the work results of the individual groups adequately and continuously is important. The network structure of collective players helps the information flow. Some positions and persons are present in different teams and boards. They react to missing pieces of information.

There are several successful examples resulting from this coordination and focus:

- *Gender analysis:* Committee members identified the necessity of gender differentiating analyses for building an information pool. A small spontaneously formed work group defines criteria for structuring and systematizing data. The faculties' women's representatives collected data. Following these procedures, the group conducted a needs assessment. The guidance group acted similarly.

- *Objectives:* All faculties must agree on objectives with the university. The project group presented basic GM information to the university's leadership, the guidance group, the senate group for equalization and the women's advisory board. The faculties' deans were also informed.

Principle 2—Strategic and Operative Controls: Objectives with the Faculties

The controlling concern leading the university and developing the organization in GM is an instrument that shapes the process in the desired direction and, if needed, corrects it. This means implementing equal opportunity politics—quality management that combines the central coordination and control of individual measures with empirical evaluation. In combination with strategic and operative controlling (Brüggemeier, 2001; Die Frauenbeauftragten der Berliner Universitäten, 2002) the following measures are applied:

- Realization of strategic and operative controls through the five "collective actors" of the GM process
- Collecting data for gender analyses regarding the number of women and men in all positions at the university and the duration of their jobs to create an information pool (empirical analyses not only show a disproportion between men's and women's status positions but also between short-term and long-term jobs, to the disadvantage of women)
- Objectives with the faculties concerning gender
- Integration of GM into the university's mission statement and profile
- Gender budgeting
- Objectives for the nonacademic staff

Objectives about gender mainstreaming touch all conceivable fields—research, lecturing and studies, human resource development, fostering of young talent, as well as social issues (i.e., compatibility of family and job).

Principle 3—Empowerment: Identification and Fostering of Talented Women at All Steps of the Career Ladder

Consistent promotion of young researchers is pursued. Talented women are identified and supported in their development of studies, by material means and through child care measures.

Starting GM by developing individual potential (Macha and Bauhofer, 2004) is based on the assumption that competencies of individual employees and their potentials are the base of organizational development. Starting with individual development makes sense for the system, initiating processes of change from below. The learning organization's development depends on the staff's development. Roloff stresses that human resource development often is not practiced adequately at universities, because they do not have an institutional understanding of human resource development. Roloff underscores the growing importance of quality management for modern universities, which includes the mobilization of individual motivation and potential of staff and students and connecting them with the institution's goals (2004).

At many universities the development of potential and fostering young talent is practiced with the end result of equalization, whether objectives or other measures aim at this goal. This is necessary as the existing inequality of opportunities is seen most clearly when looking at the low numbers of women staying in the academic field in Germany. Even though more women than ever have a university diploma, qualified women are eventually "lost" in the university system, as the image of a "leaky pipeline" stresses (Babcock and Lashever, 2003; Blome, 2005; Van Anders, 2004).

Equalization measures must focus on targeted and continual fostering of female academic junior staff. Empowerment means potential development of talented women in all phases of their career. A "culture of encouragement" has to be created (Macha, 2005) in which women can follow the goal of an academic career successfully from their initial studies to being a full professor.

Increasing the number of women in leading positions is not only important for equal opportunities but a compelling prerequisite of sociocultural change. The so-called critical mass for change in a profession's culture is given by Etzkowitz, et al. (1994), as 30% (Allmendinger, 2003; Schlegel and Burkhardt, 2005, p. 78). That implies that not until 30% of the professors are female can the traditionally male dominated culture at universities change effectively and essentially.

Principle 4—Networking in Communities: Developing the Potential of Individuals Through Supportive Groups

The principle of organizing further education in groups makes use of the intersection between organizational development and individual potential development. Individual men and women can develop their potential better in informal communities than alone (Fahrenwald and Porter, 2007). Networks traditionally have a supportive function for women and men. Through appreciative feedback they induce developments and lay a base for exploring new goals.

Through feedback individuals obtain important information for innovative actions. This makes the effects of education deeper and longer lasting. Students as well as scientists are gathered in support groups or "success teams" or "wish craft" (Sher and Gottlieb, 1989). This principle is practiced, for instance, in the workshop and training program KleVer (www.uni-augsburg.de/projekte/gendermainstreaming/klever) and in the mentoring program ProMentora (www.uni-augsburg.de/projekte/gendermainstreaming/promentora), which is vitally important for women in academic fields where they are clearly underrepresented (Sobehart and Giron, 2007).

Principle 5—Family Oriented University: Work-Life Balance for Women and Men at the University

Improving the work-life balance is a topic for women and men, acknowledged in politics and society. In particular, highly qualified women are confronted with the problem of how to combine family and work life (Macha, 2006). Studies give evidence that often women believe they must abstain from having children in order to have a science career whereas male colleagues indeed have families with three or more children (Krimmer et al., o.J.). To solve this problem a "family-friendly university" must be set up. Innovative measures like the following are introduced:

- Day care for the staff's preschool-age children;
- Vacation programs for children of the university staff
- A pool of babysitters
- A web page with information for parents (www.uni-augsburg.de/projekte/gendermain/streaming /ikbu)

Principle 6—Scientific Evaluation of the Gender Mainstreaming Process and Its Results

The current project Gender Mainstreaming at the University of Augsburg is designed as a scientific project of applied research, hence evaluation is crucial. The process and measures are transparent in their course and structure, and can be controlled and guided. Evaluation includes reasonable assessing of processes and measures as well as a better understanding and shaping of measures through controlling effects, guiding and reflecting (Reischmann, 2003). The evaluation follows the standards of the German association for evaluation (Deutsche Gesellschaft für Evaluation), the so-called DeGEval-Standards (www. degeval.de/calimero/tools/proxy). The four basic features of evaluation are usefulness, fairness, accuracy and feasibility.

Since anchoring GM in an organization like a university is a complex process and must be scientifically analyzed as such, after dealing with diverse concepts of evaluation (Beywl et al., 1987; Guba and Lincoln, 1989; Keiner, 2001; Merkens, 2004; Reischmann, 2003; Stockmann, 2004; Wottawa and Thierau, 1990) for the current project the model of "participative evaluation" by Ulrich and Wenzel (2003) was chosen. This method is distinguished by the possibility of taking the involved persons' perspectives into consideration and integrating these into the GM process, that is, by interviewing the participants regarding the various measures. Evaluation is seen as a process which is mutually designed as one of interaction and intervention. Led by hypotheses, methods of evaluation are planned, including interviews, monitoring, testing and analyzing written material. That is how new hypotheses are generated. The GM process is investigated with an analysis of process and structure. Formative evaluation of the program's development, implementation and summative evaluation are accomplished (Reischmann, 2003). Formative evaluation is carried out during the project so that the participants can be involved and, if necessary, correction can take place. It is process oriented. Summative evaluation makes up the balance, collecting the project's results after measures and phases. It is outcome oriented.

Many changes have already occurred. The reform process of GM passed through five phases:

- Phase 1 (2003–2004): The concept was designed and formulated, drawing on a national comparison of university politics (Macha and Handschuh-Heiss, 2004). The concept was enhanced by brainstorming within the project group and at national and international conferences, and then interconnected with national research organizations about GM, such as the CEWS and at other universities, among them Ludwig-Maximilians-Universität in Munich, the University of Pittsburgh and Duquesne University in Pittsburgh. The evaluation concept was designed and tested at the same time. The GM concept was approved by the university senate and university leadership. Implementation began.

- Phase 2 (2004): The GM concept was made public, communicated within and outside the university by informing the university's leadership, its boards and the public. Individual measures were substantiated and initiated. Evaluation started, collecting data about process and GM measures.
- Phase 3 (2005): The consolidation of processes, implementation of measures and evaluation data collection took place.
- Phase 4 (2005): The control process initiated improvement, changing measures if necessary, modifying the evaluation plan if needed.
- Phase 5 (2006–2007): The emphasis lies on evaluating the collected data and writing a report. The GM process continues. There is a continual dissemination into all parts of the university.

Although the evaluation is not yet finished, some trends have emerged. Individual measures that have been realized since 2004 are well established and well liked by participants, especially IKBU, enhancing or enabling a balance between work life and family life, and the programs KleVer and ProMentora for fostering young female scientists in all phases of their career. The measures' relevance for everyday life can clearly be seen when considering the participants' comments. Shortly after a KleVer workshop a participant expressed appreciation for the "really successful training" and shared, "In those two days I learned so much that I was well prepared for an appraisal interview with my boss and, due to the trainer, I was able to advance my requests."

Even university employees, who can no longer profit from the measures, gave feedback. For instance, when the vacation program for school children was announced a mother of grown-up children who has been working at the university for a long time remarked she would have wished for such an option 20 years ago. Increasing demand and good appraisals in feedback surveys document the measures' acceptance and effectiveness. The generated evaluation data are used for shaping and optimizing the measures.

By cooperating and connecting the groups and boards, the so-called collective actors' potential for taking actions is used and synergetic effects are set free. The successful realization of the individual measures is connected positively to the GM process. The topic of equal opportunities was established by the workshop "Gender Mainstreaming at the University of Augsburg" as well as copious communication. A "culture of encouragement" (Macha, 2005) is being created.

Female students are inspired to aim for high professional goals in an academic career. GM implementation also has effects outside the university. The University of Augsburg can present itself as an attractive employer for talented young women scientists with and without children. More applications for professorships are received. In all fields a process of participative emancipation is released. Structural and cultural change is initiated, assuring gender equalization politics.

Evaluation data shows change at all levels of the university:

- *Interaction:* The gender perspective is considered more in all decisions by faculties and chairs. Sensitization concerning the construction of gender and gender relations exists.
- *System:* Data collection for gender analyses has been optimized and continued. Gender analyses are the basis of all university objectives and achievement criteria.
- *Faculty:* Objectives contain gender specific expectations and quantifiable goals.
- *Individual:* Through GM measures the principle of women's, mothers', fathers' and single parents' empowerment is slowly but surely functioning.

OUTLOOK

By implementing GM, the University of Augsburg's self-observation has changed; the category "gender" is the focus. Concerning the gender level, one may conclude that the conception of gender-equal opportunities for the sexes has increased. This self-observation can be further institutionalized as an all-embracing "gender-watch system." So another lasting result of the project's evaluation is to supply the university with the necessary premises for self-help in order to develop instruments of self evaluation, such as gender checks, gender statements, gender reports, gender impact assessments and so on. This fosters the continuation of controlling equalization on a permanent basis, which can restore a prominent position in the universities' equalization competition to the University of Augsburg.

REFERENCES

Acker, J. (1991). Hierarchies, jobs, bodies: A theory of gendered organizations. In J. Lorber and S. A. Farrell (Eds.). *The social construction of gender*. Newbury Park/London/New Delhi, 162–179.

Allmendinger, J. (2003). Strukturmerkmale universitärer Personalselektion und deren Folgen für die Beschäftigung von Frauen. In: Wobbe, T. (Hrsg.): Zwischen Vorderbühne und Hinterbühne. Beiträge zum Wandel der Geschlechterbeziehungen in der Wissenschaft vom 17. Jahrhundert bis zur Gegenwart, Bielefeld, S. 259–277.

Baaken, U./ Plöger, L. (Hrsg.) (2002): Gender Mainstreaming. Konzepte und Strategien zur Implementierung an Hochschulen, Bielefeld.

Babcock, L., and S. Laschever. (2003). Women don't ask: Negotiation and the gender divide. Princeton, NJ.

Beywl, W. u. a. (1987). Evaluation von Berufswahlvorbereitung. Fallstudie zur responsiven Evaluation, Opladen.

Blome, E. u. a. (2005). Handbuch zur universitären Gleichstellungspolitik. Von der Frauenförderung zum Gendermanagement? Wiesbaden.

Bothfeld, S./Gronbach, S./ Riedmüller, B. (Hrsg.) (2002). Gender Mainstreaming—eine Innovation in der Gleichstellungspolitik. Zwischenberichte aus der politischen Praxis, Frankfurt a.M.

Brüggemeier, M. (2001). Controlling. In: Hanft, A. (Hrsg.). Grundbegriffe des Hochschulmanagements, Neuwied/Kriftel, S. 58–67.

Center of Excellence Women and Science (Hrsg.) (2003). Hochschulranking nach Gleichstellungsaspekten, Bonn.

Center of Excellence Women and Science (Hrsg.) (2005). Hochschulranking nach Gleichstellungsaspekten, Bonn.

Coleman, J. S. (1990). *Foundations of social theory.* Cambridge, MA/London.

Die Frauenbeauftragten der Berliner Universitäten (2002). Zielvereinbarungen als Instrument erfolgreicher Gleichstellungspolitik. Ein Handbuch, Kirchlinteln.

Engler, S. (2001). „In Einsamkeit und Freiheit"? Zur Konstruktion der wissenschaftlichen Persönlichkeit auf dem Weg zur Professur, Konstanz.

Ernst, S./Warwas, J./Kirsch-Auwärter, E. (Hrsg.) (2005). Wissenstransform. Wissensmanagement in gleichstellungsorientierten Netzwerken, Münster.

Etzkowitz, Henry, Carol Kemelgor, Michael Neuschatz, Brian Uzzi, and Joseph Alonzo. (1994). The paradox of critical mass for women in science. *Science* 266, 51–54.

Färber, C. (2002). Frauen auf die Lehrstühle durch Gender Mainstreaming? Ein neues gleichstellungspolitisches Konzept und seine Bedeutung für den Hochschulbereich. In Bothfeld, S./Gronbach, S./Riedmüller, B. (Hrsg.). Gender Mainstreaming—eine Innovation in der Gleichstellungspolitik. Zwischenberichte aus der politischen Praxis, Frankfurt a.M., S. 107–131.

Fahrenwald, C./Porter, M. (2007). Weiterbildung als Cultural Change—Transatlantische Studie über Frauen in pädagogischen Führungspositionen. In: Macha, H./Fahrenwald, C. (Hrsg.). Gender Mainstreaming und Weiterbildung—Organisationsentwicklung durch Potentialentwicklung. Opladen and Farmington Hills, S. 131–147.

French, W. L./ Bell, C. H. (1994). Organisationsentwicklung. Sozialwissenschaftliche Strategien zur Organisationsveränderung (4. Auflage), Bern.

Frey, R./Kuhl, M. (2003). Wohin mit Gender Mainstreaming? Zum Für und Wider einer geschlechterpolitischen Strategie. In: gender…politik…online. Dezember, S. 2–14 (Internet-Adresse der Zeitschrift: web.fu-berlin.de/gpo).

Gildemeister, R./Wetterer, A. (1992). Wie Geschlechter gemacht werden. Die soziale Konstruktion der Zweigeschlechtlichkeit und ihre Reifizierung in der Frauenforschung. In Knapp, G.-A./Wetterer, A. (Hrsg.). Traditionen Brüche. Entwicklungen feministischer Theorie, Freiburg/Br., S. 201–254.

Guba, E. G./Lincoln, Y. S. (1989). *Fourth generation evaluation.* Newbury Park.

Hark, S. (2005). Dissidente Partizipation. Eine Diskursgeschichte des Feminismus, Frankfurt a.M.

Heath, S. (1992). Difference. In *The sexual subject: A screen reader in sexuality.* London/New York, S. 47–106.

Jung, D. (2005). Gender Mainstreaming als Lernprozess—Methodische Voraussetzungen zur nachhaltigen Umsetzung. In Jung, D./Krannich, M. (Hrsg.). Die Praxis des Gender Mainstreaming auf dem Prüfstand. Stärken und Schwächen der nationalen Umsetzungspraxis, Frankfurt a.M., S. 11–21.

Kahlert, H. (2003). Gender Mainstreaming an Hochschulen. Anleitung zum qualitätsbewussten Handeln, Opladen.

Kanter, R. M. (1977). *Men and women of the corporation.* New York.

Kessler, S./ McKenna, W. (1978). *Gender: An ethnomethodological approach.* New York.

Konzept zur Frauenförderung und Gleichstellung (2001). Universität Augsburg.

Köthel-Raithelhuber, U. (2004). Mit Gender Mainstreaming: Neue Ansätze der Hochschulsteuerung. Gender Mainstreaming im Reformprozess an der Johannes Gutenberg-Universität Mainz. Abschlussbericht im Auftrag der Frauenbeauftragten der Universität, Mainz.

Krais, B. (Hrsg.) (2000). Wissenschaftskultur und Geschlechterordnung. Über die verborgenen Mechanismen männlicher Dominanz in der akademischen Welt, Frankfurt/New York.

Krell, G./Mückenberger, U./Tondorf, K. (2001). Gender Mainstreaming: Chancengleichheit (nicht nur) für Politik und Verwaltung. In: Krell, G. (Hrsg.). Chancengleichheit durch Personalentwicklung (3. Auflage), Wiesbaden, S. 59–75.

Krimmer, H. u.a. (o.J.). Karrierewege von ProfessorInnen an Hochschulen in Deutschland, Münster.

Kuhlmann, S. (2004). Evaluation in der Forschungs- und Innovationspolitik. In Stockmann, R. (Hrsg.). Evaluationsforschung. Grundlagen und ausgewählte Forschungsfelder (2. überarb. und aktual. Auflage), Opladen, S. 287–308.

Lind, I. (2004). Aufstieg oder Ausstieg? Karrierewege von Wissenschaftlerinnen. Ein Forschungsüberblick, Bielefeld.

Löther, A. (Hrsg.) (2004). Erfolg und Wirksamkeit von Gleichstellungsmaßnahmen an Hochschulen, Bielefeld.

Lorber, J. (1999). Gender-Paradoxien, Opladen.

Macha, H. (2000). Erfolgreiche Frauen. Wie sie wurden, was sie sind, Frankfurt/New York.

———. (2005). Frauen und Elite. In: Spiegel Special 1/2005, S. 74–75.

———. (2006). Work-Life-Balance und Frauenbiographien. In Schlüter, A. (Hrsg.). Kind und Karriere? Bildungs- und Karrierewege von Frauen. Wissen—Erfahrungen—biographisches Lernen, Opladen.

Macha, H./Bauhofer, W. (2004). Weiterbildung als Potentialentwicklung und Kompetenzerwerb—Prämissen und Handlungsfelder. In Bender, W. u.a. (Hrsg.). Lernen und Handeln, Schwalbach/Ts., S. 300–316.

Macha, H./Fahrenwald, C. (2007). Zur Einführung: Gender Mainstreaming und Weiterbildung. In Macha, H./Fahrenwald, C. (Hrsg.). Gender Mainstreaming und Weiterbildung—Organisationsentwicklung durch Potentialentwicklung. Opladen and Farmington Hills, S. 9–14.

Macha, H./Handschuh-Heiß, S. (2004). Konzept Gender Mainstreaming an der Universität Augsburg (Unveröffentlichtes Manuskript).

Macha, H./Handschuh-Heiß, S. (2005a). Gender Mainstreaming und Wissensmanagement—Theorie, Konzepte, Umsetzung und Evaluation. In Ernst, S./ Warwas, J./Kirsch-Auwärter, E. (Hrsg.). wissenstransform. Wissensmanagement in gleichstellungsorientierten Netzwerken, Münster, S. 23–39.

Macha, H./Handschuh-Heiß, S. (2005b) Gender Mainstreaming an Hochschulen als Instrument der Organisationsentwicklung. In Burkhardt, A./König, K. (Hrsg.). Zweckbündnis statt Zwangsehe. Gender Mainstreaming und Hochschulreform, Bonn, S. 209–225.

Mayrhofer, W./Meyer, M./Steyrer, J. (2005). Macht? Erfolg? Reich? Glücklich? Einflussfaktoren auf Karrieren, Wien.

Merkens, Hans (Hrsg.). (2004). Evaluation in der Erziehungswissenschaft, Wiesbaden.

Metz-Göckel, S. (2007). Gender Mainstreaming und Geschlechterforschung—kein einfaches Verhältnis. In Macha, H./Fahrenwald, C. (Hrsg.). Gender Mainstreaming und Weiterbildung—Organisationsentwicklung durch Potentialentwicklung. Opladen and Farmington Hills, S. 101–116.

Meuser, M. (2004). Gender Mainstreaming: Fortschreibung oder Auflösung der Geschlechterdifferenz? Zum Verhältnis von Geschlechterforschung und Geschlechterpolitik. In Meuder, M./Neusüß, C. (Hrsg.). Gender Mainstreaming. Konzepte, Handlungsfelder, Instrumente, Bonn, S. 322–336.

Nassehi, A. (2003). Geschlecht im System. Die Ontologisierung des Körpers und die Asymmetrie der Geschlechter. In Pasero, U./Weinbach, C. (Hrsg.). Frauen, Männer, Gender Trouble, Frankfurt a.M., S. 80–104.

Nohr, B./Veth, S. (Hrsg.). (2002). Gender Mainstreaming. Kritische Reflexionen einer neuen Strategie, Berlin.

Rastetter, D. (1994). Sexualität und Herrschaft in Organisationen, Opladen.

Reinmann-Rothmeier, G. (2001). Wissensmanagement in der Forschung. Gedanken zu einem integrativen Forschungs-Szenario (Forschungsbericht Nr. 132), Ludwig-Maximilians-Universität München.

Reischmann, J. (2003). Weiterbildungsevaluation. Lernerfolge messbar machen, Neuwied.

Rendtorff, B. (2006). Erziehung und Geschlecht. Eine Einführung, Stuttgart.

Roloff, C. (2001). Hochschulreform—Idee und Wirklichkeit in ihren Auswirkungen auf die Gleichstellungspolitik. In Batisweiler, C. u. a. (Hrsg.). Geschlechterpolitik an Hochschulen: Perspektivenwechsel. Zwischen Frauenförderung und Gender Mainstreaming, Opladen, S. 87–97.

———. (Hrsg.) (2002). Personalentwicklung, Geschlechtergerechtigkeit und Qualitätsmanagement an der Hochschule, Bielefeld.

———. (2004). QueR-Strukturen—Geschlechtergerechte Personalentwicklung im Kontext des Qualitätsmanagements. In Laske, S. u. a. (Hrsg.). Personalentwicklung und universitärer Wandel. Programm—Aufgaben—Gestaltung, München und Mering, S. 313–329.

Schlegel, U./Burkhardt, A. (2005). Förderung der Berufsfähigkeit: Stipendiatinnenprogramme in Sachsen-Anhalt im gesellschaftlichen und gleichstellungspolitischen Kontext (HoF-Arbeitsbericht 6'05), Wittenberg.

Schmitz, B. (2002). Die gläserne Decke. Machtkämpfe und untergründige Arbeit. In Christensen, B. u. a. (Hrsg.). wissen macht geschlecht. Philosophie und die Zukunft der ,condition féminine', Zürich, S. 625–632.

Schreyögg, G. (1999). Organisation. Grundlagen moderner Organisationsgestaltung (3. überarb. und erw. Auflage), Wiesbaden.

Sher, B., and Gottlieb, A. (1989). *Teamworks! Building support groups that guarantee success.* New York.

Sobehart, Helen C./Giron, Kara L. (2007). Mentoring and women in educational leadership: Theory and practice. In Macha, H./Fahrenwald, C. (Hrsg.). Gender Mainstreaming und Weiterbildung—Organisationsentwicklung durch Potentialentwicklung. Opladen and Farmington Hills, S. 148–159.

Stiegler, B. (2002). Wie Gender in den Mainstream kommt. In Bothfeld, S./Gronbach, S./Riedmüller, B. (Hrsg.). Gender Mainstreaming—eine Innovation in der Gleichstellungspolitik. Zwischenberichte aus der politischen Praxis, Frankfurt/ New York, S. 19–40.

———. (2007). Erst kamen die Frauen, nun kommt Gender in die Universität—Gender Mainstreaming als Hochschulreform. In Macha, H./Fahrenwald, C. (Hrsg.). Gender Mainstreaming und Weiterbildung—Organisationsentwicklung durch Potentialentwicklung. Opladen and Farmington Hills, S. 37–59.

Stockmann, R. (Hrsg.). (2004). Evaluationsforschung. Grundlagen und ausgewählte Forschungsfelder (2. überarb. und aktual. Auflage), Opladen.

Stößel, U. (1979). Das Datenfeedback als Instrument der Prozeßevaluation innovativer Schulentwicklungen, Frankfurt a.M.

Süßmuth, R. (2007). Der Einfluss von Frauenforschung und Frauenbewegung auf die Politik. In Macha, H./Fahrenwald, C. (Hrsg.). Gender Mainstreaming und Weiterbildung—Organisationsentwicklung durch Potentialentwicklung. Opladen and Farmington Hills, S. 15–24.

Ulrich, S./Wenzel, F. M. (2003). Partizipative Evaluation. Ein Konzept für die politische Bildung. Centrum für angewandte Politikforschung (CAP), Universität München (http://www.cap.uni-muenchen.de).

Van Anders, S. M. (2004). Why the academic pipeline leaks: Fewer men than women perceive barriers to becoming professors. *Sex Roles: A Journal of Research, 51*(9/10), S. 511–521.

Weber, M. (1972). Wirtschaft und Gesellschaft (5. revid. Auflage), Tübingen.

Wetterer, A. (2002). Arbeitsteilung und Geschlechterkonstruktion. ,Gender at Work' in theoretischer und historischer Perspektive, Konstanz.

Winterhager-Schmid, L. (1998). Konstruktionen des Weiblichen, Weinheim.

Woodward, A. E. (2004). Gender Mainstreaming als Instrument zur Innovation von Institutionen. In Meuser, M./Neusüß, C. Gender Mainstreaming. Konzepte, Handlungsfelder, Instrumente, Bonn, S. 86–102.

Wottawa H./Thierau, H. (1990). Lehrbuch Evaluation, Bern.

Zimmermann, K. (2000). Spiele mit der Macht in der Wissenschaft. Paßfähigkeit und Geschlecht als Kriterien für Berufungen, Berlin.

VOICE, PLACE AND FACE

Ways of Knowing in Brazil, Hispanic and Mixed Cultures, and the Caribbean Islands

CHAPTER 22

Overview for Part VI

SHARON ADAMS-TAYLOR AND CLAUDIA FAHRENWALD

As PART OF THIS CONFERENCE, we had the distinct pleasure of reviewing three papers under the sub-heading "Voices, Faces and Places." The three were: "Communicative Actions: The Brazilian Women in Educational Leadership," by Rosangela Malachias; "Women in Educational Leadership: The Relationship between Contextual Factors and Women's Careers in Educational Leadership," by Maria Luisa González and Flora Ida Ortiz; and "A Photographic Journey of Discovery: Women and Children Living in Dominica, West Indies," by Katherine M. Houghton. Rather than take the traditional approach and review these papers as discrete bodies of research, we decided to respond to them as they spoke to us—as a body of work on minority women filled with historical and ethnic and educational similarities.

The first message that comes through in these chapters is that gender matters, race matters, context matters, history and culture matter and leadership matters. Each author did a brilliant job presenting the intersection of politics and social structure with historical and cultural factors.

Each researcher indicates how roots, race and ethnicity are readily acknowledged and built upon in their study. González and Ortiz quote a school superintendent who explains her decision to stay in her home state of New Mexico and thus give back to New Mexico as akin to a yucca plant that is hard to uproot. They also mention a woman leader who does not feel that her path was directed a certain way because she is Hispanic but did feel that her heritage contributed to her selection for her current leadership position. Malachias opens her chapter by honoring the ancestors and offers her work in homage to two Brazilian Black women. The author also speaks of a Black Brazilian woman who is head of the teachers' association and how she used her race and ethnicity to introduce legislation on the teaching of African history and African-Brazilian culture.

The work of Houghton, González, Ortiz and Malachias illuminates the intergenerational nature of leadership and how intently and intentionally women's

leadership in particular is focused on improving the lives of children. Houghton's photographs show us the faces of two, three and sometimes four generations of women and children. The González and Ortiz analysis touches upon the influence of parents and grandparents in the success of each of the three women leaders they profiled. Malachias' chapter contains a powerful quote, where Maria Benedita de Castro de Andrade speaks about the struggles of being a woman in leadership and how she learned to confront those struggles:

> Undeniably, I need to fight every day to be respected. How have I learned to fight? When I was a little girl, my mother taught me to say with her "We are. We can." For years, we repeated this mantra together and we have survived.

Each study embraces the significance of time and gives the reader a sense of experiences and lives lived. Houghton's photographs cover a four-year time span in Dominica; Malachias' work includes a timeline beginning in 1500 with the European discovery of Brazil; and González and Ortiz cover the careers of three women in New Mexico from their beginnings until now. All three chapters address the nature of power: power over adversity, the power of the media, the power of the lens, Black power, and the power and sweet smell of success as educational leaders.

Finally, these consummate researchers speak to the importance of women finding their own pathways to success. González and Ortiz tell of success emanating from the development of strengths gained through unique contextual experiences. They give examples of two different pathways: women who went through the system to the top and women who worked in other areas of leadership and then transferred to top positions in education. Malachias talks about the Black woman president of the teachers' union who "constructed her career" by performing different functions, beginning in the lowest places and ascending to the position she now holds. Houghton's photographs tell of women who developed and built upon pathways from their unique cultural perspective and share the stories of the many ways that women find their way and help their children and their community to find theirs.

It is clear, in the writing and the presentation, that the subjects of these papers are deeply personal for these researchers. The passion comes through in the words and the photographs and immediately evokes unexpected pleasure, insight and joy.

In all three chapters the most impressive thing is that they did not focus on statistics and numbers but on individual stories. They offer us the biographical narratives of real human beings. They share with us the life stories of women from all over the world—giving them voice and face. In this way the studies represent the women in their "being" (using a term of the German philosopher Heidegger); they show us their lived experience. The women in these studies did not have theoretical frameworks when they launched their careers, nor did they entertain any strong feminist concepts. They just tried to handle matters in their own ways, with passion and strong belief in the value of their work. Their motivation and their energy are admirable.

From these chapters we learn the critical role of stories for motivating change. Even these life stories themselves are inspired by other stories. Remember the woman in Malachias' study who told of how she personally learned to fight and to resist, and her mantra, "We are, we can." Stories illustrate the performative power of language and the creative impact of words.

Images and stories are an integral part of our daily lives and therefore have the capacity to elicit emotions and to touch hearts. These personal narratives convey how women—even if they are poor, even if they belong to an ethnic minority group, even if they don't seem to have a big chance in life—how these women can deal with their demographic, personal and professional challenges, and how they finally succeed.

It is absolutely fascinating to watch these women in their career paths, to get to know them, their lives, labors and struggles. We can meet them in the marketplace during their daily shopping, we can meet them celebrating holidays, weddings and funerals. These stories foster empowerment and hope for future emancipation as a bottom-up process performed by women. These stories help to promote social justice and cultural change. Thus we learn more about the contradiction between individual and collective progress of contemporary activism.

The personal life stories of these Black and Hispanic women from South America, Central America and the United States create a dynamic interchange of visions, thoughts and worldviews. They *discover*, *uncover* and *recover* new images and meanings of women in their "being" within professional and private lives. These narratives inspire and help us to find new role models and concepts of leadership for women all over the world. They help us to discover a completely different framework of thoughts and actions than can be known from a single Western point of view.

In 1980 at the first AASA conference for women school leaders, a former AASA associate executive director, Dr. Effie H. Jones, said the questions she received over and over again were "How many women are there in educational leadership? Where are they? What are their roles? How did they get there? How are they faring?" She said, "For some reason everyone thinks that AASA has a research arm and we really don't." But Dr. Jones and her staff picked up the telephone and called all the state departments of education, local school districts and all the women she knew to ask, "How many women are there in your network? How many women are there in your state? I know you're there . . . why can't we find you? I want to know and AASA wants everyone in this country to know who you are and where you are."

> It is ironic that a profession so dominated by women at various levels finds itself underrepresented at the top. It appears that women are seen as good enough to do everything but lead. Yet, the greatest irony is that given the demands of school systems, what is needed most are the skills and insights that women bring to the task. (Paul Houston, AASA Executive Director)

Thanks to a recent collaboration among Duquesne University, the University Council for Educational Administration (UCEA) and AASA, we understand more fully the status of women leaders in K-12 and higher education in countries around the world.

A global review of women's leadership in several fields suggests that the issues keeping women out of the top positions are universal, not particular to industries or to countries. The differences are in degree and complexity.

> Now that I have traveled to Japan and China. . . . I am coming to the conclusion that there is an international universal truth . . . women—while born in equal ratios to men—seem not to rise to leadership positions in equal numbers anywhere in the world! (Sarah Jerome, AASA President)

The three studies we reviewed allow us to hear women's voices and see their faces as they take their rightful places as educational leaders. But we need more like them.

Effie Jones challenged us with her assertion that the way to increase the numbers of women in educational leadership positions was by making those changes happen. This international collaboration is a major avenue for responding to that challenge.

CHAPTER 23

Women in Educational Leadership

The Relationship between Contextual Factors and Women's Careers in Educational Leadership

María Luisa González and Flora Ida Ortiz

INTRODUCTION

WHAT IS IT ABOUT THE FIELD of educational leadership that supports individuals' persistent claim that theory and explanations offered by others do not apply to them? This chapter is an attempt to provide a response to this fundamental question.

Educational leaders head organizations that are internally and externally complex. The complexity arises internally because the purpose of educational organizations is to educate and socialize youth. The complexity arises externally because the youth who enter the organization represent a variety of groups, values and belief systems, and differing degrees of compliance with the organization's purpose. Educational leaders must wrestle with these complexities on a daily basis and attempt to demonstrate to the public that educational organizations are similar to other organizations. Success in leading educational organizations is judged by the lack of conflict, perceived stability and periodic notable accomplishments by students, as in athletics, science fairs, musical and theatrical performances and academic achievement. Such success rewards the adults who work with students in the educational setting through promotions from teaching to site administration, central office management, and finally superintending as chief executive officer of a state educational organization (in the United States).

In this chapter, we report on how contextual complexity interacts with successful educational administration leadership. Our site for examination is the state of New Mexico, and we claim that its extreme poverty and lack of resources, geographical characteristics, political, cultural and social features, and demographic properties provide an occasion to examine how context determines leadership success in educational organizations. Before examining two specific cases of educational leadership in New Mexico, we begin by presenting a historical backdrop of this state, the status of its children and women, and also demographics of educators and educational administrators in New Mexico. After this, sketches of two female educational leaders, with subsequent discussions, are offered.

GENERAL BACKDROP ON THE CONTEXT OF THE STATE OF NEW MEXICO

New Mexico is a land rich in diversity, culture and history. Located between the states of Texas and Arizona, it proudly claims its ancient indigenous roots as well as a European heritage. Civilization in New Mexican territory began in 12000 B.C. when the Sandia people created the area's first residences. The earliest evidence of agriculture in what is now New Mexico dates from 10000 to 500 B.C., when the Cochise people cultivated corn, squash and beans (Márquez, 1999). The Pueblo Indians, still residents of current New Mexico, started establishing villages with permanent buildings around A.D. 1200.

New Mexico's history started earlier than the first English settlements of the United States. For example, the first Spanish capital of New Mexico, San Juan de los Caballeros, was founded in 1598 (Márquez, 1999). By comparison, Europeans from England did not arrive on the east coast of the United States, that is, what would become Plymouth, Massachusets, until 1620 (Stratton, 1986). Thus the capital of New Mexico had been established 22 years prior to the appearance of the first Pilgrims in Plymouth. Although New Mexico is one of the oldest established settlements in the United States, it is one of the newest states in the nation. Despite being highly developed, possessing a capitol and colonies, as well as maintaining involvement in agriculture and trade long before New England's first colony was formalized, New Mexico did not achieve statehood until 1912, when it became the nation's 47th state (Simmons, 1977).

New Mexico's history is derived from three prominent ethnic groups: Native American, Hispanic (descendants from Spain and Mexico), and White (settlers of European descent) (Kirgo, 1989). New Mexico has tribal lands that are home to as many as 19 pueblos and tribes including the Apache, Pueblo, Navajo, Ute, and Zuni (Kirgo, 1989; The New Mexico Blue Book, 2007). Unlike the demographics of the United States as a whole, in New Mexico minorities constitute the majority of the population. The diversity of New Mexico's residents is also represented by the 22 languages spoken in the state—the predominant language being English, followed by Spanish, with most of the other languages spoken by Native American tribes having been in existence well before the arrival of the Spanish colonizers. Among the native languages are the Pueblo languages of Zuni, Keresan, Tiwa, Tewa, as well as the Towa dialects (Kirgo, 1989).

The various New Mexican populations live in a land that is also varied geographically. New Mexico comprises deserts as well as mountains, pine forests, meadows, and fast-flowing streams (Kirgo, 1989). The mountains allow for internationally recognized snow sports and, at the other extreme, the deserts account for some of the hottest temperatures in the nation. The beauty of the terrain has given this state the name "Land of Enchantment." Leaving the vastness of the landscape takes us to the financial status of the residents to understand the "vastness" between the haves and have-nots.

STATUS OF CHILDREN AND EDUCATION

New Mexico is one of the most poverty-stricken states in the United States. In a study by the United States Census Bureau (Percentage of Poverty, 2005), New Mexico had the second highest poverty rate, 18%, compared to the U.S. average of 13%. Gerry Bradley, research director for New Mexico Voices for Children (press conference, September 1, 2005), announced, "The fact that over one-third of our state's population is working—even, in many cases, working more than full-time—and still living in poverty should be seen as an economic crisis." A report from New Mexico Voices for Children (Border Kids Count, 2007, p. 4) stated, "Children who live in poor or low-income families are less likely to stay in school and get the preparation necessary for future success." The report also stated, "an educated workforce can attract industries that pay living wages or better, which offers hope for communities wanting to help its families break out of the cycle of poverty." New Mexico is faced with breaking the cycle of poverty for 30% of its children.

School teachers, principals and superintendents are directed to serve New Mexico's extremely ethnically diverse student population. New Mexico demographics are based on the three predominant groups: 57% are White children (non-Hispanic), 51% are Hispanic

children, and 13% are American Indian children. In contrast, ethnic teachers comprise only one-third of the total faculty in New Mexico (New Mexico Public Education Department, May 9, 2006). One finds the contrast with the nation in a recent article by Ramos (May 1, 2007) that states, "Ethnic minorities represent 14% of the teaching population nationwide while ethnic minority students comprise 36%." Table 23.1 compares New Mexico's and the United States' ethnic minority representation in the classroom.

As depicted in table 23.1, New Mexico has a higher percentage of ethnic minority teachers than the nation, but the difference in the percentage between ethnic minority students and teachers is 30%. A possible effect of the lack of teacher representation in the schools is the high dropout rate among minorities. Every year nearly 13% of the students in New Mexico high schools drop out. This means that the state of New Mexico loses almost $26,000 over the lifetime of each high school dropout in wages and taxes. With about 12,700 of New Mexico's children dropping out of high school every year, this translates into $3.3 billion lost in wages, taxes and productivity. Thus, the cycle of poverty continues to envelop children in its web.

STATUS OF WOMEN IN NEW MEXICO

According to the 2000 United States Census, New Mexico had a total population of 1,819,046, 51% of this group being female. Forty-five percent of these women identified themselves as White, 42% Hispanic, and 10% American Indian; the remainder identified as "other." Sadly, New Mexico is one of the worst states for women to find economic equality. For example, the median annual income for New Mexican women is $25,600, 42nd in the nation. New Mexico ranks 29th of 50 in the ratio of discrepancy between women's earnings and men's earnings. When comparing full-time, year-round, employed women with only White, non-Hispanic men, New Mexican females rank 49th among their peers from other states in terms of salary equality. The *Bare Bones Budget Survey* (2003) indicates that

Table 23.1. Comparison of New Mexico and the United States in Percentage of Ethnic-Minority Students and Teachers

	Students	Teachers	Difference between Students and Teachers
United States	36	14	22
New Mexico	61	31	30

poverty in New Mexico is double what the federal poverty level suggests. Overall, New Mexico received a "D" for women's social and economic autonomy, ranking 42nd in the nation, according to a 2004 study of the states (New Mexico Commission on the Status of Women, January 2007). On the other hand, when one looks at political involvement the data are a bit more promising. For example, New Mexico can claim two of the mere five women of color in the nation elected to statewide positions. Of New Mexico's 110 senators and state representatives, 32 are female; 11 of these women are Hispanic and two are African American, but none are American Indian. "Political participation is key to ensuring that women's priorities and needs are reflected in spending and policy decisions made at all levels of government" (New Mexico Commission on the Status of Women, January 2007).

In New Mexico, according to the 2000 U.S. Census, 57% of women participate in the labor force. The percentage of women employed in management, professional and related occupations is 30%. According to a national study, most Hispanic females in the United States have either a technical job, one related to service or employment in sales (United States Census Bureau, 2002). Jobs in service and sales include vendors, food preparers and department store sales associates (including cashiers). Less than 19% of Hispanic women work in managerial positions, compared to nearly 40% of non-Hispanic White females who work in such capacities. Hispanic women are not represented fairly in the workforce. Even in the profession that is predominantly female, that is, education, Hispanic women in New Mexico make up a small percentage of the state's teachers and have even smaller representation at the superintendency level.

DEMOGRAPHICS ON TEACHERS AND ADMINISTRATORS

The best data related to teachers and those who serve at the different levels of school administration in New Mexico are contained in Appendix A of *Personnel by Ethnicity and Gender 2005–2006* (New Mexico Public Education Department, 2006). There are over 2,000 teachers in the state; approximately one in five teachers is a Hispanic female and one in two is a White female. At the principalship level, more White women than White men are principals. The same concept applies with Hispanic women, who hold more principalships than their male counterparts. This pattern holds true even in high school principalships, where women outrepresent men in both White and Hispanic categories.

Thus, 53% of principals in New Mexico are women, compared to only 44% nationally (National Center for Educational Statistics, 2006).

In terms of superintendency, nationally the average is that 13% of these positions are held by females. In comparison, New Mexico's rate is nearly 30% (Glass, Bjork and Brunner, 2000). However, for women of color in New Mexico only three American Indian women and seven Hispanic women occupy the superintendency. At the national level, 1% of all women occupying the superintendency are Latinas (Glass, Bjork and Brunner, 2000; Grogan and Brunner, 2005).

Following is the section that presents the profiles of two women. One is a Hispanic woman in the highest leadership position in the state, secretary of education, a state cabinet position. The other is a superintendent.

TWO WOMEN IN THE HIGHEST LEVELS OF EDUCATIONAL LEADERSHIP

For the purposes of this chapter, we chose to feature two women who are educational leaders in New Mexico. We start with the brief background of a superintendent from a "medium-sized" district by New Mexico's standards, followed by the highest basic education position for New Mexico, the state's secretary of education. Names have been changed to maintain some semblance of anonymity; however, their district and state affiliations identify them. We believe that the two women represent women whose leadership has been shaped and formed by the unique and multifaceted experiences in New Mexican descent and context.

Superintendent Kelly Jones—Educational Leader in a Small District

The first superintendent in our study, Dr. Kelly Jones, leads a small school district near Albuquerque, the state's urban center. She is completing her fourth year in this, her first superintendency. She had previously served as an associate superintendent and in other school positions. Following is a brief sketch of her personal and professional life.

Dr. Jones was raised in the southern part of the state in a region located a few miles from the U.S.-Mexican border, an area influenced heavily by its proximity to Mexico. Dr. Jones, who was completing her doctorate in educational leadership during the time of the interview, explained how badly she had always wanted to be a teacher—as far back as she could remember. She described her aspiration in the following manner: "When I was in high school I was a Girl Scout leader for special needs children. I also gave piano lessons to elementary students and have always loved being around children."

She went on to explain that when she graduated from high school, her parents disagreed as to whether she needed to go to college. Her father believed that only males needed a college education while her mother felt otherwise. Her mother was one of the first Hispanic women to ascend to management in the company where she was employed. Finally, Jones was permitted to attend the university under the condition that she not pursue an educational degree. Her parents' rationale was based on the fact that there was an overabundance of teachers at that time. They feared that money would be wasted obtaining a degree that would not yield steady employment.

At the university, Dr. Jones first majored in business, then sociology, followed by computer science. Other disciplines did not interest her, and she left the university to work as a receptionist at a doctor's office. Before long, she realized that if she wanted to be a teacher she would have to reach her dream on her own. She soon began to explore grants and scholarships and fortunately secured funding. She re-enrolled at the university and obtained her degree in education.

Kelly Jones began her career in education as a kindergarten teacher, serving at the same location where she had attended elementary school herself. Over the years, she acquired her master's degree and moved away from the border area. She applied for and was appointed to a teaching principal position in a small, isolated rural school with 85 students. She held that position for a year and then was selected to become the principal of an elementary school referred to as "the project school."

The school had "staff that was dysfunctional, the students were out of control, and the departing principal spent most of his time at the local doughnut shop while the secretary ran the school." When she assumed the position, the school had the lowest test scores in the district. In five years, she converted it into a Blue Ribbon School with the second-highest district scores in the state. She completely turned the school around, giving it the reputation of being the best school in town. Parents wanted to enroll their children in the school and the staff became known for their excellence and caring.

Following these accomplishments, Dr. Jones was selected for a central office position that she mentioned was "created for her." She provided expertise and mentored elementary principals. She also helped principals identify changes required in order to meet the needs of students and supported them through the change process. After assisting the schools directly in that position, she was promoted to director of human resources and then to associate superintendent for human resources.

After spending 11 years in those two positions, she left that district to become superintendent, her current role. She applied for and was appointed superintendent through a tedious interview process. She endured this search procedure, conducted by a committee of 13 individuals representing different district positions, as well as numerous principals and parents. All three finalists for the superintendency were interviewed publicly in the school cafeteria. A social followed and the candidates were subsequently rated. The next day, each one of the applicants had a private interview with the board. Dr. Jones was hired.

When Dr. Jones speaks or thinks of herself, she sees herself as Hispanic. She does not believe her ancestry either hindered or helped her career prior to stepping into the superintendency. She does, however, believe that her ancestry assisted in her appointment to the superintendency.

While discussing leadership issues, Dr. Jones stated that she "has seen men use a more dictatorial type of leadership style, whereas Latinas seem to be more collaborative and listen to all ideas before making a decision. Men appear to have a very strong network and they provide information to each other that doesn't necessarily include women." At the same time she believes that women are more "hands on than men and [women] do not delegate as much as men."

When queried about her attributes, Dr. Jones contends that her strongest personal and professional qualities are a "very strong work ethic, high energy level, and getting along with almost anyone." She explained that the most difficult aspect of her superintendent's job is "dealing with parents that are unreasonable." On the other hand, the most favorable aspect of her work is having the ability to implement district programs that make a difference for students.

Her advice to future superintendents is to "get experience leading and try to diversify administrative experiences as much as possible." She also mentions that her life has changed in that "[she] does not have close personal friends in the community." The superintendency brings about isolation; her husband, however, has been very supportive. She considers him her closest friend. "[I have] been an administrator in two districts. The enrollment has been 6,800 students and 4,600 students. They were very much alike, both considered medium-sized districts, both close to an urban area, and both noted for outstanding academics."

Dr. Monica Lopez—Statewide Educational Leader

Dr. Monica Lopez is currently the state secretary of education, an office which was created by the governor and voted into law soon after he was elected to office. The position has no precedent and no history, and is directly under the governor's jurisdiction.

Dr. Lopez described herself as a child of poverty, raised by grandparents. Born and raised in New Mexico, she is the first person in her family to graduate from high school. She explained:

> It has been a conscious decision [to stay in New Mexico throughout my career] to contribute back to a system that changed my life and my family's life forever. I always felt a sort of sense of responsibility for working here and improving our state and, therefore, I hope in the future. I don't know in what capacity, but I hope that I will be able to continue to contribute to our state. I love our state. Have you ever tried to uproot a yucca plant? Have you ever tried to dig one up? It's not an easy task. Sometimes it looks like it is almost pulled over, but it still has roots that hang onto the soil, you know. You just can't pull it up. Sometimes I think I am like a yucca plant, very hard to get uprooted and out of here.

With regard to Dr. Lopez' personal life, she was single for the greater part of her career. She was married for 11 years, had two children, divorced, and remained single for another 20 years. She claimed that this status made it easier for her to advance in her career. She is currently married and has two grandchildren while she holds the top educational leadership position in the state.

Dr. Lopez began her career in education as a substitute teacher. She served as a substitute teacher in a large urban center in New Mexico. The experience gave her a strong foundation for her entire career because that district is the largest in the state and it serves children that represent many cultural, social and economic levels. The students' demographic characteristics are quite varied. School staff located throughout diverse schools must prepare to serve children from all walks of life coming from the most affluent communities to the poorest of the poor. These circumstances provided a backdrop for Dr. Lopez's socialization in New Mexico's educational system that never intimidated or discouraged her.

After substituting for a year, she taught special education and technical skills in an alternative high school. After teaching at a "regular" inner-city high school for five years, she went to the university where she obtained her master's degree and also became licensed as a school psychologist and a diagnostician. Following these academic accomplishments she left the schools and moved into the central office realm, serving as a program coordinator for five years. She became the assistant director for special education for three years. After eight years as a central office administrator, she returned to lead directly at the site level. She explained her experiences: "Ironically, I went back to New Futures [the alternative school] and was the principal of their new school and director of their non-profit."

New Futures was interesting to Dr. Lopez because it consisted of a day care center with four nurseries for children from 6 weeks to 4 years of age. The New Futures school provided health services, food stamps and immunizations. This experience provided the knowledge about community schools that would later assist her.

Her leadership helped the school raise large amounts of money. They became entrepreneurial by selling and marketing textbooks all over the country. They raised about a quarter of a million dollars in three years. She summed up this experience as being exhilarating and one in which she also learned to work with boards.

From that alternative school, Dr. Lopez was appointed principal of a high school whose predecessor had been removed. The school was located in the poorest area of the city and served students with the lowest test scores. The high school had 2,600 students with seven to eight gangs creating student unrest that led to walkouts.

Her innovative spirit came to the fore as she established a principal's council that helped reduce the number of student fights and gang violence. She created a restructuring committee to work on curriculum and engaged the community through two organizations that brought support from distinguished alumni and people in the business community. These organizations instituted an annual ball and an auction to recognize outstanding high school graduates "so that kids could see that there were wonderful people who had graduated from their high school and had gone on to do some really incredible things." Dr. Lopez also raised money for the school and its musical instruments.

After the high school's transformation, she returned to the central office, this time as the regional superintendent covering the district's southern region.

Approximately 45,000 of the children in this region lived in poverty, and Dr. Lopez led the cluster of high schools with the highest needs.

In time, she received and accepted an offer to work with the school district located in New Mexico's capital. She was offered an associate superintendency where she worked primarily with principals. During her tenure there a tragic accident took place: a group of children went skiing as part of an extracurricular outing and several were killed in a bus crash. Throughout this time, Dr. Lopez worked with the community by calming and engaging parents in meaningful ways. She was able to assure the community that their children could be safe. Regarding this experience she explained, "The board liked the way I handled the tragedy and when the superintendent decided to leave, I was named superintendent even though I had no intention of becoming superintendent."

Upon assuming the superintendency, she discovered the district had a $2.5 million deficit. The school board suspended the district's finance committee and the school district was taken over by the state. Within two years, Dr. Lopez led the district to a financial upswing, guiding the school district through some very tough decisions. She worked with the union and the citizens' oversight committee. There was much community unrest at the time. A study conducted by an external group pointed to the need for an action plan. An executive leadership council was created consisting of the mayor, city council representatives, United Way members, representatives from banks, and others who would put all of their dollars into education around three priorities—the top priority being early childhood education. These monies were used for after-school programs and early childhood projects in the state's capital. During her tenure as superintendent, she was named New Mexico's Superintendent of the Year and also Administrator of the Year.

After serving as superintendent in the state's capital district, Dr. Lopez retired; however, shortly thereafter she was recruited to become the executive director of a statewide coalition of 31 educational organizations. These bodies were considered to be members of the most powerful network of educational administrators in the state. As part of her responsibilities, Dr. Lopez learned to lobby for educational issues affecting all of New Mexico. This position was instrumental in presenting her the opportunity to apply for the highest state educational leadership position, secretary of education, which she currently holds. As executive director of the statewide organization, she became highly visible and the organization's members recommended her to the governor, who subsequently hired her.

PRELIMINARY DISCUSSION

For the purposes of this chapter we offer discussion about certain contextual factors that we believe have influenced women in securing educational leadership roles. The context we describe is one in which early personal and professional experiences serve to sustain them throughout their challenging educational leadership positions. We see context differently from the traditional contingent leadership style (Fiedler and Chemers, 1974) that "assumes that there are wide variations in the contexts for leadership and that to be effective these contexts require different leadership responses" (Leithwood and Duke, 1999, p. 10).

We find that the formation and development of leadership for those with successful superintendency paths comes from developing strengths from unique contextual experiences. These same experiences eventually assist in supporting a repertoire of superintendency strengths that are transferable to different roles and responsibilities. In our participants, we found women who could successfully "master" their educational contexts by accumulating knowledge, attitudes, and skills from each promotion and challenging situations by remaining in the same state. They have been and continue to be part of the New Mexico landscape and have learned to succeed in it.

We found that for both women, where they were raised was an important factor. Each mentioned those who raised them—parents and grandparents—and the influence they offered. Where they were raised also affected their personal and professional nurturing. For example, both women are Hispanics who grew up in New Mexico and prefer to be identified as Hispanics rather than Chicanas or Latinas. The term "Hispanic" is primarily used by governmental agencies in the United States to identify Spanish-speaking people and includes those with Spanish ancestry. The term "Chicana" is more politically loaded and carries an activist connotation. The other, more current term, "Latina," encompasses those Spanish-speaking groups who come directly from the Latin American countries as opposed to those with European heritage (Salinas-Sosa, 1998, pp. 197–212).

One of these Hispanic women grew up in the northern part of the state and the other was raised in the southern part. Even within this one small state, the demarcation line is clearly felt. Among Latinos, the differences are most obvious, for this is not a homogeneous group of people and residing in one part of the state implies a certain cultural typology (Bejarano, 2005). People from the north often contend that they come directly from Spanish lineage and those in the south may wrestle with identity crises of trying to remain firmly placed on the U.S. side of the border. Many times individuals from both sides of the state do not want to recognize their Mexican and/or indigenous roots (Hurtado and Gurin, 2004).

For Dr. Lopez, who was raised by grandparents in the northern part of the state, her first language was Spanish and thus she went to school without initially speaking English. Conversely, Dr. Jones grew up close to the border but did not speak any Spanish. Neither Hispanic directly mentioned a need for bilingual education, nor was there any mention of meeting the needs of the "majority" of the children in New Mexico, who incidentally are Hispanic and American Indian.

Both women realized at an early age that they would be educators. One chose to go the early childhood route and the other chose special education. These professional experiences allowed them to work in specialized fields with the most vulnerable of school populations, which gave them the advantage of being able to address children's needs in larger contexts beyond the classroom. In addition, the two spent their entire administrative careers in New Mexico. Remaining in the same state helped the participants fully understand the political, cultural and social factors that led to their positions. They have been able to transfer their knowledge of the unique state context, the same context that shaped their leadership success from one job to another, even when placed in different districts.

Another important point to consider is the multilevel experience necessary to ascend to the superintendency. Dr. Lopez has a multiplicity of administrative experiences ranging from those housed directly at school sites to those in the central office realm. Each challenging position built on its predecessor, shaping the leadership persona of the educator. Like Dr. Lopez, Dr. Jones served in two district central offices and also achieved site experience. Both women gained extensive visibility through their work with the coalition of administrative organizations, a statewide network advocating for educational support.

In addition, Dr. Lopez served in administrative positions in the state's most highly visible districts because of their proximity to the state capital, which is in the center of the state. Following closely with the literature that describes women's ascension into the superintendency, Dr. Lopez was a secondary school administrator after serving in the central office (Ortiz, 1999). Dr. Jones served as an elementary principal before moving to a central office. Dr. Jones, as a woman, did hold a nontraditional role by heading human resources for one district before moving to the other side of the state (Scott, 1999). Both were successful principals who first proved themselves in very demanding schools and later in central offices before moving into the superintendency.

An interesting note to consider is that both women hold a doctorate degree. The motivation of these women to go the extra mile to be fully prepared and have the energy required is admirable. Of special significance is that both completed their studies while they held central office administrative positions. Neither this terminal degree nor any special training is a requisite for the superintendency in New Mexico.

When speaking about supportive mentorship, Dr. Lopez mentioned a White teacher from her first year teaching in the classroom. Dr. Jones spoke of a White man being the most helpful in aiding her ascension into administration. Both women described mentors, but they also discussed the importance of mentorship and the rare opportunities to find such arrangements, which is supported by the literature (Enomoto, Gardiner and Grogan, 2000; Gonzalez-Figueroa and Young, 2005; Magdaleno, 2004; Mendez-Morse, 2004; Ortiz, 2000). In both women we found educators who were excited and motivated to continue working for children.

What does the future hold for the two Hispanic women? Dr. Lopez serves in a highly vulnerable position where political appointees are removed at the whim of those in power within a few months of beginning their appointments. In this case, Dr. Lopez has outlasted her counterparts at the state capital by more than a year. Now that she has served at the highest state level, her next move might be outside her context into the national arena. She has already been a speaker at a presidential national convention. Through her experiences in New Mexico she acquired the skills, attitudes and knowledge to continue undertaking the challenge to succeed. Dr. Jones has the same energy and commitment to succeed. She seems destined to move to bigger districts within the state. If she continues to make herself visible by taking on additional leadership roles, she can potentially serve the state in a larger capacity—not excluding the national scene. Both will continue trailblazing and surpassing the odds.

These two superintendents highlight personal attributes—intent, passion—and strong beliefs in the value of education. These two cases also emphasize the context, the character of the school districts and the state call for leadership that is far-reaching and farsighted. The sense of reality and the complexity of these women's jobs are very much a part of the way they portray themselves. Their portrayal of themselves and their work, we are claiming, is a strong part of their context.

NOTE

We would like to acknowledge Dr. Karen Couch for her contributions to this study and this report. She constructed many of the questions used in the interviews.

REFERENCES CITED

Alderman, S. L., and O'Donnell, K. (2003). *New Mexico bare bones budget*. Albuquerque: New Mexico Voices for Children.

Bejarano, C. L. (2005). *¿Qué onda?: Urban youth culture and border identity*. Tucson: University of Arizona Press.

Cummins, J. (1996). *Negotiating identities: Education for empowerment in a diverse society*. Ontario: California Association for Bilingual Education.

Delpit, L. D. (1993). The silenced dialogue: Power and pedagogy in educating other people's children. In L. Weis and M. Fine (Eds.). *Beyond silenced voices: Class, race, and gender in United States schools*, pp. 119–139. Albany: State University of New York Press.

Enomoto, E. K., Gardiner, M. E., and Grogan, M. (2000). Notes to Athene: Mentoring relationships for women of color. *Urban Education, 35*(5), 567–583.

Fiedler, F. E., and Chemers, M. M. (1974). *Leadership and effective management*. Glenview, IL: Scott, Foresman.

Glass, T. E., Bjork, L., and Brunner, C. C. (2000). *The 2000 study of the American school superintendency: America's educational leaders in a time of reform*. Arlington, VA: American Association of School Administrators (ERIC Document Reproduction Service No. EA030399).

Gonzalez-Figueroa, E., and Young, A. M. (2005). Ethnic identity and mentoring among Latinas in professional roles. *Cultural Diversity and Ethnic Minority Psychology, 11*(3), 213–226.

Grogan, M., and Brunner, C. C. (2005). Women leading systems. *The School Administrator*. Retrieved June 26, 2006, from http://www.aasa.org/publications/saarticledetail.cfm.

Hurtado, A., and Gurin, P. (2004). *Chicana/o identity in a changing U.S. society*. Tucson: University of Arizona Press.

Institute for Women's Policy Research. (December 2006). Briefing paper: The best and worst state economies for women. Retrieved May 14, 2007, from http://www.iwpr.org/pdf/R334_BWStateEconomies2006.pdf.

———. (April 2007). Fact sheet: The gender wage ratio: Women's and men's earnings. Retrieved June 14, 2007, from http://www.iwpr.org/pdf/C350.pdf.

Keller, B. (1999). Women superintendents: Few and far between. *Education Week, 19*(11), 1, 22, 23.

Kirgo, J. (1989). *New Mexico: Portrait of the land and the people*. Helena, MT: American Geographic Publishing.

López, A. S. (1995). Latina issues: Fragments of historia (ella) (herstory). New York: Garland Publishing.

Leithwood, K., and Duke, D. L. (1999). A century's quest to understand school leadership. In J. Murphy and K. Seashore-Lewis (Eds.). *Handbook of research on educational administration*, pp. 45–72. San Francisco: Jossey-Bass.

Magdaleno, K. R. (2004). Lending a helping hand: Mentoring tomorrow's Latina and Latino leaders into the 21st century. Unpublished doctoral dissertation. University of California, Los Angeles.

Márquez, R. S. (1999). *New Mexico: A brief multi-history*. Albuquerque: Cosmic House.

Mendez-Morse, S. E. (2004). Constructing mentors: Latina educational leaders' role models and mentors. *Educational Administration Quarterly, 40*(4), 561–590.

National Center for Educational Statistics. (2006). Table 83: Principals in public and private elementary and secondary schools, by selected characteristics: 1993–94 and 1999–2000. Digest of Educational Statistics: 2005. Retrieved April 8, 2007, from http://nces.ed.gov/programs/digest/d05/tables/dt05_083.asp.

New Mexico Commission on the Status of Women. (January 2007). *Status of Women in the New Mexico Counties*. Albuquerque: Author.

New Mexico. Office of the Secretary of State. (2007). *The New Mexico Blue Book, 2006–2007*. Santa Fe: Author.

New Mexico Public Education Department. (May 9, 2006). *Personnel by ethnicity and gender 2005–2006*. Santa Fe: Author.

New Mexico Voices for Children. (2007). *Border kids count*. Albuquerque: Author.

Ortiz, F. I. (1999). Seeking and selecting Hispanic female public school superintendents. In C. C. Brunner (Ed.). *Sacred dreams: Women and the superintendency*, pp. 91–101. Albany: State University of New York Press.

———. (2000). Who controls succession in the superintendency? A minority perspective. *Urban Education, 35*(5), 557–566.

Ramos, D. C. (May 1, 2007). Seeking diversity: Faculty member studies reasons for ethnic underrepresentation among teachers. Retrieved June 5, 2007, from http://campusapps.fullerton.edu/news/Inside/2007/Seeking_Diversity.html.

Salinas Sosa, A. (1998). Latinos in the United States: A tapestry of diversity. In M. L. Gonzalez, A. Huerta-Macias, and J.-W. Tinajero (Eds.), *Educating Latino students: A guide to successful practice*, pp. 197–212. Lancaster, PA: Technomic.

Scott, J. (1999, April). Constructing identity through power and discourse in exemplary women public school superintendents. Paper presented at the Annual Meeting of the American Educational Research Association, Montreal, Quebec.

Simmons, M. (1977). *New Mexico: An interpretive history.* Albuquerque: University of New Mexico Press.

Stratton, E. A. (1986). *Plymouth Colony: Its history and people.* Salt Lake City, UT: Ancestry Incorporated.

The Iris Center. (n.d.). Star legacy modules: Teaching and learning in New Mexico: Considerations for diverse student populations. Retrieved May 7, 2007, from http://iris.peabody.vanderbilt.edu/tnm/chalcycle.htm.

Thomas, W. P., and Collier, V. P. (2001). A national study of school effectiveness for language minority students' long-term academic achievement. Center for Research on Education, Diversity and Excellence.

United States Census Bureau. (2002). Percent of occupation by women and Hispanic origin: 2002. Retrieved June 12, 2007, from http://www.census.gov/population/socdemo/hispanic/ppl-165/slideshow/sld022.htm.

———. (2005). Percentage of people in poverty by state using 2- and 3-year averages: 2003 to 2005. Retrieved June 13, 2007, from http://www.census.gov/hhes/www/poverty/poverty05/table8.html.

CHAPTER 24

Communicative Actions

Brazilian Women in Educational Leadership

ROSANGELA MALACHIAS

METHODOLOGICAL STATEMENT: HISTORICAL CONTEXTUALIZATION

The *transculturación* concept[1] defines a societal complexity as violence arising from cultural shock among Europeans, Native people and Africans. Simultaneously, *transculturación* also demonstrates adaptation, resistance and re-elaboration existing in different moments and conflicts.[2] Approaching disciplines—history, communication sciences, social sciences—and concepts[3] *transculturación*, *mediações* (mediation)[4] and advocacy, we will explain paradoxes about ethnic and social relations. The methodology of the study alternates between personal pronouns (I/we and it/they) to indicate a position of neutrality and a critical point of view. With this style, I am including my personal situation (I am a Black woman researcher) and I report other positions as *transcultural* and communicative practices. Some may criticize this option, but several other authors have already adopted this methodology.

An "individual" discourse contrasting with general[5] interests was identified by Barreto (2005, p. 55) in her dissertation about the lives of Lélia Gonzalez and Angela Davis. Barreto compared their "trajectories" showing their personal and general "thoughts." Paulo Freire (2001) wrote that educators have to give their opinions about fundamental questions while respecting other points of view. Researchers should be willing to investigate a subject while using care with dogmatic statements (Fals Borda, 1988). Each author can elaborate his or her own philosophy (Gramsci, 1978), and social activists have played a protagonist and "transcultural" (Malachias, 2006) role against political ideologies.

Discriminated minorities have resisted hegemonic speeches, and mediation has occurred among cultural and political actions. This action would be a contemporary *transculturación*, changing realities. Government and media spread ideological speeches, however there always is a *transcultural* reaction. This study summarizes how Brazilian social activism has contemporarily influenced federal government public policy in education, health, the labor market and media.

Therefore, we report advocacy practices made by social activism—the Black Movement, Movement of Women[6] (White women and Black[7] too)—as relevant examples of communicative actions, because individual and collective actions must be considered when we speak of leadership.

COMMUNICATIVE ACTIONS AND LEADERSHIP

History, sociology and anthropology have contributed to a large number of scientific studies about ethnicity, race and gender. Together, these areas provide a pathway for activists to include the minority groups they represent. Therefore, our intention is to pose research questions about the contradiction between individual and collective progress in contemporary activism. We believe that new analysis can be made in the communication and journalism field.

Race relations in Brazil comprise several contradictions. For years, Brazil has been considered a racially democratic society, and this ideology has remained for decades. In the 1930s, anthropologist Gilberto Freyre wrote *The Masters and the Slaves*, a book that presented Brazil to the world as a "harmonious" country free of racial prejudice. Additionally, it is important to consider the political conjuncture of this time. Getúlio Vargas was president of the country, and his government represented the principles of nationalism and development. Brazil had to maintain a national unity. Because of this, the Vargas period illustrates controversial policies. During the Vargas dictatorship (1937) the Brazilian Congress and political parties were closed. Politicians such as Antonieta de Barros could not exercise their political role. Simultaneously, Vargas promoted industrial, cultural and communicative investments. In fact, racial democracy was a perfect myth to unify the country.

However, in 1952, sociologist Florestan Fernandes and his mentor Roger Bastide produced a study titled "Racial Prejudice in the City of São Paulo." This work included aspects of the famous UNESCO investigation about racism. In the 1960s, the Paulista School (Fernandes, Ianni, Viotti and others) conducted several studies about slavery and racial relations and their conclusions challenged the Freyrean ideology.

The 1960s changed the world, and the development of feminist theory (Beauvoir, Scott) challenged male-chauvinist attitudes and sought equality for women. Specifically, this period was a time when women fought for the right to work, to feel sexual pleasure, and to think and act freely. However, in Brazil, the second dictatorship began in 1964.[8] This period was filled with military action that resulted in violence and repression of individual and societal movements.

During this time some leaders of social activism were forced to leave the country. Abdias Nascimento, an important Black leader, and several others were exiled. It was (and sometimes still is) very difficult for individuals to denounce racism, inequalities and chauvinism. Some activists chose the educational field and produced research, studies and data to support or refute ideological arguments. Nearly 20 years later, Brazilian women began to debate and write about women's rights. This women's movement has conducted several theoretical studies (Bruschini, Correa, Saffioti) investigating the intersection between human rights and gender.

Simultaneously, the Black women's movement was born, emphasizing its own values such as color, race and class. However, during this time feminism in Brazil primarily addressed the challenges of White women. In fact, this feminism reproduced an unequal speech about work and sexuality. White feminists considered Black women to have an "aggressive"[9] (Bairros, 2000, p. 15) and "emotional" speech. Gonzalez (1979) wrote an article[10] criticizing[11] the manifested resistance of White feminists in the acceptance of the demands of Black women. Gonzalez (1979) believed that "it is possible to be emotional when we have another reason, a new reason" (1979, p. 15).

According to Lélia Gonzalez, Brazilian feminists did not respond to racial inequalities and related issues because they denounced the contrastive relationship between White and Black women, housewives and domestic workers, and bosses and employees. Instead, Black women activists argued that together White women and Black women should confront gender inequality *and* social differences of class and race.

RESISTANCE AND ADVOCACY

International movements have[12] influenced Brazilian activism and increased national awareness of racial prejudice. An organized Black press originated in São Paulo (1910–1950) and was sponsored by the community and Black women who were cooks or domestic workers receiving regular salaries.[13] This kind of individual action had a collective impact. In our analysis it is a *transcultural* reaction, or a processed mediation between political and cultural activities. Martín-Barbero (1992, p. 20) defines *mediações* (mediation) as the place from which it is possible to understand the interactions of the production and reception spaces. Additionally, mediation is a critical reception of different and communicative speeches.

For almost one century, since the abolition of slavery in 1888, social movements have collaborated with individual and collective actions. Actions include participating in protests, launching and supporting community newspapers, and suggesting articles for the new constitution (1988). In 1988, slavery had been abolished for 100 years and the national media, including newspapers, magazines and television, and government as well, spread the ideological speech of racial democracy.

However, the Black movement did not want to celebrate this fact. It used this moment to include its demands in the governmental agenda, and November 20 was recognized as Black Awareness Day.[14] The constitution, public universities and survey institutes became open to responding to African Brazilian problems. Data about access to education, health and labor were included in studies. This research shift resulted in abolishing the racial democracy myth and exposed critical issues.

Women's political organizing in the 1980s occurred in the context of the struggle to establish a democratic government. A central focus for both White and Black women was the creation of a public system of health. They founded the *PAISM—Programa de Assistência Integral à Saúde da Mulher* (Program for Integrated Assistance to Women's Health) that heightened awareness about reproductive rights. White women initiated and became involved in international activism, participating in the 1994 Population and Development Conference in Cairo and in the 1995 World Conference of Women in China. Brazilian Black women did not participate in the Cairo conference, however, international nongovernmental organizations sent members of the Black women's movement to China.

Advocacy practices such as speeches to the media and political analysis and involvement promoted knowledge of international relations. In the 1990s, White and Black women decided to list some common goals (reproductive rights, sexual rights, abortion legalization, equal pay for equal work, etc.). Advocacy practices were developed to empower White and Black activist groups. Gonzalez' (1982) ideas about a Black feminism were becoming a reality. The intersection between social class, race and gender was incorporated into Brazilian feminist discourse as a result of an educational, communicative and *transcultural* movement.

During the 1980s, economic development gained new meaning in the context of globalization and capitalism and poverty increased. At the same time, national and foreign nongovernmental organizations (NGOs) initiated social projects sponsored by federal, state and municipal governments. Some of these organizations are still working to eradicate poverty and find a solution for famine and hunger. However, social exclusion continues to affect both rich and poor countries.

Hespanha (2002, 161–162) indicates that the poor-rich polarization affects both hemispheres. Structural policies should be implemented promoting better salaries as a means to creating a more equal distribution of income, health, education, a clean environment and sustainable development. These areas represent human rights issues. The Higher Human Development Indices (HDI) of Brazil show three realities: one for White men, another lower one for women, and the worst for Black people.[15] Therefore, the question becomes: Would Brazilian society be willing to include and empower Black women?

Table 24.1 illustrates the status of Brazilian women in the labor market. Comparisons of non-Black (White and yellow/Asian) and Black people (*pretos* and *pardos*/brown) may be drawn from this table. In 2007, the federal government developed the National Plan of Policies for Women. This initiative is a product of activism because it combines activist propositions with the United Nations' "Goals of the Millennium," to which Brazil is a signatory. One of the outlined goals is to know the poverty problems and challenges faced by the educational system. In this context, Brazil has had little success in reducing illiteracy and creating mechanisms for inclusion in higher education.[16] In labor markets, gender diversity has become an issue. Public companies and banks have recently promoted inclusion policies for (White)[17] women. There are, however, significant challenges since, according to data from official and recognized institutes,[18] Brazilian Black women suffer the most in areas such as economic development (see table 24.1), education and health care.

Table 24.1. Index Calculated by Hour Paid Monthly According to Gender and Color, 2004–2005

Metropolitan Cities and Federal District	Black Women	Black Men	Non-Black Women	Non-Black Men
Belo Horizonte	48.9	66.2	80.4	100.0
Distrito Federal	50.8	63.9	78.0	100.0
Porto Alegre	61.2	68.8	86.4	100.0
Recife	53.3	67.6	82.1	100.0
Salvador	39.2	49.6	82.3	100.0
São Paulo	42.2	52.9	79.5	100.0

Source: Partnership between DIEESE/Seade, MTE/FAT, and regional partners. Survey about employed and unemployed people by DIEESE.
Note: Non-Black = white and yellow/Asian. Black = pretos and pardos. Inflation rates IPCA-BH/IPEA, INPC-DF-IBGE, IPC-IEPE/RS, INPC-RMR/IBGE/PE, IPC-SEI/BA, ICV-DIEESE/SP.

For decades, public primary and secondary schools (table 24.2) have experienced a lack of government attention, while private schools have offered the best education. Paradoxically, public universities are the best post-secondary institutions in the country. Private universities tend to be more profit driven and a few of them are evaluated with scores approaching those of public universities. Upper- and middle-class families enroll their children in private primary and secondary schools that are extremely expensive and serve primarily White students. These youngsters are thus privileged with a superior education and are able to compete for spots in one of the prestigious public universities, which have more competitive *vestibulares* (entrance exams) than private universities do. Poor families do not have the resources to pay for private primary and secondary education, therefore their children study in deteriorating public schools that suffer from a variety of problems, including a shortage of teachers. In these schools, children can attend for years without learning important subjects like mathematics, chemistry and physical science because few of the nation's limited number of public school teachers are interested in working in poor, distant or violent communities. If they finish high school, these students are unable to compete with private school students in the difficult college entrance examinations administered by public universities. In summary, it is very difficult for poor people, most of whom are Black, to gain the opportunity to study in a public university. This fact indicates a serious social problem.

However, this social problem also is linked with gender issues that come into focus when examining MEC/INEP/DEAES findings about who is hired to work in IHE (institutes of higher education). "Men

Table 24.2. Faculty Members in Brazilian Public and Private Higher Education Institutions, 2000–2005

Year	Public			Private		
2000	Total	Female	Male	Total	Female	Male
Total	88.154	39.7	60.3	109.558	41.8	58.2
Not Graduate	100	41.7	58.3	100	44.8	55.2
Graduate	100	38.9	61.1	100	35.5	64.5
Specialist	100	44.5	55.5	100	42.1	57.9
Master	100	44.7	55.3	100	46.1	53.9
Doctor	100	32	68	100	37	63
2005	Total	Female	Male	Total	Female	Male
Total of Faculty members	98.033	42.6	57.4	194.471	45.2	54.8
Not Graduate	100	26.7	73.3	100	23.5	76.5
Graduate	100	43.1	56.9	100	38.1	61.9
Specialist	100	45.4	54.6	100	45.5	54.5
Master	100	46.9	53.1	100	47.8	52.2
Doctor	100	38.2	61.8	100	42.7	57.3

Source: MEC/INEP/Deaes.

comprise a majority of the faculty members in public and private universities" (Ristoff, Grosz, Giolo and Leporace, 2007). Public universities are more prestigious than private universities, and most women faculty members of the country work in private institutions. In 2000, 41.8 percent of all private university professors were women, with the figure 39.7 percent for public universities. In 2005, 45.2 percent of private university faculty were women, while 42.6 of public university faculty were women. Thus, women have enhanced their position as faculty members in public institutions; however, men are still occupying the best positions, particularly in the more prestigious public universities.

Racial and ethnic (color) data for women professors are difficult to obtain.[19] Government statistics do not indicate whether these women (and men) are White, Black, *pardas/pardos* (brown), Asian, or Indigenous. However, I can attest to the fact that the number of Black professors, both men and women, is negligible, because the access of Brazilian Black people to study and to work in IHE is very low. The University of São Paulo (USP), for instance, is ranked as the best IHE in the country. It has the largest scientific production of any Latin American university. But in terms of racial and ethnic inclusion, in 2001 Black students made up only 1.3 percent of the university's student body, along with another 7.0 percent that had self-declared as *pardos* (brown) (Azzoni and Malachias, 2004, p. 8). José Jorge de Carvalho, in a 2003 study of Black professors in Brazilian public universities, asserts that USP had about 20 Black professors compared to 4,705 White professors and Asian faculty members (Carvalho,

2003, p. 165). The USP web site gives its faculty's demographic statistics without color/race (table 24.3).

FINAL CONSIDERATIONS

The entertainment media is the engine that drives Brazil's largest communication corporations. Brazil contains a large number of people who have been educated primarily by television. Most soap operas perpetuate both racial and gender stereotypes (Barbosa, 2002). At the same time, for children who do learn to read and have the opportunity to learn from sources other than television, prejudice and stereotypes appear in children's didactic books, frequently representing Native people and Blacks, especially Black women, as servants.

A Leadership Example

The Union of Education Specialists of Municipal Public Teaching of São Paulo (SINESP) has a Black female president[20] named Maria Benedita de Castro de Andrade who advanced from low positions to the presidency. During an interview I conducted[21] with Andrade she stated that "the staff of the union is made up of 96.0 percent women and 4.0 men, including

Table 24.3. University of São Paulo, 2007

Faculty	Number	%
Total Men and Women	5,222	100.0
Men	3,412	65.3
Women	1,810	34.7
Full-time dedication	4,216	79.0
Ph.D., Post-Doctorate or above level	5,028	

principals, supervisors and deans. But sometimes I observe a chauvinist mentality among the women. I think that being in the majority does not [necessarily] mean that women have power. At the same time, in the schools, young women have a new awareness, and they want to learn more things than my generation."

The president of SINESP is politically responsible for the interests of SINESP's rights and duties, but according to Andrade, there is resistance to discussing matters of ethnicity, race and gender. In 2006 she initiated a discussion within SINESP about law 10.639/03, which mandated the teaching of African history and Afro-Brazilian culture in the city's primary and secondary schools. She explained, "It was hard yet democratic work because I had to convince the [education] specialists that this law must be obeyed. I am sure that if I were not a Black president, this subject would not have been included in the union's program."

Concluding our interview, Andrade reflected upon her past and present accomplishments, stating, "I have been an educator for 42 years. Undeniably, I need to fight every day to be respected. How did I learn to fight? When I was a little girl, my mother taught me to say with her, 'We are. We can.' For years we repeated this mantra together, and I have survived."

NOTES

1. It was elaborated upon by the Cuban ethnologist Fernando Ortiz in the 1940s. For him, European colonization in the Americas and Caribbean promoted a violent cultural shock among different people.

2. Gonzalez (1983, p. 236) used another concept by Magno (1980), "Amefrica" (Americas, Africa, including Caribbean countries, Black and Native people). In our opinion, both "Amefrica" and *transculturación* have similarities because Native and African people are considered protagonists of history and European culture would not be superior compared with other civilizations.

3. At this point, I have intentionally left untranslated the concepts of *transculturación* (Fernando Ortiz) and *mediações* (Jesus Martín-Barbero).

4. Mediation (Free translation).

5. Barreto's study talks about Brazil and the United States. Lélia Gonzalez and Angela Davis show how racism is an international subject.

6. In Brazil, the Movement of Women was initially organized by White leadership women.

7. Black women are inside both movements. However, Black men and White women did not listen to their specific concerns.

8. It finished in 1985.

9. Luiza Bairros (2000) made a mention of a Lélia Gonzalez interview at MNU Jornal, May/June/July 1991, p. 9.

10. Cultura, Etnicidade e Trabalho: Efeitos Lingüísticos e Políticos da Exploração da Mulher Negra. Pontifícia Universidade Católica—RJ. Comunicação apresentada no 8º. Encontro nacional da Latin American Studies Association. Pittsburgh, April 5–7, 1979.

11. *O modo mais sutilmente paternalista é exatamente aquele que atribui o caráter de "discurso emocional" à verdade contundente da denúncia presente na fala do excluído* (Gonzalez, 1979, p.16).

12. From international leadership: Marcus Garvey, W. E. B. Du Bois, Leopold Senghor, Martin Luther King, Jr. Malcolm X, Angela Davis, Nelson Mandela, Winnie Mandela, and others.

13. Black men had less opportunities to work than White men did. Most of them had informal jobs. White men, especially European immigrants, had formal jobs.

14. Slavery Abolition is celebrated on May 13. The National Day of Black Awareness is a celebration of the leader Zumbi dos Palmares. He was a hero who led 1,000 slaves. They lived in a *quilombo* (refugee slave settlement) in Palmares.

15. See: 2005. The National Report about Human Development concluded that Brazilian Black people are victims of institutional racism and inequality.

16. Federal universities adopted affirmative action for Black and poor people.

17. According to Ethos Institute Black women are discriminated against by companies.

18. DIEESE, Seade, IBGE, Ministry of Education (MEC), Anísio Teixeira National Institute of Studies and Research (INEP) and the Office of Statistics and Evaluation of Higher Education (DEAES).

19. The national census conducted by the Brazilian Institute of Geography and Statistics (IBGE) uses color to define ethnic and racial classification. These colors are: branca (White); preta (Black); parda (Brown, i.e., mixed race); amarela (Yellow, i.e., Asian) and Indigenous (Native people—in this case ethnic origin, not color, is used).

20. Benê gave me authorization to publish her name.

21. March 2007.

REFERENCES CITED

A Mulher na Educação Superior Brasileira. 1991–2005 / Organizadores: Dilvo Ristoff [e al.] Brasília: Instituto Nacional de Estudos e Pesquisas Educacionais Anísio Teixeira, 2007. 292 p.:il.

Arilha, Margareth, and Citeli, Maria Teresa. (orgs.) Políticas, Mercado, Ética: Demanda e desafios no campo da saúde reprodutiva no Brasil. São Paulo: Ed. 34; Comissão de Cidadania e Reprodução, 1998.

Azeredo, Sandra. Direitos Reprodutivos: A questão racial na pesquisa. São Paulo, FCC/DPE, 1991.

Bastide, Roger, e Fernandes, Florestan. Relações raciais entre negros e brancos em São Paulo. São Paulo: Anhembi, 1955.

Berquó, Elza, O Brasil e as recomendações do plano de ação do Cairo. Trabalho apresentado no Seminário Saúde Reprodutiva e na América Latina e Caribe. Temas e problemas. PROLAP/ABEP/NEPO, Caxambu, 1996.

Bourdieu, Pierre. Escritos de Educação, Petrópolis, Vozes, 1998.

Bruschini, Cristina, and Sorj, Bernardo (orgs.). Novos olhares: mulheres e relações de gênero no Brasil. São Paulo: Marco Zero/Fundação Carlos Chagas, 1994.

Cadernos Pagu-Raça e Gênero. (6/7), Núcleo de Estudos de Gênero/UNICAMP, Campinas, São Paulo, 1996.

Canclini, Nestor G. As culturas populares no capitalismo. São Paulo, Brasiliense, 1983.

————. Consumidores e cidadãos. Conflitos multiculturais da globalização. Rio de Janeiro, UFRJ, 1995.

Cappelin, Paola. Discriminação positiva: ações afirmativas em busca da igualdade, São Paulo, CFEMEA/ELAS, 1996.

Carneiro, Sueli. A organização nacional das Mulheres Negras e as perspectivas políticas. In: Cadernos Geledès nº. 4. São Paulo, Geledès Instituto da Mulher Negra, Programa de Comunicação, nov./1993.

Correa, Marisa. Sobre a invenção da mulata. Cadernos Pagu, Raça e Gênero. (6/7), Núcleo de Estudos de Gênero/UNICAMP, Campinas, São Paulo, 1996.

Correa, Sônia, and Petchesky, Rosalind. Direitos Sexuais e Reprodutivos: uma perspectiva feminista. In: PHYSIS: Rev. Saúde Coletiva. Rio de Janeiro, 6(1/2): 147–177, 1996.

D'Ambrósio, Ubiratan. Transdisciplinaridade. São Paulo, Palas Athena, 1997.

Deuze, Mark. Ethnic media, community media and participatory culture. *Journalism, 7*(3), 263–280.

Fals Borda, Orlando. Aspectos teóricos da pesquisa participante: considerações sobre o significado e o papel da ciência na participação popular. In: BRANDÃO, CR, Pesquisa Participante, São Paulo, Brasiliense, 1988.

Fanon, Frantz. Pele negra, máscara branca. Rio de Janeiro, Fator, 1980.

Fernandes, Florestan. A integração do negro na sociedade de classes. São Paulo, Ed. Dominius, 1966.

————. Ciências Sociais: na ótica do intelectual militante. *Estudos Avançados, 8*(22), 1994.

Freire, Paulo. Pedagogia da Autonomia: saberes necessários à prática educativa, São Paulo, Paz e Terra, 2000. 16ªed.

Frigotto, Gaudêncio. A interdisciplinaridade como necessidade e como problema nas Ciências Sociais. In: Revista Educação e Realidade, Faculdade de Educação da Universidade Federal do Rio Grande do Sul, vol. 18, nº. 2, jul./dez./1993, pp. 63–72.

Gohn, Maria da Glória. Teoria dos Movimentos Sociais. Paradigmas clássicos e contemporâneos. São Paulo, Loyola, 1997.

Gomes, Nilma Lino. Mulheres Negras e Educação: trajetórias de vida, histórias de luta. mimeo, sd.

Gonzalez, Lélia. Cultura, Etnicidade e Trabalho. Efeitos lingüísticos e políticos da exploração da Mulher Negra. Comunicação apresentada no 8º. Encontro Nacional da Latin American Studies Association, Pittsburgh, 5 a 7 de abril de 1979.

Gonzalez, Lélia e Hasenbalg, Carlos A. Lugar de Negro, Rio de Janeiro, Editora Marco Zero, 1982.

Gramsci, Antonio. Obras escolhidas, trad. Manuel Cruz; revisão Nei da Rocha Cunha. São Paulo, Martins Fontes, 1978.

Heilborn, Maria Luiza. Gênero e Condição Feminina: uma abordagem antropológica. In: Mulher e Políticas Públicas, IBAM/UNICEF.

Hespanha, Pedro. Mal estar e risco social num mundo globalizado: novos problemas e novos desafios para a teoria social. In: Globalização e as Ciências Sociais –Boaventura de Sousa Santos (Org.). São Paulo, Cortez, 2002.

Ianni, Octávio. A Era do Globalismo, Rio de Janeiro, Civilização Brasileira, 1997.

Kellner, Douglas. A Cultura da Mídia. Estudos culturais: identidade e política entre o moderno e o pós moderno. (Trad. Ivone Castilho Benedetti), Bauru, São Paulo, EDUSC, 2001.

Malachias, Rosangela. Ação transcultural: a visibilidade da juventude negra nos bailes Black de São Paulo (Brasil) e Havana (Cuba). Dissertação de Mestrado, São Paulo, PROLAM/USP—Programa de Pós-Graduação em Integração da América Latina da Universidade de São Paulo, outubro/1996.

————. Discursos impressos: os direitos reprodutivos reivindicados pelos Movimentos de Mulheres da América Latina e Mulheres Negras Brasileiras (1988–1995). www.lpp-uerj.net/olped/documentos/ppcor/0171.pdf.

————. Os sonhos podem acontecer. Teorias e práticas à ampliação do discurso preventivo ao abuso de drogas com a inclusão de jovens, negros e mulheres. Tese de Doutorado, São Paulo, ECA/USP, outubro de 2002.

Marco Estratégico para a UNESCO no Brasil. http.www.unesco.org.br.

Martin Barbero, Jesus. Sujeito, Comunicação e Cultura, in Revista Comunicação and Educação, São Paulo, CCA-ECA/USP, Editora Moderna, (15): 62 a 80, maio/ago, 1999.

————. De los medios a las mediaciones. México, Gustavo Gili, 1987.

Olhar sobre a Mídia. Comissão de Cidadania e Reprodução, Belo Horizonte, Mazza Edições, 2002.

Oliveira, Eliana. Mulher Negra Professora Universitária. Trajetória, Conflitos e Identidade. Brasília, Líber Livro Editora, 2006.

Ortiz, Fernando. Por la integración cubana de blancos y negros, in Órbita de Fernando Ortiz, Col. Órbita, Ediciones UNEAC, La Habana, 1973, pp. 181–191.

Pinto, Gisele. Situação das Mulheres Negras no Mercado de Trabalho: uma análise dos indicadores sociais. Trabalho apresentado no XIV Encontro Nacional de Estudos Populacionais, ABEP, Caxambu, MG, 18-22 de setembro de 2006.

Piza, Edith, e Rosemberg, Fúlvia. A cor nos censos brasileiros. In: Psicologia Social do Racismo. Rio de Janeiro, Vozes, 2002.

Por uma outra comunicação. Mídia, Mundialização Cultural e Poder. Denis de Moraes (org). Rio de Janeiro-São Paulo, Record, 2005.

Plano Nacional de Políticas para as Mulheres. Presidência da República, Secretaria Especial de políticas para as Mulheres. Brasília: DF, 2004.

Roland, Edna. Gênero e Raça e a Promoção da Igualdade, Brasília, Programa Nacional de Direitos Humanos, 1999.

Rosemberg, Fúlvia. Educação formal, Mulher e Gênero, Scielo, Brasil. Revista Estudos Feministas. ISSN 0104-026X versão impressa. Rev. Estud. Fem. v.9 nº 2 Florianópolis, 2001.

Sant'Anna, Wania. Relações Raciais no Brasil: entre a unanimidade e a paralisia. In: Perspectivas em Saúde e Direitos Reprodutivos. Informativo semestral/ The John D. and Catherine T,. MacArthur Foundation, maio/2001 / nº. 4/ano 2 (pp. 53–68).

Santos, Milton. As cidadanias mutiladas. In: O Preconceito. São Paulo, IMESP, 1996–1997.

———. Por uma outra globalização: do pensamento único ao pensamento universal. Rio de Janeiro Record, 2002.

Soares, Ismar de Oliveira. Educomunicação: um campo de mediações. In: Comunicação e Educação 19, ano VII, set./dez, 2000, pp. 12–24.

Sorj, Bernardo. Internet, Espaço Público e Marketing Político: entre a promoção da comunicação e o solipsismo moralista. Working Paper 2, Rio de Janeiro, Centro Eldestein de Pesquisas Sociais Comunicações do ISER. Referendo do Sim ao Não. Rio de Janeiro, Nº. 62, ano 25.

Souza, Lorena Francisco de, and Ratts, Alecsandro. Gênero Raça Educação e Ascensão Social: as professoras negras e suas trajetórias socioespaciais. Trabalho apresentado no 1º. Seminário Nacional de Trabalho e Gênero, 2003.

CHAPTER 25

A Photographic Journey of Discovery
Women and Children Living in Dominica, West Indies

Katherine M. Houghton

THE CULTURAL AND SOCIETAL CONTEXT OF THE STUDY: THE COMMONWEALTH OF DOMINICA, WEST INDIES

The island of the Commonwealth of Dominica is described as the "nature island of the Caribbean." The island culture is rooted in language (Patois or Creole), music, religious faith, customs, rituals and folklore. It is an eastern Caribbean island located in the Lesser Antilles between Martinique and Guadeloupe, and is recognized as a Windward Island. The landscape comprises rugged coastlines, volcanic terrain, lush countryside, dense tropical rainforests, and unpredictable flowing rivers and waterfalls. At times the weather is volatile and erratic, resulting in heavy rainfalls, landslides, earthquakes, tropical storms, and hurricanes. Dominica is described as having a "turbulent history, a vibrant cultural present, and a future as unsettled as next year's hurricane season" (Ferguson, 1997, p. 4).

The Caribbean Community (CARICOM) Secretariat confirms that the island population of Dominica is 69,810 (2004) with the majority being descendants of African slaves and the descendants of a few thousand Caribs who reside on a 3,700-acre reserve. People of African descent live throughout the island (Country Review 2000, 1999, p. 17). The island infrastructure and government is challenged by a population that is growing while Dominicans migrate to other islands, Great Britain and North America to seek educational and occupational opportunities.

Lenox Honychurch (1995), a Dominican author and historian, notes that "the West Indian pattern of high illegitimacy and low percentage of marriage features prominently in Dominican society. The problems of paternal neglence and lack of the father figure has contributed to the complex nature of our modern social issues" (p. 197). Additionally, the dynamic interplay within and between societal issues, social status, ethnicity and race, cultural identity and gender provides a context that is complex, vibrant and ever changing. In fact, Andre and Christian (2002) summarize the society as "not so much a melting pot of cultures but one with a plurality of cultures existing side by side" (p. 5).

THE RECENT HISTORICAL CONTEXT OF THE ISLAND OF DOMINICA: INDEPENDENCE TO RECENT DAY

The 1970s were "characterized by social and labor unrest, political upheaval, general discontent and in some cases, disenchantment with the legacy of colonial government" (Andre and Christian, 2002, p. 8). "Feminism came of age during that period, with women being called sisters" (Andre and Christian, 2002, p. 69). This period also led to the granting of independence from Great Britain on November 3, 1978. Since the granting of independence the island has undergone many challenges, experienced significant "black power" violence, been engrossed in color and class prejudice, and weathered many political and tropical storms—including hurricanes Luis and David.

Presently, the island and its people are making great efforts to work through their history while striving to foster equitable economic development, modernize governmental and legal systems, and overcome an ingrained subservient and slave cultural identity. Andre and Christian (2002) describe the foundation of the struggle as rooted in the country's history and "psychic scars lashed into the minds of Dominicans by centuries of Western-taught self hate and ridicule lavished upon Africa and people of African descent" (p. 45).

THE FOCUS OF THE STUDY: THE WOMEN AND CHILDREN OF DOMINICA, WEST INDIES

The focus of the study is Dominican women and children. Dominican "women comprise 50.2 percent of the population" with female-headed households "estimated at 38 percent" (Mohammed and Perkins, 1999, p. 39). The daily lives of Dominican women and children are filled with struggles to prevent impoverishment and maintain self-sufficiency. Women laborers encounter discriminatory practices in many areas of everyday life. "In farming, for instance, they find it more difficult than men to gain access to credit—the lifeblood of every smallholding—often because their names do not appear on title deeds" (Ferguson, 1997, p. 53).

Prominent occupations of Dominican women are: mothers and housewives, farming, professional and semiprofessional, such as teaching, nursing, nongovernmental organization (NGO) worker, clerical, civil servant, self-employed shopkeepers, seamstresses, caterers and bakers (Mohammed and Perkins, 1999, p. 47). Many households in Dominica are headed by women, and "teenage pregnancies are a serious problem throughout the region, and significant numbers of single mothers are under the age of 20. In many cases they have to rely on their own mothers for support, placing an extra burden on them" (Ferguson, 1997, p. 54). In addition, "family support networks are important, with women playing the major role in caring for elderly relatives" (Ferguson, 1997, p. 55).

However, findings from a study of Dominican women by Mohammed and Perkins (1999) discovered that the women studied had "made virtue out of necessity, persistently confronting many adversities to map out meaningful goals and make informed decisions about their lives. They continue to face life in these societies with joy and resilience, with warmth and affection for other women, and for their supportive or itinerant menfolk" (Mohammed and Perkins, 1999, p. 126).

A QUALITATIVE RESEARCH DESIGN: VISIONS AND IMAGES OF WOMEN AND CHILDREN LIVING IN DOMINICA, WEST INDIES

An intense qualitative research design and methodology is acted upon to achieve an in-depth study and understanding of the lived experiences of Dominican women and children. The methodology of this qualitative study is guided by a hermeneutic phenomenological field research perspective and approach. Therefore, while I lived, saw and visually inquired about the experiences and lives of these women and children I maintained "a sincere interest in learning how participants function in their ordinary pursuit and milieus and with a willingness to put aside many presumptions" (Stake, 1995, p. 1). Visual representations, themes and images emerge from this study and expose the phenomenon of "being" (Heidegger, 1962) a Dominican woman or child.

As I lived and traveled in Dominica from May 2003 to September 2006 I engaged in ordinary and commonplace activities such as going to the market and snack shops, holiday celebrations, weddings, funerals and political rallies. Bailey (2007) describes the journey of field research as "a systematic study, primarily through long-term, face-to-face interactions and observations, of everyday life. A primary goal of field research is to understand daily life from the perspectives of people in a setting or social group of interest to the researcher" (p. 2).

This qualitative research process was and is a journey that challenged me to develop a multifaceted methodology that evolved and built upon a rigorous, dynamic and all-embracing approach derived from my experiences as a white American woman living in Dominica. In fact, at times I consciously struggled to internally and externally overcome the natural differences of being a stranger in a foreign, unfamiliar, overwhelming and sometimes dangerous world. My life in Dominica overflowed with moments of photographing approximately 8,000 images from May 2003 to September 2006. On a daily basis I analyzed visual representations as I lived, researched and photographed, while interpreting those visions and experiences. I constantly worked to define my purpose and scope of this study.

However, most significantly throughout this vigorous and ever-changing process I remained present in the field and open to photographing and depicting an image, scene, impression, reflection or visual representation. I was grounded, focused and calmed by simply seeing into the images and interpreting the essence and meanings of the photographs and my solitary or mutually lived experiences. Collier and Collier (1986) note, "Well-organized visual analysis usually combines structured, detailed study with such impressionistic process as a means of seeking new insight" (p. 195).

Observations and interactions of this study were overt, unstructured and done publicly. Additionally, I maintained an observational and active perspective by viewing background and foreground experiences. In fact, Bailey (2007) encourages researchers to always be aware and analytical in the field and to see both the background and foreground and how they simultaneously act mutually. While in the midst of viewing the background and foreground experiences and images I realized that a single image or multiple images may serve to illustrate a story. I discovered that "elements of a story obviously are embedded in the data; they lie dormant until the researcher crafts them into something meaningful" (Bailey, 2007, p. 163).

PARADIGM OF THE STUDY: A FEMINIST IDEOLOGICAL STANDPOINT

This study employs a feminist conceptual and ideological framework described by Brooks and Hesse-Biber (2007) as research that fosters "empowerment and emancipation for women and other marginalized groups, and feminist researchers often apply their findings in the service of promoting social change and social justice for women" (p. 4). In addition, Duelli Klein (1983) urges feminists to engage in methods that are open, interactive and comprehensive. Similarly, Mies (1983) encourages researchers to perform studies that expose "hidden women," contribute to feminist research and promote "conscious partiality" that expands the consciousness and enhances the rapport and reciprocity within and between the researcher and the researched. In fact, "feminist standpoint epistemology requires the fusion of knowledge and practice" (Brooks, 2007, p. 55). Consequently, this study sought to combine a multifaceted, creative and rigorous research approach to understanding the lived experiences of Dominican women and children through visual images and inquiry.

THEORETICAL PERSPECTIVES AND PHILOSOPHICAL ASSUMPTIONS: PHENOMENOLOGY AND HERMENEUTIC INTERPRETATION

A hermeneutic interpretation guides the study and my journey of discovering the women and children of Dominica. This journey drew my photographic lens to express lived experiences of myself and of the women and children that I was meeting, seeing, viewing, comprehending, observing, reflecting on and gaining glimpses of along the journey. Gadamer (1975/1985 and 1989/2000) and Heidegger (1962) articulate that hermeneutics is not a solitary and isolated interpretation, but an interactive understanding of life experiences. Therefore, the lens of my camera interacted with my lived experiences to capture the essence and existence of the phenomenon of "being" a Dominican woman or child.

Throughout this dynamic, reflective and interactive process I strove to set aside my ethnocentric views, overcome biases and prejudgments and minimize apprehensions based in "being" a stranger, a minority and a vulnerable individual in a foreign land. My process is described by Moustakas (1994) as including "not only a description of the experience as it appears in consciousness but also an analysis and astute interpretation of the underlying conditions, historically,

and aesthetically, that account for the experience" (p. 10). Therefore, as I traveled and lived in Dominica I read, researched, wrote and photographed while simultaneously seeking to comprehend historical, social, societal, economic, cultural and political conditions that may give explanation and vision to experiences. Crotty (1992) describes travels, life and research as a "hermeneutic circle" that is often found in the work of Heidegger (1962).

Throughout my journey I reflected on the backward and forward movement of my hermeneutic circle with and between myself, my photography, the study and Dominican women and children. My quest within this circle was and is to expose the "being" of the women and children I encountered and to give vision to this circle of hermeneutic understanding. The circle of hermeneutic "understanding turns out to be a development of what is already understood, with the more developed understanding returning to illuminate and enlarge one's starting point" (Crotty, 1998, p. 92). Additionally, Collier and Collier (1986) "suggest that research be seen as a circular journey, beginning with open-ended processes, evolving into various stages of structured observation and analysis, and concluding again with open speculation as we translate our feelings into conclusions. This is a dynamic form that allows creative perception, fieldwork and analysis without sacrificing the specificity and responsibility of scientific study" (p. 167).

The photographic phenomenological methodology of the study fostered an increased creative and scientific awareness and analysis of everyday life while I lived, studied and photographed. Becker (1992) emphasizes that "to understand people, we must understand their context—the worlds or situations in which they live. To separate person and world is false; to be a person is to be in the world" (p. 13). Therefore, my life in Dominica and this study is interconnected with me "being" in the world of images and experiences that urged me to understand the context in which I was living and the people that I was knowing. Throughout my journey, life and research in Dominica I gleaned glimpses, images and "aspects of human cultural activity and experience from the perspective of those living through the experience" (Hultgren and Coomer, 1989, p. 41).

Therefore, the study employed research methods grounded in phenomenology and visual inquiry because it discovers the essence of experiences in the everyday life of Dominican women and children and phenomenology "presents itself as a method, and yet it implies a complete view of the world. It is disclosure of phenomena, but at the same time it is a return to the self and subject" (Thervenaz, 1962, p. 91). However, Thervenaz (1962) further explains that phenomenology "is above all method—a method for changing our relation to the world, for becoming more acutely aware of it" (p. 57). He summarizes the purpose of phenomenology as focusing on "the point of contact where being and consciousness meet" and "aims at disclosing the structures of consciousness as consciousness, of experience as experience" (pp. 20, 21). Benjamin, cited in Emmison and Smith (2000), emphasizes the interconnectedness between photographic images and consciousness. He suggests that photographic images have a "magical value" and that the photograph is a "space informed by human consciousness" (p. 14).

Practicing phenomenology and visual inquiry is a dialectic process of discovering multiple layers of consciousness and experiences. Therefore, uncovering understandings gained from my layered journey of visual discovery reveals that this study provided me the privilege of connecting myself to the world and becoming a part of this world. In fact, Van Manen (1984) relates that "in doing research we question the world's very secrets and intimacies which are constitutive of the world, and which bring the world into being for us and in us" (Van Manen, 1984, p. 4). Hence, as I lived, studied and experienced Dominica I was brought to a world of understanding of my lived experiences, shared experiences and the experiences of others in the world.

THE RESEARCHER AND PHOTOGRAPHER: BEING DRAWN AND CALLED TO PROVIDE A LENS TO THE PHENOMENON

For many personal and professional reasons I have come to understand that my "being" (Heidegger, 1962) is "called" (Heidegger, 1962) to visually depict and seek understanding of the lived experiences of Dominican women and children that I encountered during my life in Dominica. Therefore, I have been summoned to this experience as a human being, a professional, a photographer and a researcher. I studied and lived to see with a vision that opened my eyes, pointed my lens and fostered trustworthy methods and theoretical perspectives that would inspire meaningful images and authenticity of visual representation and interpretation. Additionally, because I was focused, present and engaged in images and visions, this self-engagement allowed me "to be led by the questions and the natural unfolding of the inquiry as it is lived" (Hultgren and Coomer, 1989, p. xxx).

Since it was essential to have my lens focused solely on the lives of Dominican women and children I intentionally surrendered myself to experiences and practiced a phenomenological methodology that was directed "back to the things themselves" (Husserl, 1931). This intentional process established authenticity, fostered visual inquiry and exposed an understanding and essence of the lived experiences of Dominican women and children. I sought to make visible and give sight to their lives and existence. As a photographer and researcher in this hermeneutic process I sought a phenomenological and visual methodology of inquiry. Specifically, I immersed myself in the research process, "dwelt" (Heidegger 1962, p. 47) in a world of images, and was privileged to be given "the opportunity for an authentic gaze into the soul of another" (Silverman, 2000, p. 821). Overall, the gazing into the souls of Dominican women and children through my photographic lens has been a crossing between quiet reflective times to moments of intense emotions and thoughts. Often, my thoughts and emotions overflow with visions, sightings and images of Dominican women and children that called and recalled me to the phenomenon.

Often I was drawn to the phenomenon and visual representation and found myself withdrawing from it to provide the opportunity to newly view and see openly the visions and images. Thereby, I established impressions, reflections, perceptions, and further understandings and possibilities while sharing lived experiences with Dominican women and children. This dialectic process encouraged the "horizons of experience" to widen. "At first it only seems to tell us about our own inner states but in knowing oneself one also comes to know about the external world and other people" (Dilthey, 1976, p. 162).

THE RESEARCHER: PHOTOGRAPHER AND PHENOMENOLOGIST

The role of the researcher and photographer requires a significant professional and personal responsibility. Pink (2001) explains that the researcher's photography "may be related equally to their professional fieldwork narratives or personal biographies. Moreover, photography and photographs can represent an explicit meeting point (or continuity) between personal and professional identities" (Pink, 2001, p. 26). Therefore, my role as researcher and photographer demanded that I fully engage in the research process and develop authentic and trustworthy relationships while adhering to rigorous methodologies and impeccable ethical standards.

The research process honored the American Sociological Association (ASA) code of ethics and guidelines (1999). The guidelines indicate that informed consent is not required when "research involves no more than minimal risk for research participants," "research could not practically be carried out were informed consent to be required," and during "naturalistic observations in public places" (p. 12). In addition to these guidelines I sought to "cultivate genuine interest in other people, willingness to learn from lived experience, and respectful empathy for others" (Becker, 1992, pp. 39, 40).

As the researcher it is my responsibility to deeply understand and reflect upon the interplay between the lived experiences and images of Dominican women and children and my lived experiences. During those reflective times I was "critically thinking about how one's status, characteristics, values, and history, as well as the numerous choices one has made during the research affect the results" (Bailey, 2007, p. 6). This search to understand my images and stories contributes to the process of exposing and discovering the essence and existence of Dominican women and children. Therefore, throughout this study I intentionally focused, remained open and reminded myself I was and am a "reflective partner" (Habermas, 1990) in the research process. As I maintained the role of "reflective partner" I simultaneously interacted with and observed experiences while understanding that I must remain objective, acknowledge biases, determine limitations of the study and identify influences of my lived experiences.

Hesse-Biber (2007) explains that "strong reflectivity is the manifestation of strong objectivity through method. It requires the researcher to be cognizant and critically reflective about the different ways her positionality can serve as a hindrance and a resource toward achieving knowledge throughout the research process" (Hesse-Biber, 2007, p. 115). Therefore, I strive to work with my positionality in service to the study and attempt to have this positionality be a resource to the research process. Combining my positionality and reflective approaches based in a rigorous qualitative research design with visual inquiry and analysis provides the framework for the development of exposing knowledge and images of the lives of Dominican women and children.

Throughout my life in Dominica I consciously lived and studied while challenging myself to understand my positionality and practice visual methods of inquiry described by Pink (2001). Pink (2001)

urges photographic researchers to have a reflective approach that involves knowing "in particular cultural settings, how they frame particular images, and why they choose particular subjects" (p. 57). Additionally, Daines (1989) emphasizes that "it is easy to say 'I understand' or to interpret information through the lens of one's own lived experience without attempting to move beyond—or behind—that experience to glimpse and become a part of other perspectives or to bring these to bear on one's interpretation. Yet the responsibility to move beyond and behind is an important dimension of the interpretive sciences, for it unites their purposes and underlies their methodologies" (p. 45).

As I moved beyond and behind the images during the research process I remained grounded by my background in fine arts and photography, qualitative research methodology and commitment to giving sight to underrepresented women and children of the world. Although at times I found the research process to be exhaustive and overwhelming, I was guided by the knowledge that "it is difficult, sometimes impossible, to observe accurately phenomena we do not understand, and the camera provides a solution to this problem" (Collier and Collier, 1986, p. 19).

As I practiced visual inquiry through a phenomenological mode I gained an understanding that knowledge is co-created and that what is known, perceived or visualized is influenced by the standpoint of the knower, perceiver or viewer. Because of this knowing, perceiving and viewing I truly began to realize the meaning of the beliefs expressed by Russo (1991) and "how my survival is intricately linked with the survival of women of color and that real freedom can be a reality only when all of us are free" (p. 308). In the hope of further developing this standpoint I strove to be proficient in a reflective mode of analysis and discover my own experiences, prejudices, preunderstandings and worldviews throughout my life and research in Dominica.

EXPOSING PHOTOGRAPHIC IMAGES TO GAIN A COMPREHENSIVE UNDERSTANDING OF THE PHENOMENON

As I viewed and reviewed photographs and wrote and rewrote, I simultaneously found myself photographing and analyzing until meaningful understanding was unveiled. As the phenomenon was illuminated through photographic phenomenological inquiry I discovered that photographs hold "intense human significance and communication" and that "the secret of such records lies in the nature of rapport, not in photographic technique" (Collier and Collier, 1986, p. 214). I consciously and consistently made "an attempt to get closer to the view from the inside" (p. 214) and sought permission from Dominican women and children with verbal and nonverbal dialogue and cues before or while shooting photographs. As I became less of a stranger to others it was almost as if the camera became part of my conversations, views and photographs. I developed a thankful and powerful relationship with my camera. My camera provided me the ability to focus, see, connect, give insight and communicate with others and myself in ways I had not imagined. The more I photographed the more I enhanced my visual inquiry and observational skills. Collier and Collier (1986) reaffirm that visual research "should sharpen our vision, so that with or without the camera, we become skilled and knowledgeable observers of our surroundings" (Collier and Collier, 1986, p. 207). As I was snapping, experiencing, learning, participating, focusing, scanning, processing and analyzing my journey I discovered that "the critical eye of the camera is an essential tool in gathering accurate visual information" and "its sharp focus might help us see more and with greater accuracy" (Collier and Collier, 1986, p. 5).

VISUAL REPRESENTATION, VERIFICATION AND ANALYSIS OF THE PHENOMENON

Since there is minimal research and limited literature on the lives of Dominican women and children I primarily discovered the essence of their lived experiences while distinguishing unified meanings and themes derived from my photographs. Visual analysis included an awareness of my personal perspectives, a comprehensive visual depiction of experiences and the extraction and interpretation of significant themes and patterns that emerge from the photographs. "The purpose of a good research design and of different procedures applied within it is to facilitate the discovery and definition of patterns" (Collier and Collier, 1986, p. 195). Therefore, after numerous viewings and reviewings I began to discover contexts, common themes, patterns and experiences among and within the images. I found this aspect of the research process to be challenging, creative, complex and holistic. In fact, discoveries from this study reinforced that "unique experiences generate common themes that enable phenomenologists to illuminate the essential structures of life" (Becker, 1992, p. 23).

The process of theme analysis is "recovering the theme or themes that are embodied and dramatized in the evolving meanings and imagery" (Van Manen, 1990, p. 78). This analysis requires "the elimination of supposition and the raising of knowledge above every possible doubt" (Moustakas, 1994, p. 26) and "thematizing" (Heidegger, 1962, p. 414). The purpose of "thematizing is to free the entities we encounter with-in-the-world, and to free them in such a way that they can 'throw themselves against' a pure discovery" (Heidegger, 1962, p. 414). Theme analysis combined with authenticity criteria provides the foundation of research verification throughout this study. The rigorous process of "thematizing," theme analysis and theme verification promotes credible research methods and trustworthy discoveries from this study.

High standards of research quality, trustworthiness and authenticity were rigorously pursued throughout the discovery of images, themes and influences. While photographing Dominican women and children and analyzing sources of information I ensured that high standards of good research were maintained and I consistently strove to understand the context of the image or experience. According to Banks (2001), good research acknowledges that "in order to do good social research, a researcher has to enter into that process self-consciously, not pretend that they can somehow transcend their humanity and stand outside, merely observing" (p. 112). Additionally, this research design ensures "that the researcher is kept honest, asks hard questions about methods, meanings, and interpretations" (Creswell, 1998, p. 202).

Images are integral to our daily lives; therefore, images provide understanding of the daily lives of Dominican women and children. Banks (2001) asserts that Euro-American societies regard sight and vision casually and leisurely, and, since Euro-American societies are oral and written based societies, the visual and visible aspects of culture and life have been marginalized, compartmentalized and constrained. Therefore, research methodologies incorporating visual inquiry and analysis of the lives of Dominican women and children will expose new findings beyond language-based discourse.

This study in essence promotes thought by the process of "reading" visual images and expands the meaning and understanding of the existence of Dominican women and children and their life-world. Banks (2001) declares, "When we read a photograph . . . we are tuning in to conversations between people, including but not limited to the creator of the visual image and his or her audience" (p. 10). Wright (cited in Banks, 2001) further explains that an approach of reading photographs involves "looking through, looking at, and looking behind" the image (p. 10). Looking through the photographs, looking at the images presented in my daily life and looking behind my past and present images I was called to depict visions literally or figuratively every moment I lived in Dominica.

Oftentimes, I would gaze upon the environment and context and either snap an image with my camera or snap an image with my mind in preparation for another opportunity to view this or a similar image, theme, story or context in the future. In fact, eventually when I would view a future image illustrating a similar vision from the past I shot multiple images depending on the opportunity or story that was unfolding. I did not just capture images or visions; rather, I sought to come to an understanding of my experiences and the lives of Dominican women and children while grappling to "get the picture" (a common English expression used to describe comprehension).

The images' meaning and character became evident as I sought verification of their patterns and themes. The knowledge derived from the images and photographs exposes the viewer to glimpses of the phenomenon. The phenomenon is revealed and becomes thematically evident as the researcher or viewer openly, consciously and continually reviews and returns to the image or multiple images. The reviewing and analyzing process is dynamic and never ending; therefore, to seek conclusions about the images is a temporal endeavor that is complex and challenging.

However, I am certain that the comprehensive, open, trustworthy and structured methods of analysis and verification of this study give sight to the lives of Dominican women and children. In fact, Collier and Collier (1986) explain that "the ideal analysis process allows the data to lead to its own conclusions through a dynamic interplay between open and structured procedures" (p. 172). Consequently, the image viewer's analysis of the photograph or multiple photographs often involves interaction between an analytical review and an emotional response. This vibrant interplay seeks an understanding of the phenomenon, and common or universal meanings are unveiled about the essence of "being" a woman or child living in Dominica.

CONCLUSION: A PHOTOGRAPHIC JOURNEY OF DISCOVERING THE PHENOMENON OF WOMEN AND CHILDREN LIVING IN DOMINICA

This study confirms the significance of visual inquiry and phenomenological methodology and reveals glimpses of the lived experiences of Dominican women and children during the time frame of May 2003 to September 2006. Those lived experiences are illustrated in over 8,000 photographs, which have been thoroughly analyzed and reanalyzed throughout this study. From this analysis the photographs selected for this chapter represent common themes, patterns and experiences of Dominican women and children. Common themes and experiences derived from this study indicate that the lives of Dominican women and children are abundant with activities such as going to school, laboring outside or working indoors, shopping in the market, enjoying time on the beach or by a river, acknowledging nationalism, celebrating country holidays and festivals, campaigning for political parties, socializing at "snackettes" and attending church services.

The photographs selected for this chapter embody the lives of women and children and demonstrate relationships and roles such as mother and child, vendor and consumer, market huckster and shopper, grandmother and grandchild, schoolteacher and child, worshiper and religious official, and carnival parade revelers and spectators. The photographs were taken at different times of the day, afternoon or evening. The images depict diverse locations throughout the island and demonstrate a variety of activities and events.

The purpose of my research and photography is not to impose my worldview, but rather expose others to multiple views and layers of the lives of women and children living in Dominica. Therefore, there is no one or correct way to view these images. Instead the images create a connection between the viewer and the photograph that illuminates aspects of the lives and experiences of the women and children of Dominica. The viewer may have instances of a combined perspective that is both symbolic and realistic. This simultaneous perspective creates a dynamic interchange of visions, thoughts and worldviews. Encountering the visual is a process that has neither beginning nor ending. In fact, the process is not linear in nature but rather holistic, intense and all consuming. Experiences and images are adduced in defining realities, truths and worldviews. The process of definition does not seek to end or complete; instead it seeks to discover, uncover and recover imagery.

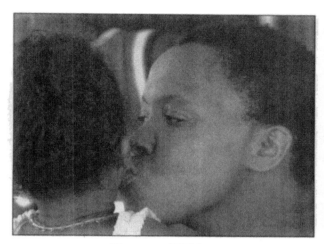

Women and Children

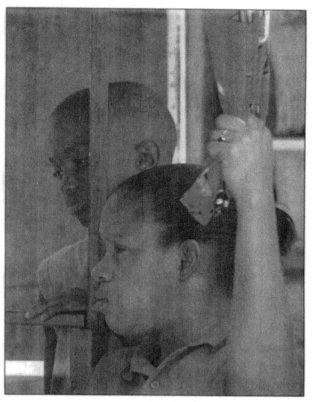

Women and Children: Work

Women at Work

Children and Work

Children and Education

Women and Children: Religious Faith

Children and Play

Women and Children: Politics

Women and Children in the Market

Women and Children Celebrate Dominica

My camera serves as a conduit linking past, present and future experiences and images. This temporal approach provides the catalyst for giving sight to the images that I was, am and will be drawn to depict and expose. I have found that photographs have the capacity to elicit emotions, communicate information and be artistically engaging. In fact, many times throughout this journey I reflected upon the meanings of American phrases such as "a picture is worth a thousand words" or "the camera cannot lie." Therefore, I invite the viewer to experience glimpses of the lives of Dominican women and children by seeing, analyzing, reflecting upon and experiencing the selected photographs in this chapter.

REFERENCES CITED

American Sociological Society. (1999). Code of ethics and policies and procedures. ASA Committee on Professional Ethics, pp. 1–28.

Andre, I. W., and Christian, G. J. (2002). *In search of eden.* Brampton, Ontario: Pond Casse Press.

Arminio, J. (1994). Waking up white: A phenomenological journey into racial being. Unpublished doctoral dissertation, University of Maryland, College Park.

Bach, E. D., and Staller, K. M. (2007). The feminist practice of ethnography. In S. N. Hesse-Biber and P. Leavy (Eds.). *Feminist Research Practices,* pp. 187–221. Thousand Oaks, CA: Sage.

Bailey, C. A. (2007). *A guide to qualitative field research.* Thousand Oaks, CA: Sage.

Banks, M. (2001). *Visual methods in social research.* Thousand Oaks, CA: Sage.

Becker, C. S. (1992). *Living and relating.* Thousand Oaks, CA: Sage.

Bowles, G., and Duelli Klein, R. (Eds.). (1983). *Theories of women's studies.* New York: Routledge and Kegan Paul.

Brooks, A. (2007). Feminist standpoint epistemology: Building knowledge and empowerment through women's lived experience. In S. N. Hesse-Biber and P. Leavy (Eds.). *Feminist Research Practices,* pp. 53–82. Thousand Oaks, CA: Sage.

Brooks, A., and Hesse-Biber, S. N. (2007). An invitation to feminist research. In S. N. Hesse-Biber and P. Leavy (Eds.). *Feminist Research Practices,* pp. 1–24. Thousand Oaks, CA: Sage.

Caribbean Community (CARICOM). (2004). Member country profile: Dominica. (Online.) Available: www.caricom.org.

Collier, J., and Collier, M. (1986). *Visual anthropology: Photography as a research method.* Albuquerque: University of New Mexico Press.

Country Review 2000. (1999). *Dominica.* Houston, TX: CountryWatch.com.

Creswell, J. W. (1998). *Qualitative inquiry and research design: Choosing among five traditions.* Thousand Oaks, CA: Sage.

Crotty, M. (1998). *The foundations of social research.* Thousand Oaks, CA: Sage.

Daines, J. R. (1989). Verstehen: A more comprehensive conception of understanding through hermeneutics. In F. H. Hultgren and D. L. Coomer (Eds.). *Alternative modes of inquiry in home economics research,* pp. 45–55. Peoria, IL: Glencoe Publishing Company.

Dilthey, W. (1976). The rise of hermeneutics. In P. Connerton (Ed.). *Critical sociology: Selected readings,* pp. 104–116. New York: Penguin.

Denzin, N. K., and Lincoln, Y. S. (Eds.). (2000). *Handbook of qualitative research.* Thousand Oaks, CA: Sage.

Duelli Klein, R. (1983). How to do what we want to do: Thoughts about feminist research. In G. Bowles and R. Duelli Klein (Eds.). *Theories of women's studies,* pp. 88–101. New York: Routledge and Kegan Paul.

Emmison, M., and Smith P. (2000). *Researching the visual.* Thousand Oaks, CA: Sage.

Fine, M. (1992). *Disruptive voices: The possibilities of feminist research.* Ann Arbor: University of Michigan Press.

Gadamer, H.-G. (1976). *Philosophical hermeneutics* (D. E. Linge, trans.). Los Angeles: University of California Press. (Original work published 1960–1972.)

———. (1985). *Truth and method.* (1st ed.). (G. Barden and J. Cumming, trans.). New York: The Crossroad Publishing Company. (Original work published 1960, translated in 1975.)

———. (2000). *Truth and method.* (2nd ed.). (J. Weinsheimer and D. G. Marshall, trans.). New York: The Crossroad Publishing Company. (Original work published 1960, second revision 1989.)

Gilligan, C. (1982). *In a different voice: Psychological theory and women's development.* Cambridge, MA: Harvard University Press.

Guba, E. G., and Lincoln, Y. S. (1989). *Fourth generation evaluation.* Thousand Oaks, CA: Sage.

Ferguson, J. (1997). *Eastern Caribbean.* Brooklyn, NY: Interlink Publishing Group.

Habermas, J. (1990). *Moral consciousness and communicative action.* (C. Lenhardt and S. Nicholsen, trans.). Cambridge, MA: MIT Press. (Original work published 1983.)

Heidegger, M. (1962). *Being and time.* (7th ed.). (J. Macquarrie and E. Robinson, trans.). New York: Harper and Row. (Original work published 1927.)

Heidegger, M. (1966). *Discourse on thinking.* (J. M. Anderson and E. H. Freund, trans.). New York: Harper and Row. (Original work published 1959.)

Heidegger, M. (1971). *Poetry, language, thought.* (A. Hofstadter, trans.). New York: Harper and Row.

Honychurch, L. (1995). *The Dominica story.* London: Macmillan Education.

Hultgren, F. H. and Coomer, D. L. (Eds.). (1989). *Alternative modes of inquiry in home economics research.* Peoria, IL: Glencoe Publishing Company.

Husserl, E. (1931). *Ideas: General introduction to pure phenomenology.* London: George Allen and Unwin.

Johnson-Odin, C. (1991). Common themes, different contexts: Third world women and feminism. In C. T. Mohanty, A. Russo, and L. Torres (Eds.). *Third world women and the politics of feminism,* pp. 314–327. Bloomington: Indiana University Press.

Lincoln, Y. S., and Guba E. G. (2000). Paradigmatic controversies, contradictions, and emerging confluences. In N. K. Denzin and Y. S. Lincoln (Eds.). *Handbook of qualitative research,* pp. 163–188. Thousand Oaks, CA: Sage.

Maxwell, J. A. (1996). *Qualitative research design: An interactive approach.* Thousand Oaks, CA: Sage.

Merriam, S. B. (1998). *Qualitative research and case study applications in education.* San Francisco, CA: Jossey-Bass.

Mies, M. (1983). Towards a methodology for feminist research. In G. Bowles and R. Duelli Klein (Eds.). *Theories of women's studies,* pp. 117–139. New York: Routledge and Kegan Paul.

Miles, M. B., and Huberman, A. M. (1994). *Qualitative data analysis.* Thousand Oaks, CA: Sage.

Mohammed, P., and Perkins, A. (1999). *Caribbean women at the crossroads.* Kingston, Jamaica: Canoe Press, University of the West Indies.

Moustakas, C. (1994). *Phenomenological research methods.* Thousand Oaks, CA: Sage.

Pink, S. (2001). *Doing visual ethnography.* Thousand Oaks, CA: Sage.

Prosser, J. (1998). *Image-based research.* New York: RoutledgeFarmer.

Silverman, D. (2000). Analyzing talk and text. In N. K. Denzin and Y. S. Lincoln (Eds.). *Handbook of qualitative research,* pp. 821–834. Thousand Oaks, CA: Sage.

Stake, R. E. (1995). *The art of case study.* Thousand Oaks, CA: Sage.

Thevenaz, P. (1962). *What is phenomenology?* Chicago, IL: Quadrangle Books.

Van Manen, M. (1984). *Doing phenomenological research and writing: An introduction.* The University of Alberta: Publication Services. Monograph No. 7.

———. (1990). *Researching the lived experience.* Thousand Oaks, CA: Sage.

Energy, Spirit and Light

The Journey's End and Beginning

HELEN C. SOBEHART

WE HAVE COMPLETED the first steps of our journey. Unlike the opening story about Ann Bancroft's first Antarctic attempt when her beginning was influenced by others, we began this journey at a time and place of our own choosing—July 2007 in Rome, Italy. However, similar to Ann's later journey with Liv, we burned the right fuel in a gentle kettle of an age-old nunnery, we fanned a great flame to melt some icy barriers of knowledge, and we used the water of our actions for energy to move on.

Just as Ann and Liv did not consider their successful Antarctic traverse as the end of their journey, neither can we see this as an end. On our last day, the group came together in what Margaret and Charol would call "collective leadership." It was amazing. These outstanding human beings, who had come together from the soil of every continent, sat together in unified voices to agree upon goals that would further the cause of gender equity in educational leadership and touch the lives of our sons, daughters and generations beyond. We asked ourselves what we could do to give back to the world, sharing information and wisdom to all within our reach—in person and in virtual environments.

Taking the lead from Liv and Ann, we set goals for ourselves that implicitly carried the will to "be friends on the other side," the other side of the work that we began. Our overall goal is to document the status of diverse women in educational leadership across continents. In addition, our goals are:

o To document statistically, update and disseminate where women are in the education continuum, as students, workers and as educators at all levels
o To document the ways that women attain positions of formal leadership within schools and universities
o To investigate the extent to which, if at all, formal and informal programs and processes facilitate the preparation and development of leaders for diversity and gender equity (the extent to which they are mainstreamed into educational programs and organizational structures)

o To collect experiences of women in educational leadership internationally and document their institutional impact
o To question and monitor what is happening as an international group—a gender watch system
o To cooperate in developing more gender inclusive leadership theories related to school effectiveness and to link this to human rights
o To return powerfully and purposefully in the future to build and expand our community
o To develop research teams around focused areas

As we gain a better understanding of gender issues through the statistics and qualitative information mentioned above, we can develop or modify theoretical frameworks of leadership that have been male-dominated for so very long. We don't imply an intentional male domination, though in some cases we know that is true. We do mean, however, that an issue seen through varied eyes and intellects is an issue better understood. An issue better understood makes us better able to make a strategic impact on the condition of the underrepresented and underserved.

We chose a goal to stay together while ever increasing our collegial sphere. Like the vapor rising from a steaming cauldron, our energy could easily dissipate in a thousand directions. We made a promise to each other not to let that happen. At the end of the final day we gave each other a lapel insignia as a gift, pinning it onto each other's collars as we read, "I pass this symbol of friendship on to you. Sharing our profession as educators has given us common ground. As a team we have become better then we are alone. I hope you will remember the things I have passed on to you and you to me. Working together has created a bond between us that will always remain." (The Master Teacher, Inc.) Tears of joy and kinship were shed.

As the group's chair, I gave each of my newfound friends a picture of the conference program cover so that they could proudly hang it in their offices or other spaces where people would notice it and ask about it. When people ask, what shall we say? First, we can share the specific research questions and methodologies generated by our goals:

- What is the status of women in educational leadership across continents?
- How have the lived experiences of conference participants influenced their life and professional/leadership decisions?
- What are conceptions of leadership in different countries and what social regularities frame those conceptions?
- How do women navigate cultural constraints in order to become leaders?
- To what extent do girls have access to basic education?
- What are the primary issues within leadership training programs that prevent or advance diversity and gender equity?
- What strategies effectively facilitate change to the status quo and how do those changes become institutionalized?
- Are women able to actualize their human rights in their own countries within internationally recognized frameworks, and are their human rights guaranteed?
- How can we provide inspiration and access to young women to seek positions of leadership?

We will seek answers through a gender audit; frameworks such as Schein's cultural categories; visualization; portraiture; spiritual frames; human rights frames such as that of the United Nations Human Rights Commission; gender mainstreaming organizational analysis; and partnerships with mutually interested organizations such as the Arnesen/Bancroft network. We will share our findings.

We have created a listserv for the group so that we can continue to communicate on a regular basis. While as of this writing a website does not yet exist, we will announce its creation broadly, via the websites of UCEA (www.ucea.org), AASA (www.aasa.org), Duquesne University (www.duq.edu) and other media.

We have started to construct a gender audit which we intend to use for research and to carry out our "gender watch" goal. Statistics and attributes in the audit are compelling. (See appendix E.1 at the end of this chapter.) The current audit represents only the countries of our initial group. Nevertheless, the statistics of underrepresentation are an affront to social justice. As Sister Hellen noted, we would consider such an imbalance to be cheating in the world of probability statistics and gambling. How sad that what is unacceptable in games of chance is so acceptable in the human condition. This qualitative information shows how inequity gambles with lives. Though barriers can be as simple as subconscious attitudes which prevent women from being hired into top educational seats, they can be as vicious as an accepted cultural norm noted by a research subject—that the raping of Melanesian women is taken about as seriously as a schoolchild losing a pencil.

This situation needs our energy to spread like a spirit. People of all countries, genders, races and religions need to see it. We need to show it to them. We need to put it in front of policy makers, civic leaders, cultural leaders, our neighbors, our families. We need to do this with the passionate spirit which has been fueled by the flame ignited in Rome.

This takes me back to the logo created for our conference, the cover for this book. Why that image? The picture was designed by a graphic artist from Duquesne University after just a brief conversation about some of the issues which we have now shared with you. We talked about fire, flame, energy, spirit, light, learning and the vast terrain of the world.

The day I received the design, I met Charlie Dougherty, who penned the eloquent preface to this book. In my enthusiasm, I pulled out the picture and said, "Look at our logo for the conference." Charlie looked at it, smiling, and said, "It really is well done. I like it a lot. But why are you burning that woman in the flame?" While I jokingly said that he should be grateful, since we originally considered burning a man, I realized that the woman wasn't burning, even though the flame was all around her. St. Hildegard of Bingen had done what we must do. She was a twelfth-century nun and mystic who influenced kings and popes of the day against all odds. She believed in the ability of the spirit to transcend time and space. Hildegard's spirit had silently traveled across time to join our group. The picture and the message were from her.

Hildegard powerfully influenced leaders of her time and beyond, though she lived in a cloistered setting. She claimed her position by engaging a monk to write down her transcendent visions. Her visions symbolized wisdom as a woman and spirit as light. In her sixties, she left the cloister to preach, standing for social justice on public and religious platforms. She made no apologies for her strong stance about alleviating the suffering of the underrepresented and summoning to justice those who abused their power. She *was* her message. Her visions are the reason why our logo inspires.

Hildegard, in her transcendent way, just like Ann and Liv in their earthly way, told us how the journey must be. We must *be* the message in every action. We must share the light of information and social justice, especially in the darkest places. As contemporary author Jennifer James (1997) said, "Participation in a wisdom journey requires you to believe that the powers of the universe are not only on our side, but within you. You must feel that passion is your genuine life force" (p. 28).

So as you end the journey of this book, you are called to the flame and the spirit it creates. You must believe that you are the passion that can transform the universe, or at least your piece of it, as flame transforms ice and turns it into energy. You are the light that leads the spirit of social justice to where it needs to be, rather than allowing it to evaporate into nothingness. You can speak it loudly from bully pulpits, as Hildegard did in her old age, but you can spread it silently through the images you leave in the minds and hearts of others.

Ultimately we must *be* the image in our logo. In her book *Scivias* (Ways of Knowing), Hildegard described the ethereal journey we must now take, the light we must draw from the flame of social justice, and the energy we must use to inspire others around the world and into the future. Our logo carries on her vision and ours: "The woman was in the flame, but not consumed by it. Rather, it came from her."

Peace and strength on our shared journey. We join you in the light.

REFERENCES CITED

Hildegard of Bingen. (1990). *Scivias*. (C. Hart and J. Bishop, trans.). Classics of western spirituality. New York: Paulist Press.

James, J. (1997). *Twenty steps to wisdom: A guide to self-knowledge and spiritual well-being*. New York: Newmarket Press.

Gender Audit

Taking Stock of Women Leading Education across Continents

KNOWING WHERE WOMEN ARE IN THE EDUCATIONAL SYSTEM

Percentage of girls in primary schools

- Bangladesh – 50%
- Germany – 49.1% (2006/2007)
- Greece – 48.6%
- Hong Kong – 48%
- Pakistan – 42%
- South Africa – 48.7%
- Tanzania – 49%
- United Kingdom – 100% (very small proportion home schooled)

Percentage of girls in secondary schools

- Bangladesh – 50%
- Germany – 49.3% (42.3% graduating degree level; 50.6% graduating higher level) 2006–2007
- Greece – 47%
- Hong Kong – 49%
- Pakistan – 24%
- South Africa – 50.3%
- Tanzania – 47%
- United Kingdom – 100% (very small proportion home schooled)

Percentage of women in college

- Bangladesh – 41%
- Germany – 55.2% (2006–2007)
- Greece – 53%
- Hong Kong – 66%
- Pakistan – 46%
- South Africa – 53.1%
- Tanzania – 35%
- United Kingdom – full-time 55%, part-time 65%

Percentage of women in graduate school

- Bangladesh – 22%

- Germany – 47.8% (2004)
- Greece – 50.3%
- Hong Kong – 46%
- Pakistan – 49%
- South Africa – 53% (contact), 57% (distance)
- Tanzania – 21% (Ph.D.), 30% (master's)
- United Kingdom – 47% (higher degrees [masters and doctorates] by research), 55% (higher degrees [masters and doctorates] taught)

Percentage of women in the professorship by rank and discipline

- Bangladesh – 17%
- Germany – 16.6% (2004)
- Greece – professors 15%, associate professors 26%, assistant professors 32%, lecturers 40.6%
- Hong Kong – professors 8%, readers 10%, senior lecturers 15%
- South Africa – 42%
- Tanzania – 11% Ph.D. holders
- United Kingdom – professors 19%, senior lecturers 33.5%, lecturers 46.8%

Percentage of women leaders by role/title in PK-12

- Bangladesh – primary teachers 36%, secondary teachers 19%, secondary heads of government 29%, private secondary school heads 20%
- Greece – principals 34%, assistant principals 68%, assistant superintendent, 17.5%, superintendent, 7%
- Hong Kong – primary 50%, secondary 30%
- Pakistan – 50%
- Tanzania – 13% (secondary education)
- United Kingdom – primary principals 61.8%, primary teachers 88.1%, secondary principals 31.6%, secondary teachers 56.4%

Percentage of women leaders by role/title in higher education

- Germany – 15.5% total (2005); rector 6.0%,

president 12.7%, pro-rector 17.9%, vice president 20.8%, chancellor 17.0%

- Hong Kong – professor 8%, reader 10%, senior lecturer 15%,
- Pakistan – 42.5% colleges, 13% universities
- South Africa – 4% vice chancellors
- Tanzania – 4.5% (only 3 top positions surveyed)
- United Kingdom – vice chancellors (head of university) 13.2%, further education college principals 27.5%

FORMAL AND INFORMAL PREPARATION FOR LEADERSHIP

Process by which to become a PK-12 administrator
- Bangladesh – Only workshops after being appointed
- Germany – Administrators nominated by the school departments of the federal states
- Greece – From most to least importance:

    1. At least 12 years of full-time teaching
    2. Interview with selection committee
    3. Personality factors
    4. Administration training

- Pakistan – Seniority
- South Africa – Bachelor's degree in any field
- Tanzania – Secondary/undergraduate education plus short- or long-term training
- United Kingdom – National Professional Qualification for Headship is required; prior to that there is a course for aspirant leaders called Leading from the Middle

Percentage of women in administrator preparation programs as instructors

- Bangladesh – 23%
- Germany –N/A (Germany has no state administration preparation program, only in some of the federal states where no data are gathered about instructors)
- Pakistan – 36%

Gender visibility in the curriculum

- Pakistan – Yes
- United Kingdom – In relation to an audit the following specific recommendations arise:

1. Every effort should continue to be made to ensure an equal balance of men and women coaches and tutors.
2. It is often difficult for people to recognize unconscious disempowerment, especially if it reflects the society at large. The programs should take a lead in ensuring that course content includes consideration of gender stereotypes and leadership. Discussion can focus on gender stereotypes for men and women and would inform debate about leadership in general.
3. The lists of references in Learning to Lead (a national program in the UK) should include literature that is relevant to women in leadership in the current British context.
4. Tutor training should include gender issues, giving tutors "permission" to address, for example, women leading teams of men, in the course.
5. Issues of work/life balance for both women and men could be addressed directly at meetings with a view to identifying positive ways through the issues raised here and elsewhere.
6. Consideration should be given to inviting senior women role models to talk to participants.
7. Women do not necessarily see themselves as potential senior leaders and tend to look only at the next stage of career. Coleman's survey of head teachers (2005) also found that many women heads in comparison to their male colleagues had not planned their career. Support for career planning for women is therefore recommended and lack of confidence may also be a specific area to address and investigate further. Mentoring and networking should be considered.
8. There will need to be sensitivity in the way that gender issues are addressed. Women and men are both wary of positive discrimination and feminism. It is often thought that there is no longer a gender "problem."
9. Flexible arrangements should be in place for women participants who are pregnant or who go on maternity leave.
10. Middle leaders in schools who are not teachers (most often women) should be welcomed in the course.

GETTING THE JOBS

Strategies for success

- Germany –There are a lot of different programs especially for women at German universities/graduate schools, for example, mentoring programs, leadership workshops, and the like.
- Greece
    1. More women mentors
    2. Administration training
    3. Help with family
- Tanzania – Education and training

Barriers/process to formal leadership positions

- Bangladesh
    1. Culture where women have traditionally not worked outside the home once married.
    2. Marriage can be as early as age 14.
    3. Women are expected to shoulder all domestic responsibility even when working and defer to male peers.
- Germany – When it comes to evaluation of the gender mainstreaming strategy, coming into focus are not only promising factors and results but also areas for improvement. Gender mainstreaming only gives a method. The central goal of the strategy is to increase the share of female scientists and students in fields where they are underrepresented. Therefore, passive promotion is not enough—active promotion is necessary. In order to get rid of the current deficit of equity, the responsibility lies not only with the female gender. The attitude and the way of acting of every individual is decisive. According to Allmendinger and others the so-called critical mass necessary for a changing of subject cultures and communication models is 30% (2003). Kahlert (2003) points out that an important prerequisite for the top-down strategy mentioned at the beginning is that the management has to have a certain level of consciousness and commitment. A further difficulty emerging from working with gender mainstreaming is the lack of regular data surveys. Descriptive statistics giving reasons for a premature stop in an educational pathway are not kept. The university landscape in Germany is very diverse. In view of this heterogeneity it is evaluation's task to support both the claim on comparison as well as the claim on reflecting the culture of each individual university (Quirin J. Bauer, Gender mainstreaming at German universities, in preparation).
- Greece
    1. Family responsibilities
    2. Lack of women mentors
    3. Feelings of uncertainty about leadership and administration skills
    4. Challenges of administration
    5. Negative attitudes of male colleagues
    6. Complicated process of applying for administration positions
    7. Biases of the selection committees (until recently consisting of males only)
- Pakistan – Single-sex institutions offer a space for women to perform as leaders but in mixed-sex contexts there are very few opportunities.
- Tanzania – Lack of education and training.

REFERENCES CITED

Allmendinger, J. (2003). Strukturmerkmale universitärer Personalselektion und deren Folgen für die Beschäftigung von Frauen. In: Wobbe, T. (Hrsg.). Zwischen Vorderbühne und Hinterbühne. Beiträge zum Wandel der Geschlechterbeziehungen in der Wissenschaft vom 17. Jahrhundert bis zur Gegenwart, Bielefeld, S. 259–277.

Bauer, Q. J., and Gruber, S. (2007). Gender mainstreaming at universities: Successful strategies of implementation. Paper presented at the Women Leading Education Conference, Rome, Italy.

Coleman, M. (2005). Gender audit of Leading from the Middle. Final Report to NCSL.

Kahlert, H. (2003). Gender Mainstreaming an Hochschulen. Anleitung zum qualitätsbewussten Handeln, Opladen.

About the Editor and Contributors

ABOUT THE EDITOR

Dr. Helen C. Sobehart has been an educator since 1969. She is president of Cardinal Stritch University in Milwaukee (the largest Franciscan university in the United States); associate provost/academic vice president of Duquesne University in Pittsburgh, Pennsylvania; and director of the Duquesne University School of Education Leadership Institute and Interdisciplinary Doctoral Program for Educational Leaders. She was a finalist for AAUW's prestigious "Scholar in Residence" Award, received the Gold Star Award for Mentoring of Schools Leaders from the Pittsburgh Council on Public Education, and was 2008 recipient of the Dr. Effie H. Jones Humanitarian Award from AASA. Prior to that, she was a superintendent in the Fox Chapel Area School District (Pennsylvania). She served by gubernatorial appointment on the Pennsylvania Advisory Council for Special Education, was recognized by the Pennsylvania State Senate for "her immeasurable contribution to educational progress," and was appointed to U.S. Department of Education committees.

Helen has served on the board of NEED (Negro Emergency Education Drive), the Homeless Children Emergency Fund, Leadership Pittsburgh and the Bradley Center for Children and Youth. She chairs the Women's Special Interest Group of the University Council for Educational Administration, publishing and presenting nationally and internationally on issues related to leadership, women's leadership specifically. Her life's commitment has been to those who are marginalized or underserved.

Helen holds a bachelor's degree in psychology/sociology from Slippery Rock University, a master's degree in special education from Duquesne University and a doctorate in history from Carnegie-Mellon University. She is married and has two sons, a daughter-in-law and the best grandson in the world (just like every other grandmother).

ABOUT THE CONTRIBUTORS

Sharon Adams-Taylor, M.A., M.P.H., is associate executive director of the American Association of School Administrators (AASA). As such, she is responsible for programs related to minority and women school leaders and equity, health and social programs to improve the lives of children. She directed AASA's Women Administrators Conference for six years and participated in a panel that ultimately led to this global conference.

Liv Arnesen, a self-proclaimed "keen" but not fanatical outdoors enthusiast, is most interested in the development of adults and children. Through her diverse roles as a polar explorer, educator and motivational leader, Arnesen ignites passion in others to reach beyond their normal boundaries and achieve their dreams. In February 2001, Arnesen and American polar explorer Ann Bancroft became the first women in history to sail and ski across Antarctica's landmass—completing a 94-day, 1,717-mile trek. In 1996, Arnesen climbed the north side of Mount Everest, getting to within 6,200 feet of the summit before altitude sickness forced her to descend. In 1994, she became the first woman in the world to ski solo and unsupported to the South Pole—a 50-day expedition of 745 miles—and in 1992, she led the first unsupported women's crossing of the Greenland Ice Cap.

Dr. Anastasia Athanasoula-Reppa has a B.A. in sociology, political sciences and public administration (Panteion University in Athens), M.Sc. and Ph.D. in educational policy and administration (Panteion University), and holds undergraduate diplomas in pedagogy (Pedagogical and Technological School in Athens) and open and distance learning (Hellenic Open University). She has worked as a civil servant and as a teacher in secondary schools. She was elected as a member of teaching and research staff in Pedagogical and Technological School (ASPETE) in Athens in educational policy and administration, and became a full professor in the same institution. She is vice president of the Department of Pedagogical Studies at ASPETE.

Ann Bancroft is one of the world's preeminent polar explorers and an internationally recognized leader who is dedicated to inspiring women, girls and audiences around the world to unleash the power of their dreams. Bancroft's teamwork and leadership skills have undergone severe tests during her polar expeditions and provided her with opportunities to shatter female stereotypes. She is a member of the Women's Hall of Fame (1995) and was named *Ms. Magazine*'s "Woman of the Year" (1987). In February 2001, Bancroft and Norwegian polar explorer Liv Arnesen became the first women to sail and ski across Antarctica. In 1993, she led the American Women's Expedition to the South Pole, a four-woman, 67-day expedition of 660 miles on skis, earning the distinction of being the first woman to cross the ice to both the North and South Poles. In 1992, Bancroft led the first American women's east-to-west crossing of Greenland, and in 1986, she dogsledded 1,000 miles from the Northwest Territories in Canada to the North Pole as the only female member of the Steger International Polar Expedition.

Sister Dr. Hellen A. Bandiho was born and raised in Tanzania and belongs to the community of the Sisters of St. Therese. Currently, she is dean of the Faculty of Business Administration at St. Augustine University of Tanzania (SAUT). Hellen taught grade school and junior college in Tanzania before obtaining a B.A. and an M.B.A. from Edgewood College in Madison, Wisconsin. Her doctorate is from Duquesne University's Interdisciplinary Doctoral Program in Educational Leadership. Hellen is an advocate for women's education at all levels; she started a scholarship fund for female students at SAUT to enable academically capable but impoverished students to complete their studies. Her research interests are in management and leadership in both business and education.

Dr. Dorothy Bassett is dean of Duquesne University's School of Leadership and Professional Advancement. She previously served as director of information technology initiatives at Carnegie Mellon University. In addition, Dr. Bassett led a number of corporate and international programs under the auspices of such organizations as Robert Bosch GmBH, the United Nations High Commissioner for Refugees, U.S. Agency for International Development and the Pew Charitable Trusts. Dr. Bassett received a Ph.D. in public and international affairs from the University of Pittsburgh.

Quirin Johannes Bauer, M.A., is scientific assistant in the project "Gender Mainstreaming at Universities—Balancing and Optimizing" at the University of Augsburg, course leader at the University of Applied Sciences of Augsburg in the project "STARTK-LAR—Training for International Students for Study" in Germany, and deputy to the University Woman Representative. He obtained his M.A. from the University of Augsburg. Since 2004 he has been a member of the Committee of Equalization of the Senate and a member in the supervision team of the Gender Mainstreaming Project at the University of Augsburg.

Dr. Bettie Bertram has been an educator for 15 years and is currently supervisor of special education/ESL for the Upper Adams School District in Pennsylvania. She holds a doctorate in educational leadership from Duquesne University and a master's degree from Western Maryland College. She holds certifications in the areas of supervisor of curriculum/instruction, superintendent, administration K-12, and supervisor of special education. She has provided professional development for school districts, colleges and the Pennsylvania Department of Education. Bettie is the 2007 winner of the Richard D. Miller Award, given by the American Association of School Administrators to outstanding graduate students in school administration. Her research focuses on women leaders and spirituality.

Dr. Jill Blackmore is professor of education in the Faculty of Education at Deakin University and director of the Educational Futures and Innovation Research Cluster. She serves on several editorial boards of international journals including *British Educational Research Journal, International Journal of Leadership in Education,* and *American Educational Research Journal.* Her research interests include feminist approaches to globalization and education policy, administrative and organizational theory, educational leadership and reform, organizational change and innovation, teachers' and academics' work and related policy implications. Her publications include *Troubling Women: Feminism, Leadership and Educational Change* (1999), *Counterpoints on the Quality and Impact of Educational Research* (2006), coedited with J. Wright and J. Harwood, and *Performing and Re-forming Leaders: Gender, Educational Restructuring and Organizational Change* (2007), with Judyth Sachs.

Dr. JoAnne E. Burley is executive director of the Pittsburgh Council on Higher Education (PCHE), a consortium of ten colleges and universities in Allegheny County, Pennsylvania. Collectively, PCHE colleges and universities educate more than 54,000 full-time,

24,000 part-time students and 20,000 noncredit students annually. Previously, Dr. Burley was the chancellor (CEO) of the Pennsylvania State University, McKeesport Campus. She received her B.S. degree from the Pennsylvania State University, M.A. from Fairfield University and Ph.D. from the University of Pittsburgh. As an active scholar and researcher, Dr. Burley has authored and coauthored many publications including the textbook *Perspectives: From Adult Literacy to Continuing Education*, and is the recipient of numerous awards and recognitions.

Dr. Mustafa Celikten obtained a Ph.D. from the University of Wisconsin at Madison. Currently he is an associate professor in the Department of Educational Administration at the School of Education, University of Erciyes, Turkey. His research focuses on women administrators, school culture and organizational change.

Dr. Marianne Coleman is a reader in educational leadership management and assistant dean of research at the Institute of Education, University of London, with responsibility for the support of research and publications among colleagues. She is an experienced researcher on leadership in schools, particularly focusing on gender issues in leadership. Her most recent work in this area has been funded by the National College for School Leadership in England.

Dr. Joyce A. Dana worked for 34 years in public schools in Missouri, Kansas, and New York in roles that ranged from teaching to superintendent of schools. She currently teaches school and community relations, politics, and ethics in the Educational Leadership doctoral program at Saint Louis University. Her abiding research interest is the experience and welfare of women leaders. Dr. Dana was recognized by the American Association of School Administrators as an Effie H. Jones Humanitarian.

Dr. Charles Dougherty was elected 12th president of Duquesne University in May 2001. Dougherty is a nationally recognized scholar and expert in health care ethics, and has served on numerous health care advisory commissions and projects. Most recently, Dougherty has worked with the Not-for-Profit Hospital Trustees Project at the Hastings Center and the New York Academy of Medicine, as well as the National Coalition on Catholic Health Care. Dougherty has also served as a commissioner for the State of Nebraska

Accountability and Disclosure Commission, a government ethics panel. He has published extensively on the subject of ethics and health care. His publications on the subject include two books published by Oxford University Press and more than 50 scholarly articles. He received his master's and doctoral degrees in philosophy from the University of Notre Dame in 1973 and 1975; he received his bachelor's degree in philosophy from St. Bonaventure University in 1971.

Dr. Claudia Fahrenwald is research associate and lecturer in the Department of Education at the University of Augsburg. She studied philosophy, literature and psychology at Munich, Berlin and Augsburg. She earned her doctorate in philosophy and comparative literature in 1999. From 2000 to 2002 she joined the Research Group for Gender Studies at the University of Augsburg. Since 2002, her expertise has been sought at the German Department of Education. Most recently, she coedited with Hildegard Macha *Gender Mainstreaming and Weiterbildung: Organisationsentwicklung durch Potentialentwicklung*.

Dr. María Luisa González, Regents Professor of Educational Management and Development and director for the Center for Border and Indigenous Educational Leadership, has been a teacher, principal, researcher and evaluator in Texas and New Mexico. She has published widely in the fields of educational administration and ELL/LEP students (students with limited English proficiency). Her book *Educating Latino Students: A Guide for Successful Practice* provides practical advice for administrators and is widely used and cited in administrator preparation programs.

Dr. Marilyn L. Grady is professor of educational administration at the University of Nebraska, Lincoln. She is founder of the Women in Educational Leadership Conference, now in its 21st year, and is editor of the *Journal of Women in Educational Leadership*. She is an active speaker and author of numerous publications on educational leadership with an emphasis on women. She holds a Ph.D. in educational administration from Ohio State University.

Dr. Margaret Grogan is currently dean of the School of Educational Studies at Claremont Graduate University in California., She was formerly professor and chair of the Department of Educational Leadership and Policy Analysis at the University of Missouri, Columbia. She has taught and been an administrator in Australia and Japan. She has written many articles and chapters on educational leadership. Together with Cryss Brunner, she authored the book *Women Leading School Systems: Uncommon Roads to Fulfillment* (2007).

Susanne Gruber is scientific assistant at the University of Augsburg in the research project "Gender Mainstreaming at Universities: Balancing and Optimizing." Her work has included evaluation in the Initiative Child Care for Employees of the University of Augsburg project, awarded by the Ministry of Sciences of Bavaria, and other social science research related to women, youth and the elderly.

Juan Han is a Ph.D. candidate in the field of curriculum and instruction in South China Normal University. She devotes much time to the study of gender and education. She completed graduate studies at South China Normal University in the field of comparative education. She was a secondary school teacher teaching politics for nine years. In recent years she has been an associate on a research project about girls' educational opportunity and quality in China, has presented reports about gender and education issues for teachers and secondary students in Guangzhou, and is a university women's studies teacher. Her research on girls' secondary schools in China will form the core of her doctoral dissertation. Her publications include "The development of gender consciousness education in higher education in China."

Dr. Stephanie Handschuh-Heiss is a sociologist and a research assistant participating in the Gender Mainstreaming at the University of Augsburg project in Augsburg, Germany. Her doctoral thesis was completed magna cum laude, and she has published widely on organizational culture and gender issues.

Dr. Esther Sui-chu Ho is associate professor and director of the Hong Kong Center for International Student Assessment, Faculty of Education, The Chinese University of Hong Kong. She holds B.S., M.A., and Ph.D. degrees, and was consultant for the Macau-PISA project and the China-PISA project. Esther was a Fulbright Scholar at Pennsylvania State University; research associate for Education and Development in South China; teaching assistant and research assistant at the University of British Columbia, Canada; and teaching consultant for the World Bank in the District Primary Educational Program, India. She was

principal investigator of the Home School Collaboration Project and the Hong Kong PISA Project, and has taught a wide variety of courses ranging from educational policy and practice to parent involvement and research methods.

Dr. Katherine M. Houghton has worked in higher education administration on land and sea for over twenty years in both the United States and Caribbean. She has circumnavigated the world twice as administrator on the Semester at Sea Program, University of Pittsburgh, and Institute for Shipboard Education. She was dean of academic administration at Ross University, Island of Dominica. Presently, Katherine is the vice president/dean of academics of The Art Institute of Charleston. She has been featured as a keynote speaker and presenter on topics including leadership in higher education, multicultural programming, students with invisible handicaps and global issues affecting women and children. Katherine's most recent scholarly pursuits combine her background as a photographer, extensive international travel, expertise in qualitative research and her commitment to furthering the cause of underrepresented women and children.

Dr. Alice Merab Kagoda attended Makerere University, Kampala, Uganda, graduating with a B.A. degree and concurrent diploma in education and a master's degree in education. She later graduated from the University of Alberta, Canada, with a Ph.D. in international/intercultural education. She worked as a secondary school teacher in various districts of Uganda, and was appointed deputy head teacher for A-level day schools by the Ministry of Education, posted in one of the largest government-aided schools in Kampala City. She was appointed university lecturer in the School of Education, Department of Social Science and Arts Education, Makerere University, and became deputy dean of the School of Education, her current position. She is a member of several women's organizations, including the Uganda Association of University Women.

Dr. Angeliki Lazaridou is assistant professor at Intercollege, Cyprus, where she teaches undergraduate students, and an affiliate of Open University of Cyprus and Green Open University, where she teaches graduate students. Her teaching and research focus on educational administration at the graduate level and general pedagogy at the undergraduate level. Her qualifications include an undergraduate degree in education from the University of Athens, Greece;

a master's degree in educational psychology; and a Ph.D. in educational administration and leadership, both from the University of Alberta in Edmonton, Canada. Dr. Lazaridou has participated in research projects and presented at national and international conferences.

Dr. Pamela Lenz is principal of Springfield Elementary School in the Northwestern School District (Pennsylvania) and adjunct professor in educational leadership at Gannon University. She was presented the 2006 Dissertation of the Year Award by AERA's Leadership for School Improvement Special Interest Group. Pam also received the S. D. Shankland Award from the American Association of School Administrators and was named a UCEA Clark Scholar. A Pennsylvania Association of School Administrators Research Fellow, Pam was co-recipient of the 2003 Henderson Prize for Educational Leaders from Duquesne University, where she earned a doctoral degree in educational leadership.

Dr. Jacky Lumby is a professor of education at the University of Southampton, England. Her main interests are in leadership and management, particularly diversity issues and leadership of high school and post-compulsory education. She is also interested in adopting an international perspective, challenging the appropriateness of ethnocentric concepts, theories and suggested practice in many educational administration texts. Her most recent book (with Marianne Coleman) considers diversity and leadership. She is co-editor of *International Studies in Educational Administration*, and a member of the Council of the British Educational Leadership, Management and Administration Society.

Dr. Linda L. Lyman is professor in the Department of Educational Administration and Foundations at Illinois State University, where she teachers master's and doctoral students seeking leadership positions in schools. Her academic degrees are a B.A. in English, Northwestern University, 1963; an M.A.T. in secondary education, Harvard University, 1964; and a Ph.D. in administration, curriculum, and instruction, University of Nebraska, Lincoln, 1990. She served as executive director of Illinois Women Administrators for four years. She spent the spring semester of 2005 in Greece at Aristotle University as a Fulbright scholar. Her research, publications and presentations focus on leadership, with an emphasis on issues of caring, poverty and gender.

Dr. Hildegard Macha studied at the Universities of Würzburg, Kiel and Bonn, and examined as a teacher 1974 at Bonn. She obtained her Ph.D. with the paper "Emotional Education," and her habilitation with the paper "Theories of Identity." (Both were later published in book form.) She has been professor for the science of education and adult education at the University of Augsburg since 1992. She has been dean of philosophical faculty, a member of University Senate, and a member of Faculty Council. Hildegard is leader of a research group for gender studies and women's representative of the University of Augsburg. Her current research projects are "Gender Mainstreaming at 16 Universities of Germany: Balancing and Optimizing"; "Further Education for Teachers"; "Gender Mainstreaming at the University of Augsburg"; and "Handbook of Family Research."

Dr. Rosangela Malachias is journalist and a Black Movement activist. Her master's thesis (1996) at PROLAM Latin America Program, University of São Paulo (USP), Brazil, compared African Cuban and African Brazilian youngsters. She was a MacArthur Foundation Fellow (1997–1999) with the Interactive Youth Project against drug use, HIV and STD; and was in 2001 a SYLLF Fellow (Japan). In 2002, Malachias was the first Black woman to receive a doctoral degree in the Department of Communications and Arts of USP. With other Black women, she launched the Media and Ethnicity Office to promote courses and offer consultation. She was academic consultant in the Race Development and Social Inequality Program, a consortium comprising USP, Federal University of Bahia, Howard University and Vanderbilt University (2003–2007).

Xiaoyan Niu is an English teacher in Guangzhou Xiguan Foreign Language School, located in Guangzhou, Guangdong, China. She completed graduate studies at South China Normal University in the field of curriculum and instruction. She took part in a research project on English immersion instruction beginning in 2005. From 1999 to 2005, she worked as a middle school English teacher. During this time, she noticed that girls and boys were interested in different subjects. As a result, girls were better at liberal arts while boys were better at science, which had great influence on the major they chose after they entered university. She also noticed an imbalance in women's participation in educational leadership in middle schools. Her other research interests include female students' psychology and education. She is concerned with improving education equity between boys and girls in secondary school and tries hard to ensure that equity in her daily work, including encouraging girls to pursue scientific education.

Dr. Flora Ida Ortiz is professor emerita at University of California, Riverside. She holds a B.M. degree from the University of Denver and M.A. and Ph.D. degrees from the University of New Mexico. Her teaching and research interests include school careers, socialization processes, organizational theory and the superintendency. Representative titles from recent publications include: (2001) Using social capital in interpreting the careers of three Latina superintendents. *Educational Administration Quarterly, 37*(1), 58–85; (2000) Who controls succession? A minority perspective. *Urban Education, 35*(5), 557–566; *Career Patterns in Education: Women, Men and Minorities in Public School Administration.* New York: J. F. Bergin (1994).

Dr. Thidziambi Phendla is a newly appointed full professor of educational management in the Department of Teacher Education at the University of Venda in South Africa. She has taught courses in leadership and community building, leadership and gender equality, and education management. She was the first director of IICBA, the International Institute for Capacity Building in Africa, UNESCO-IICBA, Pretoria Node, United Nations Educational, Scientific, Cultural Organization, a center within the Faculty of Education of the University of Pretoria. Thidziambi's passion is work focused around issues of leadership, educational change, developing and training women in leadership and social justice.

Professor Haiyan Qiang is a Chinese scholar in the field of comparative education, who is currently teaching in the Faculty of Education at South China Normal University (SCNU), located in Guangzhou, Guangdong, China. She completed graduate studies at the University of Massachusetts, and was a visiting academic fellow at the Institute of Education, University of London, and in the Ontario Institute for Studies in Education, University of Toronto. She was an associate director of the Center for Women's Studies at Shaanxi Normal University and plays the same role in the Women's Study Center at SCNU. She was director in China for "Women and Minorities as Educational Change Agents," a SULCP project supported by CIDA (Canadian International Development Agency). Recently, she was the chief leader of a priority research project, "Girls' Education: Quality and Equity." She

has written two books and many papers on women in education, published in academic journals both in China and internationally.

Dr. Saeeda Shah is currently a lecturer at the School of Education, University of Leicester, U.K., teaching/supervising master's and doctoral students. Previously, she taught for many years in higher education in Pakistan, holding senior management positions, her last position being dean of faculty at the University of Azad Jammu and Kashmir, Pakistan. She has published widely on leadership, gender, ethnicity, and Islam and society. She has been involved in the volunteer sector as well, working with communities in Pakistan and England. She participated in many United Nations Human Rights Commission sessions in Geneva in her work for human rights, particularly those of women and youth.

Dr. Charol Shakeshaft is chairperson of educational leadership at Virginia Commonwealth University. She obtained her Ph.D. from Texas A&M University. Her research primarily focuses on gender and leadership, at-risk youth and the educational effectiveness of technology use. She has been studying equity in schools for more than 25 years, documenting gendered practice in the classroom and in school administration. She is an internationally recognized researcher in the area of gender patterns in educational delivery and classroom interactions. Her work on equity in schools has taken her into school systems across the United States, Australia, China, Japan, Canada and Europe, where she has helped educators make schools more welcoming to females.

Dr. Jill Sperandio is assistant professor in the International School Educational Leadership program at Lehigh University (Pennsylvania). She obtained a B.A. degree with honors at the University of Wales and an M.Ed. degree from Worcester State College, Massachusetts. Her professional career has spanned all aspects of international education, as teacher, principal, teacher trainer, program evaluator and college lecturer. First teaching in a national secondary school in Uganda, she moved to teaching, administrative and teacher training positions in international schools in Kuwait, Malta, Tanzania, Venezuela, Azerbaijan and Holland, while completing her doctorate at University of Chicago. She is currently researching, publishing and presenting on gender issues in Bangladesh and Uganda, together with women in leadership preparation programs in the United States.

Dr. Jane Strachan is associate professor at the University of Waikato, Hamilton, New Zealand. Over the past 20 years, her teaching and research interests have focused on educational leadership, women, social justice, gender, policy development and Pacific education. Recently, she has lived and worked in Vanuatu, assisting the government with national education and women's human rights policy development and research. Currently, in addition to supervising master's and doctoral students in the educational leadership program, Jane is directing a three-year project with the School of Education in the Solomon Islands designed to build teacher education there, funded by NZAID, the development agency of the New Zealand Ministry of Foreign Affairs and Trade.

Dr. Eileen Zungolo earned her bachelor's, master's and doctoral degrees from Teachers College, Columbia University. Her career has included a number of years in clinical nursing practice, in acute and pediatric clinical settings. In addition, she has worked in higher education in nursing for over 30 years. A former president of the National League for Nursing, Dr. Zungolo has served many national and regional professional organizations. Over the course of her career she has received many awards and honors, including a Fulbright scholarship to Thailand. She received the Leader of Leaders Award from the National Student Nurses Association in 2005. Since 2002, Dr. Zungolo has served as dean and professor of nursing at Duquesne University in Pittsburgh.

9 781578 869961